Violent and Sexual Offenders

Violent and Sexual Offenders

Assessment, treatment and management

Edited by

Jane L. Ireland, Carol A. Ireland and Philip Birch

WILLAN
PUBLISHING

Published by

Willan Publishing
Culmcott House
Mill Street, Uffculme
Cullompton, Devon
EX15 3AT, UK
Tel: +44(0)1884 840337
Fax: +44(0)1884 840251
e-mail: info@willanpublishing.co.uk
website: www.willanpublishing.co.uk

Published simultaneously in the USA and Canada by

Willan Publishing
c/o ISBS, 920 NE 58th Ave, Suite 300,
Portland, Oregon 97213-3786, USA
Tel: +001(0)503 287 3093
Fax: +001(0)503 280 8832
e-mail: info@isbs.com
website: www.isbs.com

First published 2009

ISBN   978-1-84392-382-4 paperback
       978-1-84392-383-1 hardback

British Library Cataloguing-in-Publication Data

A catalogue record for this book is available from the British Library.

FSC
Mixed Sources
Product group from well-managed
forests and other controlled sources
Cert no. SGS-COC-2482
www.fsc.org
© 1996 Forest Stewardship Council

Project managed by Deer Park Productions, Tavistock, Devon
Typeset by GCS, Leighton Buzzard, Bedfordshire
Printed and bound by T.J. International Ltd, Padstow, Cornwall

Contents

Part 1   Assessment

Part 2   Treatment

Part 3   Management

List of figures and tables

Figures

Tables

List of abbreviations

ABC   Antecedents, Behaviours and Consequences model
ACC   Aggression Choice Chain
ACPC   Area Child Protection Committee
ARAI   Actuarial Risk Assessment Instrument
ASAP   Aid to Safety Assessment and Planning
ASPD   Antisocial Personality Disorder
AUC   Area Under the Curve

BPD   Borderline Personality Disorder
B-SAFER   Brief Spousal Assault Form for the Evaluation of Risk

CBT   Cognitive-Behavioural Therapy
CEOP   Child Exploitation and Online Protection [Centre]
COSA   Circles of Support and Accountability

DA   Danger Assessment
DRAMS   Dynamic Risk Assessment and Management System
DVSI   Domestic Violence Screening Inventory

ERASOR   Estimate of Risk of Adolescent Sexual Offender
            Recidivism

GES   Group Environment Scale
GLM   Good Lives Model

HCR-20	Historical, Clinical and Risk Management Guide – 20
HRDC	Human Resource Development Canada
HSF	Healthy Sexual Functioning programme
IBAQ	Internet Behaviour and Attitudes Questionnaire
IPV	Intimate Partner Violence
JSOAP	Juvenile Sex Offender Assessment Protocol
LMV-E	Life Minus Violence – Enhanced
LSI-R	Level of Service Inventory – Revised
MAPPA	Multi-Agency Public Protection Arrangements
MIP	Mood Induction Procedure
MMPI	Minnesota Multiphasic Personality Inventory
MORM	Multifactor Offender Readiness Model
MSI-II	Multiphasic Sex Inventory – II
NACC	Non-Aggression Choice Chain
NACRO	National Association for the Care and Resettlement of Offenders
NSPCC	National Society for the Prevention of Cruelty to Children
OASys	Offender Assessment System
ODARA	Ontario Domestic Assault Risk Assessment
OPB	Offence Parallel Behaviour
PCC	Psychology of Criminal Conduct
PCL-R	Psychopathy Checklist – Revised
PROTECT	Prosecutorial Remedies and Other Tools to end the Exploitation of Children Act 2003 (US)
RECON	Relationship and Context-based
RMP	Risk Management Plan
RRASOR	Rapid Risk Assessment for Sex Offender Recidivism
RSVP	Risk of Sexual Violence Protocol
SARA	Spousal Assault Risk Assessment guide
SARN	Structured Assessment of Risk and Need
SFO	Serious Further Offence
SOMA	Sex Offender Management Assistance programme (US)

SOO	Sex Offender Order
SORAG	Sex Offender Risk Appraisal Guide
SORC	Setting conditions, Organism variables, Response variables, Consequences
SOTP	Sex Offender Treatment Programme
SPJ	Structured Professional Judgment
SRM-RP	Self-Regulation Model of the Relapse Process
SSRI	Serotonin Selective Re-uptake Inhibitor
SOTEP	Sex Offender Treatment Evaluation Project
SVR-20	Sexual Violence Risk Scale – 20
UCJ	Unstructured Clinical Judgment
UCLA	University of California at Los Angeles
URICA	University of Rhode Island Change Assessment scale
VRAG	Violence Risk Appraisal Guide
VRS:SO	Violence Risk Scale: Sex Offender version
WAIS-III	Wechsler Adult Intelligence Scale – III

Notes on contributors

Stefanie Ashton Wigman is a demonstrator and PhD student at the University of Central Lancashire, Preston. She received her undergraduate degree from this university and began her research work in 2003, investigating former-intimate harassment and associated behaviours and traits in undergraduate, prison and large-scale crime survey samples. She has published journal articles on topics such as male stalking victims, and the roles of attachment, jealousy and dependency in former-intimate harassment.

Anthony R. Beech is Professor of Criminological Psychology at the Centre for Forensic and Family Psychology, University of Birmingham. He has published over 140 papers, books and book chapters, mainly on the assessment and treatment of sexual offenders. His work is regarded as having had a major influence on assessment and treatment in the UK. He has recently completed an authored book with Tony Ward and Devon Polaschek entitled *Theories of Sexual Offending* and an edited book with Theresa Gannon, Tony Ward and Dawn Fisher entitled *Aggressive Offenders' Cognition: Theory, Research and Practice*, both in the Wiley series in Forensic Clinical Psychology.

Philip Birch is a senior lecturer in the Division of Criminal and Community Justice and a university associate in the Applied Criminology Centre at the University of Huddersfield. His research interests include sex offenders, domestic violence, sex work and rape and sexual assault. Philip has also worked as a practitioner within the field of criminology; for the past five years he has held a number of posts within the Crime and Disorder Reduction Partnerships in

Kirklees, Bolton and Oldham Metropolitan Councils (UK). Over the last few years Philip has presented a number of conference papers on the issues of sex offenders, domestic violence and sex work. He is currently an elected member on the Executive Committee within the British Society of Criminology, of which he has been a member for over seven years. Philip is also a member of the Social Policy Association and NOTA (National Organisation for the Treatment of Abusers).

Douglas P. Boer is Associate Professor and Director of Clinical Psychology at the University of Waikato in Hamilton, New Zealand, and also Adjunct Professor of Disability Studies at RMIT University in Melbourne. He is also Associate Editor of the e-journal *Sex Offender Treatment* and the New Zealand editor of the journal *Sexual Abuse in Australia and New Zealand: An Interdisciplinary Journal*. Prior to 2006, Dr Boer was employed by the Correctional Service of Canada (CSC) for 15 years in a variety of contexts including sex offender therapist, institutional psychologist, sex offender programme director, senior and regional psychologist. While working for CSC, he also published a number of articles and structured clinical guideline manuals for use with offenders, most notably the Sexual Violence Risk – 20 (SVR-20) with a number of co-authors from Simon Fraser University.

Thomas Considine worked as a probation officer for West Yorkshire Probation Service for nine years. In this capacity he covered a broad range of main grade activities including report writing and the supervision of offenders. He also delivered a broad range of training activities including the use and implementation of risk assessment tools. He joined the University of Huddersfield in 2005 as a Senior Lecturer in Applied Criminology and Police Studies which are both part of the Division of Criminal and Community Justice. He is currently Course Leader of the Police Studies course and his teaching responsibilities predominantly cover victims and victimolgy as well as risk assessment and related issues around domestic violence and sexual/violent offenders.

Kevin S. Douglas is Associate Professor and Coordinator of the Law and Forensic Psychology Program in the Department of Psychology at Simon Fraser University. He is also Guest Professor of Applied Criminology at Mid-Sweden University, Sweden. He has a law degree from the University of British Columbia (2000) and a PhD in clinical (forensic) psychology from Simon Fraser University (2002). His research focuses on forensic assessment broadly, and violence risk assessment and psychopathy specifically. He is a co-author of the HCR-20 Violence Risk Assessment Scheme, which has been the subject of more than 50 evaluations, has been translated into 16 languages, and is used in correctional, forensic and psychiatric facilities across many countries. He has approximately 85 publications on topics including risk assessment and management, crime and violence, psychopathy, and forensic assessment broadly. In 2005, he was awarded the Saleem Shah Award for Early Career Excellence in Psychology and Law from the American Psychology-Law Society and the American Academy of Forensic Psychology. He was also awarded a Career Scholar Award from the Michael Smith Foundation for Health Research (a British Columbia health research funding agency).

Nicola Graham-Kevan is a Chartered Psychologist, Chartered Scientist and Fellow of the International Society for Research on Aggression (ISRA). Dr Graham-Kevan is the president of the International Family Aggression Society and has published over 20 papers, articles and book chapters, the majority of which are on intimate partner violence. Dr Graham-Kevan has presented at over 20 conferences, many of which were international, and has delivered invited keynote speeches both nationally and internationally.

Laura S. Guy is a PhD candidate in the clinical psychology programme (law and psychology stream) at Simon Fraser University under the supervision of Dr Kevin Douglas. She completed her undergraduate work at McGill University, including one year of study at the University of New South Wales. Laura obtained her Masters degree in clinical (forensic) psychology at Sam Houston State University under the supervision of Dr John Edens. She has published on topics related to violence risk assessment, psychopathic personality disorder, legal decision-making and the assessment of malingered psychopathology.

Stephen D. Hart is a professor in the Department of Psychology and a Member of the Mental Health, Law, and Policy Institute at Simon Fraser University in Canada, and also a Visiting Professor in the Faculty of Psychology at the University of Bergen in Norway. His work focuses on clinical-forensic assessment in criminal and civil settings, and especially on the assessment of violence risk and psychopathic personality disorder.

Leigh Harkins is a chartered forensic psychologist and a lecturer at the Centre for Forensic and Family Psychology at the University of Birmingham. Dr Harkins has published a number of papers, articles and book chapters, primarily in the area of sexual offender treatment effectiveness. Dr Harkins has previous experience in the assessment and treatment of offenders within the Correctional Service of Canada and at the Centre for Addiction and Mental Health in Toronto.

Bill Hebenton is Director of the Criminology Programme in the School of Law at the University of Manchester. He worked with the Home Office and ACPO on the early approach to the policing of sexual offenders in the community in the late 1990s, and completed the first evaluation of the pilot areas for lay-advisers to Multi-Agency Public Protection Arrangements in England and Wales. His current research interests lie mainly in comparative criminological research and in particular crime and punishment in the Greater China region; he is currently completing a socio-historical study of the development of criminology in China. He has held Visiting posts at the Institute of Sociology, Academia Sinica (Taiwan), the Graduate School of Criminology, National Taipei University (Taiwan) and the East China University of Politics and Law, Shanghai. He is a member of the editorial board of *Crime and Criminal Justice International*.

Carol A. Ireland is a chartered forensic psychologist and chartered scientist. She is Chair for the British Psychological Society's Division of Forensic Psychology. She has worked in HM Prison Service, and currently works for Mersey Care NHS Trust, where she is one of the leads for Sex Offender Therapies and is the lead for Crisis Negotiation. She also works at the University of Central Lancashire, teaching on Consultancy and Professional Practice. Dr Ireland has published a number of papers relating to sexual offending and crisis negotiation. She has also presented at a wide variety of national and international conferences on topics such as sexual offending, the role of cognitive impairments in offending and crisis negotiation.

Jane L. Ireland is a chartered forensic psychologist and Fellow of the International Society for Research on Aggression (ISRA). Professor Ireland holds a full professorial chair in the area of aggression research and is also a Violence Treatment Lead within Mersey Care NHS Trust, based within High Secure Psychological Services. Professor Ireland is a former Chair of the British Psychological Society's Division of Forensic Psychology, is current Chair of the British Psychological Society's Expert Witness Advisory Group and a representative at the Royal Courts of Justice. Professor Ireland has published over 60 papers, articles and book chapters, the majority of which are on intra-group aggression and management. Professor Ireland is a consultant and trainer for the Canadian Correctional Services and Japan's Forensic Psychiatric Services on aggression treatment and management.

Jennifer A.A. Lavoie is a PhD candidate in the Law and Psychology program at Simon Fraser University, Burnaby, BC. She is currently an Addiction and Mental Health Services (RAMHPS) scholar and a Research Officer with BC Mental Health and Addiction Services. She received an Honours degree in Psychology at Carleton University, Ottawa, and completed her Master's degree in the same field at Simon Fraser University. Her research contributes to a growing body of literature seeking to understand relationships between dynamic risk factors for adverse outcomes (such as violence, victimization, and self-harming behaviours) among mentally disordered populations. Her dissertation work explores the role of situational stress and coping in predicting prospective anger, violence, and other adverse outcomes among psychiatric outpatients.

Tim Jones is a senior lecturer at the University of Gloucestershire, an Associate Fellow of the British Psychological Society and a Chartered Psychologist. Prior to joining the University of Gloucestershire he completed a number of post-doctoral and academic positions. Tim is interested in the relationship between physical, psychological and virtual spaces and how individuals are able to move between such spaces (either physically or virtually) and the resulting demands (perceptually, cognitively and inter-personally) placed upon them. Researching the construct of space has most recently involved him investigating how memory can act as a barrier to regeneration projects and the role of the Internet in reinforcing sexual fantasies – although the two areas of application are vastly different the model of space can be applied to each. Tim retains close links with the centre for Criminal Justice Policy & Research at Birmingham City University where he currently co-supervises a PhD candidate investigating the relationship between Schizotypy Personality Disorder and crime.

P. Randall Kropp is a clinical and forensic psychologist specialising in the assessment and management of violent offenders. He works for the Forensic Psychiatric Services Commission of British Columbia, Canada, and is Adjunct Professor of Psychology at Simon Fraser University. He has conducted workshops on psycho-legal issues and risk assessment in 15 countries on five continents. He has frequently consulted with provincial, state and federal governments on matters related to violence against women and children. He has published numerous journal articles, book chapters and research reports, and is co-author of several works on risk assessment, including the *Manual for the Spousal Assault Risk Assessment Guide (SARA)*, the *Manual for the Sexual Violence Risk – 20 (SVR-20)* and the *Risk for Sexual Violence Protocol (RSVP)*.

Werner Tschan is the current president of AETAP (Association of European Threat Assessment Professionals). He is a leading expert in the prevention of interpersonal violence ranking from workplace violence, stalking, domestic and sexual violence. He serves as a Program Director at Zurich University for a postgraduate training course on intervention in and prevention of sexual violence. He works as a psychiatrist in private practice. He dedicated much of his career to the prevention of interpersonal violence and has been involved in many projects over the years. He lectures worldwide on various aspects of interpersonal violence and provides practical solutions based on a large 'frontline' expertise.

David Wilson is Professor of Criminology at Birmingham City University, and Editor of *The Howard Journal of Criminal Justice*. His published work includes *Innocence Betrayed: Paedophiles, the Media and Society* (Polity Press) and most recently *Serial Killers: Hunting Britons and their Victims, 1960–2006* (Waterside Press). He is the Vice Chair of the Howard League for Penal Reform and is currently Chair of the Commission on English Prisons Today.

Rachel Worthington is Deputy Head of Psychology and Programmes at HMP Risley, UK. She is trained in the family of HMP Sex Offender Treatment programmes and has extensive experience of completing a variety of risk assessments and treatments with sexual offenders in secure hospital and prison settings as well as in the community. She is also a lecturer on the MSc in Forensic Psychology at the University of Central Lancashire, lecturing in the assessment and treatment of violent and sexual offenders. Her special interest and research experience has been in exploring the experiences of staff working with offenders and she is currently co-editor for the Division of Forensic Psychology publication, *Forensic Update*.

Foreword

David P. Farrington

It is a great pleasure for me to welcome this outstandingly important book, which greatly advances our knowledge about risk assessment and treatment of violence, sex, domestic violence and stalking offenders. The coverage of the relatively new topic of stalking is especially noteworthy. All the chapters are well-written and highly informative. The editors should be congratulated for assembling this excellent collection and for their own superb contributions.

It is a great source of satisfaction to me to see the extent to which the field has developed since I edited *Prediction in Criminology* more than 20 years ago (Farrington and Tarling 1985). It is interesting how the term 'prediction' became a dirty word, possibly because some people thought that it had deterministic connotations. There were also worries about the stigmatising effects of giving a person a label such as 'dangerous'. Of course, all predictions are probabilistic and essentially concern the outcomes of groups rather than individuals. The term 'risk assessment' has proved to be more acceptable and durable. Nevertheless, many of the issues discussed in our book, such as how to select and combine predictor variables into an instrument, how to measure predictive efficiency and the amount of shrinkage in predictive efficiency between construction and validation samples, are still challenging.

This book makes many important points about risk assessment. For example, it is essential to measure clinical needs as well as risk and to use these in devising a treatment plan. Second, it is desirable to make risk assessment more positive, for example by including protective factors as well as risk factors, by focusing on strengths and by collaborating more with offenders; otherwise, offenders may be too worried about the potential consequences for them of risk assessment to cooperate. Third, dynamic as well as static instruments are important in order to assess change over time and hence to predict when offenders can safely be released. Fourth, risk and needs assessment instruments should be incorporated within a structured clinical judgment approach.

A great advance in recent years has been the use of the area under the ROC curve (AUC) as a measure of predictive accuracy. Nowadays, the AUCs of many risk assessment instruments are being systematically compared. However, rather than trying to decide which instrument is 'best', it would be better to extract the most important items from several different instruments to develop new devices. It is unfortunate that some owners of instruments (not represented in this book!) seem to be mainly concerned to make money by selling them rather than to advance knowledge about assessment. The conflict between commercial and academic considerations militates against the continuous improvement and evolution of instruments.

All assessment instruments need to be based on fundamental research on explanations of violence, sex offending and other forms of behaviour, and especially on knowledge gained in prospective longitudinal studies of individual development over time (see, for example, Farrington 2005, 2007). More within-individual analyses in longitudinal studies are needed, comparing changes in offending over time that follow changes in explanatory variables over time. For example, we found that changes within individuals in delinquent peers were not followed by changes in delinquency, even though delinquent peers and delinquency were highly correlated between individuals at the same time (Farrington *et al.*, 2002). In contrast, decreases in parental supervision within individuals over time did predict increases in delinquency, suggesting that poor parental supervision might be a causal risk factor.

Current risk assessment instruments largely operate between individuals: high-risk people are compared with low-risk people. This encourages the use of static devices. Dynamic risk assessment instruments that predict within individuals over time would be more relevant to intervention. These instruments could identify time periods when people are especially at risk of offending. They could be based on results obtained in longitudinal studies supplemented by repeated measures of situational factors.

These issues, and many other up-to-the-minute issues central to the assessment and treatment of violent, sex and other offenders, are all discussed in this excellent book. It should be essential reading for forensic psychologists and for other scholars, practitioners and policy-makers who are concerned with these types of offenders. It should help to reduce the prevalence and incidence of these troubling social problems.

David P. Farrington
Professor of Psychological Criminology
Cambridge University

References

Farrington, D.P. (ed.) (2005) *Integrated Developmental and Life-Course Theories of Offending*, Advances in Criminology Theory, Vol. 14. New Brunswick, NJ: Transaction.

Farrington, D.P. (2007) 'Origins of violent behaviour over the life span', in D.J. Flannery, A.T. Vaszonyi and I.D. Waldman (eds), *The Cambridge Handbook of Violent Behaviour and Aggression*. Cambridge: Cambridge University Press, pp. 19–48.

Farrington, D.P. and Tarling, R. (eds) (1985) *Prediction in Criminology*. Albany, NY: State University of New York Press.

Farrington, D.P., Loeber, R., Yin, Y. and Anderson, S.J. (2002) 'Are within-individual causes of delinquency the same as between-individual causes?', *Criminal Behaviour and Mental Health*, 12: 53–68.

This book is dedicated to our mother whose journalistic interest in violent crime was undoubtedly responsible for our chosen career. Thanks mum.
Jane L. Ireland and Carol A. Ireland

Dedicated to my mum and dad for their continued support and encouragement.
Philip Birch

Part I

Assessment

Chapter I

Violence risk assessment: principles and models bridging prediction to management

Jennifer A.A. Lavoie, Laura S. Guy and Kevin S. Douglas

Interpersonal violence is a social concern that cuts across geographical, religious and racial boundaries. Preventing violence is desirable not only in terms of averting physical and emotional harm, but also because it constitutes a major international public health issue. The World Health Organisation estimated that in the year 2000 there were approximately 1.66 million deaths due directly to violence (e.g. Krug *et al.* 2002). The costs of violence can be observed from a monetary perspective as well; the dollar figure for consequences of violence to society (e.g. in terms of correctional and judicial costs, medical and mental health interventions for victims and perpetrators, absenteeism from work, police/fire services, etc.) has been estimated to be in the billions (e.g. Miller *et al.* 1996). A viable avenue for containing these human and financial costs is violence risk assessment. If conducted carefully, such assessments have the potential to evaluate and manage risk of future violence and thus can play a critical role in preventing violence (Douglas *et al.* 1999; Douglas and Kropp 2002).

Violence risk assessments are required in more than a dozen legal and quasi-legal situations (Lyon *et al.* 2001; Shah 1978), including civil commitment, bail determination, juvenile transfer and decertification, release decision-making (hospitals, correctional facilities), specialised penal decisions (i.e. sexually violent predator laws in the US, dangerous offender legislation in Canada, and dangerous and severe personality disorder law in the UK), and in clinical practice more broadly (e.g. as they pertain to *Tarasoff*-type duties). The stakes involved in risk assessments are high and the costs associated with errors are serious: such assessments implicate important social values such as protection of the public and individual civil liberties (see Schopp 1996). Individuals who are assessed incorrectly as being at high risk for violence may face involuntary civil commitment, mandated outpatient treatment, forced administration of medication and loss of a host of constitutionally protected civil liberties (see Monahan *et al.* 2001). Individuals who are assessed incorrectly as not being at risk for violence and hence permitted to retain their freedom may violate others' civil rights and legally protected interests to be free from injury by others.

Over the past several decades, the expanding role of violence risk assessment in the practice of forensic-clinical psychology and psychiatry in part has resulted from a series of developments in the legal arena. Whereas the basis for involuntary hospitalisation was once 'need for treatment', this criterion was replaced in the 1960s by 'dangerousness to others'. In the 1972 case *Lessard* v. *Schmidt*, a federal district court in Milwaukee ruled Wisconsin's commitment law to be unconstitutional. The effect of the decision was to replace the traditional *parens patriae* grounds for commitment in the United States with a fairly strict 'dangerousness' standard. Also during the 1970s, imposing tort liability on clinicians who negligently failed to protect potential victims saw its genesis (*Tarasoff* v. *Regents of the University of California* 1976). During the following decade, in the 1980s, many states enacted statutes authorising involuntary treatment in the community for otherwise 'dangerous' patients. The 1990s saw risk assessments of violence being explicitly mandated in the Americans with Disabilities Act 1990, which protected the employment rights of people with disabilities unless those disabilities resulted in an employee becoming a 'direct threat' of violence to co-workers or customers.

The field of violence risk assessment has undergone a tremendous metamorphosis during the past three decades. Whereas research conducted in the 1970s and early 1980s about mental health professionals' ability to predict violence seemed unpromising, today there exist a substantial number of research studies that provide evidence of ability to predict reoffending with much improved accuracy relative to previous years. Undoubtedly, this advancement is owed in large part to researchers having identified the specific factors that demonstrate robust empirical associations with various types of reoffending among different groups. In fact, a sufficiently large number of studies has been completed to warrant quantitative syntheses within divergent areas of the literature, including mentally disordered offenders (Bonta *et al.* 1998), sexual offenders (Hanson and Morton-Bourgon 2005), stalkers (Rosenfeld 2004), prisoners (Gendreau *et al.* 1997), adult offenders (Gendreau *et al.* 1996), juveniles (Cottle *et al.* 2001; Heilbrun *et al.* 2005) and delinquent girls (Hubbard and Pratt 2002).

A seemingly natural progression in light of the accruing knowledge base on specific risk factors was the development (and subsequent proliferation) of risk-assessment instruments and decision-support tools that incorporate these factors in one way or another. Collectively, these tools reflect various approaches to the clinical task of violence risk assessment. The obvious question that arises, then, is: how best do we approach the task of violence risk assessment and management? Over the last decade especially there has been a fair amount of commentary and empirical work that may serve to guide practising clinicians. In the present chapter, we will review these efforts, focusing on conceptual developments and practical challenges in the risk-assessment field, how these developments and challenges are incorporated into prevailing models of risk assessment and management (including an overview of representative instruments developed within these models), and where we see the future of the field headed.

Developments in the risk assessment field: from prediction to management of risk

For decades, prediction was a central focus in violence risk assessment; empirical contributions to the field at that time were pervaded by this particular perspective. More recently, the task has come to be regarded as an assessment of risk rather than as a prediction, with the concomitant goal being violence prevention (Hart 1998). This shift highlighted the importance of viewing risk as an ongoing, changing entity as opposed to one in which one-time, yes/no predictions would be appropriate (Douglas *et al.* 1999; Otto 2000; Steadman 2000; Webster *et al.* 2000). Indeed, some scholars have defined risk assessment as 'the process of speculating in an informed way about the aggressive acts a person might commit and to determine the steps that should be taken to prevent those acts and minimize their negative consequences' (Kropp *et al.* 2002: 147; also see Hart 1998). Such scenario planning is useful because it calls for the specification of conditions that may exacerbate or mitigate risk, rather than an 'on-off, context-free prediction of dangerousness based on a consistent algorithm' (Mulvey and Lidz 1995: 136; also see Skeem *et al.* 2000), a desirable, though unattainable, goal.

Clearly, in order for violence risk to be reduced, the factors that elevate risk for violence must be *reducible*. Risk predictors can be classified broadly into two types: static and dynamic (Bonta 1996; Douglas and Skeem 2005). Static variables are those that generally do not change with time, whereas dynamic variables are amenable to change. Dynamic variables may change rapidly (i.e. intoxication, negative mood states) or slowly (i.e. personality or attitudinal factors). The early, prediction-focused approach to violence risk assessment was associated with research that focused on static risk factors. Of particular interest to researchers and practitioners, whose efforts focus on risk reduction, are dynamic risk variables that, when changed, are associated with a reduction in risk for criminal behaviour (i.e. criminogenic needs factors; see Andrews and Bonta 2006).

Research on the role of dynamic risk factors in violence risk assessment represents a relatively recent empirical effort, and much less evidence regarding this type of risk factor is available – primarily because of the resource-intensive type of research design required to study them. Andrews and Bonta (2006) differentiate between various types of risk factors, as well as the nature of the information that they can provide about their relation with criminal behaviour, as a function of research design. A *correlate* of criminal behaviour is established via cross-sectional study designs (i.e. extreme groups or survey designs), and indicates the strength of the association between a variable and past criminal behaviour. *Predictors* are risk factors made known vis-à-vis longitudinal designs and thus reflect the relation between changes in a variable and associated changes in future criminal behaviour. Most stringent are investigations of the effects of deliberate interventions; using a true experimental design will yield information about the *causal* relation between a variable and criminal behaviour. Similar distinctions have been made in the field of psychiatry (Kraemer *et al.* 1997).

The distinction between the roles and applications of dynamic versus static factors is readily apparent when viewed within a legal decision-making context pertaining to potential for future violence (Heilbrun 1997; Heilbrun *et al.* 1998). Heilbrun (1997) described two models – the *prediction model* and the *management model* – that may be applicable depending on the given circumstances. Not surprisingly, the goal within the former is violence prediction whereas the goal within the latter is risk reduction. An assessment is made only once within the prediction model but on multiple occasions within the management model. The sensitivity to change in risk status is low in the prediction model but essential in the management model.

The distinctions between these risk factors are not merely academic but rather are important in applied decision-making contexts. The type of risk assessment being conducted will dictate the consideration of different types of risk factors. Referring to the assessment of risk for sexual violence, Hanson and Harris (1998) commented:

> Static, fixed predictors, such as gender or criminal record, can be useful for evaluating long-term risk potential (e.g. dangerous offender applications). Stable dynamic factors, such as personality disorders or deviant sexual preferences, may also be used for long-term risk assessments, but they are crucial for assessing enduring changes (e.g. treatment outcome, parole release). In contrast, acute, rapidly changing factors, such as negative mood or alcohol intoxication, can signal the timing of reoffence, and are particularly useful for monitoring risk during community supervision. (p. 2)

Moreover, more than one model of risk assessment may be appropriate under some circumstances. For example, during the civil commitment process, the prediction-oriented model initially may be more suitable when an individual's risk to self or others is being evaluated. Following commitment, however, the management-oriented risk assessment model would be more useful in terms of treatment planning.

Although the benefits of focusing on risk prevention, management and reduction are clear, in order to do so one first must be able to identify risk status with accuracy. Risk assessment and reduction thus are irreconcilably intertwined. In the following section, we will expand upon this theme by elucidating guiding principles and outlining practical challenges associated with risk assessment and management. In other words, what types of guidance can clinicians expect to receive from a sound risk assessment scheme? Following this, we will evaluate leading models of violence risk assessment vis-à-vis our guiding principles.

Practical assessment challenges and guiding principles

Without doubt, *violent* human behaviour is tremendously intricate, multi-faceted and difficult to forecast with precision. It is essential, then, that any approach designed to assess violence risk condense its complexity in order to arrive at timely, practical and meaningful risk-relevant conclusions. There are a number of challenges in constructing an assessment instrument that embodies this quality. Outlined below are five principles recommended for any risk assessment procedure to possess (and hence to be evaluated).

Principle 1: Reliable identification of accurate violence risk factors

Decision-makers must be aware of, and be able to reliably identify, accurate risk factors in order to determine the level of risk posed by an individual. Decades of empirical research investigating various types of violent behaviour has been particularly dedicated to uncovering reliable risk factors (for reviews, see Douglas and Webster 1999; Monahan and Steadman 1994; Otto 2000). Given this body of work, any useful risk assessment instrument should comprise relevant scientifically supported risk factors. Further, the instrument must clearly and precisely define (i.e. operationalise) these risk factors in order to (a) foster agreement between decision-makers as to the presence of the risk factor in a given case (i.e. promote inter-rater reliability) and (b) maintain the relationship between the risk factor and violence.

To illustrate, research has identified the construct of psychopathy as a robust risk factor for future violent behavior (for a review, see Douglas *et al.* 2006). However, there are numerous approaches to defining and measuring psychopathy; some methods are superior to others in accurately capturing the construct. A meaningful risk assessment procedure that incorporates psychopathy must define it so as to reflect the most empirically valid conceptualisation and measurement. Careful and contemplative operationalisation will optimise the likelihood that the assessed risk factor will relate to violence as intended.

Principle 2: Comprehensive coverage of violence risk factors

The second challenge to clinicians is the ability to consider almost all of the known key risk factors relevant to the specific type of violence of interest. A risk assessment procedure or measure must therefore contain most identified risk factors. Upon deliberating each factor, clinicians may choose to focus on factors that are pertinent to the case at hand and similarly discard irrelevant factors if necessary to arrive at a violence risk decision. An incomprehensive coverage of violence risk factors is perilous when potentially important and pertinent risk factors exist for a case but fail to be considered by the clinician subsequently resulting in (a) an inappropriately lower (or higher) estimated risk status, and/or (b) unpredicted violence.

Principle 3: Relevance of risk assessment scheme to risk management and risk reduction

In many circumstances, once a decision-maker has identified the most important risk factors present in a given case, the next step is to make recommendations for treatment, management and risk reduction. Many consider the ability for a risk assessment approach to inform these types of risk management decisions to be vital (Douglas *et al.* 2001), given that clinicians are regularly required to assist in managing the risk of their clients, or at minimum are responsible for making recommendations regarding how to do so.

A risk assessment procedure that facilitates the construction of a promising risk reduction plan must encompass two features: (a) violence risk factors that can be feasibly targeted for treatment; and (b) a mechanism for linking the assessment of these risk factors to recommendations concerning their management (a point that will be discussed under Principle 4). In order for clinicians to attend to risk factors to which intervention may be applied, the risk assessment procedure should contain *dynamic* violence risk factors (Douglas and Skeem 2005).

Unfortunately, little guidance is available to assist clinicians who are responsible for the ongoing monitoring, treating and decision-making concerning at-risk individuals. The preponderance of extant research emphasises 'risk status', or identifying individuals at higher levels of risk compared to other individuals (Douglas and Skeem 2005; Mulvey *et al.* 1996). Risk status often accentuates static risk factors for violence, allowing little opportunity for risk level to change over time. Therefore, risk status itself is of limited utility when the task is monitoring or treating an at-risk individual. While being at high risk for violence as a function of the presence of many static risk factors might provide clinicians with information regarding the *intensity* of intervention needed to stem prospective violence, this knowledge does little to guide specific management efforts toward meaningful targets (Douglas and Kropp 2002).

Importantly, however, risk for violence ebbs and flows over time within each individual. In order to be maximally effective in reducing violence potential within a person, clinicians must extend their assessment beyond baseline *risk status* which underscores inter-individual variability to evaluating *risk state* which emphasises intra-individual variability in potential for prospective violence (Skeem and Mulvey 2002). Risk state may be defined as a person's propensity to engage in violent behaviour at a given time that is predicated on specific changes in psychological, biological and social variables in his or her life (Skeem and Mulvey 2002). Central to this notion is an acknowledgement that risk factors vary in the degree to which they are changeable, ranging from highly static variables (e.g. gender, race, history of violence) to highly dynamic ones (e.g. intoxication, weapon availability; Heilbrun 1997; see also Kazdin *et al.* 1997; Kraemer *et al.* 1997).

The main objective in many risk assessment and management contexts is to evaluate factors and their variability over time, rather than assuming that single-point time estimates will remain valid indefinitely (Douglas *et al.* 1999; Douglas and Kropp 2002; Douglas and Skeem 2005; Webster *et al.* 2000). Indeed, 'an individual's risk [state] may be seen as changing over time and in response to interventions, as contrasted with the single, unchanging risk [status] estimate yielded under the prediction model by actuarial tools that use static (unchangeable through planned intervention) risk factors (Dvoskin and Heilbrun 2001: 8).

Clearly, the field must develop sound methods for evaluating changeable features of risk and systematic procedures for targeting these aspects to reduce violence (Dvoskin and Heilbrun 2001). With an enhanced ability to assess ongoing change in violence potential, clinicians could make better decisions about *when* intervention is needed to mitigate acute exacerbations of risk, *how much* individuals respond to intervention and *whether* levels of supervision should be modified. These payoffs would be most pronounced among the treatment of high-risk individuals in the community, where effective risk monitoring and reduction could stem the occurrence of violence.

Principle 4: Clear and logical method of communicating risk decisions

The task of how best to summarise and communicate an individual's risk estimate can be challenging. Some instruments provide numerical or probabilistic estimates of risk that are valid for a particular time frame (i.e. that a given individual is 68 per cent likely to be violent over the next six months) based on the scoring of the risk factors that are present (i.e. Quinsey *et al.* 1998). By itself, this approach alone is inadequate for reducing risk because it is unclear what actions should follow the probabilistic statement. In fact, at times such estimates might actually be misleading because they tend to be quite statistically unstable across samples. Risk assessment approaches should give rise to categorical, descriptive risk statements that are tied both to estimated risk level and the associated intensity of management that is anticipated to reduce risk. For example, a statement of 'high risk' (as opposed to moderate or low risk) would suggest the presence of several risk factors (or a few very salient ones for the given individual) that, relative to other persons, indicates that a person is likely to act violently in the future if interventions are not engaged, that a high level of management is required to restrict the risk and that the management plan should comprise specific interventions that relate to the known dynamic risk factors. Thus the risk communication system should compel, facilitate and specify action. Clinicians should not only communicate the degree of risk posed, but how best to reduce it. Notably, research suggests that clinicians prefer a management-oriented, prescriptive and categorical risk communication approach over simple probability or numeric estimates of future risk (Heilbrun *et al.* 2000). The end result is clinically relevant, yet scientifically based, risk estimates.

Principle 5: Reviewable and accountable decision process

Critically, a risk assessment approach should be entirely reviewable by others (e.g. judges, lawyers). Because many of these decisions transpire in legally relevant contexts, it is important that third parties are able to reconstruct how decisions were made so that they may be contested if necessary. Further, the decision-making process should be transparent given the significant personal implications that arise from these decisions (e.g. being deprived of the right to liberty). Finally, for continuity of care, clinicians should document information derived from risk assessment processes in detail to assist other correctional or mental health personnel. As such, the assessment process should state unambiguously the risk factors included, the scoring rules and the principles followed to integrate risk factors into a final risk decision.

Together, these five principles can provide the basis for meaningful and practical violence risk assessment and management. Next we discuss the three dominant models of risk assessment and how they present against the principles we have recommended.

Models of decision-making in risk assessment

Generally, decision-making approaches to risk assessment fall into two broad categories: unstructured and structured decisions. Clinical assessment comprises the former approach; actuarial-based decisions and structured professional judgment (SPJ) comprise the latter. Here, we will review the historical background of the major risk assessment models and examine their objectives, strengths and weaknesses. Each approach is also evaluated in light of the principles outlined previously.

Clinical approach: the first generation

Traditionally, the most common approach to risk assessment is unstructured clinical judgment. Assessors exercise absolute discretion over selecting which information to consider, and how to interpret and synthesise information to render a decision (Grove and Meehl 1996). The clinical approach has been described as an 'informal, in the head, impressionistic, subjective conclusion, reached (somehow) by a human clinical judge' (Grove and Meehl 1996: 294). Flexibility is the strength of clinical prediction; clinicians can adapt their decision-making to accentuate idiosyncratic case features that are particularly salient or unique (Hart 1998). This approach, however, has many shortcomings. The technique tends to lack consistency because clinicians focus on diverse sources of information and can subsequently form contrary conclusions (Dawes *et al.* 1989). Moreover, the clinical approach tends to preclude transparency. It is difficult to challenge a clinical judgment because assessors often fail to specify their method for arriving at their final decision (Grove *et al.* 2000). Finally, decisions based on unaided clinical judgment, despite being better than chance, are less accurate then those based on structured approaches (Mossman 1994), with some commentators arguing that they are not much more accurate than chance prediction (Cocozza and Steadman 1976; Dawes *et al.* 1989; Ennis and Emery 1978; Faust and Ziskin 1988; Grove and Meehl 1996; Meehl 1954; Thornberry and Jacoby 1979).

While much of the early research was beleaguered by methodological flaws, additional research efforts have been made to evaluate clinical predictions of violence. For example, Rofman *et al.* (1980) found some support for short-term clinical predictions of inpatient violence in a retrospective study comparing psychiatric patients committed on grounds of danger paired with an unmatched group of patients committed for alternate reasons. In a study of unstructured, dichotomous prediction of inpatient violence among psychiatric patients, Janofsky *et al.* (1988) found that psychiatrists were unable to forecast physical violence above chance levels. Hoptman *et al.* (1999) asked psychiatrists to rate the likelihood that forensic patients would engage in institutional physical violence within three months. Clinician predictions were significantly more accurate than chance (overall rate of correct prediction was 71 per cent). Sepejak *et al.* (1983) who had mental health professionals rate the dangerousness of 598 pre-trial forensic remandees reported a positive predictive power of 56 per cent, but a false positive rate of 61 per cent.

Studies employing stronger methodologies have assisted in clarifying these equivocal research findings (see Lidz *et al.* 1993). McNiel and colleagues, who examined predictions of violence in the context of civil commitment of psychiatric patients, have shown consistently that clinicians can forecast inpatient violence at better than chance levels (McNeil and Binder 1987, 1991, 1995; McNeil *et al.* 1998). Lidz *et al.* (1993), in one of the strongest studies on clinical prediction, reported that clinicians' predictions were moderately accurate, although they were no better than chance for women and were outperformed by a brief actuarial screen. Other studies have failed to find strong support for unstructured clinical risk assessments. Monahan (1981) cited a series of errors typical of clinical judgment that led to prediction inaccuracy. The most common fault was failing to consider base rate information. Other errors included a lack of integration of situational/contextual information, reliance on invalid risk factors and a failure to clearly specify the criterion variable.

In essence, the performance of unstructured clinical judgment considering our five principles of risk assessment is weak. In light of Principles 1 and 2, the clinical approach must be rated as 'poor' because there is only inconsistent empirical evidence that the method is reliable, makes use of accurate risk factors and does so comprehensively. The clinical approach should be considered 'fair' in fulfilling Principle 3 given its flexibility and inherent relatedness to treatment and intervention. However, for Principles 4 and 5, the clinical approach must be rated as 'poor' because no rules are present that specify what risk factors are to be considered, how they are defined, how a final decision is reached, what that decision means in terms of risk level or management needs or how the decision is to be communicated. A paucity of rules is the major drawback of the unstructured approach.

Actuarial approach: the second generation

In response to the shortcomings of the unstructured clinical approach, many scholars, clinicians and commentators in the risk assessment field strove to impose increased structure upon the risk decision process. The actuarial approach involves applying a predetermined set of decision rules, such as a formula or algorithm, to render a judgment (Dawes *et al.* 1989; Meehl 1954; Monahan 1981). Grove and Meehl (1996) described the actuarial process as 'a formal method, [that] uses an equation, a formula ... to arrive at a probability or expected value, of some outcome' (p. 294). This approach has been further portrayed as well-specified, mechanical, and wholly reproducible (Grove *et al.* 2000). Actuarial predictors are empirically validated, being selected because they have been demonstrated to be independently related to violence in a particular construction sample.

The strength of actuarial prediction is the reliable and valid identification of accurate risk factors. Because actuarial methods use an explicit coding procedure, the use of this approach should result in the same decision among a given data set each time. A structured rule set also facilitates transparency (i.e. decisions are reviewable and accountable). Usually, actuarial instruments are statistically optimised in that variables are weighted according to their relationship to the criterion variable (Dawes *et al.* 1989). Many instruments consist of a checklist of risk factors that are independently scored; the combination (simple summation or more complex combinatory procedures) of these scores equals the estimated actuarial probability of violence attributed to an individual.

A typical example of an actuarial measure is the Violence Risk Appraisal Guide (VRAG) developed by Quinsey *et al.* (1998). The VRAG is a twelve-item instrument constructed from a derivation sample of Canadian male offenders ($N = 618$) who were receiving treatment in a forensic facility, or were found either not guilty by reason of insanity or unfit or incompetent to stand trial. The instrument was construed using a pseudo-retrospective design, in which a regression analysis identified twelve variables that each predicted a dichotomous outcome (i.e. any new criminal charge for a violent offence or comparable institutional behaviour). Quinsey and colleagues (1998) reported that the VRAG was strongly associated with subsequent violence (*Mult R* = 0.44).

There is general consensus that the actuarial approach is superior to the unstructured clinical model in terms of predictive accuracy among the same samples. Grove and colleagues (2000) conducted a meta-analysis of 136 studies that directly compared actuarial and clinical prediction methods. Overall, approximately half of the studies favoured actuarial prediction, half of the studies indicated no difference between the two approaches, and a minority (6 per cent) favoured clinical prediction. Actuarial prediction resulted in an approximate 10 per cent increment in hit rate compared to clinical prediction. Grove *et al.* concluded that the research 'modestly favours mechanical prediction' (2000: 21).

Despite this advantage, the actuarial approach has many limitations in the risk assessment context. By design, actuarial models that are statistically developed optimise their predictive ability in the sample upon which they were constructed in part by taking advantage of chance associations and therefore may not generalise or apply as well when extended beyond derivation samples (Gottfredson and Gottfredson 1986). For instance, Blair *et al.* (in press) reported meta-analytic findings that the mean correlation between actuarial instruments such as the VRAG and violence in cross-validation studies was substantially smaller than it was in development samples. This effect was even more pronounced when the cross-validation was done by independent researchers not involved with the development of the instrument. For instance, the correlation of 0.44 for the VRAG in the development sample 'shrank' to 0.30 in independent cross-validation studies. Second, deriving valid actuarial judgments in the risk assessment field can be challenging when in many practical situations decision-makers are concerned about predicting behaviour in circumstances that are incongruent with the actuarial protocol (Litwack 2001). For example, actuarial instruments based on lengthy follow-up periods are of limited use for clinicians who are concerned with imminent violence, because the algorithmic scoring rules were determined with a particular set of conditions in place. A third concern with actuarial models is that they tend to ignore low base rate factors and potentially vital case-specific information. Because risk factors are predetermined, additional information is not considered (Melton *et al.* 1997). Further, actuarial models have been criticised for their rigidity, their lack of sensitivity to change and their tendency to exclude dynamic risk factors. Moreover, reliance on factors with empirically demonstrated predictive power can result in the inclusion of risk factors that may be legally or ethically objectionable (e.g. gender, race). Lastly, actuarial instruments may fail optimally to inform violence prevention, intervention and risk management (Dvoskin and Heilbrun 2001; Hart 1998).

We consider the actuarial method to be 'good' with respect to Principle 1 because the approach involves the reliable identification of accurate risk factors. The approach is assessed as 'fair' in embodying Principle 2 because risk factor coverage on actuarial tests often omits potentially important risk factors (typically dynamic ones). It is evaluated as 'fair' for Principle 3 because, although the actuarial approach might be able to inform the necessary intensity of risk management, it is generally less able to specify the types of risk management strategies that would be most useful. The approach is similarly rated as 'fair' with respect to Principle 4 because, although it produces logically derived estimates of risk level, it tends not to do so in a manner than specifies, aids or compels risk-reducing interventions. Finally, we rate the actuarial approach as 'good' in adhering to Principle 5. It is intrinsically reviewable and transparent due to the clarity in conveying which risk factors entered into the decision.

Structured professional judgment approach: the third generation

The structured professional judgment (SPJ) model of decision-making (e.g. Borum 1996; Douglas and Kropp 2002; Hart 1998) is characterised by adherence to explicit guidelines that are grounded in the scientific literature. This model is intended to capitalise on some of the attributes associated with actuarial decision-making that promote reliability and accountability, while concurrently allowing professional flexibility that is practically relevant and responsive to each case (Douglas et al. 1999; Hart 1998).

Evaluators using the SPJ approach review all relevant clinical data to determine the presence of specific risk factors. On the basis of these factors, their relevance to the individual case and the anticipated intensity of intervention required to reduce risk, evaluators render an overall judgment of risk – that is, a structured final risk judgment of low, moderate or high. In contrast to actuarial approaches, no fixed or explicit rules for combining items are prescribed to arrive at the final risk judgment. Indeed, professional discretion is viewed as potentially valuable and appropriate for the assessment of risk, so long as it is buffered by the requisite structure to reduce the complexity of the clinical task and guide clinical discretion. Structure is imposed on the decision-making process in several ways: (a) by identifying the specific risk factors to be considered; (b) by operationalising these risk factors and recommending the best method of obtaining data; (c) by specifying fixed scoring guidelines for each risk factor; and (d) by providing guidance for rendering final judgments of categorical risk level (Douglas et al. 2003).

Professional judgment benefits from this sort of structure in several ways (see Boer et al. 1997). First, such guidelines can make risk assessments more systematic and therefore promote increased agreement among clinicians. Second, guidelines can improve the accuracy of predictions because risk factors are selected on the basis of empirically demonstrated associations with violence. Third, guidelines have the potential to facilitate the planning and delivery of interventions. Finally, because they are intentionally developed to be transparent, such guidelines may facilitate the objective evaluation of the adequacy of risk assessments in the course of routine quality assurance or critical incident reviews.

The risk factors specified in SPJ measures reflect a set of core factors that the scientific and professional literature broadly identify as having important, empirical associations with the type of violence under consideration. Consequently, SPJ measures are intended to be more generalisable across samples and settings relative to actuarial measures. Both static and dynamic risk factors are included in SPJ measures; the inclusion of the latter reflects the model's emphasis on risk management (versus prediction). Moreover, because dynamic factors by definition can change over time, final risk judgments made within the SPJ framework have an 'expiry date' or 'shelf life' and therefore must be updated as necessary.

The first set of structured professional guidelines developed to assess general violence was the HCR-20 (Webster *et al.* 1997). First published in 1995 (Webster *et al.* 1995), the HCR-20 was constructed with input from various groups of stakeholders, including researchers, clinicians and administrators. Drafts were revised in consultation with a wide variety of colleagues; the revision of the initial preliminary 1995 version reflected critical feedback from users of the first version (see Douglas *et al.* 2001). The HCR-20 is so-named for its inclusion of twenty risk factors in Historical, Clinical and Risk management domains. The factors were selected rationally following a comprehensive review of the scientific research available at that time. The HCR-20 currently is being revised and, as one part of the development of the third version, a comprehensive evaluation of the research and professional literature published since 1997 was conducted (Guy and Wilson 2007) to inform decisions regarding the continued importance of the various risk factors and to identify ways in which the operationalisation of the factors potentially may be refined to reflect current research. Substantial empirical evidence has accrued that supports the use of the HCR-20 as a reliable and valid tool for assessing violence (Nikolova *et al.* 2006; Douglas *et al.* 2007).

Although most research using SPJ measures has examined their performance when used actuarially (i.e. by summing scores on the individual risk factors), several published studies have demonstrated that the structured final decisions do predict violence and, often, do so at levels equalling or surpassing actuarial predictions (either by the instruments themselves used in an actuarial manner or in comparison to actuarial instruments). Of the eleven peer-reviewed published studies that we were able to locate, five reported that the SPJ final judgment demonstrated *incremental* validity compared to actuarial decisions for predicting violence (de Vogel and de Ruiter 2006; Douglas *et al.* 2003; Douglas *et al.* 2005; Enebrink *et al.* 2006; Kropp and Hart 2000); two reported that the SPJ final judgment yielded larger effect sizes than an actuarial decision (de Vogel *et al.* 2004, de Vogel and de Ruiter 2005); two presented analyses indicating equivalent predictive utility of the two indices (Catchpole and Gretton 2003; Douglas *et al.* 2005); and two did not support the relative superiority of the SPJ final judgment (Sjösted and Långström 2002; Viljoen *et al.* 2008). Taken together, these results indicate that clinical decisions, when made within a specific, structured framework, offer valid assessments of violence risk.

In terms of how the SPJ approach fares with respect to the five principles, we rate it as follows. For Principles 1 to 3, we regard the SPJ model as good because it provides reliable identification of a comprehensive set of management-relevant and accurate risk factors. All SPJ measures include dynamic risk factors, and test manuals specify the relevance of these factors to risk management. The model also is 'good' with respect to Principles 4 and 5; although in principle the model espouses the values represented by these two principles, in practice most SPJ measures could benefit from enhanced structure for making the final risk judgments.

Future directions and conclusions

As the reader might have surmised, we support maximising the relevance of violence risk assessment to risk management and risk reduction efforts. For this reason we view (a) dynamic risk, and (b) randomised control trials as two potential areas of research that represent the most promising avenues for furthering the development of risk assessment scholarship. Continued efforts to identify the most promising changeable or dynamic risk factors will inform the second goal of implementing violence reduction interventions that flow from sound risk assessment procedures.

However, these two areas of scholarship are incredibly difficult to research. As reported by Douglas and Skeem (2005), studies on dynamic risk need to be able to address the following issues (in addition to using a prospective design and repeated measurements over time):

- a variety of potential trajectories that risk factors may follow so as to capture, as accurately as possible, the 'true' change in risk factors over time;

- both stable and time-specific components of a construct;

- mediational effects of one variable on another (i.e. does a third variable explain why two others are related?);

- moderating effects of variables (i.e. does the relationship between two variables change as a function of a third variable, such as having differential strength across gender?);

- incremental predictive improvement of dynamic risk factors beyond static or historical ones, as well as potential interactions between static and dynamic factors;

- interactions between risk factors (i.e. do changes in substance use and symptoms of mental illness interact to increase the risk of violence?);

- uni-directional and bi-directional effects of risk factors on one another and on violence. Bi-directional effects are sometimes referred to as reciprocal or transactional effects, and essentially mean that two constructs influence one another as time passes (symptoms cause substance use, which in turn worsens symptoms, which in turn further increases substance use).

Once progress has been made in terms of identifying the strongest dynamic risk factors, the nature of how they change, and what mediates or moderates their change, then researchers can turn their efforts to designing treatment studies that incorporate these dynamic risk factors and the treatments (or management strategies broadly) that might ameliorate them (see Douglas and Kropp 2002, for an extended discussion). This will be the true test of whether our risk assessment procedures can actually *prevent* further violence.

References

Andrews, D.A. and Bonta, J. (2006) *The Psychology of Criminal Conduct*, 4th edn. Cincinnati, OH: Anderson Publishing.

Blair, P.R., Marcus, D.K. and Boccaccini, M.T. (in press) 'Is there an allegiance effect for assessment instruments? Actuarial risk assessment as an exemplar', *Clinical Psychology: Science and Practice*.

Boer, D.P., Hart, S.D., Kropp, P.R. and Webster, C.D. (1997) *Sexual Violence Risk-20*. Burnaby, BC: Simon Fraser University and British Columbia Forensic Psychiatric Services Commission.

Bonta, J. (1996) 'Risk-needs assessment and treatment', in A.T. Harland (ed.), *Choosing Correctional Options that Work: Defining the Demand and Evaluating the Supply*. Thousand Oaks, CA: Sage, pp. 18–32.

Bonta, J., Law, M. and Hanson, K. (1998) 'The prediction of criminal and violent recidivism among mentally disordered offenders: a meta-analysis', *Psychological Bulletin*, 123: 123–42.

Borum, R. (1996) 'Improving the clinical practice of violence risk assessment: technology, guidelines, and training', *American Psychologist*, 51: 945–56.

Catchpole, R.E.H. and Gretton, H.M. (2003) 'The predictive validity of risk assessment with violent young offenders: a 1-year examination of criminal outcome', *Criminal Justice and Behavior*, 30: 688–708.

Cocozza, J.J. and Steadman, H.J. (1976) 'The failure of psychiatric predictions of dangerousness: clear and convincing evidence', *Rutgers Law Review*, 29: 1084–101.

Cottle, C.C., Lee, R.J. and Heilbrun, K. (2001) 'The prediction of criminal recidivism in juveniles: a meta-analysis', *Criminal Justice and Behavior*, 28: 367–94.

Dawes, R.M., Faust, D. and Meehl, P.E. (1989) 'Clinical versus actuarial judgement', *Science*, 243: 1668–74.

de Vogel, V. (2002) 'Interrater reliability and predictive validity of the SVR-20 and the Static-99: a retrospective study', in M. Dernevik (Chair), *Using Structured Clinical Risk Assessment and Management in Europe: The ENSRA Network*. Symposium presented at the annual meeting of the International Association of Forensic Mental Health Services, Munich, Germany, March.

de Vogel, V. and de Ruiter, C. (2005) 'The HCR-20 in personality disordered female offenders: a comparison with a matched sample of males', *Clinical Psychology and Psychotherapy*, 12: 226–40.

de Vogel, V. and de Ruiter, C. (2006) 'Structured professional judgment of violence risk in forensic clinical practice: a prospective study into the predictive validity of the Dutch HCR-20', *Psychology, Crime and Law*, 12: 321–36.

de Vogel, V., de Ruiter, C., van Beek, D. and Mead, G. (2004) 'Predictive validity of the SVR-20 and Static-99 in a Dutch sample of treated sex offenders', *Law and Human Behavior*, 28: 235–51.

Dempster, R.J. (1998) 'Prediction of Sexually Violent Recidivism: A Comparison of Risk Assessment Instruments'. Unpublished master's thesis, Simon Fraser University, Burnaby, BC, Canada.

Douglas, K.S., Cox, D.N. and Webster, C.D. (1999) 'Violence risk assessment: science and practice', *Legal and Criminological Psychology*, 4: 149–84.

Douglas, K.S., Guy, L.S. and Weir, J. (2007) *HCR-20 Violence Risk Assessment Scheme: Overview and Annotated Bibliography*. Available online: http://kdouglas.files.wordpress.com.

Douglas, K.S. and Kropp, P.R. (2002) 'A prevention-based paradigm for violence risk assessment: clinical and research applications', *Criminal Justice and Behavior*, 29: 617–58.

Douglas, K.S., Ogloff, J.R.P. and Hart, S. (2003) 'Evaluation of a model of violence risk assessment among forensic psychiatric patients', *Psychiatric Services*, 54: 1372–9.

Douglas, K.S., Ogloff, R.P., Nicholls, T.L. and Grant, I. (1999) 'Assessing risk for violence among psychiatric patients: the HCR-20 violence risk assessment scheme and the Psychopathy Checklist: Screening Version', *Journal of Consulting and Clinical Psychology*, 67: 917–30.

Douglas, K.S. and Skeem, J.L. (2005) 'Violence risk assessment: getting specific about being dynamic', *Psychology, Public Policy, and Law*, 11: 347–83.

Douglas, K.S., Vincent, G.M. and Edens, J.F. (2006) 'Risk for criminal recidivism: the role of psychopathy', in C. Patrick (ed.), *Handbook of Psychopathy*. New York: Guilford, pp. 533–54.

Douglas, K.S. and Webster, C.D. (1999) 'Predicting violence in mentally and personality disordered individuals', in R. Roesch, S.D. Hart and J.R.P. Ogloff (eds), *Psychology and Law: The State of the Discipline*. New York: Plenum, pp. 175–239.

Douglas, K.S., Webster, C.D., Hart, S.D., Eaves, D. and Ogloff, J.R.P. (eds) (2001) *HCR-20: Violence Risk Management Companion Guide*. Burnaby, BC, Canada: Mental Health, Law, and Policy Institute, Simon Fraser University, and Department of Mental Health Law and Policy, University of South Florida.

Douglas, K.S., Yeomans, M. and Boer, D.P. (2005) 'Comparative validity analysis of multiple measures of violence risk in a sample of criminal offenders', *Criminal Justice and Behavior*, 32: 479–510.

Doyle, M. (2000) 'Risk assessment and management', in C. Chaloner and M. Coffey (eds), *Forensic Mental Health Nursing: Current Approaches*. Oxford: Blackwell Science, pp. 140–70.

Doyle, M. and Dolan, M. (2004) 'Violence Risk Assessment: combining actuarial and clinical information to structure clinical judgements for the formulation and management of risk', *Journal of Psychiatric and Mental Health Nursing*, 9: 649–57.

Dvoskin, J. A. and Heilbrun, K. (2001) 'Risk assessment and release decision-making: toward resolving the great debate', *Journal of the American Academy of Psychiatry and the Law*, 29: 6–10.

Enebrink, P., Långström, N. and Gumpert, C.H. (2006) 'Predicting aggressive and disruptive behavior in referred 6- to 12-year-old boys: prospective validation of the EARL-20B risk/needs checklist', *Assessment*, 13: 356–67.

Ennis, B.J. and Emery, R.D. (1978) *The Rights of Mental Patients*. New York: Avon Books.

Ennis, B.J. and Litwack, T.R. (1974) 'Psychiatry and the presumption of expertise: flipping coins in the courtroom', *California Law Review*, 62: 693–752.

Faust, D. and Ziskin, J. (1988) 'The expert witness in psychology and psychiatry', *Science*, 241: 31–5.

Gendreau, P., Goggin, C.E. and Law, M.A. (1997) 'Predicting prison misconducts', *Criminal Justice and Behavior*, 24: 414–31.

Gendreau, P., Little, T. and Goggin, C. (1996) 'A meta-analysis of the predictors of adult offender recidivism: what works', *Criminology*, 34: 575–607.

Gottfredson, S.D. and Gottfredson, D.M. (1986) 'Accuracy of prediction models', in A. Blumstein, J. Cohen, J.A. Roth and C. Visher (eds), *Criminal Careers and 'Career Criminals'*. Washington, DC: National Academy Press, pp. 212–90.

Gretton, H. and Abramowitz, C. (2002) 'The Structured Assessment of Violence Risk in Youth (SAVRY): comparing contributions of SAVRY items to clinical risk estimates and criminal outcomes', in P. Bartel (Chair), *The Structured Assessment of Violence Risk in Youth (SAVRY): The Validity and Application of Risk Assessment in Violent Youth*. Symposium presented at the biennial meeting of the American Psychology-Law Society (Div. 41, APA), Austin, TX, March.

Grove, W.M. and Meehl, P.E. (1996) 'Comparative efficiency of informal (subjective, impressionistic) and formal (mechanical, algorithmic) prediction procedures: the clinical-statistical controversy', *Psychology, Public Policy, and Law*, 2: 293–323.

Grove, W.M., Zald, D.H., Lebow, B.S., Snitz, B.E. and Nelson, C. (2000) 'Clinical versus mechanical prediction: a meta-analysis', *Psychological Assessment*, 12: 19–30.

Guy, L.S. and Wilson, C.M. (2007) *Empirical Support for the HCR-20: A Critical Analysis of the Violence Literature*. Burnaby, BC, Canada: Mental Health, Law, and Policy Institute, Simon Fraser University. Available online: http://kdouglas.files.wordpress.com/2007/09/hcr-20-report-2007.pdf.

Hanson, R.K. and Bussière, M.T. (1998) 'Predicting relapse: a meta-analysis of sexual offender recidivism studies', *Journal of Consulting and Clinical Psychology*, 66: 348–62.

Hanson, R.K. and Harris, A.J.R. (1998) *Dynamic Predictors of Sexual Recidivism*, User Report No. 1998–01. Ottawa, ON: Department of the Solicitor General of Canada.

Hanson, R.K. and Morton-Bourgon, K.E. (2005) 'The characteristics of persistent sexual offenders: a meta-analysis of recidivism studies', *Journal of Consulting and Clinical Psychology*, 73(6): 1154–63.

Hart, S. (1998) 'The role of psychopathy in assessing risk for violence: conceptual and methodological issues', *Legal Criminological Psychology*, 3: 121–37.

Heilbrun, K. (1997) 'Prediction versus management models relevant to risk assessment: the importance of legal decision-making context', *Law and Human Behavior*, 21: 347–59.

Heilbrun, K., Lee, R. and Cottle, C.C. (2005) 'Risk factors and intervention outcomes: meta-analyses of juvenile offending', in K. Heilbrun,

N.E.S. Goldstein and R.E. Redding (eds), *Juvenile Delinquency: Prevention, Assessment, and Intervention*. Oxford: Oxford University Press, pp. 111–33.

Heilbrun, K., Nezu, C., Keeney, M., Chung, S. and Wasserman, A. (1998) 'Sexual offending: linking assessment, intervention, and decision making', *Psychology, Public Policy, and Law*, 4: 138–74.

Heilbrun, K., O'Neill, M.L., Strohman, L.K., Bowman, Q. and Philipson, J. (2000) 'Expert approaches to communicating violence risks', *Law and Human Behavior*, 24: 137–48.

Hoptman, M.J., Yates, K.F., Patalinjug, M.B., Wack, R.C. and Convit, A. (1999) 'Clinical prediction of assaultive behaviour among male psychiatric patients at a maximum-security forensic facility', *Psychiatric Services*, 50: 1461–6.

Hubbard, D.J. and Pratt, T.C. (2002) 'A meta-analysis of the predictors of delinquency among girls', *Journal of Offender Rehabilitation*, 34: 1–13.

Janofsky, J.S., Spears, S. and Neubauer, D.N. (1988) 'Psychiatrists' accuracy in predicting violent behaviour on an inpatient unit', *Hospital and Community Psychiatry*, 39: 1090–4.

Janus, E.S. and Meehl, P.E. (1997) 'Assessing the legal standard for predictions of dangerousness in sex offender commitment proceedings', *Psychology, Public Policy, and Law*, 3: 33–64.

Kazdin, A.E., Kraemer, H.C., Kessler, R.C., Kupfer, D.J. and Offard, D. R. (1997) 'Contributions of risk-factor research to developmental psychopathology', *Clinical Psychology Review*, 17: 375–406.

Kraemer, H.C., Kazdin, A.E., Offord, D.R., Kessler, R.C., Jensen, P.S. and Kupfer, D. J. (1997) 'Coming to terms with the terms of risk', *Archives of General Psychiatry*, 54: 337–43.

Kropp, P.R. and Hart, S.D. (2000) 'The Spousal Assault Risk Assessment (SARA) Guide: reliability and validity in adult male offenders', *Law and Human Behavior*, 24: 101–18.

Kropp, P.R., Hart, S.D., Lyon, D.R. and LePard, D.A. (2002) 'Managing stalkers: coordinating treatment and supervision', in J.C.W. Boon and L. Sheridan (eds), *Stalking and Psychosexual Obsession: Psychological Perspectives for Prevention, Policing and Treatment*. Chichester: Wiley, pp. 141–63.

Krug, E.G., Dahlberg, L.L., Mercy, J.A., Zwi, A.B. and Lozano, R. (eds) (2002) *World Report on Violence and Health*. Geneva: World Health Organization.

Lessard v. *Schmidt*, 349 F. Supp. 1078 (E.D. Wis. 1972).

Lidz, C.W., Mulvey, E.P. and Gardner, W. (1993) 'The accuracy of predictions of violence to others', *Journal of the Medical Association*, 269: 1007–11.

Litwack, T.R. (2001) 'Actuarial versus clinical assessments of dangerousness', *Psychology, Public Policy, and Law*, 7: 409–43.

Lyon, D.R., Hart, S.D. and Webster, C.D. (2001) 'Violence and risk assessment', in R.A. Schuller and J.R.P. Ogloff (eds), *Introduction to Psychology and Law: Canadian Perspectives*. Toronto, ON: University of Toronto Press, pp. 314–50.

McNeil, D.E. and Binder, R.L. (1987) 'Predictive validity of judgements of dangerousness in emergency civil commitment', *American Journal of Psychiatry*, 144: 197–200.

McNeil, D.E. and Binder, R.L. (1991) 'Clinical assessment of the risk of violence among psychiatric on patients', *American Journal of Psychiatry*, 148: 1317–21.

McNeil, D.E. and Binder, R.L. (1995) 'Correlates of accuracy in the assessment of psychiatric inpatients' risk of violence', *American Journal of Psychiatry*, 152: 901–6.

McNeil, D.E., Binder, R.L. and Greenfield, T.K. (1988) 'Predictors of violence in civilly committed acute psychiatric patients', *American Journal of Psychiatry*, 145: 965–70.

Meehl, P.E. (1954) *Clinical versus Statistical Prediction: A Theoretical Analysis and Review of the Evidence*. Minneapolis, MN: University of Minneapolis Press.

Melton, G.B., Petrila, J., Poythress, N.G. and Slobogin, C. (1997) *Psychological Evaluations for the Courts: A Handbook for Mental Health Professionals and Lawyers*, 2nd edn. New York: Guilford.

Miller, T.R., Cohen, M.A. and Wiersema, B. (1996) *Victim Costs and Consequences: A New Look*, Final Summary Report presented to the National Institute of Justice. Washington, DC: Department of Justice.

Monahan, J. (1981) *Predicting Violent Behaviour: An Assessment of Clinical Techniques*. Beverley Hills, CA: Sage.

Monahan, J. (1984) 'The prediction of violent behavior: toward a second generation of theory and policy', *American Journal of Psychiatry*, 141: 10–15.

Monahan, J. and Steadman, H.J. (eds) (1994) *Violence and Mental Disorder: Developments in Risk Assessment*. Chicago, IL: University of Chicago Press.

Monahan, J., Steadman, H.J., Silver, E., Applebaum, P.S., Robbins, P.C. and Mulvey, E.P. *et al.* (2001) *Rethinking Risk Assessment: The MacArthur Study of Mental Disorder and Violence*. New York: Oxford University Press.

Mossman, D. (1994) 'Assessing predictions of violence: being accurate about accuracy', *Journal of Consulting and Clinical Psychology*, 62: 783–92.

Mulvey, E. and Lidz, C. (1995) 'Conditional prediction: a model for research on dangerousness to others in a new era', *International Journal of Law and Psychiatry*, 18: 129–43.

Mulvey, E., Lidz, C., Gardner, W. and Shaw, E. (1996) 'Clinical versus actuarial predictions of violence in patients with mental illnesses', *Journal of Consulting and Clinical Psychology*, 64: 602–9.

Nikolova, N., Collins, M.J., Guy, L.S., Lavoie, J., Reeves, K., Wilson, C.M. and Douglas, K.S. (2006) *HCR-20 Violence Risk Assessment Scheme: A Quantitative Synthesis of Its Application, Reliability and Validity*. Poster presented at the annual conference of the American Psychology-Law Society, St Petersburg, Florida, March.

Otto, R.K. (2000) 'Assessing and managing violence risk in outpatient settings', *Journal of Clinical Psychology*, 56: 1239–62.

Quinsey, V.L., Harris, G.T., Rice, G.T. and Cormier, C.A. (1998) *Violent Offenders: Appraising and Managing Risk*. Washington, DC: American Psychological Association.

Rofman, E.S., Askinazi, C. and Fant, E. (1980) 'The prediction of dangerous behavior in emergency civil commitment', *American Journal of Psychiatry*, 137: 1061–4.

Rosenfeld, B. (2004) 'Violence risk factors in stalking and obsessional harassment: a review and preliminary meta-analysis', *Criminal Justice and Behavior*, 31: 9–36.

Schopp, R.F. (1996) 'Communicating risk assessments: accuracy, efficacy, and responsibility', *American Psychologist*, 51: 939–44.

Sepejak, D.S., Menzies, R.J., Webster, C.D. and Jensen, F.A.S. (1983) 'Clinical predictions of dangerousness: two-year follow-up of 408 pretrial forensic cases', *Bulletin of the America Academy of Psychiatry and the Law*, 11: 171–81.

Shah, S.A. (1978) 'Dangerousness: a paradigm for exploring some issues in law and psychology', *American Psychologist*, 33: 224–38.

Sjösted, G. and Långström, N. (2002) 'Assessment of risk for criminal recidivism among rapists: a comparison of four different measures', *Psychology, Crime, and Law*, 8: 25–40.

Skeem, J. and Mulvey, E. (2002) 'Monitoring the violence potential of mentally disordered offenders being treated in the community', in A. Buchanan (ed.), *Care of the Mentally Disordered Offender in the Community*. New York: Oxford University Press, pp. 111–42.

Skeem, J., Mulvey, E. and Lidz, C. (2000) 'Building clinicians' decisional models into tests of predictive validity: the accuracy of contextualized predictions of violence', *Law and Human Behavior*, 24: 607–28.

Steadman, H.J. (2000) 'From dangerousness to risk assessment of community violence: taking stock at the turn of the century', *Journal of the American Academy of Psychiatry and the Law*, 28: 265–71.

Steadman, H.J. and Cocozza, J.J. (1974) *Careers of the Criminally Insane: Excessive Social Control of Deviance*. Lexington, MA: Lexington Books.

Steadman, H.J., Monahan, J., Appelbaum, P.S., Grisso, T., Mulvey, E.P., Roth, L.H., Robbins, P.C. and Klassen, D. (1994) 'Designing a new generation of risk assessment research', in J. Monahan and H.J. Steadman (eds), *Violence and Mental Disorder: Developments in Risk Assessment*. Chicago: University of Chicago Press, pp. 297–318.

Steadman, H.J., Monahan, J., Robbins, P.C., Appelbaum, P., Grisso, T., Klassen, D., Mulvey, E.P. and Roth, L. (1993) 'From dangerousness to risk assessment: implications for appropriate research strategies', in S. Hodgins (ed.), *Mental Disorder and Crime*. Thousand Oaks, CA: Sage, pp. 39–62.

Tarasoff v. *Regents of University of California* (1976) 17 Cal. 3d 425.

Thornberry, T.P. and Jacoby, J.E. (1979) *The Criminally Insane: A Follow-up of Mentally Ill Offenders*. Chicago, IL: University of Chicago Press.

Viljoen, J.L., Scalora, M., Cuadra, L., Bader, S., Chavez, V., Ullman, D. and Lawrence, L. (2008) 'Assessing risk for violence in adolescents who have sexually offended: a comparison of the J-SOAP-II, J-SORRAT-II, and SAVRY', *Criminal Justice and Behavior*, 35: 5–33.

Webster, C.D., Douglas, K.S., Belfrage, H. and Link, B. (2000) 'Capturing change: an approach to managing violence and improving mental health', in S. Hodgins and R. Müller-Isberner (eds), *Violence Among the Mentally Ill*. Dordrecht: Kluwer Academic, pp. 119–44.

Webster, C.D., Douglas, K., Eaves, D. and Hart, S. (1997) *HCR-20: Assessing Risk for Violence, Version 2*. Burnaby, BC: Simon Fraser University.

Webster, C.D., Eaves, D., Douglas, K.S. and Wintrup, A. (1995) *The HCR-20 Scheme: The Assessment of Dangerousness and Risk*. Burnaby, BC: Simon Fraser University and British Columbia Forensic Psychiatric Services Commission.

Chapter 2

Sex offender risk assessment: research, evaluation, 'best-practice' recommendations and future directions

Douglas P. Boer and Stephen D. Hart

Risk assessment of sexual offenders remains a controversial and important topic in forensic psychiatry and psychology. Academics argue the strengths and weaknesses of 'unstructured clinical judgment' versus 'actuarial' versus 'structured professional judgment' assessment strategies with something approaching religious zeal. Practitioners meanwhile, *nolen volens*, are requested to do assessments and therefore continue to do their best to minimise errors of overestimating or underestimating the reoffence risk of violent offenders for correctional agencies, the courts and other decision-makers in the absence of agreement over best practice and in the absence of convincing data of instrument superiority. Overestimation of risk can result in the needless prolonging of incarceration, overly intensive treatment or supervision for low-risk offenders, with the underestimation of risk resulting in additional risk for victimisation of the public by high-risk offenders who may be released prematurely or provided with inadequate levels of treatment or supervision. Egregious levels of either sort of error are unacceptable. Practitioners seek leadership from the research literature for indications of what might constitute best practice.

Unfortunately, it is our opinion that there is more polemic argument in the risk assessment literature as to what is the best type of approach to risk assessment than there is evidence of concern for public safety. It is our argument in this chapter that if we are truly concerned about public safety via effective risk management (as the ultimate objective of all risk assessment work), then the academic arguments should be less important given that the main concern of all researchers and clinicians should be that of determining the safest, best model of practice to benefit both the public and offenders themselves. Our aim in this chapter is to look at the current state of risk assessment of sexual offenders and then recommend a parsimonious 'best practice' approach based on the currently available research.

Unstructured clinical judgment

The most basic sort of risk assessment approach is unstructured clinical judgment or UCJ, which refers to decisions unguided by tests or professional guidelines. Although it requires no special procedures and is easily tailored to individual cases, it is also typically considered by reviewers to be the least useful approach to risk assessment. This is in large part because it fails to provide a clear basis for the decisions reached by individual clinicians (e.g. Monahan 1995; Quinsey *et al.* 2006). But this is not to say that UCJ risk assessment is only based on guesswork or that all psychologists or psychiatrists who base their risk judgments on their clinical intuition and experience are always (or even mostly!) incorrect. Most clinicians, whether or not they use specific tests or guidelines, base their assessment strategies and findings on clinical hypotheses and also follow diagnostic indicators on which to base their risk judgments. As a result, UCJ tends to be better than chance with respect to both inter-clinician agreement (reliability) and predictive accuracy (validity), but inferior to decisions made using actuarial or structured professional judgment (SPJ) approaches. However, research suggests that the predictive accuracy of UCJ may actually be improving over time (e.g. Hanson and Morton-Bourgon 2004, 2007), presumably because clinicians are consumers of the scientific and professional literature and as a result are paying greater attention to important scientifically validated risk factors such as sexual deviance and antisocial lifestyle, or because they have learned from various SPJ guidelines (e.g. Schalock and Luckasson 2005).

Schalock and Luckasson (2005) have offered some general recommendations for improving UCJ. These authors focused specifically on risk assessments of clients who are intellectually disabled, but with little effort the recommended strategies are generalisable to almost any clinical forensic or correctional assessment situation. Each of the following clinical judgment strategies is addressed in its own chapter and the following summary is intended only to give a sense of the erudite content of Schalock and Luckasson's book; strategy titles given in italics are the same as in the original. We have also paraphrased the clinical judgment strategies that these authors have suggested that pertain more directly to intervention given that the main point of a good assessment is to inform the management of the client.

1 *Conducting a thorough social history* – is the social history comprehensive and does it cover all relevant aspects of the client's functioning?

2 *Aligning data and its collection to the question at hand* – was the information sought or the file data or interview questions being used related to the referral question?

3 *Applying broad-based assessment strategies* – were assessment measures used that were relevant to the intervention methods recommended?

4 *Implementing intervention best practices* – are the interventions being recommended based on research-supported knowledge and do these interventions lend themselves to analysis?

5 *Planning, implementing, and evaluating individualised supports* – are the intervention plans being recommended clear enough so that major areas of the client's life are being addressed?

6 *Reflecting cultural competence and linguistic diversity* – is the assessment plan sensitive to the client's cultural and linguistic background in addition to the client's strengths and limitations?

In sum, much of the current risk assessment literature assumes that UCJ is a poor decision-making strategy. However, its weaknesses have probably been overstated, and reliance on recommendations such as those of Schalock and Luckasson (2005) may further improve the exercise of UCJ.

Actuarial risk assessment instruments

Actuarial risk assessment instruments (ARAIs) are highly structured tests (see in particular Chapter 5 of the current volume for a summary of relevant ARAIs). They often (although not necessarily) comprise items that have been shown statistically to be related to risk. The construction of such tests for the prediction of any outcome usually is based on a 'known groups' or 'criterion groups' design. In a sample of offenders or patients who were followed up in the community, variables are selected that statistically discriminate between known recidivists and non-recidivists. A final combinatoric algorithm is derived based on selected variables that optimises the prediction of recidivism (more correctly, 'post-diction', given that the test is constructed with historical data). Of course, the usefulness of the resulting 'test' (really a statistical equation) depends on the extent to which it discriminates between recidivists and non-recidivists in new samples. Unfortunately, differences in legal context, uniqueness of the offender being assessed, race and culture, length of time in the community without a new offence, and age at time of release from custody, among other variables, may degrade the usefulness of the actuarial test. Also, ARAIs attempt to estimate the likelihood that an offender may commit another offence of the sort being assessed. Likelihood is an important aspect of risk, but clearly not the only aspect of risk that we are concerned about when doing a risk assessment. As we have noted elsewhere (e.g. Boer *et al.* 1997), risk is a multi-faceted phenomenon and includes the nature, duration and frequency of future violence, as well as the imminence and severity of any future violent act.

Recent meta-analyses (e.g. Hanson and Morton-Bourgon 2004, 2007) show that various ARAIs for assessing sexual violence risk are all about equal in terms of predictive accuracy. In 2004, Hanson and Morton-Bourgon found that ARAIs were roughly 'moderate' in terms of their overall predictive accuracy; in 2007, the findings were virtually identical. There are some studies that argue that some ARAIs work better than others, but these sorts of claims are generally made by test authors or researchers with a vested interest in the results. For example, Harris *et al.* (2003) examined the predictive accuracy of four ARAIs for sexual offenders in four samples of sex offenders. The Violence Risk Appraisal Guide (VRAG) and the Sex Offender Risk Appraisal Guide (SORAG) (both authored by Quinsey *et al.* 1998/2006) were found to have better predictive accuracy than either the Static-99 (Hanson and Thornton 1999) or Rapid Risk Assessment for Sex Offender Recidivism (RRASOR: Hanson 1997). In Hanson and Morton-Bourgon's meta-analyses (2004, 2007), the opposite is found to be true, but when confidence interval data is taken into account (which Hanson and Morton-Bourgon describe in both of their meta-analyses), then it appears that all ARAIs designed for sex offender risk assessment seem to have similar predictive accuracy.

Boer (2006) suggested that the similar predictive accuracy of various ARAIs may be due to their inclusion of similar items. For example, Craig *et al.* (2003) found seventeen static variables related to increased sexual offence recidivism, which they then grouped into four broad domains (Craig *et al.* 2005: 67):

1 *Developmental factors* – juvenile sexual offences, poor family background and victim of sexual abuse.

2 *Sexual interest factors* – male victim, paraphilias (atypical sexual outlets) and extra-familial victims.

3 *Forensic factors* – past criminal history, past sexual convictions, past violent convictions, time spent in custody, non-contact sex offences, stranger victims and multiple victims.

4 *Clinical factors* – age of offender (negatively correlated), lower IQ, marital or relationship history, discontinuation in community treatment programmes and psychopathy (PCL-R).

Similarly, a meta-analysis of recidivism studies by Hanson and Morton-Bourgon (2005) grouped risk factors into six broad domains:

1 *Sexual deviancy* – deviant sexual interests, such as children, rape and other paraphilias, as well as sexual preoccupations and gender dysphoria.

2 *Antisocial orientation* – antisocial personality (e.g. antisocial personality disorder, psychopathy, Minnesota Multiphasic Personality Inventory Scale IV), antisocial traits (e.g. lifestyle instability, substance abuse, hostility), and a history of rule violation (e.g. childhood criminality, history of nonsexual crime, violation of conditional release).

3 *Sexual attitudes* – tolerance of sexual crime, support for adult–child sex and low sex knowledge.

4 *Intimacy deficits* – poor social skills, negative social influences, conflicts in intimate relationships, emotional identification with children and loneliness.

5 *General psychological problems* – internalisation of psychological problems (e.g. anxiety and low self-esteem, as well as major mental illness).

6 *Clinical presentation* – denial, minimisation, lack of victim empathy, low motivation for treatment and poor progress.

Existing ARAIs include primarily items related to past offences – those that would fall into the 'forensic' domain of Craig *et al.* (2005) or the 'antisocial orientation' domain of Hanson and Morton-Bourgon (2005). Some items related to past offences may also be related to the 'sexual interest' or 'sexual deviancy' domain of Craig *et al.* (2005) and Hanson and Morton-Bourgon (2005). But existing ARAIs have few items from the other risk factor domains, and even those risk factors included are often defined in a rather limited or rigid manner. For example, risk factors such as sexual deviancy and antisocial orientation are defined indirectly in terms of criminal charges and convictions or offence-related behaviours as opposed to directly on the basis of clinical assessments of sexual interests, antisocial attitudes and so forth. Similarly, intimacy problems are defined in several ARAIs in terms of the person's longest marital or common-law relationship, ignoring the person's age or the quality of the relationships.

A major limitation of most ARAIs is their near-complete exclusion of dynamic risk factors. For example, Craig *et al.* (2005: 70–1), differentiating between stable (slowly changing) and acute (quickly changing) dynamic risk factors, identified the following domains:

Stable dynamic risk factors

1 *Sexual interest factors* – deviant sexual urges, sexual deviance – children (as measured by penile plethysmography) and attitudes tolerant of sexual assault.

2 *Clinical factors* – cognitive distortions, lack of victim empathy, low self-esteem, anger, substance abuse, impulsivity and personality disorder.

Acute dynamic risk factors

1 *Sexual interest factors* – frequency of sexual fantasies.

2 *Treatment behaviour factors* – delinquent behaviour during treatment, deterioration in dynamic risk during treatment, poor treatment cooperation, deterioration in awareness of high-risk situations and relapse prevention strategies, short duration of treatment programme and poor cooperation with supervision.

3 *Clinical factors* – isolation, unemployment, deviant social influences, chaotic lifestyle, poor social support, affective disorders and substance abuse.

As already noted previously, Hanson and Morton-Bourgon (2005) identified six domains of dynamic risk factors. However, few of these dynamic factors have become items in any of the Hanson tests – except sometimes by inference (e.g. sexual deviance is not directly measured by phallometry but is inferred from sexual behaviour – despite the literature being very equivocal about the validity of such inferences) and very important items (e.g. sexual attitudes) have been eliminated from tests explicitly designed to assess dynamic risk (e.g. STABLE 2007, by Hanson and Harris 2007a).

The exclusion of so many established static risk factors and putative dynamic risk factors from ARAIs is surprising. While the general rationale for why some items make it onto an actuarial test and some do not is presumably that of predictive validity (or, more accurately, the incremental predictive validity of each item following the initial item on any particular actuarial test), it is worth noting that some of the items appear not to be included because some variables are simply too difficult to measure (e.g. antisocial attitudes, clinical presentation) or require a PCL-R score (Hare 1991, 2003) or the diagnosis of mental or personality disorder and thus make the test unadoptable (and therefore less likely to be used) except by mental health professionals who have the right to diagnose. Perhaps the simplistic items in the Static-99 versus those in the SORAG reflect this more pedestrian rationale, that is the items are not necessarily the 'best' items, but the items with both good predictive validity and acceptable levels of inter-rater reliability with non-professional users. Whatever the reason, these content deficiencies have led some authors to develop new tests to supplement their existing ARAIs (e.g. Hanson and Harris 2007a, 2007b).

Finally, it ought not escape anyone's attention that the majority of the above items, static or dynamic, are actually included in most of the structured professional judgment instruments, such as the SVR-20 (Sexual Violence Risk Scale: Boer *et al.*, 1997).

Structured professional judgment

The SPJ approach to risk assessment is also referred to as 'guided clinical judgment' or 'structured clinical guidelines' in the risk assessment literature. Regardless of terminology, the use of these guidelines assumes that (a) the assessment is being done by a trained professional, and (b) the guidelines specify the important risk factors that should be considered, at a minimum, by the evaluator, but in the final analysis, and (c) the evaluator exercises discretion with respect to how information about risk factors is combined to reach a final judgment regarding risk.

SPJ guidelines for assessing risk for sexual violence have been widely adopted by experienced clinicians around the world because of the flexibility of the method. These instruments allow for a very wide analysis of risk including not just likelihood of reoffence, but also its nature, imminence and severity (lethality). They also encourage systematic consideration of a broad range of factors that are relevant to risk assessment and management decisions, including issues related to sexual disorders (paraphilias) that may be reflected in criminal behaviour, such as sadism, fetishism or paedophilia.

The Sexual Violence Risk-20 (SVR-20; Boer *et al.* 1997) is a good example of an SPJ instrument. It comprises twenty risk factors in three domains.

- *Psychosocial adjustment* includes sexual deviation, victim of child abuse, psychopathy, major mental illness, substance use problems, suicidal/homicidal ideation, relationship problems, employment problems, past non-sexual violent offences, past non-violent offences and past supervision failures.

- *Sexual offences* includes high-density sex offences, multiple sex offence types, physical harm to victim(s) in sex offences, uses weapons or threats of death in sex offences, escalation in frequency or severity of sex offences, extreme minimisation or denial of sex offences and attitudes that support or condone sex offences.

- *Future plans* includes the lack of realistic plans and a negative attitude toward intervention.

The inclusion of each item was supported by systematic review of the scientific and professional literatures.

The SVR-20 has been evaluated by a variety of researchers in a variety of sites and is the best-validated SPJ for the risk assessment of sexual offenders. According to several empirical studies (e.g. de Vogel *et al.* 2004) and even meta-analyses (e.g. Hanson and Morton-Bourgon 2004), judgments of risk made using the SVR-20 have predictive validity that is equal or even superior to that of ARAIs in small independent studies and in large meta-analytic reviews.

The SVR-20 is currently being updated to reflect developments in the research literature and changes in treatment foci over the past decade. Although the content of the revised SVR-20 will remain similar to that of the original guidelines in broad terms, a number of specific changes have been made: the definitions of some risk factors have been clarified; two specific risk factors were collapsed to create a more general risk factor; and two new risk factors (reflecting problems related to sexuality and psychological coercion of victims) were added. *Psychosocial adjustment* now includes sexual deviance, problems with sexual health, problems related to child abuse, personality disorder, major mental illness, substance abuse problems, suicidal/ violent ideation, relationship problems, employment problems, and non-sexual offending. *Sexual offences* now includes frequent sexual offences, diverse sex offences, actual or threatened physical harm, psychological coercion, escalation in frequency or severity, extreme minimisation or denial of sex offences, and attitudes that support or condone sex offences. *Future plans* now includes lacking realistic plans, negative attitude toward intervention, and negative attitude toward supervision. In addition to content changes, the way in which risk factors are coded have been modified to facilitate the identification of protective factors (e.g. personal strengths or resources) as well as risk factors. The revisions ensure that the SVR-20 will be comprehensive in scope, sensitive to both dynamic and static aspects of risk and useful in the development of risk management plans.

The revised SVR-20 no doubt will be subject to the same criticisms as the original manual. First, some critics will object to the inclusion of risk factors in the guidelines that are not established in the scientific literature as predictors of sexual reoffence. But because the revised SVR-20 – like the original – uses a broad definition of risk, the risk factors may be predictive of the nature, severity or imminence of reoffence rather than the likelihood, or they may be related to risk management rather than the likelihood of reoffence. Second, some will object to the fact that the guidelines will be published 'without validation research'. But this criticism reflects a fundamental misunderstanding of the SPJ approach. It is true that the content of the revised SVR-20 was not based on a single piece of empirical research; instead, it was based on a systematic review of scores – even hundreds – of empirical studies, as well as a review of the professional literature. We do not understand why decisions about the content of a risk assessment instrument should be based on what happened in a specific cohort of offenders released from a specific institution during a specific time period; if the goal is generalisable guidelines, then surely the guidelines should be based on a more general review? Third, some will object to the fact that the revised SVR-20 will not yield a quantitative estimate of the probability of reoffence. This is correct; the goal of the SVR-20 is to guide management decisions and prevent reoffence, not to predict what might happen if we do nothing or sit by passively and let the future bring what it may. The primary reason for developing SPJ guidelines was to provide a sensible alternative to predictive ARAIs.

Current status of risk assessment research

It is probably accurate to say that the only topic related to risk assessment in which there is substantial agreement among researchers is the definitions regarding types of risk assessment methodologies at the beginning of this chapter. Adherents of any one sort of approach are often very steadfast in their admiration of their own sort of assessment practice or instruments. There are very ardent – and sometimes foolhardy – claims of superiority of one approach over the others, and both ARAI and SPJ claims of superiority over against UCJ approaches. There are actuarial tests that we feel naively suggest the use of very few variables (sometimes as few as four!) to 'calculate' the overall risk posed by an offender. No actuarial tests account for improvements with treatment, although some authors (e.g. Marshall *et al.* 1999) suggest that treated offenders reoffend at half the rate of untreated offenders. Similarly, SPJ instruments could improve by paying greater attention to dynamic factors, such as treatment gains or age-related changes in sexual health (e.g. Barbaree *et al.* 2008).

In 1999 it was argued that risk assessment research had progressed to where it offered direction to clinicians in terms of improving the accuracy of predictions (Douglas *et al.* 1999). In that same article, Douglas and colleagues reviewed ARAI and SPJ data on a number of samples with a number of different SPJs and related ARAIs and found that the SPJ approaches routinely outperformed (had better predictive validity) the ARAIs across subject domains (e.g. sex offender risk assessment, spousal abuse risk assessment, violent offender risk assessment). Other studies have found similar sorts of results. That being said, we cannot state with certainty that if ARAIs were developed for more specific purposes (e.g. assessing lethality, imminence, nature) they could not, in theory, outperform the SPJs, but to date ARAIs have not shown much promise in risk assessment except in terms of likelihood prediction.

If anything, the ARAI–SPJ debate seems to have intensified in recent years. Hart *et al.* (2007) questioned the usefulness of ARAI to predict the likelihood of reoffence in individual cases due to an overlap in confidence intervals among risk levels. Their research indicated that the Static-99 and VRAG yielded only two or three distinct (i.e. non-overlapping) predictions at the group level – low- and high-risk groups – and at the individual level may be completely unable to make distinct predictions. In these authors' opinion, 'ARAIs cannot be used to estimate an individual's risk for future violence with any reasonable degree of certainty and should be used with great caution or not at all' (Hart *et al.* 2007: 60). In contrast, Hanson and Morton-Bourgon (2007), focusing on group-level data, concluded that actuarial tests had better predictive validity than SPJs on average.

In sum, there are problems with the risk assessment literature. Issues such as how to handle missing data or how to use dynamic (i.e. changeable) variables when accounting for changes as a result of treatment are rarely addressed by risk assessment test authors. Further, clinicians, trained as scientist-practitioners, must not be fooled by the claims of the research literature. All too often, the research literature is compiled by the test developers who must, to varying degrees, suffer from the 'allegiance effect' – the tendency to find that one's data supports the supremacy of one's own test versus that of others. We see this effect in action when a researcher discounts data that supports a competitor's test or somehow massages the data or the presentation of meta-analytic data to show that his or her test magically outperforms competitors' tests. The result of the allegiance effect in test research is not restricted to getting one's data published when it may not be warranted, but if grandiose conclusions dissuade test users from using valid methodology, that researcher may unintentionally cause bad clinical practice with potentially catastrophic consequences for potential victims.

In addition to the above warnings, we would add that we as test consumers must be very careful not to conclude that any test or set of guidelines can replace good clinical acumen, but to be aware that the opposite conclusion appears true as well – clinical acumen is, without proper structure or foundation, no match for a good test. Paradoxical as the last sentence sounds (and is on a superficial level), the essence of the dilemma is that a good risk assessment needs both our clinical wisdom and the input from structured assessment procedures such as ARAIs or SPJ guidelines tests. When clinicians use a well-known test such as the Minnesota Multiphasic Personality Inventory (MMPI) in a mental health assessment, they also use their clinical observation skills and diagnostic acumen to come up with a complete clinical picture of the patient. If clinicians' observations do not match the results of the MMPI profile, clinicians are trained to form their clinical opinion primarily based on their observations and make reference to the differing test data. Risk assessors should do the same. There is no point in blind allegiance to one's clinical intuition or hypothesis-driven diagnosis of risk if the research literature suggests that actuarial or SPJ results provide useful information regarding risk. However, it would seem equally foolhardy to abandon one's clinical hypotheses when dealing with clients who are each unique and may be quite different from the standardisation sample of the most useful actuarial test, or who have idiosyncratic risk factors that are not captured in the most relevant SPJ.

Hanson and Morton-Bourgon (2007) suggested that 'for those wishing to understand their cases, there are a number of risk assessment tools available, although the research on these instruments is much less developed than the research on empirical actuarial measures' and these authors go on to suggest the SVR-20 as one such measure (that presumably would help assessors understand their cases). The rather odd implication of this comment is that some people who conduct risk assessments do not wish to understand their cases! However, that is perhaps a philosophical difference between those who do research and those who practise; we are in the latter category.

The SVR-20 (Boer *et al*. 1997) was promoted initially as an aide-memoire or report-writing assessment and guide. It was a fortuitous finding that the risk levels predicated on supervision and treatment needs were found to have good predictive validity. A large amount of independent research has shown that well-guided professional judgment allows clinicians to make allowances for the uniqueness of their clients and that such judgments have better predictive validity than actuarial tests on average. Logically, this makes some sense: the individual is never accurately represented by the group average. The corollary is also true: a group of individual predictions (e.g. via the SVR-20) ought to outperform a group average (when the SVR-20 is used actuarially it does not predict as well as when it is used in an SPJ manner). So it is no surprise that the SVR-20 continues to perform as well as or better than the Static-99 and other ARAIs in terms of predictive validity. The research will always be somewhat equivocal – it is simply too difficult to accumulate samples of the magnitude possible using ARAIs with something as complex as the SVR-20.

However, it does appear that the complexity of the client is worth it. We want to get to know our client because it is only by knowing the client that we do our job – protecting the public and reducing victims by understanding our client and their violent propensities

– something ARAIs cannot ever tell us. In fact, the revised SVR-20 (scheduled for publication in 2008) remains complex and will again require a great deal of validation research, but it promises to provide additional insights into the client being assessed and hopefully will continue to show acceptable levels of predictive validity.

In sum, the research literature remains highly polarised. In some ways, the research enterprise in this area seems slightly out of touch with the reality of the clinicians' plight – conducting assessments, writing reports and managing risk in the face of complex and conflicting data. Meanwhile, we can take some solace from Litwack (2001), who sagely noted that 'although clinicians who engage in risk assessments certainly should be knowledgeable about arguably relevant actuarial assessment schemes and other assessment guides (e.g. the HCR-20), it is premature, at best, to replace clinical risk assessments with actuarial assessments' (p. 409). We should note that Litwack was commenting on Quinsey *et al*'s (1999) polemic view against all forms of clinical risk assessment, UCJ and SPJ, and that the Historical, Clinical and Risk management guide (HCR-20, Webster *et al.* 1997) is another SPJ risk assessment measure on which the SVR-20 was largely modelled.

Conclusions and best-practice recommendations

There is much that we now know about risk assessment with sexual offenders. However, we acknowledge that there is also a great deal that we are unsure about and, as a result, we need to assess risk and make our recommendations regarding case management with caution. We would prefer to err on the side of caution; we are of the view that we would prefer convicted offenders to do more time in jail/secure settings than harm another person. However, we would also like our risk assessment research to advance to the point where those men who are safe to release are released and reduce the cost of detaining offenders unnecessarily.

Regardless of the state of the risk assessment literature, courts and parole boards around the world demand risk assessments on which to base their decisions. It is our responsibility to provide our best risk formulation on the individual client while acknowledging the limitations of our field. Further, it is also our responsibility to advise policy- and law-makers regarding effective risk methodologies and to encourage research in this regard. Clearly we have a responsible job, as not only do we provide the basis for decisions that affect the offender's life, but also decisions that could affect the life of potential victims.

Recently one of us (DPB) was asked to make 'best practice' recommendations at a conference at the University of São Paulo, Brazil (Boer 2007). In the Brazilian context it would be safe to assume that an actuarial test developed elsewhere would need to be validated in Brazil before use as anything other than a potential indicator of relative risk (one would assume that those who scored higher would be higher risk than those who scored lower). Actuarial tests are only completely useful when validated in the setting in which they are to be used. It makes no sense to do otherwise as such tests are derived and have any claim to predictive accuracy only when used with members of a population wherein which such tests have been evaluated. Doing otherwise may yield meaningless results, or worse, underestimate risk and result in a dangerous offender gaining the opportunity to create new victims.

The items that comprise SPJ instruments are derived from the international research literature and the overall assessment guide is then applied to the individual. Some of the SPJs have been shown to have validity in a variety of countries, but this does not necessarily mean that a commonly used SPJ would necessarily work in the Brazilian context. However, we would argue that the SPJ items are less sample-dependent than are those in an actuarial test. Hence, the SVR-20, based on the fact that it has already proven to work in number of countries, was recommended as a basic SPJ for examination in Brazil.

However, Boer (2006) also suggested that it is worthwhile to examine what is probably the best of the actuarial measures, the Static-99, for adoption in any new setting. Boer (2006) suggested that a convergent appraisal of risk – coming at the risk picture of a client from a number of directions – may well provide the best and most well-rounded appraisal of risk. Hence the Static-99 was also recommended for adoption in Brazil (keeping in mind the warnings of Hart *et al.* 2007) with appropriate cautions for the development of a cross-validation study to ensure that the Static-99 and the SVR-20 were valid in the Brazilian justice system. In fact, the Static-99 will be recommended as part of the convergent approach to risk assessment promoted in the revised SVR-20 manual as an 'actuarial baseline' for those who wish to anchor their structured professional judgments.

In our view, the more complete the risk picture, the more likely we are to develop effective risk management strategies for that individual offender – and that is the entire point of doing risk assessments on sexual offenders. If there are philosophical differences among test authors and researchers, such issues are solely of academic interest until the research provides certainty in terms of what works best. In the interim, those in charge of research must provide leadership to practitioners that is reasonable and not merely based on personal polemics, as the latter practice could lead to poor practice and place the public safety in jeopardy.

References

Barbaree, H.E., Langton, C.M., Blanchard, R. and Boer, D.P. (2008) 'Predicting recidivism in sex offenders using the SVR-20: the contribution of age-at-release', *International Journal of Forensic Mental Health*, 7: 1 (in press).

Boer, D.P. (2006) 'Sexual offender risk assessment strategies: is there a convergence of opinion yet?', *Sexual Offender Treatment*, 1: 1–4.

Boer, D.P. (2007) *The Current Status of Risk Assessment of Sexual Offenders*. Invited plenary address presented at the meetings of the Brazilian Association for the Treatment of Sexual Offenders, University of São Paulo, São Paulo, Brazil, November.

Boer, D.P., Hart, S.D., Kropp, P.R. and Webster, C.D. (1997) *Manual for the Sexual Violence Risk – 20: Professional Guidelines for Assessing Risk of Sexual Violence*. Vancouver, BC: Mental Health, Law, and Policy Institute.

Craig, L.A., Browne, K.D. and Stringer, I. (2003) 'Risk scales and factors predictive of sexual offence recidivism', *Trauma, Violence and Abuse*, 4: 45–68.

Craig, L.A., Browne, K.D., Stringer, I. and Beech, A. (2005) 'Sexual recidivism: a review of static, dynamic and actuarial predictors', *Journal of Sexual Aggression*, 11 (1): 65–84.

de Vogel, V., de Ruiter, C., van Beek, D. and Mead, G. (2004) 'Predictive validity of the SVR-20 and Static-99 in a Dutch sample of treated sex offenders', *Law and Human Behavior*, 28 (3): 235–51.

Douglas, K.S., Cox, D.N. and Webster, C.D. (1999) 'Violence risk assessment: science and practice', *Legal and Criminological Psychology*, 4: 149–84.

Hanson, R.K. (1997) *The Development of a Brief Actuarial Risk Scale for Sexual Offense Recidivism*. Ottawa, ON: Department of the Solicitor General of Canada.

Hanson, R.K. and Harris, A.J.R. (2007a) *Acute 2007 Scoring Guide*. Ottawa, ON: Public Safety and Emergency Preparedness Canada.

Hanson, R.K. and Harris, A.J.R. (2007b) *Stable 2007 Master Scoring Guide*. Ottawa, ON: Public Safety and Emergency Preparedness Canada.

Hanson, R.K. and Morton-Bourgon, K.E. (2004) *Predictors of Sexual Recidivism: An Updated Meta-analysis*. Ottawa, ON: Public Safety and Emergency Preparedness Canada.

Hanson, R.K. and Morton-Bourgon, K.E. (2005) 'The characteristics of persistent sexual offenders: a meta-analysis of recidivism studies', *Journal of Consulting and Clinical Psychology*, 73 (6): 1154–63.

Hanson, R.K. and Morton-Bourgon, K.E. (2007) *The Accuracy of Recidivism Risk Assessments for Sexual Offenders: A Meta-Analysis*. Ottawa, ON: Public Safety and Emergency Preparedness Canada.

Hanson, R.K. and Thornton, D. (1999) *Static 99: Improving Actuarial Risk Assessments for Sex Offenders*. Ottawa, ON: Department of the Solicitor General of Canada.

Hare, R.D. (1991) *The Revised Psychopathy Checklist*. Toronto, ON: Multi-Health Systems.

Hare, R.D. (2003) *Hare PCL-R*, 2nd edn. New York: Multi-Health Systems.

Harris, G.T., Rice, M.E., Quinsey, V.L., Lalumière, M.L., Boer, D.P. and Lang, C. (2003) 'A multi-site comparison of actuarial risk instruments for sex offenders', *Psychological Assessment*, 15 (3): 413–25.

Hart, S.D., Michie, C. and Cooke, D.J. (2007) 'Precision of actuarial risk assessment instruments', *British Journal of Psychiatry*, 190 (49): 60–5.

Langton, C.M., Barbaree, H.E., Seto, M.C., Peacock, E.J., Harkins, L. and Hansen, K.T. (2007) 'Actuarial assessment of risk for re-offence among adult sex offenders: evaluating the predictive accuracy of the Static-2002 and five other instruments', *Criminal Justice and Behavior*, 34: 37–59.

Litwack, T.R. (2001) 'Actuarial versus clinical assessments of dangerousness', *Psychology, Public Policy, and Law*, 7 (2): 409–33.

Marshall, W.L., Anderson, D. and Fernandez, Y. (1999) *Cognitive Behavioural Treatment of Sexual Offenders*. Chichester: John Wiley & Sons.

Monahan, J. (1995) *The Clinical Prediction of Violent Behavior*. Northvale, NJ: Jason Aronson (original work published in 1981).

Quinsey, V.L., Harris, G.T., Rice, M.E. and Cormier, C.A. (1999/2006) *Violent Offenders: Appraising and Managing Risk*. Washington, DC: American Psychological Association.

Schalock, R.L. and Luckasson, R. (2005) *Clinical Judgment*. Washington, DC: American Association on Mental Retardation.

Sjöstedt, G. and Långström, N. (2002) 'Assessment of risk for criminal recidivism among rapists: a comparison of four different measures', *Psychology, Crime, and Law*, 8: 25–40.

Webster, C.D., Douglas, K.S., Eaves, D. and Hart, S.D. (1997) *HCR-20: Assessing Risk for Violence, Version 2*. Burnaby, BC: Simon Fraser University, Mental Health, Law, and Policy Institute.

Chapter 3

Intimate partner violence risk assessment

P. Randall Kropp

In recent years there has been a surge in research and commentary on intimate partner violence risk assessment. A number of comprehensive literature reviews have now been published on risk factors for intimate partner violence (Bennett Cattaneo and Goodman 2005; Dutton and Kropp 2000; Hilton and Harris 2005; Riggs *et al.* 2000; Schumacher *et al.* 2001; Vest *et al.* 2002) and femicide (Aldridge and Browne 2003; Campbell *et al.* 2001). There have also been a number of efforts to develop risk assessment tools to assist front-line professionals in assessing and managing risk in these cases. They include the Danger Assessment (DA: Campbell, 1995), the Domestic Violence Screening Inventory (DVSI: Williams and Houghton 2004), the Spousal Assault Risk Assessment Guide (SARA: Kropp *et al.* 1995, 1999) and the Ontario Domestic Assault Risk Assessment (ODARA: Hilton *et al.* 2004). However, with increased attention to risk assessment in this field some controversy has emerged about a number of practical, professional and ethical issues. For example, there is little agreement in the field regarding how to define risk, how to establish professional standards for conducting assessments, how we should communicate risk information and what is the most appropriate method for assessing risk.

These issues will continue to be debated as the field evolves. The basic arguments have been discussed elsewhere (see Bennett Cattaneo and Goodman 2005; Hilton and Harris 2005; Kropp 2004) and will not be elaborated upon in this brief chapter. Instead, I will review what is known about risk factors for domestic violence. However, this chapter will go beyond a consideration of offender-based risk factors and assessment. There is now increased recognition that intimate partner violence is a form of targeted violence and risk assessment should therefore incorporate a victim's concerns and circumstances. Therefore this chapter will be divided into two main sections: perpetrator risk factors and victim considerations. I will conclude with suggestions for a process whereby offender- and victim-based information can be integrated into a comprehensive risk management plan.

Perpetrator risk factors

Those conducting risk assessments for intimate partner violence must necessarily consider a number of factors associated with the perpetrator and his circumstances. As noted, a number of literature reviews have summarised purported offender risk factors for intimate partner violence. These reviews reflect a burgeoning literature in the past fifteen years that has seen hundreds of studies focusing on risk factors. Most researchers emphasise the importance of establishing the empirical validity of a risk factor before using it in practice. This is laudable, but focusing only on an empirical criterion for inclusion of risk factors can be problematic. A number of potentially important risk factors are relatively rare or difficult to measure reliably, and therefore might not appear in an empirical literature review or meta-analysis. For example, suicidal ideation in the offender has been excluded as an important risk factor in some literature reviews because it has not been reliably associated with intimate partner violence recidivism, broadly defined. However, it would be a mistake to ignore suicidal ideation as a warning sign in an offender who has recently separated from their partner and made threats to harm or kill them. The association between suicide and homicide is well known in such cases. Herein is a fundamental ethical question for front-line workers: how does one balance practical and common-sense considerations if they conflict with what 'science' tells us about risk assessment? One answer might be that we should consider both empirical and *professional* knowledge about risk factors. Of course, this is also controversial since many clinicians or practitioners might be wrong in their assumptions about what is, or is not, related to intimate partner violence. Therefore risk factors should only be considered if they have a solid theoretical foundation or there exists some professional consensus regarding their importance.

It follows that the review of risk factors presented here includes risk factors that are discussed either in the empirical or professional literatures. Further, the risk factors are included here not only because they are relevant to the probability or likelihood of recidivism; their relationship to the severity, nature, frequency and imminence of future partner violence is also considered. I have included ten basic risk themes that should be considered regarding every perpetrator. These themes also form the basis for the Brief Spousal Assault Form for the Evaluation of Risk, or B-SAFER, a recent effort to develop a risk assessment tool for front-line workers (Kropp 2007; Kropp et al. 2005). They are: (1) past physical or sexual violence in relationships; (2) violent threats, ideation or intent; (3) escalation of violence; (4) violations of civil or criminal court orders; (5) attitudes supporting domestic violence; (6) other criminality; (7) relationship problems; (8) employment and/or financial problems; (9) substance abuse; (10) mental disorder.

Past physical or sexual violence in relationships

Men who have demonstrated physically assaultive behaviour in either past or current intimate relationships are at risk for future intimate partner violence (Campbell et al. 2001; Dutton and Kropp 2000; Fagan et al. 1983; Gondolf 1988a; Harrell and Smith 1996; Healy et al. 1988; Hilton et al. 2004; Riggs et al. 2000; Saunders and Browne 2002; Sonkin 1987; Williams and Houghton 2004). Recidivism rate estimates for intimate partner violence range from 30 to 70 per cent over a period of two years (Dutton 1995); these rates seem to apply regardless of whether or not the offender is arrested or completes treatment (Gondolf 2001; Hamberger and Hastings 1993).

In addition, typologies of spousal assaulters often indicate that the most severe patterns involve sexual assault (Gondolf 1988a; Snyder and Fruchtman 1981). Men who have sexually assaulted their partners are also at greater risk of violent recidivism (Campbell et al. 2001; Goldsmith 1990; Stuart and Campbell 1989; Walker 1989). The significant recidivism of spousal assaulters may reflect patterns of behaviour learned in the assaulter's family of origin, as a significant number of these men experienced or witnessed violence as children (Caesar 1988; Saunders 1993; Schumacher et al. 2001).

Violent threats, ideation or intent

Thoughts or threats of causing harm to others are clearly relevant to risk assessment. Violent ideation includes thoughts, urges and fantasies about killing or causing harm to others. It also includes intent, threats or attempts to cause harm or death to others (including victim's friends or family members). Such ideation is particularly problematic if it is experienced as persistent and intrusive, involves high-lethality methods or is associated with moderate- to high-intent. Violent ideation may be inferred from behaviour as well as from threatening statements. Such inferences are more likely to be accurate when based on a pattern of behaviour rather than a single act. It is common sense to consider threatening behaviour when conducting a spousal violence risk assessment, but there is also empirical support for this risk factor. Men who make credible threats of death (i.e. men feared intensely by their partners) are at increased risk of violent recidivism (Gondolf 1988a; Sonkin 1987; Dutton and Kropp 2000; Hart 1992; Stuart and Campbell 1989; Walker 1989). Also, spousal assaulters who have used or threatened to use a weapon are at increased risk for violent recidivism and spousal homicide (Campbell *et al.* 2001; Sonkin *et al.* 1985).

Harassing or stalking behaviour is a form of threatening behaviour that is of particular relevance to spousal violence. Stalking in the form of unwanted communication, watching, following or threatening can intentionally or recklessly create a sense of fear in victims. There is increasing evidence that such fear is justifiable given the link between the stalking of ex-intimate partners and violence (Burgess *et al.* 1997; Kropp *et al.* 2002; Palarea *et al.* 1999; Douglas and Dutton 2001). Stalking and threats are also risk factors for escalation into life-threatening violence (McFarlane *et al.* 2002). In general, any behaviour or credible threat that generates significant fear in the victim should be considered relevant as some evidence suggests that such fear may be predictive of violence (Gondolf 2001; Weisz *et al.* 2000). Overall, this factor is likely a risk marker that reflects the presence of mental illness, serious distress or attitudes that support or condone intimate partner violence.

Escalation of violence

Abusive relationships may be characterised by distinctive patterns or cycles of violence. One important pattern involves a recent escalation in the frequency or severity of assault. Escalation means the violence or threats have increased in severity or frequency over time. Increased severity indicates that, relative to earlier acts, the individual's recent acts of violence were more likely to involve direct contact with victims, serious physical harm to victims or use of weapons or credible threats of death. This pattern is associated with imminent risk for violent recidivism (Hart 1992; Sonkin 1987; Stuart and Campbell 1989; Weisz, *et al.* 2000) and may reflect a 'trajectory of violence' across time (Greenland 1985). Escalation of intimate partner violence is often associated with life-threatening assaults (Campbell 1995; Campbell *et al.* 2003).

Although it is not entirely clear why this pattern of violence occurs in some relationships but not others (Mahoney *et al.* 2001), there may be a number of explanations for the escalation of violence in some relationships. For example, this pattern may reflect the instrumental, reinforcing aspects of the use of violence in intimate relationships. In other words, if the abuser obtains the outcome that he desires through violence, he will be more likely to use this strategy in the future. Escalation may also be related to desensitisation to the use of violence over time, recent stressors or the onset/recurrence of mental illness.

Violations of civil or criminal court orders

There is abundant evidence in the literature that offenders who have violated the terms of conditional release (full parole, day parole, mandatory supervision, temporary absence) or community supervision (bail, probation) are more likely to recidivate than are other offenders (Andrews and Bonta 1996 2003; Hart *et al.* 1988). This relationship holds true when violent recidivism is the criterion (Quinsey *et al.* 1998).

Although there is little direct evidence bearing on this issue with respect to spousal violence specifically, based on the axiom that past behaviour is a good predictor of future behaviour, wife assaulters with a history of violating the 'no contact' provisions of a civil or criminal court protective order (e.g. bail, probation, parole, restraining order, peace bonds) are likely to be at risk for violent recidivism.

This factor is a risk marker that may reflect generally antisocial attitudes, attitudes that support or condone intimate partner violence, severe distress and employment or financial status. Thus some research suggests that while protection orders are often helpful (Holt *et al.* 2003) abusers that have a lower stake in conformity are more likely to violate such orders (Carlson *et al.* 1999; Sherman *et al.* 1992).

Attitudes supporting domestic violence

It is often noted in the professional literature that most serious and persistent offenders minimise the seriousness of past violence, deflect personal responsibility for past violence or even deny their involvement in past violence altogether. This is true of violent offenders in general and spousal assaulters in particular (Dutton 1995; Dutton and Kropp 2000; Hare 1991; Riggs *et al.* 2000; Saunders 1992; Webster *et al.* 1985).

In spousal assaulters, extreme minimisation or denial is associated with an unwillingness to desist assaultive behaviour or to participate and complete treatment programmes, which in turn is related to an increased risk of violent recidivism (Gondolf and White 2001; Hanson and Wallace-Capretta 2000; Shepard *et al.* 2002; Sonkin 1987). It is also plausible that minimisation and denial will affect the degree to which an offender complies with other risk management strategies such as monitoring and supervision.

Research and clinical observation also suggest that a number of socio-political, religious, (sub-)cultural, and personal attitudes differentiate men who have recently assaulted their partners from those who have not (e.g. Campbell *et al.* 2001; Saunders 1992). For instance, spousal assaulters support or condone intimate partner violence by implicitly or explicitly encouraging patriarchy (male prerogative), possessiveness, misogyny and/or the use of violence to resolve conflicts. These attitudes and beliefs are associated with increased risk of violent recidivism and femicide (Campbell *et al.* 2003; Daly and Wilson 1998; Hanson and Wallace-Capretta 2000; Sonkin 1987; Riggs *et al.* 2000; Schumacher *et al.* 2001).

This factor may be causally related to future intimate partner violence given that attitudes have been shown to directly influence behaviour under certain circumstances (e.g. Ajzen and Fischbein 1980). There is some evidence suggesting that these attitudes might be learned as a result of experiencing or witnessing family violence in childhood (Kessler *et al.* 2001; Riggs *et al.* 2000; Schumacher *et al.* 2001).

Other criminality

An offender with a history of violence is at increased risk for intimate partner violence, even if the past violence was not directed at his intimate partner. Both clinicians and researchers have noted that 'generally violent men' (those who are violent both in and out of home) often engage in more frequent and severe intimate partner violence than do other wife assaulters (Cadsky and Crawford 1988; Fagan *et al.* 1983; Gondolf 1988a; Hilton *et al.* 2001; Hilton *et al.* 2004;

Saunders 1992; Sonkin 1987; Stuart and Campbell 1989; Tweed and Dutton 1998). Past non-familial violence has also been cited as a risk factor for spousal violence recidivism and life-threatening violence (Campbell *et al.* 2003; Gondolf and White 2001; Hanson and Wallace-Capretta 2000; Jones and Gondolf 2001). In addition, offenders whose violence is directed solely at family members tend to engage in repetitive violence (Dutton 1995; Dutton and Hart 1992).

Research also demonstrates that a history of general (non-violent) criminality is a risk factor for violence among criminal offenders and forensic patients (Hare 1991; Harris *et al.* 1993; Monahan 1981; Monahan *et al.* 2001; Quinsey *et al.* 1998). Non-violent criminality has also been implicated in the risk for spousal violence (Dutton and Kropp 2000; Gondolf and White 2001; Hanson and Wallace-Capretta 2000; Hilton and Harris 2005; Hilton *et al.* 2004).

Relationship problems

Many clinicians have observed that risk of violence appears to be highest for spousal assaulters when relationship problems are evident, for example when: (a) the man is living with his partner, but she wants to end the relationship; (b) the man is separated from his partner, but he wants to renew the relationship; (c) there has been a sudden and/or recent separation (Campbell *et al.* 2001; Dutton and Kropp 2000; Kennedy and Dutton 1989; Kyriacou *et al.* 1999; Riggs *et al.* 2000). Murder of a female partner is also most likely to occur in the context of marital separation or divorce (Campbell *et al.* 2001; Daly and Wilson 1998; Wilson and Daly 1993).

Many couples seeking marital therapy report relationship aggression (Riggs *et al.* 2000). Indeed, probably most relationship violence occurs in the context of an argument or conflict (Cascardi and Vivian 1995; Stamp and Samburin 1995). Schumacher *et al.* (2001) reviewed six empirical studies that found statistically significant relationships between spousal violence and marital discord. It is likely that stress associated with finances, child rearing and power dynamics is often channelled in the form of violence. Relationship problems may be linked with intimate partner violence through a common association with personality disorder. Alternately, men with patriarchal attitudes (e.g. male proprietariness) may be more likely to resort to violence in the context of a woman's attempts to end the relationship.

Relationship problems may also be linked to intimate partner violence in a causal manner. Offenders with relationship problems may suffer from increased levels of distress, which might then increase the likelihood that they will resort to violence to resolve conflicts. In this way, relationship problems may be associated with both increased likelihood and frequency of future intimate partner violence. Recent relationship problems may also be associated with the imminence of intimate partner violence.

Employment and/or financial problems

Employment problems are associated with risk for criminality and general violence (Andrews and Bonta 1996 2003). For instance, a sudden, recent change in employment status (e.g. being laid off or fired) is associated with increased risk of violence (McNeil 1993). Low income, unstable employment and financial stresses are also among the most commonly cited risk factors for spousal assault (Carlson *et al.* 1999; Dutton and Kropp 2000; Hanson and Wallace-Capretta 2000; Hotaling and Sugarman 1986; Kyriacou *et al.* 1999; Riggs *et al.* 2001; Schumacher *et al.* 2000; Sherman *et al.* 1992; Stuart and Campbell 1989). Unemployment has also been cited as a risk factor for life-threatening and lethal spousal violence (Campbell *et al.* 2003).

Like relationship problems, employment problems may be a risk marker that predicts intimate partner violence because it is associated with personality disorder. Alternatively, employment problems may be linked to intimate partner violence in a causal manner by increasing general psychological distress, which in turn may lead men to displace work-related frustration and anger onto their families (Saunders 1993). Thus a history of employment problems may be associated with an increased likelihood and frequency of future intimate partner violence, and recent problems with the imminence of intimate partner violence.

Substance abuse

Problems with substance use include impairments of the individual's psychosocial adjustment (e.g. health, relationships, work or legal problems) related to the use of illicit drugs, as well as misuse of licit drugs (e.g. alcohol, prescribed medications). More serious problems include substantial impairment of the individual's health or social functioning (e.g. overdose, physical illness, arrest, job loss or a markedly inordinate amount of time spent obtaining and using substances). Offenders with a history of family violence (including spousal assault) are more likely than those with no such history to abuse substances (Dutton and Hart 1992; Gondolf and White 2001;

Riggs *et al.* 2000; Schumacher *et al.* 2001; Tolman and Bennett 1990), and the co-morbidity of substance abuse and spousal violence is commonly reported (Dutton and Kropp 2000; Kessler *et al.* 2001).

Recent substance use is associated with risk for violent recidivism among spousal assaulters and is considered one of the most critical dynamic or time-varying risk factors (Gondolf 2001; Hanson and Wallace-Capretta 2000; Hilton and Harris 2005; Jones and Gondolf 2001; Saunders 1992; Stuart and Campbell 1989). Finally, substance misuse may also contribute to assaults resulting in serious injury or death (Campbell *et al.* 2001; Farr 2002; Kyriacou *et al.* 1999).

The nature of the association between substance use and intimate partner violence is not clear. Substance use may simply be a risk marker, indirectly signalling the presence of personality disorder or other psychosocial maladjustment. Substance use may also set the stage for spousal assault by increasing conflict in the marital relationship. For instance, Saunders (1993) suggested that chronic substance use may induce family arguments about excessive drinking.

Alternatively, substance use may be a casual factor. Substance use may result in an increased likelihood of behavioural disinhibition among individuals with a history of intimate partner violence, or spousal assaulters may deliberately use substances to disinhibit themselves when they are considering intimate partner violence. Regardless, substance use probably is associated with the likelihood and frequency of future intimate partner violence, as well as with its severity and nature (e.g. reactive/impulsive). Active substance use may be associated with the imminence of future violence.

Mental disorder

Although mental disorder is not the sole or even primary cause of violence, the risk assessment literature suggests that symptoms of major mental disorder (e.g. psychotic and/or manic symptoms) are associated with violent behaviour in general (Borum *et al.* 1996; Monahan *et al.* 2001) and spousal violence in particular (Gondolf 1998; Kessler *et al.* 2001, Magdol *et al.* 1997; Schumacher *et al.* 2001).

In addition, suicidality is often indicative of a state of 'crisis' for the offender, and is generally considered a risk factor for spousal violence, including homicide (Campbell 1995; Goldsmith 1990; Saunders 1992; Stuart and Campbell 1989). Research suggests there is a link between dangerousness to self and others (Convit *et al.* 1988; Menzies *et al.* 1985), and most homicides that are followed by suicides occur against a female spouse (Campbell *et al.* 2001).

Personality disorders characterised by anger, impulsivity and behavioural instability (e.g. antisocial, borderline, narcissistic or histrionic personality disorder) are also associated with increased risk for spousal violence (Dutton 1995; Dutton and Kropp 2000; Gondolf 1998; Healy *et al.* 1998; Huss and Langhinrichsen-Rohling 2000; Jones and Gondolf 2001; Kessler *et al.* 2001; Magdol *et al.* 1997; Riggs *et al.* 2000; Schumacher *et al.* 2001).

Mental disorder is likely a causal factor that leads to impulsive or irrational decisions to act violently towards an intimate partner. It is probably associated with the likelihood and frequency of future intimate partner violence. In addition, active symptoms of major mental disorder may be associated with the imminence of future intimate partner violence (e.g. Binder and McNeil 1988; Link and Stueve 1994). Mental disorder can also have an indirect impact on risk by undermining effective risk management. In other words, symptoms of mental disorder can interfere with an offender's ability or motivation to comply with treatment and supervision (e.g. to participate in a batterer's intervention programme).

Victim considerations

Information integrity is important to the reliability of risk assessments. Offender-based risk assessments are often compromised by the reality that offenders are disinclined to volunteer information that could result in unfavourable decisions about their sentencing, release, access to their family and so forth. Offenders also often minimise or deny their responsibility for their offending. Thus assessments based only upon the self-report of the offender are not typically recommended; collateral information is important. Most experts appear to agree that information from the victim should be considered in intimate partner violence risk assessments (Bennett Cattaneo 2007; Hilton *et al.* 2004; Kropp 2004). For example, the DA (Campbell 1995) is designed entirely for use with victims. Similarly, the authors of the SARA guide (Kropp *et al.* 1999) strongly recommend interviewing victims in the course of a risk assessment. Some have investigated empirically the effect of victim estimates of their own danger. Weisz *et al.* (2000) reported that survivors' predictions of re-assault were significantly associated with the reoccurrence of severe violence, and Gondolf (2001) found that the most significant predictors of domestic violence reoffence were offender drunkenness and women's perceptions of safety. It seems, therefore, that victims can play a critically important role in risk assessments. But it is also important to consider that victims' own perceptions of safety are not always accurate (Weisz *et al.* 2000). Victims can also grossly minimise or underestimate the risk posed by their partners. Campbell *et al.* (2001) reported that victims underestimated their spouse's risk in 47 per cent and 53 per cent of actual and attempted femicides, respectively. Thus in the course of conducting a risk assessment it is important to consider factors that might influence victims' perceptions of risk, the accuracy of the information they provide and their motivation to engage in safety planning.

A victim should never be held responsible for an offender's abusive and violent behaviour. However, there are a number victim-related barriers, or *vulnerability* factors, that could affect a victim's ability or motivation to take self-protective actions. These factors should be considered in a risk assessment. In many situations there are limitations to what can be done to manage and control an offender's behaviour. In such cases it is important to work closely with victims to make them safe. This notion is nothing new; the importance of victim safety planning is well established in the intimate partner violence field (Hart and Stuehling 1992). However, it is often the case that those working with offenders and victims do so in isolation and important information regarding offenders and victims is not shared. Indeed, much of the risk assessment literature has ignored the role of victim vulnerability factors, although there have been some exceptions of late (Belfrage and Strand 2008; Hilton *et al.* 2004). The discussion next summarises five victim vulnerability factors that should be a part of any risk assessment for intimate partner violence: (1) inconsistent behaviour and/or attitudes toward perpetrator; (2) extreme fear of perpetrator; (3) inadequate access to resources; (4) unsafe living situation; (5) personal problems.

Inconsistent behaviour and/or attitudes toward perpetrator

For various reasons such as fear, love, unassertiveness or sensitivity to the perpetrator's feelings, a victim might display inconsistent behaviour toward a perpetrator. In situations involving an imminent or recent separation, an ambiguous response by the victim is subject to misinterpretation and cognitive distortion by the perpetrator (e.g. 'She's sending me mixed messages'). Some victims might even attempt to cope with the stress of the situation by approaching an ex-intimate partner through reasoning, communicating or pleading with them (Brewster 2000; Nicastro *et al.* 2000; Sheridan and Davies 2001; Spitzberg 2002). Of course, some contact with an ex-intimate partner can be an unavoidable hazard due to a shared work environment or joint custody of children (Buel 1999; Hardesty and Campbell 2004; Hart 2000; Pearson *et al.* 2001). In other cases, a victim may use violence themself, but this can in turn increase the risk of severe injury due to retaliation from the abuser (Das Dasgupta *et al.* 2002; Straus 1999).

A victim's opinion or belief about the perpetrator and their abusive behaviour can affect their level of self-protective behaviour. Thus it is important to consider whether a victim has any inconsistent attitudes toward the perpetrator. Many victims minimise or deny that the abuser's behaviour is wrong or dangerous (Barnett 2001; Campbell 1995; Logan *et al.* 2006; Walker 1984; Walker and Meloy 1998). Other victims may blame themselves for their abuser's behaviour, believe that the perpetrator's actions are partially justified or feel guilt about their choice of partner (Barnett *et al.* 1996; Ferraro and Johnson 1983; Gondolf 1998; Logan *et al.* 2006; Vézina and Hébert 2007). A victim may also possess social, religious or cultural beliefs that create ambivalence about ending an abusive situation, or prevent them from seeking help from the civil or criminal justice systems (Fischer and Rose 1995; Henning and Klesges 2002; LaViolette and Barnett 2000; Yoshihama 2000).

Extreme fear of perpetrator
Victims are often traumatised and fearful as a result of the abuse they have suffered. Distress of this nature can increase a victim's feelings of vulnerability and helplessness, and thus interfere with their ability, energy and motivation to take self-protective actions (Barnett 2001; Davies *et al.* 1998; Dutton 1992; Gorde *et al.* 2004; Fischer and Rose 1995; Logan *et al.* 2004). A victim's fear is usually realistic, and I have noted that victims' assessments of their own risk are empirically associated with spousal violence recidivism (Bennett Cattaneo and Goodman 2003; Bennett Cattaneo 2007; Heckert and Gondolf 2004; Weisz *et al.* 2000). Further, a victim's concerns about the safety of children or other dependents (e.g. the elderly or disabled) can also hinder their self-protective efforts (Buel 1999; Brewster 2003; Jaffe *et al.* 2004; McFarlane *et al.* 1999; Mechanic *et al.* 2000).

Inadequate access to resources
A victim is likely to be more vulnerable if they lack the knowledge, ability or motivation to access resources such as legal counsel, advocacy and shelter. Thus a victim may be unaware of laws, legal rights, legal remedies and other resources, or they may be reluctant to use those resources. Alternatively, a victim might be motivated

to access resources that are simply not available; this is often the case for victims in isolated communities (Davies *et al.* 1998; Logan *et al.* 2004). Further, victims who are elderly, have disabilities or are recent immigrants or refugees may have insufficient access to resources and increased reliance on the abuser (Cook *et al.* 2004; Nosek and Howland 1998; Orloff and Little 1999; Ulrich 1995). Lack of economic resources has been associated with a victim's ability to leave an abusive relationship (Aguirre 1985; Cole 2001; Davies 2001; Gondolf 1988b; Pence and Lizdas 1998; Strube 1988). Inadequate access to resources has been associated with domestic violence risk and revictimisation (Barnett 2001; Bell 2001; Bennett Cattaneo and Goodman 2005; Bybee and Sullivan 2002; Hilton *et al.* 2004; Sullivan 1991; Sullivan and Bybee 1999). Logically, victim safety planning is a meaningless exercise if adequate resources are not available.

Unsafe living situation
Some victims have unsafe living situations due to inadequate physical security in their homes, workplaces or transportation. The absence of a secure living situation has some empirical support as a predictor of domestic violence recidivism (Hilton *et al.* 2004). Many victims choose to remain in an unsafe situation with the abuser because they still love them or are either afraid or unable to leave (Barnett 2001; Buel 1999; Dutton 1992; Griffing *et al.* 2002; LaViolette and Barnett 2000). In situations involving the imminent or recent separation of the abuser and victim, risk management often must involve practical improvements to the security where victims live, work and travel (Baker *et al.* 2003; Davies *et al.* 1998; Goodman *et al.* 1999; Hart and Stuehling 1992; Menard 2001). For example, it is often necessary to: (a) improve visibility around the home or workplace; (b) decrease access to buildings by improving locks or other security measures; or (c) provide cell phones or personal alarms to victims. In some cases, it is impossible to ensure the safety of victims in a particular site and extreme measures such as relocation of the victims' residences or workplaces might be necessary (Human Resource Development Canada 2000; Kropp *et al.* 2002).

Personal problems
Victims of spousal violence often experience mental health, substance use, employment or legal problems that can increase their feelings of vulnerability and helplessness and thus interfere with their ability, energy and motivation to take self-protective actions. Common mental health problems include anxiety, post-traumatic stress symptoms,

depression and suicidality (Anderson *et al.* 2003; Astin *et al.* 1993; Barnett 2001; Cascardi *et al.* 1995; Davies *et al.* 1998; Einstadt and Bancroft 1999; Gleason 1993; Golding 1999; Gorde *et al.* 2004; Jones *et al.* 2001; Laffaye and Stein 2003; LaViolette and Barnett 2000; Nurius *et al.* 2003; Stark and Flitcraft 1995). It has been noted that substance use can place a domestic violence victim at further risk if they and the perpetrator are co-dependent on substances, if they depend on the perpetrator to provide drugs or if the victim's intoxication causes them to approach rather than avoid the perpetrator (Hart and Stuehling 1992; Hilton *et al.* 2004; Gilbert *et al.* 2001; Logan *et al.* 2006; Miller *et al.* 1989).

Problems with employment or finances have been associated with decisions not to leave abusive relationships due to victims' fears about being able to support themselves and their dependents (Bell 2003; Cole 2001; Davies *et al.* 1998; Johnson 1992; Logan *et al.* 2004; Rhodes and McKenzie 1998; Strube 1988). Similarly, unemployment can contribute to abused spouses' feelings of social isolation and self-efficacy (Davies 2001; Moe and Bell 2004; Nurius *et al.* 2003), which often occur in the context of financially controlling behaviours by the perpetrator (Brewster 2003). Finally, a victim who is involved in criminal activity (e.g. using or selling illicit drugs, prostitution) may fear the legal consequences of contacting the police in an abusive situation.

Concluding comments

There is some debate in the spousal violence risk assessment literature about the best way of combining risk factors to form an opinion about violence risk. Much of the discussion centres on the degree of professional discretion that should be exercised in evaluations of risk (see Hilton *et al.* 2004; Hilton and Harris 2005; Kropp 2004; Kropp and Hart 2000; Litwack 2001; Quinsey *et al.* 2001; Williams and Houghton 2004). However, the final decision about risk level, whether it is expressed in relative terms (e.g. high, moderate, low) or as a precise probability for reoffence, is largely irrelevant to the practical decisions made every day by those working with offenders and victims. The primary question facing those professionals and, importantly, the perpetrators and victims is: 'how do we prevent future violence from taking place?' Thus the value in a risk assessment lies in its ability to generate reasonable and practical ideas about risk management strategies. The perpetrator and victim risk factors in this chapter can be used in this way. They can be applied formally using instruments with explicit coding instructions, such as the SARA, B-SAFER, ODARA or the Aid to Safety Assessment and Planning (ASAP: BC Institute Against Family Violence 2006), or they can be referred to in a more informal way. However, a systematic and structured approach is typically recommended to ensure a comprehensive and objective risk assessment (Campbell 1995; Hilton and Harris 2005; Kropp 2004). Regardless, the information gathered about these factors can be integrated into a comprehensive risk management plan. They can be used to formulate plans for *monitoring, supervision* and *treatment* of the perpetrator and *safety planning* for the victim.

First, *monitoring* involves the surveillance of the perpetrator. Those supervising perpetrators should consider the most appropriate ways to monitor changes in risk, particularly when circumstances arise that might increase the imminent risk for violence. Monitoring typically will involve regular contacts with perpetrators and victims to assess dynamic risk factors such as relationship problems, employment problems, substance abuse, victim security and so forth. Second, *supervision* involves restrictions on activity, movement, association or communication. Once again, consideration of perpetrator and victim factors can help decisions about release, supervision conditions, restrictions on weapons and use of substances, restraining orders and so forth. Third, consideration of perpetrator factors will generate a hypothesis about appropriate *treatment*, which could include spousal violence programming, substance abuse intervention, medication, crisis intervention and hospitalisation. Finally, the victim vulnerability factors are particularly relevant to the formulation of a *victim safety plan*. Here the goal is to enhance the physical security or self-protective skills of the victim through support, counselling and the improvement of security at home or the workplace.

In sum, a risk assessment for intimate partner violence must include consideration of a range of perpetrator and victim factors. These factors should be combined to formulate a comprehensive risk management plan that includes four domains – monitoring, supervision, treatment and victim safety planning. It is hoped that these basic principles will assist the reader to achieve the true goals of the risk assessment process: the enhancement of victim safety and the prevention of violence.

References

Aguirre, B.E. (1985) 'Why do they return? Abused wives in shelters', *Social Work*, 30: 350–4.

Ajzen, I. and Fischbein, M. (1980) *Understanding Attitudes and Predicting Social Behavior*. Englewood Cliffs, NJ: Prentice-Hall.

Aldridge, M.L. and Browne, K.D. (2003) 'Perpetrators of spousal homicide: a review', *Trauma, Violence and Abuse*, 4: 265–76.

Anderson, D.K., Saunders, D.G., Yoshihama, M., Bybee, D.I. and Sullivan, C.M. (2003) 'Long-term trends in depression among women from abusive partners', *Violence Against Women*, 9 (7): 807–38.

Andrews, D.A. and Bonta, J. (1996) *The Level of Service Inventory – Revised: User's Manual*. Toronto, ON: Multi-Health Systems.

Andrews, D.A. and Bonta, J. (2003) *The Psychology of Criminal Conduct*, 3rd edn. Cincinnati, OH: Anderson.

Astin, M.C., Lawrence, K.J. and Foy, D.W. (1993) 'Post-traumatic stress disorder among battered women: risk and resiliency factors', *Violence and Victims*, 8 (1): 17–28.

Baker, C.K., Cook, S.L. and Norris, F.H. (2003) 'Domestic violence and housing problems: a contextual analysis of women's help-seeking, received informal support, and formal system response', *Violence Against Women*, 9 (7): 754–83.

Barnett, O.W. (2001) 'Why battered women do not leave. Part 2: External inhibiting factors – social support and internal inhibiting factors', *Trauma, Violence, and Abuse*, 2: 3–35.

Barnett, O.W., Martinez, T.E. and Keyson, M. (1996) 'The relationship between violence, social support, and self-blame in battered women', *Journal of Interpersonal Violence*, 11 (2): 221–33.

BC Institute Against Family Violence (2006) *Aid to Safety Assessment and Planning (ASAP) Manual*. New Westminster, BC: Justice Institute of BC.

Belfrage, H. and Strand, S. (2008) 'Structured spousal violence risk assessment: combining risk factors and victim vulnerability factors', *International Journal of Forensic Mental Health*, 7 (1): 39–46.

Bell, H. (2001) 'Cycles within cycles: domestic violence, welfare, and low-wage work', *Violence Against Women*, 9 (10): 1245–62.

Bennett Cattaneo, L.B. (2007) 'Contributors to assessments of risk in intimate partner violence: how victims and professionals differ', *Journal of Community Psychology*, 35 (1): 57–75.

Bennett Cattaneo, L. and Goodman, L.A. (2005) 'Risk factors for reabuse in intimate partner violence: a cross-disciplinary critical review', *Trauma, Violence, and Abuse*, 6: 141–75.

Binder, R.L. and McNeil, D.E. (1988) 'The effects of diagnosis and context on dangerousness', *American Journal of Psychiatry*, 145: 728–32.

Borum, R., Swartz, M. and Swanson, J. (1996) 'Assessing and managing violence risk in clinical practice', *Journal of Practicing Psychiatry and Behavioral Health*, 4: 205–15.

Brewster, M.P. (2000) 'Stalking by former intimates: verbal threats and other predictors of physical violence', *Violence and Victims*, 15: 41–54.

Brewster, M.P. (2003) 'Power and control dynamics in prestalking and stalking situations', *Journal of Family Violence*, 18 (4): 207–17.

Buel, S. M. (1999) 'Fifty obstacles to leaving, a.k.a., why abuse victims stay', *Colorado Lawyer*, 28 (10). Also available online at: http://www.cobar.org/tcl/.

Burgess, A.W., Baker, T., Greening, D., Hartman, C.R., Burgess, A.G., Douglas, J.E., and Halloran, R. (1997) 'Stalking behaviors within domestic violence', *Journal of Family Violence*, 12: 389–403.

Bybee, D.I. and Sullivan, C.M. (2002) 'The process through which an advocacy intervention resulted in positive change for battered women over time', *American Journal of Community Psychology*, 30 (1): 103–32.

Cadsky, O. and Crawford, M. (1988) 'Establishing batterer typologies in a clinical sample of men who assault their female partners. Special issue: Wife battering: a Canadian perspective', *Canadian Journal of Community Mental Health*, 7: 119–27.

Caesar, P.L. (1988) 'Exposure to violence in the families-of-origin among wife abusers and maritally nonviolent men. Special issue: Wife assaulters', *Violence and Victims*, 3: 49–63.

Campbell, J.C. (1995) 'Prediction of homicide of and by battered women', in J.C. Campbell (ed.), *Assessing Dangerousness: Violence by Sexual Offenders, Batterers, and Child Abusers*. Thousand Oaks, CA: Sage, pp. 96–113.

Campbell, J.C. (2001) 'Abuse during pregnancy: a quintessential threat to maternal and child health – so when do we start to act?', *Canadian Medical Association Journal*, 164 (11): 1578–9.

Campbell, J.C., Sharps, P. and Glass, N. (2001) 'Risk assessment for intimate partner homicide', in G.F. Pinard and L. Pagani (eds), *Clinical Assessment of Dangerousness: Empirical Contributions*. New York: Cambridge University Press, pp. 137–57.

Campbell, J.C., Webster, D., Koziol-McLain, J., Block, C., Campbell, D., Curry, M.A., Gary, F., Glass, N., McFarlane, J., Sachs, C., Sharps, P., Ulrich, Y., Wilt, S.A., Manganello, J., Xu, X., Schollenberger, J., Frye, V. and Laughon, K. (2003) 'Risk factors for femicide in abusive relationships: results from a multi-site case control study', *American Journal of Public Health*, 93: 1089–97.

Carlson, M.J., Harris, S.D. and Holden, G.W. (1999) 'Protective orders and domestic violence: risk factors for reabuse', *Journal of Family Violence*, 14 (2): 205–26.

Cascardi, M. and Vivian, D. (1995) 'Context specific episodes of marital violence: gender and severity of violence differences', *Journal of Family Violence*, 10: 265–93.

Cascardi, M., O'Leary, D., Lawrence, E.E. and Schlee, K.A. (1995) 'Characteristics of women physically abused by their spouses and who seek treatment regarding marital conflict', *Journal of Counselling and Clinical Psychology*, 63 (4): 616–23.

Cole, P.R. (2001) 'Impoverished women in violent partnerships: designing services to fit their reality', *Violence Against Women*, 7 (2): 222–3.

Convit, A., Jaeger, J., Lin, S.P., Meisner, M. and Volavka, J. (1988) 'Predicting assaultiveness in psychiatric inpatients: a pilot study', *Hospital and Community Psychiatry*, 39: 429–34.

Cook, S., Woolard, J.L. and McCollum, H.C. (2004) 'The strengths, competence, and resilience of women facing domestic violence: how can research and policy support them?', in K.I. Maton and C.J. Schellenbach (eds), *Investing in Children, Youth, Families and Communities: Strengths-based Research and Policy*. Washington, DC: American Psychological Association, pp. 97–115.

Daly, M. and Wilson, M. (1998) 'An evolutionary psychological perspective on homicide', in M.D. Smith and M. Zahn (eds), *Homicide: A Sourcebook of Social Research*. Thousand Oaks, CA: Sage, pp. 58–71.

Das Dasgupta, S. and Manavi (2002) 'A framework for understanding women's use of nonlethal violence in intimate heterosexual relationships', *Violence Against Women*, 8 (11): 1364–89.

Davies, J. (2001) 'Building opportunities for battered women's safety and self-sufficiency'. Available online: http://www.vawnet.org/vnl/library/general/welprac1.htm.

Davies, J., Lyon, E. and Monti-Catania, D. (1998) *Safety Planning with Battered Women: Complex Lives, Difficult Choices*. Thousand Oaks, CA: Sage.

Douglas, K.S. and Dutton, D.G. (2001) 'Assessing the link between stalking and domestic violence', *Aggression and Violent Behavior*, 6: 519–46.

Dutton, D.G. (1995) *The Domestic Assault of Women: Psychological and Criminal Justice Perspectives* (rev. edn). Vancouver, BC: UBC Press.

Dutton, D.G. and Hart, S.D. (1992) 'Evidence for long-term, specific effects of childhood abuse on criminal behavior in men', *International Journal of Offender Therapy and Comparative Criminology*, 36: 129–37.

Dutton, D.G. and Kropp, P.R. (2000) 'A review of domestic violence risk instruments', *Trauma, Violence, and Abuse*, 1: 171–81.

Dutton, M.A. (1992) *Empowering and Healing the Battered Woman: A Model for Assessment and Intervention*. New York: Springer.

Eisenstadt, S.A. and Bancroft, L. (1999) 'Domestic violence', *New England Journal of Medicine*, 341 (12): 886–92.

Fagan, J.A., Stewart, D.K. and Hansen, K.V. (1983) 'Violent men or violent husbands? Background factors and situational correlates', in D. Finkelhor, R.J. Gelles, G.T. Hotaling and M.A. Straus (eds), *The Dark Side of Families: Current Family Violence Research*. Newbury Park, CA: Sage, pp. 49–67.

Farr, K.A. (2002) 'Battered women who were "being killed and survived it": straight talk from survivors', *Violence and Victims*, 17: 267–81.

Ferraro, K.J. and Johnson, J.M. (1983) 'How women experience battering: the process of victimization', *Social Problems*, 30 (3): 325–39.

Fischer, K. and Rose, M. (1995) 'When enough is enough: battered women's decision making about court order of protection', *Crime and Delinquency*, 41: 414–29.

Gilbert, L., El-Bassel, N., Rajah, V., Folena, A. and Frye, V. (2001) 'Linking drug-related activities with experiences of partner violence: a focus group study of women in methadone treatment', *Violence and Victims*, 16 (5): 517–36.

Gleason, W.J. (1993) 'Mental disorders in battered women: an empirical study', *Violence and Victims*, 8 (1): 53–68.

Golding, J.M. (1999) 'Intimate partner violence as a risk factor for mental disorders: a meta-analysis', *Journal of Family Violence*, 14 (2): 99–132.

Goldsmith, H.R. (1990) 'Men who abuse their spouses: an approach to assessing future risk', *Journal of Offender Counseling, Services and Rehabilitation*, 15: 45–56.

Gondolf, E.W. (1988a) 'The effect of batterer counselling on shelter outcome', *Journal of Interpersonal Violence*, 3 (3): 275–89.

Gondolf, E.W. (1988b) 'Who are those guys? Toward a behavioral typology of batterers', *Violence and Victims*, 3: 187–203.

Gondolf, E.W. (1998c) *Assessing Woman Battering in Mental Health Services*. Thousand Oaks, CA: Sage.

Gondolf, E.W. (2001) *Batterer Intervention Systems: Issues, Outcomes, and Recommendations*. Thousand Oaks, CA: Sage.

Gondolf, E.W. and White, R.J. (2001) 'Batterer program participants who repeatedly reassault: psychopathic tendencies and other disorders', *Journal of Interpersonal Violence*, 16: 361–80.

Goodman, L., Bennett, L. and Dutton, M.A. (1999) 'Obstacles to victim's cooperation with the criminal prosecution of their abusers: the role of social support', *Violence and Victims*, 14 (4): 427–44.

Gorde, M.W., Helfrich, C.A. and Finlayson, M.L. (2004) 'Trauma symptoms and life skill needs of domestic violence victims', *Journal of Interpersonal Violence*, 19 (6): 306–19.

Greenland, C. (1985) 'Dangerousness, mental disorder, and politics', in C. D. Webster, M.H. Ben-Aron and S.J. Hucker (eds), *Dangerousness: Probability and Prediction, Psychiatry and Public Policy*. New York: Cambridge University Press, pp. 25–40.

Griffing, S., Ragin, D.F., Madry, L., Bingham, L.E. and Primm, B.J. (2002) 'Domestic violence survivors' self-identified reasons for returning to abusive relationships', *Journal of Interpersonal Violence*, 17 (3): 306–19.

Hamberger, L.K. and Hastings, J.E. (1993) 'Court-mandated treatment of men who assault their partner: issues, controversies, and outcomes', in N.Z. Hilton (ed.), *Legal Responses to Wife Assault: Current Trends and Evaluation*. Newbury Park, CA: Sage, pp. 188–229.

Hanson, R.K. and Wallace-Capretta, S. (2000) *Predicting Recidivism Among Male Batterers*, User Report 2000-06. Ottawa, ON: Department of the Solicitor General of Canada.

Hardesty, J.L. and Campbell, J.C. (2004) '"He still controls me through the children": post separation safety planning for battered women and their children', in P.G. Jaffe (ed.), *Ending Domestic Violence in the Lives of Children and Parents: Promising Practices for Safety, Healing and Prevention.* Toronto, ON: University of Toronto Press.

Hare, R.D. (1991) *The Hare Psychopathy Checklist – Revised.* Toronto, ON: Multi-Health Systems.

Harrell, A. and Smith, B. (1996) 'Effects of restraining orders on domestic violence victims', in E. Buzawa and C. Buzawa (eds), *Do Arrests and Restraining Orders Work?* Thousand Oaks, CA: Sage, pp. 214–42.

Harris, G.T., Rice, M.E. and Quinsey, V.L. (1993) 'Violent recidivism of mentally disordered offenders: the development of a statistical prediction instrument', *Criminal Justice and Behavior*, 20: 315–35.

Hart, B.J. (1992) *Program Standards for Batterer Intervention Services.* Reading, PA: Pennsylvania Coalition Against Domestic Violence.

Hart, B.J. (2000) 'The legal road to freedom'. Available online: http://www.mincava.umn.edu/hart/legalro.htm.

Hart, B. and Stuehling, J. (1992) 'Personalized safety plan'. Available online: http://www.mincava.umn.edu/hart/persona.htm.

Hart, S.D., Kropp, P.R. and Hare, R.D. (1988) 'Performance of male psychopaths following conditional release from prison', *Journal of Consulting and Clinical Psychology*, 56: 227–32.

Healy, K., Smith, C. and O'Sullivan, C. (1998) *Batterer Intervention: Program Approaches and Criminal Justice Strategies*, NCJ 168638. Washington, DC: National Institute of Justice.

Heckert, D.A. and Gondolf, E.W. (2004) 'Battered women's perceptions of risk versus risk factors and instruments in predicting repeat reassault', *Journal of Interpersonal Violence*, 19 (7): 778–800.

Henning, K.R. and Klesges, L.M. (2002) 'Utilization of counseling and support services by female victims of domestic violence', *Violence and Victims*, 17 (5): 623–36.

Hilton, N.Z. and Harris, G.T. (2005) 'Predicting wife assault: a critical review and implications for policy and practice', *Trauma, Violence, and Abuse*, 6 (1): 3–23.

Hilton, N.Z., Harris, G.T. and Rice, M.E. (2001) 'Predicting violence by serious wife assaulters', *Journal of Interpersonal Violence*, 16: 408–23.

Hilton, N.Z., Harris, G.T., Rice, M.E., Lang, C. and Cormier, C.A. (2004) 'A brief actuarial assessment for the prediction of wife assault recidivism: the ODARA', *Psychological Assessment*, 16 (3): 267–75.

Holt, V.L., Kernic, M.A., Wolf, M.E. and Rivara, F.P. (2003) 'Do protection orders affect the likelihood of future partner violence and injury?', *American Journal of Preventive Medicine*, 24: 16–21.

Hotaling, G.T. and Sugarman, D.B. (1986) 'An analysis of risk markers in husband-to-wife violence: the current state of knowledge', *Violence and Victims*, 1: 101–24.

Human Resource Development Canada (HRDC) (2000) *New Identities for Victims of Abuse: Client Survey.* Ottawa, ON: HRDC.

Huss, M.T. and Langhinrichsen-Rohling, J. (2000) 'Identification of the psychopathic batterer: the clinical, legal, and policy implications', *Aggression and Violent Behavior*, 5: 403–22.

Jaffe, P.G., Baker, L.L. and Cunningham, A.J. (2004) *Protecting Children from Domestic Violence: Strategies for Community Intervention*. New York: Guilford Press.

Johnson, I. (1992) 'Economic, situational, and psychological correlates of the decision-making process of battered women', *Families in Society*, 73 (3): 168–76.

Jones, A.S. and Gondolf, E.W. (2001) 'Time-varying risk factors for reassault among batterer program participants', *Journal of Family Violence*, 16: 345–59.

Jones, L., Hughes, M. and Unterstaller, U. (2001) 'Post-traumatic stress disorder (PTSD) in victims of domestic violence: a review of the research', *Trauma, Violence, and Abuse*, 2 (2): 99–119.

Kennedy, L.W. and Dutton, D.G. (1989) 'The incidence of wife assault in Alberta', *Canadian Journal of Behavioral Science*, 21: 40–54.

Kessler, R.C., Molnar, B.E., Feurer, I.D. and Appelbaum, M. (2001) 'Patterns and mental health predictors of domestic violence in the United States: results from the National Comorbidity Survey', *International Journal of Law and Psychiatry*, 24: 487–508.

Kropp, P.R. (2004) 'Some questions about spousal violence risk assessment', *Violence Against Women*, 10: 676–97.

Kropp, P.R. (2007) 'The development of the SARA and the B-SAFER', in A.C. Baldry and F.W. Winkel (eds), *Assessing Risk of Spousal Assault: An International Approach*. Hauppauge, NY: Nova Science.

Kropp, P.R. and Hart, S.D. (2000) 'The Spousal Assault Risk Assessment (SARA) Guide: reliability and validity in adult male offenders', *Law and Human Behavior*, 24: 101–18.

Kropp, P.R., Hart, S.D. and Belfrage, H. (2005) *The Brief Spousal Assault Form for the Evaluation of Risk (B-SAFER)*. Vancouver, BC: Proactive Resolutions.

Kropp, P.R., Hart, S.D. and Lyon, D.R. (2002) 'Risk assessment of stalkers: some problems and possible solutions', *Criminal Justice and Behavior*, 29: 590–616.

Kropp, P.R., Hart, S.D., Webster, C.D. and Eaves, D. (1995) *Manual for the Spousal Assault Risk Assessment Guide*, 2nd edn. Vancouver, BC: British Columbia Institute on Family Violence.

Kropp, P.R., Hart, S.D., Webster, C.D. and Eaves, D. (1999) *Spousal Assault Risk Assessment Guide (SARA)*. Toronto, ON: Multi-Health Systems.

Kyriacou, D.N., Anglin, D., Taliaferro, E., Stone, S., Tubb, T., Linden, J.A., Muelleman, R., Barton, E. and Kraus, J.F. (1999) 'Risk factors for injury to women from domestic violence', *New England Journal of Medicine*, 341: 1882–98.

Laffaye, C. and Stein, M.B. (2003) 'Post-traumatic stress disorder and health-related quality of life in female victims of intimate partner violence', *Violence and Victims*, 18 (2): 227–38.

LaViolette, A.D. and Barnett, O.W. (2000) *It Could Happen to Anyone: Why Battered Women Stay*, 2nd edn. Thousand Oaks, CA: Sage.

Link, B.G. and Stueve, A. (1994) 'Psychotic symptoms and the violent/illegal behavior of mental patients compared to community controls', in J. Monahan and H.J. Steadman (eds), *Violence and Mental Disorder: Developments in Risk Assessment*. Chicago, IL: University of Chicago Press, pp. 137–59.

Litwack, T.R. (2001) 'Actuarial versus clinical assessments of dangerousness', *Psychology, Public Policy, and Law*, 7: 409–43.

Logan, T.K., Stevenson, E., Evans, L. and Leukefeld, C. (2004) 'Rural and urban women's perceptions of barriers to health, mental health, and criminal justice services: implications for victim services', *Violence and Victims*, 19 (1): 37–62.

Logan, T.K., Walker, R., Jordan, C.E. and Leukefeld, C.G. (2006) *Women and Victimization: Contributing Factors, Interventions, and Implications*. Washington, DC: American Psychological Association.

McFarlane, J., Campbell, J.C. and Watson, K. (2002) 'Intimate partner stalking and femicide: urgent implications for women's safety', *Behavioral Sciences and the Law*, 20: 51–68.

McFarlane, J.M., Campbell, J.C., Wilt, S., Sachs, C.J., Ulrich, Y. and Xu, X. (1999) 'Stalking and intimate partner femicide', *Homicide Studies*, 3: 300–16.

Magdol, L., Moffitt, T.E., Caspi, A., Newman, D.L., Fagan, J. and Silva, P.A. (1997) 'Gender differences in partner violence in a birth cohort of 21-year-olds: bridging the gap between clinical and epidemiological approaches', *Journal of Consulting and Clinical Psychology*, 65: 68–78.

Mahoney, P., Williams, L.M. and West, C.M. (2001) 'Violence against women by intimate relationship partners', in C.M. Renzetti, J.L. Edleson and R. Kennedy Bergen (eds), *Sourcebook on Violence Against Women*. Thousand Oaks, CA: Sage.

Mechanic, M.B., Weaver, T.L. and Resick, P.A. (2000) 'Intimate partner violence and stalking behavior: exploration patterns and correlates in a sample of acutely battered women', *Violence and Victims*, 15: 55–72.

Menard, A. (2001) 'Domestic violence and housing: key policy and program challenges', *Violence Against Women*, 7 (6): 707–20.

Menzies, R.J., Webster, C.D. and Sepejak, D.S. (1985) 'The dimensions of dangerousness: evaluating the accuracy of psychometric predictions of violence among forensic patients', *Law and Human Behaviour*, 9: 49–70.

Miller, B.A., Downs, W. and Gondoli, D.M. (1989) 'Spousal violence among alcoholic women as compared to a random household sample of women', *Journal of Studies on Alcohol*, 50 (6): 533–40.

Moe, A.M. and Bell, M.P. (2004) 'Abject economics: the effects of battering and violence on women's work and employability', *Violence Against Women*, 10 (1): 29–55.

Monahan, J. (1981) *Predicting Violent Behavior: An Assessment of Clinical Techniques*. Beverly Hills, CA: Sage.

Monahan, J., Steadman, H.J., Silver, E., Appelbaum, P.S., Robbins, P.C., Mulvey, E.P., Roth, L.H, Grisso, T. and Banks, S. (2001) *Rethinking Risk Assessment: The MacArthur Study of Mental Disorder and Violence*. New York: Oxford University Press.

Nicastro, A.M., Cousins, A.V. and Spitzberg, B.H. (2000) 'The tactical face of stalking', *Journal of Criminal Justice*, 28: 69–82.

Nosek, M. and Howland, C. (1998) *Abuse and Women with Disabilities*. Available online: http://www.vawnet.org/vnl/library/general/AR_disab.html.

Nurius, P.S., Furrey, J. and Berliner, L. (1992) 'Coping capacity among women with abusive partners', *Violence and Victims*, 7 (3): 229–43.

Nurius, P.S., Macy, R.J., Bhuyan, R., Holt, V.L., Kernic, M.A. and Riavara, F.P. (2003) 'Contextualizing depression and physical functioning in battered women: adding vulnerability and resources to the analysis', *Journal of Interpersonal Violence*, 18 (12): 1141–31.

Orloff, L.E. and Little, R. (1999) *Somewhere to Turn: Making Domestic Violence Services Accessible to Battered Immigrant Women: A "How To" Manual for Battered Women's Advocates and Service Providers*. Washington, DC: Ayuda.

Palarea, R.E., Zona, M.A., Lane, J.C. and Langhinrichsen-Rohling, J. (1999) 'The dangerous nature of intimate relationship stalking: threats, violence, and associated risk factors', *Behavioral Sciences and the Law*, 17: 269–83.

Pearson, J., Griswold, E.A. and Thoennes, N. (2001) 'Balancing safety and self-sufficiency: lessons on serving victims of domestic violence for child support and public assistance agencies', *Violence Against Women*, 7 (2): 176–92.

Pence, E. and Lizdas, K. (1998) *The Duluth Safety and Accountability Audit: A Guide to Assessing Institutional Responses to Domestic Violence*. Duluth, MN: Domestic Abuse Intervention Project.

Quinsey, V.L., Harris, G.T., Rice, G.T. and Cormier, C.A. (1998) *Violent Offenders: Appraising and Managing Risk*. Washington, DC: American Psychological Association.

Rhodes, N.R. and McKenzie, E.B. (1998) 'Why do battered women stay? Three decades of research', *Aggression and Violent Behaviour*, 3 (4): 391–406.

Riggs, D.S., Caulfield, M.B. and Street, A.E. (2000) 'Risk for domestic violence: factors associated with perpetration and victimization', *Journal of Clinical Psychology*, 56: 1289–316.

Rooney, J. and Hanson, R.K. (2001) 'Predicting attrition from treatment programs for abusive men', *Journal of Family Violence*, 16: 131–49.

Saunders, D.G. (1992) 'Woman battering', in R.T. Ammerman and M. Hersen (eds), *Assessment of Family Violence: A Clinical and Legal Sourcebook*. New York: Wiley, pp. 208–35.

Saunders, D.G. (1993) 'Husbands who assault: multiple profiles requiring multiple responses', in N.Z. Hilton (ed.), *Legal Responses to Wife Assault: Current Trends and Evaluation*. Newbury Park, CA: Sage, pp. 9–34.

Saunders, D.G. and Browne, A. (2002) 'Intimate partner homicide', in R. T. Ammerman and M. Hersen (eds), *Case Studies in Family Violence*. New York: Kluwer Academic/Plenum, pp. 415–49.

Schumacher, J.A., Feldbau-Kohn, S., Slep, A.M.S. and Heyman, R.E. (2001) 'Risk factors for male-to-female partner physical abuse', *Aggression and Violent Behavior*, 6: 281–352.

Shepard, M.F., Falk, D.R. and Elliott, B.A. (2002) 'Enhancing coordinated community responses to reduce recidivism in cases of domestic violence', *Journal of Interpersonal Violence*, 17: 551–69.

Sheridan, L. and Davies, G.M. (2001) 'Violence and the prior victim-stalker relationship', *Criminal Behaviour and Mental Health*, 11: 102–16.

Sherman, L.W., Smith, D.A., Schmidt, J.D. and Rogan, D.P. (1992) 'Crime, punishment and the stake in conformity: legal and informal control of domestic violence', *American Sociological Review*, 57: 680–90.

Snyder, D.K. and Fruchtman, L.A. (1981) 'Differential patterns of wife abuse: a data-based typology', *Journal of Consulting and Clinical Psychology*, 49: 878–85.

Sonkin, D.J. (1987) 'The assessment of court-mandated male batterers', in D.J. Sonkin (ed.), *Domestic Violence on Trial: Psychological and Legal Dimensions of Family Violence*. New York: Springer, pp. 174–96.

Sonkin, D., Martin, D. and Walker, L. (1985) *The Male Batterer: A Treatment Approach*. New York: Springer.

Spitzberg, B.H. (2002) 'The tactical topography of stalking victimization and management', *Trauma Violence Abuse*, 3: 261–88.

Stamp, G.H. and Sabourin, T.C. (1995) 'Accounting for violence: an analysis of male spousal abuse narratives', *Journal of Applied Community Research*, 23: 284–307.

Stark, E. and Flitcraft, A. (1995) Killing the beast within: women battering and female suicidality', *International Journal of Health Services*, 25 (1): 43–64.

Straus, M. (1999) 'The controversy over domestic violence by women: a methodological, theoretical, and sociology of science analysis', in X.B. Arriaga and S. Oskamp (eds), *Violence in Intimate Relationships*. Thousand Oaks, CA: Sage, pp. 17–44.

Strube, M.J. (1988) 'The decision to leave an abusive relationship: empirical indication and theoretical issues', *Psychological Bulletin*, 104 (2): 236–50.

Stuart, E.P. and Campbell, J.C. (1989) 'Assessment of patterns of dangerousness with battered women', *Issues in Mental Health Nursing*, 10: 245–60.

Sullivan, C.M. (1991) 'The provision of advocacy services to women leaving abusive partners: an exploratory study', *Journal of Interpersonal Violence*, 6 (1): 41–54.

Sullivan, C.M. and Bybee, D.I. (1999) 'Reducing violence using community-based advocacy for women with abusive partners', *Journal of Consulting and Clinical Psychology*, 67 (1): 43–53.

Sullivan, C.M., Basta, J., Tan, C. and Davidson, W.S. (1992) 'After the crisis: a needs assessment of women leaving a domestic violence shelter', *Violence and Victims*, 7 (3): 267–75.

Tolman, R.M. and Bennett, L.W. (1990) 'A review of research on men who batter', *Journal of Interpersonal Violence*, 5: 87–118.

Tweed, R.G. and Dutton, D.G. (1998) 'A comparison of impulsive and instrumental subgroups of batterers', *Violence and Victims*, 13: 217–30.

Ulrich, Y.C. (1995) 'What helped most in leaving spousal abuse: implications for interventions', in J.C. Campbell (ed.), *Empowering Survivors of Abuse: Health Care for Battered Women and Their Children*. Thousand Oaks, CA: Sage, pp. 70–8.

Vest, J.R., Catlin, T.K., Chen, J.J. and Brownson, R.C. (2002) 'Multistate analysis of factors associated with intimate partner violence', *American Journal of Preventative Medicine*, 22 (3): 156–64.

Vézina, J. and Hébert, M. (2007) 'Risk factors for victimization in romantic relationships of young women: a review of empirical studies and implications for prevention', *Trauma, Violence, and Abuse*, 8 (1): 33–66.

Walker, L.E. (1984) *The Battered Woman Syndrome*. New York: Springer.

Walker, L.E. (1989) 'Psychology and violence against women', *American Psychologist*, 44: 695–702.

Walker, L.E. and Meloy, M.J. (1998) 'Stalking and domestic violence', in M.J. Meloy (ed.), *The Psychology of Stalking: Clinical and Forensic Perspectives*. San Diego, CA: Academic Press, pp. 139–61.

Webster, C.D., Dickens, B.M. and Addario, S. (1985) *Constructing Dangerousness: Scientific, Legal and Policy Implications*. Toronto, ON: Centre of Criminology, University of Toronto.

Weisz, A.N., Tolman, R.M. and Saunders, D.G. (2000) 'Assessing the risk of severe domestic violence: the importance of survivors' predictions', *Journal of Interpersonal Violence*, 15: 75–90.

Williams, K. and Houghton, A.B. (2004) 'Assessing the risk of domestic violence reoffending: a validation study', *Law and Human Behavior*, 24 (4): 437–55.

Wilson, M. and Daly, M. (1993) 'Spousal homicide risk and estrangement', *Violence and Victims*, 8: 3–16.

Yoshihama, M. (2000) 'Reinterpreting strength and safety in a socio-cultural context: dynamics of domestic violence and experiences of women of Japanese descent', *Children and Youth Services Review*, 22 (3/4): 207–29.

Chapter 4

Conducting individualised theory-driven assessments of violent offenders

Jane L. Ireland

The clinical and academic literature exploring aggression and approaches to its therapy and management focuses on what is termed 'habitual aggression' (Huesmann 1998; Martens 2000). Habitual aggression describes individuals whose aggression has occurred more than once, suggesting a development or continuation of an aggressive behaviour pattern. Habitual aggression is a useful concept with which to commence this chapter, since the populations who come into contact with professional services for aggression management needs will generally fall into this group of aggressors. It is this group of individuals which the current chapter will most concern itself with.

The chapter will commence by providing an introduction to the importance of attending to the correct literature base when trying to assess habitual aggression and the importance of concepts such as motivation, adaptation and client strength. All of these will be attended to in turn prior to detailed consideration of the frameworks which can be employed and the areas which should be the focus of assessment. To illustrate some of the points made, examples from a long-term violence treatment programme, the Life Minus Violence programme (see Ireland 2007), will be referred to, including the revised version of this programme, Life Minus Violence – Enhanced. The purpose of this is simply to provide some worked examples by illustrating a treatment programme which has been developed with attention to the aggression literature.

Any assessment needs to ensure that it attends to the correct literature base. There is a tendency within the forensic field to utilise the antisocial literature base when describing and communicating recommendations for managing aggression (Ireland 2007). Although overlap undoubtedly exists between these two sets of literature, with some researchers explaining aggression using existing theories of antisocial behaviour (e.g. Poulin and Boivin 2000), there are also clear differences (Tremblay and Côté 2005). For example, the antisocial literature includes behaviours which clearly fall outside definitions of aggression, e.g. risky sexual behaviour, drug-taking (Ireland 2007). The failure of some researchers and clinicians to attend to the aggression literature has resulted in a narrow overview, with assessment and treatment strategies describing themselves as aggression focused (e.g. Violence Reduction Programme: Wong *et al.* 2007) but which are in fact centred on antisocial behaviour. They also utilise potentially problematic integrations of theory not originally developed or adapted for forensic applications (e.g. the Stages of Change model).

Indeed, treatment programmes such as the Violence Reduction Programme take their theory from the responsivity literature, commonly referred to as the 'What Works' literature (e.g. McGuire and Priestley 2000), and not from the international literature base available on aggression theory. Responsivity issues (e.g. personality style, levels of impulsivity, levels of psychopathy, mental illness, learning styles, acquired brain injuries, etc.) are undoubtedly important in determining the individual presentation of a client, specifically *how* treatment, and indeed assessment, should be conducted. Responsivity issues do not, however, provide guidance on the *content* of the treatment or assessment approaches. For this, there has to be attention placed on the core aggression literature.

Motivation is a pertinent example of the importance of accounting for the aggression literature, an issue often missed if current perspectives on aggression are not attended to. There is an increasing acceptance that aggression should be described less by its *nature* and more by its *motivation* (e.g. Raine *et al.* 2006; Tremblay *et al.* 2007). With regard to the latter, the focus has been on reactive and proactive aggression.

Reactive aggression has been described as an uncontrolled form of aggression occurring in the context of provocation (real or perceived), frustration or threat. It has its roots in the 'frustration-anger' theory of aggression which postulates that aggression is triggered by the blocking of a goal, is accompanied by high arousal, namely anger, and represents an immediate or impulsive response to the source of the provocation or threat (Berkowitz 1989). A basic example would be an adult becoming angry following an insult and immediately assaulting or verbally berating the source of this insult. Proactive aggression, sometimes referred to as planned, instrumental or predatory aggression, is more in keeping with social learning models of aggression (Bandura 1973). These describe aggression as an acquired behaviour that is driven and reinforced by the actual or anticipated rewards which follow it (i.e. the reinforcing consequences). The aggression is largely planned, with classic examples including acts of robbery.

There has, however, been a move in recent years towards acceptance of the concept of a 'mixed-motive' aggressor and the notion that motives can alter over time (e.g. Bushman and Anderson 2001; Vitaro and Brendgen 2005; Tremblay and Côté 2005; Gendreau and Archer 2005). Furthermore, it is argued that the true 'proactive only' aggressor is rare (if indeed non-existent: Vitaro and Brendgen 2005). It has also been suggested that they are more likely to be individuals with high interpersonal style scores on measures of clinical psychopathy, namely presenting with interpersonal traits such as callousness, lack of affect and guilt (Cornell *et al.* 1996).

The focus on aggression motivation is an important one, and assessment should place emphasis on understanding the motivation and consequent *functions* of behaviours, as opposed to focusing on how aggression presents in terms of its nature alone. Focusing on the nature of aggression is likely to be of less use in actually changing the behaviour of others than concentrating on motive.

Equally important underpinning principles for assessment should be the related concepts of adaptation and client strength, with the former recognising that aggression may have adaptive qualities and thus it cannot routinely be treated within a deficit model. The more classical and integrated models of information processing which have been routinely applied to understand aggressive behaviour (e.g. Huesmann 1998) argue against using deficit models, highlighting how aggression can be adaptive and carry real benefits to the perpetrators. Downplaying the benefits for aggressors is therefore likely to prove of limited effectiveness.

In recognition of aggression as an adaptive behaviour, applications of information processing models for understanding aggression within forensic settings have been emerging in recent years (e.g. Ireland and Murray 2005). This is certainly not a new concept, however. Indeed earlier writings such as those by Galtung (1964), a peace researcher, argue for the historical benefits of aggression in promoting change, defining aggression rather more broadly than more recent definitions where the focus is solely on intent to cause fear or harm (e.g.

Shantz and Hartup 1992). Indeed Galtung adopted a very broad definition of aggression, defining it as 'drives toward change, even against the will of others' (p. 95), and in doing so arguing how 'one can turn the coin and look at the other face: aggression as the driving force in history, as the motivational force which moves mountains' (p. 95).

Indeed Galtung describes 'extreme aggression' as that more akin to the negative aggression that manifests itself in victim injury while also recognising the adaptive qualities of some aggression. Aggression in Galtung's writings is more a product of environmental pressures and changes in social structure, produced when an individual is exposed to rank disequilibrium. Thus to adopt a purely individually driven psychopathological approach that considers aggression a product solely of an individuals' deficits and failings would not provide a complete picture. Rather, aggression should be considered a product of environmental influences within which an individual is playing a part. Assessment in this sense can be holistic only if it moves beyond the individual to an outline of how they are interacting with their environment and how the environment is promoting (rank) disequilibrium.

This moves us to the next related area of individuality, that of recognising client strength. Too often in the clinical and academic literature we can focus on the problems with an individual's behaviour, ignoring their strengths. The aggression literature is perhaps an excellent example of this, where the focus has been on what causes aggression instead of what causes non-aggression. The latter falls more within the domain of 'peace research'. Focusing on positive elements of presentation, namely what makes an individual peaceful, is crucial and in part a product of attention to 'positive psychology', which argues for a focus on a strength-based approach as opposed to an approach where weaknesses are focused on and in effect repaired, i.e. 'We need to ask practitioners to recognise that much of their best work they already do in the consulting room is to amplify client's strengths rather than repair their weaknesses' (Seligman 2002: 5). In essence the work of Seligman argues for the concept of 'learned optimism' (Seligman 2006), namely the ability to change and to reach goals using positive means. Although applied more to the prevention of mental illness, the philosophy of this approach has much to offer for the management of other facets of individual presentation causing difficulty, such as aggression. The cornerstone for developing optimism for change is the recognition of existing strength in a client. This has to therefore represent a

71

core component of an assessment approach while at the same time balancing it with recognition of client weaknesses.

Regardless of differences in the specific approach and literature base attended to, there is developing consensus in the literature that in order to promote the therapeutic success of aggression management intervention, a focused assessment of individual clients is required (Wong *et al.* 2007). The ensuing sections aim to provide some guidance with regards to what a focused assessment of client need in this area should attend to. Aggression assessment is, however, a vast area to cover and it is not the intention that the current chapter will do justice to all areas of potential value. Rather it aims to provide some core issues for consideration that will enhance existing aggression assessments.

Approaches to conducting aggression assessments

If the focus is to produce a holistic and individualised assessment of offender need that accounts for aggression motivation and existing strengths, then it is of vital importance to include an offender's developmental history and to complete a functional assessment of their behaviour. Both will be discussed in turn. Assessing developmental history is, however, a cornerstone of all aggression assessments and thus will be presented first.

Developmental history I: accounting for background

The notion of accounting for the background of a habitual aggressor in trying to understand their behaviour is not a new concept and, indeed, Galtung in the 1960s reflected on how aggression 'should be studied at its roots, at the very points where it emerges' (Galtung 1964: 95). However, what is reflected on less is how developmental changes in an individual's lifespan can inform assessment and treatment. As you will note from earlier chapters, the background of an offender is of core importance when determining future risk. However, *background* is not synonymous with *development*, although they are often referred to in this way. Development refers to *change*, whereas background is a more static concept. It is change, however, that is of core importance in understanding how aggression has altered over an individual's background and in trying to determine what has influenced and/or maintained change.

This is particularly important in understanding habitual aggressors. There is here a need to increasingly accept that no one is simply born aggressive, rather individuals fail to learn how to be non-aggressive. This failure may be a product of individual and/or environmental factors, such as a lack of opportunity to learn non-aggression or exposure to high-status role models using aggression. Indeed, there is increasing evidence that control over physically violent behaviour is mostly learned by humans during early childhood (Tremblay and Côté 2005).

This is further captured by Hobbes (cited by Hartup 2005), who states how 'A wicked person was simply a child who had not grown up' (p. xiii). The notion of an individual being developmentally 'frozen' is an important one when assessing the therapeutic needs of an aggressive individual, since our focus should be on understanding when and how this occurred. Over the past three decades investigators have shifted their attention from the *aggressive act* to the *aggressive individual*, with increased attention now to true developmental perspectives, using longitudinal approaches to examine *changes over time within individuals* (Tremblay and Côté 2005).

Ensuring a developmental perspective is adopted is important in understanding both the change over time in an individual and also the causal chain of events over time that explains the development (Tremblay and Côté 2005). Equally, it remains important that a simplistic approach to understanding the development of aggression is to be avoided. It cannot, for example, be suggested that one event results in a specific outcome (A + B = C), but it needs to be acknowledged that the relationship between cause and outcome with regards to aggression development is more complex (Tremblay and Côté 2005). A good example of this may be an assumption that proactive aggressors are not characterised by emotional regulation difficulties (e.g. anger) in comparison to reactive aggressors. Developmental research has not borne this finding out, reporting that anger correlates both with reactive and proactive aggression (Dodge and Coie 1987). This point will be returned to later.

Despite some difficulties in pinning down in absolute terms aggression motivation, there is an acceptance that accounting for the factors associated with motivation is crucial (Vitaro and Brendgen 2005). With regard to developmental factors, reactive aggressors are reported to present with a history of social environment hostility, including maltreatment (Vitaro and Brendgen 2005), with parents who are more controlling and punitive than for proactive children. For 'reactive-only' aggressors there is also more evidence of physical abuse in their history than for 'proactively only' and 'proactive-reactive' individuals (Dodge *et al.* 1997). Research also suggests that reactive aggressors appear less tolerated by their peers both in childhood and adolescence, and present with increased histories of victimisation, disruption at school and general adjustment difficulties (see Vitaro and Brendgen (2005) for a review).

Proactive aggressors, however, are argued to present with a history of exposure to successful aggression models, with their aggression positively reinforced (Vitaro and Brendgen 2005). There is evidence that they have positive family relations when compared to their 'proactive-reactive' counterparts (with some suggestion that reactive aggressors can engender rejection in their caregivers). They also report less parental monitoring and fewer household rules than reactive aggressors and non-aggressors (Poulin and Dishion 2000). Some studies have reported proactive aggressors to be at an increased risk for *later* delinquency, conduct disorders, criminality and substance use difficulties (for a review see Vitaro and Brendgen 2005).

Proactive aggressors also tend to be more tolerated and accepted by their peers. They have a greater number of friends than reactive aggressors and, in particular, have friends displaying similar types of aggression to themselves (Poulin and Dishion 2000; Poulin and Boivin 2000; Vitaro and Brendgen 2005). The peer group appears particularly important for proactive aggressors, with the peer group in this instance found to encourage and reinforce the aggression of the proactive aggressor. This is not, however, found among reactive aggressors (Poulin and Dishion 2000). However, there are factors external to the peer group that appear to influence the link between aggression and peer status for proactive aggressors, such as local norms regarding the use of aggression (Vitaro and Brendgen 2005).

In addition to examining the background correlates of reactive and/or proactive aggression, there is an increasing focus on attempts to develop models that can offer an understanding of the developmental pathways associated with aggression motivation. Two models proposing to explain the development of reactive and proactive aggression include the following:

- *Parallel development model.* This views proactive and reactive aggression as originating from different background factors and developing almost independently in parallel, i.e. with reactive aggressors exposed to a threatening and unpredictable environment and/or abusive parenting, and proactive aggressors, in contrast, exposed to a supportive environment that fosters the use of aggression as goal-seeking behaviour (Dodge 1991; Vitaro and Brendgen 2005).

- *Sequential development model* (Vitaro and Brendgen 2005). This focuses on the role of temperamental and neurophysiological elements in reactive aggression but not proactive, with environmental factors emphasised in proactive aggression. It argues that children with specific temperamental or neurophysiological characteristics are predisposed to display aggression as they interact with their environment. If their reactive aggression is successful in alleviating stress and obtaining a goal, learning should take place (e.g. a child learning that their temper tantrum is successful at obtaining the sweets that they want).

It is argued that, gradually, purely *proactive* aggression may be used to obtain goals, particularly in a permissive familial or peer environment which fosters such behaviour and does not inhibit it. Thus this model suggests that reactive aggression 'might precede and open the way to proactive aggression' (Vitaro and Brendgen 2005: 191). Indeed, there is support from research indicating that reactive aggression appears in childhood earlier than proactive aggression, with reactive aggression predicting subsequent proactive aggression (but not vice versa, i.e. proactive aggression does not predict subsequent reactive aggression).

It is also important to stress at this point that although aggression models tend to focus on the maladaptive nature of aggression, the adaptive quality of aggression cannot be ignored (e.g. Tremblay and Nagin 2005; Ireland and Murray 2005). Aggression is just one of a range of strategies that an individual can utilise in order to obtain a goal, with other strategies including cooperation and conflict resolution. Some developmental models of (physical) aggression argue simply that some individuals, for whatever reason, will learn non-aggressive strategies more quickly than others (Tremblay and Nagin 2005).

Developmental history II: accounting for learning history

Equally important with regard to understanding the development of aggression across an individuals' lifespan is the role of learning history and how aggression is reinforced over time. Consideration of the consequences of enacted behaviour represents the latter stages of information processing models (e.g. Huesmann 1998: with the former stages representing how a situation is judged and perceived, the choices available to deal with the situation and the enactment of the chosen behaviour). Consideration of consequences, however, is the point at which learning takes place, i.e. where an individual learns if their (aggressive) response has positive consequences. The consequences in this sense represent rewards or reinforcers, namely events likely to *strengthen* a future expression of the behaviour, and not an event designed to weaken behaviour (e.g. punishment such as arrest and conviction for an assault).

Aggression researchers have made good use of learning theory, applying it to social situations, i.e. 'social learning theory' or 'social learning models' (e.g. Bandura 1973). Such models focus on the internal and external reinforcements for violent behaviour, and how this varies across individuals and across time and contexts (Bettman 2000). They help explain how individuals who are habitually aggressive continue their behaviour because of the rewards that this can hold for them. For example, aggressors are known to consider the consequences of their actions differently to non-aggressors, attaching more value to the positive and rewarding outcomes of aggression (e.g. Ireland and Archer 2002), and to believe aggression to be necessary and effective (Archer and Haigh 1997). The notion of consequences is thus of particular importance when it comes to completing functional assessments of aggressive behaviour, an issue that will be focused on in the ensuing section.

Social learning theories also highlight a role for observational learning, and how this may have been developed and reinforced across an individual's history. These theories recognise that individuals can learn consequences by observing the behaviour of others. For example, in a study of highly aggressive incarcerated youths, *witnessing* severe violence was related to perceived positive outcomes for the use of aggression (e.g. Shahinfar *et al.* 2001). Observational learning is also strongest if the observed aggression is being enacted by an individual whom the observer values (e.g. a role model) and, more specifically, identifies with (Bandura 1973).

Identifying the patterns of reinforcement for aggression and how this has developed over time is thus important. The rewards associated with aggression can include two types of reinforcement, positive and negative. Both are examples of operant conditioning and assist in strengthening behaviour. With regard to each:

1 Positive reinforcement (i.e. a gain) could include increased status from peers after a demonstration of violent behaviour, resolution of the conflict, feelings of self-efficacy, etc. Positive reinforcement is one of the strongest reinforcements for encouraging the reoccurrence of behaviour.

2 Negative reinforcement is the removal of something unpleasant such as a negative emotion (e.g. anger) or threat. Negative reinforcement strengthens behaviour because a negative condition is either stopped or avoided. It is different to the notion of punishment, which focuses on weakening behaviour by applying something thought to be unpleasant (e.g. such as being convicted after committing an offence).

Both negative and positive reinforcement can lead to an individual learning that responding in a certain way carries with it certain rewards. Only an assessment of the development of aggression over time is likely to identify the true reinforcers for aggressive behaviour, which then need to be addressed in treatment.

It is also important to account not just for the reinforcers but also how the individual conceptualises and evaluates them. This is again where information processing models of aggression come in and demonstrate their significant application to the completion of thorough assessments of aggression. Information processing models capture the importance of cognition, in particular how an individual interprets and *evaluates* the consequences of their actions and how this fits in with existing 'scripts' which are enacted when an event takes place. Scripts in this sense refer to 'guides for social action' (Huesmann 1998). They are stored scenarios which assist individuals to choose actions, influenced by the learned consequences of events. This is illustrated in Figure 4.1.

It is important to note at this point that it would be incorrect to assume that habitually aggressive individuals only have aggressive

---

Basic script
If A happens, then B will follow, and I find that if I do C this stops A.

Aggressive script
'If I get hit first [A], my peers will laugh at me and I will lose status [B], so I hit first to stop getting hit and to increase my status [C].

Figure 4.1 An example of a basic script and an aggressive script formula

scripts in their repertoire of possible responses (i.e. that they only have options such as 'C' as indicated in Figure 4.1). Research has not supported this, and in fact has argued that habitual aggressors present with a limited *range* of non-aggressive scripts. Thus all individuals will have a non-aggressive script that they can choose to enact in any given conflict situation; for habitual aggressors the problem arises when this script, for some reason, is blocked. Their ensuing scripts are likely to be aggressive due to this lack of further non-aggressive scripts (Ireland and Archer 2002). During assessment, therefore, our goal is to determine the range of non-aggressive scripts that an aggressor presents with and what has prevented a wider range from developing.

Similarly, emotion is recognised to play a significant role in the selection and enactment of an aggressive script, assisting to prime an individual's choice of scripts (e.g. Huesmann 1998). As noted earlier, emotion is not a factor solely relating to reactive aggression, but it is also important to account for within proactive aggression. Comprehensive information-processing models such as the unified model of Huesmann (1998) and applications of this integrated model (e.g. Ireland and Murray 2005) consider emotions to drive the selection of cognitions and beliefs, which in turn can influence the selection of aggressive scripts.

Consider a physiological change in an individual with a history of managing anger poorly. If this individual experiences a raised heart rate and increased sweating during a conflict situation they may interpret this as evidence that they are becoming angry. Enter anger cognitions such as 'why are people getting at me', 'they are making me angry' or 'why won't they leave me alone', and this will raise the perception of anger further. The physiological changes and how they are interpreted, coupled with increasing angry cognitions, will lead an individual to seek a script which has been successful for them in the past. If this individual habitually diffuses their feelings of anger by shouting at others, then this is the script that will be accessed more readily, as it is likely to be ranked higher in their repertoire of likely responses (Ireland and Murray 2005). This is particularly the case if a non-aggressive script (e.g. walking away) is for some reason blocked (e.g. an individual is obstructing their exit or they are emotionally overloaded).

Further underlying the evaluation of consequences are the beliefs that an individual has. With aggressive behaviour, the most driving and influencing beliefs are normative beliefs, namely the beliefs an individual has that they believe others also hold (Bushman and

Huesmann 2001). An example of a normative belief may be 'all young men think it is okay to hit someone if they hit you first'. Normative beliefs have also been described as 'what is right for me' beliefs such as 'an eye for an eye, a tooth for a tooth' (Huesmann 1998).

Although normative beliefs are related to social norms, they differ in that they are individually held beliefs and not societal beliefs (although there may sometimes be a link between the two). Normative beliefs form an important part of an individual's developmental history and are developed largely as a result of the judgments of significant others and an individual's own perception of their behaviour. They are used to evaluate the behaviour of others, to guide the search for social scripts, and to filter out inappropriate scripts and behaviours. In essence, normative beliefs help to make the decision to choose aggression and to evaluate it positively when aggression is enacted. They are also related closely to the concept of 'hostile attribution bias' which is a perception error that can be traced to developmental experiences.

Hostile attribution biases (e.g. Dodge and Crick 1990) relate to ambiguous situations which are interpreted in a hostile manner. Once interpreted in this way they can prime a normative belief and trigger an aggressive script which will then drive a response. An example of how this may occur is indicated in Figure 4.2.

Individuals do, however, differ with regard to the desirability of consequence(s). Thus the extent to which they value consequence(s)

Ambiguous situation	Someone pushing into you in a queue
Interpretation (hostile attribution)	They did that on purpose to try and boss me around
Normative belief	If someone pushes you and tries to boss you around, you should always push back to show them who is in charge
Evaluation	Pushing back has worked for me before and I did not lose face in front of others last time
Aggressive script triggered	A script focused on pushing the perceived protagonist back

Figure 4.2 Biases, beliefs and evaluations triggering a response

and why becomes important. For some individuals respect from peers may be most important, whereas for others ending the conflict is of most value. Their existing aggressive scripts will help them decide why a consequence is important. In Figures 4.1 and 4.2, for example, there is a suggestion that it is status and respect from peers which will drive their aggressive responding.

Importantly, responses considered to have positive rewarding consequences are likely to be stored 'higher up' in an individual's repertoire of potential choices to a social situation. If an individual identifies the consequences of an aggressive response as positive, then an aggressive response should be expected to be accessed sooner in the future, particularly if they judge that the aggressive script once enacted is likely to be successful, i.e. the 'do-ability' of a script (Huesmann 1998). Of interest also is what the individual did in order to discount negative consequences, namely likely negative outcomes for themselves. Some may also misperceive the likely consequences of an aggressive act simply because their scripts are inaccurate in predicting consequences for the current situation (Huesmann 1998). This then becomes a focus for intervention where you try to correct these judgment errors once identified via assessment.

Thus, in short, a holistic and individually driven assessment of an aggressive individual will cover all of the developmental areas of importance, accounting for:

- background influences, including early experiences and modelling;
- learning history, including reinforcers for aggressive and non-aggressive behaviour (tangible and/or emotional reinforcers) and evaluation of the associated consequences;
- identification of normative beliefs;
- the origins of hostile attribution biases;
- existing skills, such as the range of non-aggressive scripts an individual has.

A potentially useful tool in pulling together the variables of developmental interest is a 'life map'. Such maps are used within the Life Minus Violence – Enhanced programme and its earlier predecessor (see Ireland 2007). They are used as part of the assessment treatment blocks to capture not only the variables in an individual's background, but also to determine how these variables may have changed across a lifespan. An example of a life map which could be completed with an offender is indicated in Figure 4.3.

Figure 4.3 Example of a summary life map

© Life Minus Violence Programme – Enhanced (LMV-E)

Each of the representative circles in Figure 4.3 indicate a component of background known to relate to aggression development. Each map is completed separately for childhood, adolescence and adulthood. Thus an offender will create three life maps. They include an age timeline where the offender can mark times of aggression use and also times when aggression could have been used but was not. Finally, offenders are asked to produce a 'theme' sheet once all life maps are complete in which they note:

- Five general patterns that I have noticed throughout my life are ...
- When I am aggressive I have noticed I ...
- When I am aggressive it tends to be towards ...
- My reasons for aggression seem to be ...
- The following stops me from being aggressive ...
- I have noticed that when I am not aggressive I ...
- The skills I used when I am not being aggressive are ...

Although approaches such as life maps touch on learning history and the identification of existing skills, these are ascertained more clearly via functional assessment. Only functional assessment can help with a detailed analysis of what promotes and inhibits aggressive behaviour. Life maps are simply useful approaches in pulling together the background factors evidenced, and in determining the level of insight that a client has into the role of their history in aggression development. How these then fit into a framework of learning and how the environment drove a specific behavioural response is the focus of functional assessment.

Incorporating functional assessment

Functional assessment is one of the oldest methods of psychological assessment available (e.g. Sturmey 1996; Goldiamond 1975), although it has had a somewhat tempestuous relationship with assessment procedures, falling in and out of favour as a tool and finding itself applied to only a small class of behaviours (e.g. self-injurious behaviour, the management of challenging behaviour among learning disability populations: Leslie and O'Reilly 1999) when in fact its application is much broader. Functional assessment is becoming more recognised again as a method of assessment and has been applied more recently to understanding a range of presentations, including personality disorder (Nelson-Gray and Farmer 1999a, 1999b), aggression (Daffern et al. 2007) and other offending behaviour (Jones 2004).

Functional assessment is the opposite of the *structural* approach to understanding behaviour, where you would note what the behaviour looked like and then place it into a pre-determined category. Structural approaches are most useful when the behaviours being considered are observable physical complaints. Essentially, structural approaches are derived from medical disease models (Sturmey 1996). *Functional* approaches are different in that they consider the environment in which the behaviour is taking place and the tactical advantage that the behaviour may be having for the individual (e.g. Goldiamond 1975). Thus functional approaches are interested not in the outward presentation of behaviour but in why the behaviour is taking place.

Structural approaches to non-medical conditions are ineffective as they treat the symptoms and not the cause. In this way the treatment will not generalise outside of the environment in which the behaviour is occurring (Leslie and O'Reilly 1999). Functional approaches are designed to understand, and thereby treat, the individual causes of outward behaviour (e.g. aggression) by focusing on what is maintaining and strengthening the behaviour (i.e. reinforcement) and what is preventing the individual from using other behaviour (e.g. is it a skills deficit? environmental deprivation? is aggression a preferable choice?).

It is important to note at this point, however, that functional assessment should be used to determine not only the motivation for aggression, but also the motivation for non-aggression. The latter is a particularly valuable point often missed when assessments are conducted, with a focus instead on aggressive behaviour as opposed to those occasions where an offender does not commit an act of aggression when they could have chosen to do so. Indeed, functional assessment was originally designed to assess adaptive and successful behaviours; thus protective factors can be identified. However, in applied settings functional assessment has been used more routinely for problematic behaviours (e.g. Sturmey 1996). The failure of clinicians to routinely assess for non-aggression is a likely result of a tendency to perceive protective factors incorrectly as the 'absence of risk factors'. Protective factors are what is occurring when an offender is not being aggressive and not risk factors that are missing from their background.

Functional assessment is the only comprehensive method by which aggression motivation can be individually explored with an offender. There are psychometric measures either in use or in development which will assist with understanding motivation (e.g. see Gudjonsson and Sigurdsson 2004) but these tend to be research measures. They are not designed to comprehensively identify where the motivation for the individual offender developed or the individual cognitions, beliefs and environmental conditions which promoted the behaviour.

This section will now provide an application of functional assessment to aggression, illustrating the importance of this approach in determining and individualising client needs. It will do so by outlining a SORC assessment approach (Lee-Evans 1994). The SORC (**S**: setting conditions; **O**: organism variables; **R**: response variables; **C**: consequences) is chosen as it incorporates developmental history and learning experiences. SORC analyses are also being used increasingly in the applied field (e.g. Nelson-Gray and Farmer 1999a, 1999b). There are other versions of functional assessments available such as the ABC model (Antecedents, Behaviour and Consequences: e.g. Leslie and O'Reilly 1999) but these do not explicitly incorporate developmental history.

SORC analyses should be completed via the incorporation of a thorough review of the collateral information available on an offender, and by interviewing the offender and significant others (i.e. those likely to know the offender well on a daily basis such as primary nurses or personal officers). In essence, functional assessments are nothing more than the product of a thematic review of all other assessments undertaken, e.g. interviews, observations, collateral review, life maps, etc. The aim of the assessment is to obtain an outline of antecedents, background factors, behaviour displayed and reinforcing consequences. A description of these elements of a functional assessment are presented here in brief, with two simple worked examples which can be referred to throughout this description indicated in Table 4.1 and Table 4.2.

Setting conditions (S)

These essentially refer to the triggers for the behaviour, often referred to as antecedents. Antecedents are important for two theoretical reasons (Lee-Evans 1994): first, through a classical conditioning route an antecedent should elicit conditioned emotional responses, for example anxiety, arousal, etc.; and second, through an operant conditioning route, they provide a marker for the possibility that displaying a certain behaviour (e.g. aggression) will lead to a specific consequence (e.g. success). It is important to be as precise about preceding antecedents for a specific behaviour as possible, so that the antecedent can be linked to the behaviour. There are three sets of antecedents to be aware of: specific triggers, external conditions and internal conditions.

Specific triggers refer to the events or actions that precede the behaviour and can include proximal or distal events. External conditions refer to environmental factors such as where the individual is at the time of the behaviour. This can include something referred to in the information processing literature as an environmental 'hotspot', i.e. a location that an individual has associated with aggression, which results in the automatic priming of various aggressive cognitions and emotions (Huesmann 1998). Internal conditions refer to internal states such as mood states and cognitions, etc.

Organism variables (O)

This element represents the developmental background that the individual presents with, including evidence of existing beliefs and past behaviour, which has made the current act of aggression more predictable. In essence 'organism variables' refer to everything known about the individual and their background before they were presented with the antecedent stimuli (Nelson-Gray and Farmer 1999a). It can include individual learning history, repertoires of knowledge, beliefs, skill base, etc. Many of the examples can be drawn from the life map (see Figure 4.3).

Response variables (R)

This represents the behaviour displayed. The behaviour should be defined as clearly as possible and include, at the least, an indication of its duration, frequency and intensity. SORC analyses should be completed for each aggressive incident of interest. In some instances more than one functional assessment may be required for one incident, a concept referred to as 'serial functional assessment' (Gresswell and Hollin 1992). When outlining a functional assessment for aggression, the response variable represents the actual aggression displayed. There are various methods of presenting the behaviour, with the most common representing the tripartite response system and the response chain (Lee-Evans 1994).

Both methods represent ways of presenting how the behaviour was structured. The former asks for behaviour to be broken down into physiological responses, cognitions and motor responses, e.g. physiological – heart rate increasing, sweating, knot in stomach; cognitions – who does he think he is? no one talks to me like this in front of my mates, I hate being made to feel like this, my friends will make fun of me if I do nothing; and motor response – hits Mr X ten times with a broken chair leg over the course of five minutes (see Table 4.1).

Table 4.1 Brief worked example of SORC aggressive assessment for Mr Y.

Incident		
Grievous Bodily Harm towards an adult male (Mr X) by Mr Y		
(S) Setting conditions	**Specific triggers**	Mr X calls Mr Y an offensive name in front of his peers and ridicules him.
	External conditions	Occurs in front of Mr Y's peers in a public house where he has previously engaged in physical fights.
	Internal conditions	Mr Y is drinking and feels inebriated.
		He begins to experience feelings of humiliation, anger and physiological responses associated with this (e.g. heart rate increasing, sweating and knot in stomach).
		Cognitions include: 'Who does he think he is?'; 'No one talks to me like this in front of my mates' 'I hate being made to feel like this' 'My friends will make fun of me if I do nothing'.
(O) Organism variables	**Normative beliefs**	You have to be prepared to defend your honour with aggression if necessary
		A man who is ridiculed in front of his friends and does nothing will lose face.
		Aggression can calm you down.
	Previous behaviour	Presents with a history of aggression towards male peers, particularly in the context of alcohol use and if he feels ridiculed in front of others.

Table 4.1 continued

Incident		
Grievous Bodily Harm towards an adult male (Mr X) by Mr Y		
	Background	History of using aggression to resolve conflict and to promote status.
		A history of being rejected and humiliated by his peers as a child.
		Difficulties in managing emotion.
		Observed father getting into fights with others when he had been drinking. Respected his father.
		A history of substance use difficulties and poor coping, including self-injurious behaviour, as a child and adolescent.
		His peers expect him to defend himself.
(R) Response variables	**Intensity, duration, frequency**	Mr Y becomes verbally abusive to Mr X, and threatens him. Mr Y then hits Mr X ten times with a broken chair leg over the course of five minutes, causing serious injury
(C) Consequences	**Positive reinforcement**	Mr Y's friends support his actions and he perceives that there has been no loss of face.
	Negative reinforcement	Removal of negative feelings i.e. anger and humiliation
Functions of aggression: To maintain status; To cope with negative emotions		

Response chains are similar, although they focus on behaviour and emotions being displayed in a linear fashion, with the aim that skills/ alternative responses that can serve to break the chain of events can be taught at each 'link'. Response chains are particularly helpful in presenting how behaviours and emotions can be interspersed with one another, for example:

(Link 1)   Mr Y goes out drinking with his friends.
(Link 2)   Mr Y's friends begin to ridicule him for not drinking enough.
(Link 3)   Mr Y feels humiliated.
(Link 4)   Mr Y begins to drink more.
(Link 5)   Mr Y begins to become inebriated.
(Link 6)   Mr X makes a negative comment to Mr Y in front of Mr Y's peers.
(Link 7)   Mr Y begins to feel angry and humiliated.
(Link 8)   Mr Y considers the comment to be hostile and threatens Mr X.
(Link 9)   Mr X retaliates by calling Mr Y an offensive name.
(Link 10)   Mr Y becomes angrier and more humiliated.
(Link 11)   Mr Y becomes verbally abusive prior to assaulting Mr X.

Although both the tripartite response system and the response chain are described within the response (R) element of the SORC, they can also form part of the setting conditions (S) and thus elements of both of them are referred to in the 'internal conditions' section (see Tables 4.1 and 4.2).

Consequences (C)

As outlined earlier, consequences in this instance refer to the reinforcing aspects of the behaviour demonstrated as opposed to the penalties. Reinforcers are the core component of actual learning and include positive reinforcement (i.e. gains) and negative reinforcement (i.e. the removal of aversive [negative] stimuli). It is in this element of functional assessment that the actual learning of behaviour is depicted. Importantly, reinforcement only has to be intermittent in order to maintain behaviour (Nelson-Gray and Farmer 1999b), with the immediate or short-term consequences more powerful in achieving this, i.e. 'It is a simple behavioural truism that the closer the consequences are to the behaviour, the more likely they are to have an impact on the behaviour' (Jones 2004: 37).

Determining the function

Following the production of a basic functional assessment for the chosen example of aggression, the next step is to determine the actual function or motivation of the behaviour. The reinforcing elements of the behaviour (i.e. consequences, C) can be the most valuable in terms of providing an indication of likely functions, since they reflect both the antecedents and also the organism variables. The following are a few points on the clarification of functions.

First, the function of a behaviour can change over time. Aggression develops across an individual's lifespan (Tremblay and Côté 2005), and so should its functions. Second, functional analyses can be either simple or complex, and there is not always a linear relationship between the apparent nature of the aggression and its function. Thus what may seem like a simple act of aggression can have a complex function and vice versa. Third, there can be more than one function for a behaviour, with some behaviours looking very similar (e.g. throwing items versus slamming doors) but which may in fact have very different functions (Sturmey 1996). Fourth, the determined functions should be tied clearly into treatment. This is what makes functional assessment such a valuable individualised approach.

Closing this section and remembering non-aggression

It is also important to close this section by noting how functional assessment is a *therapeutic* assessment tool and is indeed integral to both the assessment and treatment components of some violence treatment programmes (e.g. Life Minus Violence – Enhanced). They are completed with clients and not 'on them', with the aim that a shared understanding can be at least partially reached. Thus, although they should be pivotal to the assessment arm of aggression intervention, functional assessment does help to begin the process for individualised and focused treatment.

Finally, a note needs to be made again here for the importance of exploring non-aggression. Table 4.1 provides a worked example of a SORC for an act of aggression, but it should equally be applied to non-aggression. A worked example for this is illustrated in Table 4.2. It will be obvious from Table 4.2 that the 'O' part of the functional assessment (organism variables) remains the same. Rather, what changes in this example are some aspects of the setting conditions (S), the response variables (R) and the consequences (C). Comparing the two incidents (i.e. Tables 4.1 and 4.2) would suggest a number of factors likely to protect Mr Y from displaying aggression, such as:

Table 4.2 Brief worked example of SORC non-aggressive assessment for Mr Y.

Incident		
Mr Y becoming angry but walking away from a potential fight		
(S) Setting conditions	**Specific triggers**	Mr B calls Mr Y an offensive name and threatens him.
	External conditions	Mr Y is sat watching football on television at Mr B's house. Mr B has been drinking.
	Internal conditions	Mr Y begins to feel anger. Physiological responses associated with this (e.g. heart rate increasing, sweating and knot in stomach).
		Cognitions included: 'He has been drinking, ignore him'; 'I'll talk to him when he is sober'; 'I can't reason with him now'; 'I need to leave'.
(O) Organism variables	**Normative beliefs**	You have to be prepared to defend your honour with aggression if necessary.
		A man who is ridiculed in front of his friends and does nothing will lose face.
		Aggression can calm you down.
	Previous behaviour	Presents with a history of aggression towards male peers, particularly in the context of alcohol use and if feels ridiculed in front of others.
		History of using aggression to resolve conflict and to promote status.
	Background	A history of being rejected and humiliated by his peers as a child.

Table 4.1 continued

Incident		
Mr Y becoming angry but walking away from a potential fight		
		Difficulties in managing emotion.
		Observed father getting into fights with others when he had been drinking. Respected his father.
		A history of substance use difficulties and poor coping, including self-injurious behaviour, as a child and adolescent.
		His peers expect him to defend himself.
(R) Response variables	**Intensity, duration, frequency**	Mr Y makes an excuse and leaves Mr B's house.
(C) Consequences	**Positive reinforcement**	Mr Y praises himself for being able to control himself and feels positive emotion due to this.
	Negative reinforcement	Absenting himself from the aversive stimulus (Mr B) reduces Mr Y's feelings of anger.
Functions of non-aggression: to cope with negative emotion; to resolve conflict		

- the absence of a peer group;
- the absence of inebriation on the part of Mr Y, which could have previously served as a disinhibitor;
- the absence of combined feelings of anger *and* humiliation, with anger only evident in the second example;
- the presence of alternative, non-aggressive cognitions in example two, e.g. 'He has been drinking, ignore him'; 'I'll talk to him when he is sober'; 'I can't reason with him now'; 'I need to leave'.

Although this is only a simple example, it does illustrate the importance of completing non-aggressive functional assessments. Without this, accessing the potential protective factors (i.e. what is present when non-aggression occurs in a high-risk situation) becomes virtually impossible. All habitual aggressors will have examples of situations in which they could have been aggressive but chose not to. Habitual aggressors are certainly not aggressive 24 hours a day, seven days a week. The difficulty is simply in accessing these situations with a client group who are used to describing their 'failures' (i.e. aggression) and not their 'successes' (e.g. when aggression was avoided). This again highlights the importance of reframing experiences for clients: recognising their strengths while not downplaying their weaknesses, and moving them towards the concept of learned optimism as opposed to learned helplessness (Seligman 2005).

Conclusions

This chapter has touched upon what is a complex and broad area of clinical work and empirical study. It has aimed to illustrate the complexity of this area by describing the developmental and learning history components relevant to aggression and its motivations. In summary, there are perhaps eight golden rules which aggression assessment should abide by to reach a comprehensive assessment. These are as follows:

1 Identifying the motivations (functions) for aggression and recognising that motivation can change over time and across behaviours.

2 Identifying the same for non-aggression, with a focus on locating protective factors.

3 Identifying areas of an individual's background known to relate to the development of aggression, and charting how these factors have influenced behaviour and changed over time.

4 Exploring normative beliefs and the causes of hostile attribution biases.

5 Exploring an offender's perception of the consequences of their aggression, including how they have evaluated consequences, how they have discounted the likely and actual penalties associated with their aggression, and any evidence of judgment errors in consequence evaluation.

6 Recognising that aggression may have adaptive qualities and not automatically assuming therefore that the treatment target is skill acquisition or enhancement.

7 Acknowledging the role of the environment in determining the negative and positive reinforcements for aggression.

8 Moving away from adopting oversimplisitic individual psychopathological models of understanding aggression.

It is hoped that readers will leave with the message that human behaviour is complex and that any notion of having a generic assessment to cover the needs of all habitual aggressors is an impossible goal to reach. All habitual aggressors are individuals, and their aggressive acts are therefore unique. Rather, what we have are frameworks to help us structure the varied and sometimes overwhelming information that we can obtain on an individual's background in order to try and tailor any intervention as closely to their individual needs as possible. Life maps and functional assessment, which have been illustrated here, are just two core examples of frameworks that can assist in making sense of this sometimes complex process.

Acknowledgements

Thanks are extended to Sharon Xuereb for her useful and insightful comments on an earlier draft of this chapter.

References

Archer, J. and Haigh, A. (1997) 'Do beliefs about aggression predict self-reported aggression?', *British Journal of Social Psychology*, 36: 83–105.

Bandura, A. (1973) *Aggression: A Social Learning Analysis*. New York: Holt.

Berkowitz, L. (1989) 'Frustration-aggression hypothesis: examination and reformulation', *Psychological Bulletin*, 106 (1): 59–73.

Bettman, M. (2000) *Correctional Service of Canada: Violence Prevention Program, Accreditation Case File*, Internal Report. Ottawa, ON: Correctional Service of Canada. Online: http://www.canada.gov.ca.

Bushman, B.J. and Anderson, C.A. (2001) 'Is it time to pull the plug on the hostile versus instrumental aggression dichotomy?', *Psychological Review*, 108: 273–9.

Bushman, B.J. and Huesmann, L.R. (2001) 'Effects of televised violence on aggression', in D. Singer and J. Singer (eds), *Handbook of Children and the Media*. Thousand Oaks, CA: Sage, pp. 223–54.

Cornell, D.G., Warren, J., Hawk, G., Stafford, E., Oram, G. and Pine, D. (1996) 'Psychopathy in instrumental and reactive violent offenders', *Journal of Consulting and Clinical Psychology*, 64: 783–90.

Daffern, M., Howells, K. and Ogloff, J. (2007) 'What's the point? Towards a methodology for assessing the function of psychiatric inpatient aggression', *Behaviour Research and Therapy*, 45: 101–11.

Dodge, K.A. (1991) 'The structure and function of reactive and proactive aggression', in D.J. Pepler and K.H. Rubin (eds), *The Development and Treatment of Childhood Aggression*. Hillsdale, NJ: Erlbaum, pp. 201–18.

Dodge, K.A. and Coie, J.D. (1987) 'Social information processing factors in reactive and proactive aggression in children's peer groups', *Journal of Personality and Social Psychology*, 53: 1146–58.

Dodge, K.A. and Crick, N.R. (1990) 'Social information-processing bases of aggressive behavior in children', *Personality and Social Psychology Bulletin*, 16: 8–22.

Dodge, K.E., Lochman, J.E., Harnish, J.D., Bates, J. and Pettit, G.S. (1997) 'Reactive and proactive aggression in school children and psychiatrically impaired chronically assaultive youth', *Journal of Abnormal Psychology*, 106: 37–51.

Galtung, J. (1964) 'A structural theory of aggression', *Journal of Peace Research*, 1: 95–119.

Gendreau, P.L. and Archer, J.A. (2005) 'Subtypes of aggression in humans and animals', in R.E. Tremblay, W.W. Hartup and J. Archer (eds), *Developmental Origins of Aggression*. New York: Guilford Press.

Goldiamond, I. (1975) 'Alternate sets as a framework for behavioural formulation and research', *Behaviorism*, 3: 49–86.

Gresswell, D.M. and Hollin, C. (1992) 'Towards a new methodology of making sense of case material: an illustrative case involving attempted multiple murder', *Clinical Behaviour and Mental Health*, 2: 329–41.

Gudjonsson, G.H. and Sigurdsson, J.F. (2004) 'Motivation for offending and personality', *Legal and Criminological Psychology*, 9: 69–81.

Hartup, W.W. (2005) 'Preface', in R.E. Tremblay, W.W. Hartup and J. Archer (eds), *Developmental Origins of Aggression*. New York: Guilford Press, pp. xiii–xiv.

Huesmann, L.R. (1998) 'The role of social information processing and cognitive schema in the acquisition and maintenance of habitual aggressive behavior', in R.G. Geen and E. Donnerstein (eds), *Human Aggression: Theories, Research, and Implications for Social Policy*. San Diego, CA: Academic Press, pp. 73–109.

Ireland, J.L. (2007) 'Introducing a new violence treatment programme: Life Minus Violence', *Forensic Update*, July.

Ireland, J.L. and Archer, J. (2002) 'The perceived consequences of responding to bullying with aggression: a study of male and female adult prisoners', *Aggressive Behavior*, 28: 257–72

Ireland, J.L. and Murray, E. (2005) 'Social problem-solving and bullying: are prison bullies really impaired problem solvers?', in J.L. Ireland (ed.), *Bullying Among Prisoners: Innovations in Theory and Research*. Cullompton: Willan.

Jones, L. (2004) 'Offence Paralleling Behaviour (OPB) as a framework for assessment and interventions with offenders', in A. Needs and G. Towl (eds), *Applying Psychology to Forensic Practice*. Blackwell: British Psychological Society, pp. 34–63.

Lee-Evans, J.M. (1994) 'Background to behavioural analysis', in M. McMurran and J. Hodge (eds), *The Assessment of Criminal Behaviours of Clients in Secure Settings*. London: Jessica Kingsley, pp. 6–33.

Leslie, J.C. and O'Reilly, M.F. (1999) 'Assessing behavior in applied settings', in J.C. Leslie and M.F. O'Reilly, *Behaviour Analysis: Foundations and Applications to Psychology*. Reading: Harwood Academic, pp. 151–81.

McGuire, J. and Priestly, P. (2000) 'Reviewing What Works: past, present and future', in J. McGuire (ed.), *What Works: Reducing Reoffending. Guidelines from Research and Practice*. Chichester: John Wiley & Sons.

Martens, A. (2000) 'Antisocial and psychopathic personality disorders: causes, course, and remission', *International Journal of Offender Therapy and Comparative Criminology*, 44: 406–30.

Nelson-Gray, R.O. and Farmer, R.F. (1999a) 'Behavioral assessment of personality disorders', *Behaviour Research and Therapy*, 37: 347–68.

Nelson-Gray, R.O. and Farmer, R.F. (1999b) 'Functional analysis and response covariation in the assessment of personality disorders: a reply to Staats and to Bissett and Hayes', *Behaviour Research and Therapy*, 37: 385–94.

Poulin, F.R. and Boivin, M. (2000) 'The role of proactive and reactive aggression in the formation and development of boys' friendships', *Developmental Psychology*, 36: 233–40.

Poulin, F. and Dishion, T.J. (2000) *The Peer and Family Experiences of Proactively and Reactively Aggressive Pre-adolescents*. Paper presented at the biennial meeting of the Society for Research on Adolescence, Chicago.

Raine, A., Dodge, K., Loeber, R., Gatzke-Kopp, L., Lynam, D., Reynolds, C., Stouthamer-Loeber, M. and Liu, J. (2006) 'The reactive-proactive aggression questionnaire: differential correlates of reactive and proactive aggression in adolescent boys', *Aggressive Behavior*, 32: 159–71.

Seligman, M.E.P. (2002) 'Positive psychology, positive prevention and positive therapy', in C.R. Snyder and S.L. Lopez (eds), *Handbook of Positive Psychology*. New York: Oxford University Press, pp. 3–9.

Seligman, M.E.P. (2006) *Learned Optimism: How to Change Your Mind and Your Life*. New York: Vintage Publishing.

Shahinfar, A., Kupersmidt, J.B. and Matza, L.S. (2001) 'The relation between exposure to violence and social information processing among incarcerated adolescents', *Journal of Abnormal Psychology*, 110: 136–41.

Shantz, C.U. and Hartup, W.W. (eds) (1992) *Conflict in Child and Adolescent Development*. New York: Cambridge University Press.

Skinner, B.F. (1953) *Science and Human Behavior*. New York: Macmillan.

Sturmey, P. (1996) *Functional Analysis in Clinical Psychology*. London: John Wiley & Sons.

Tremblay, R.E. and Côté, S. (2005) 'The developmental origins of aggression: where are we going?', in R.E. Tremblay, W.W. Hartup and J. Archer (eds), *Developmental Origins of Aggression*. New York: Guilford Press, pp. 447–64.

Tremblay, R.E. and Nagin, D.S. (2005) 'The developmental origins of physical aggression in humans', in R.E. Tremblay, W.W. Hartup and J. Archer (eds), *Developmental Origins of Aggression*. New York: Guilford Press, pp. 83–106.

Tremblay, R.E., Mihic, L., Graham, K. and Jelley, J. (2007) 'Role of motivation to respond to provocation, the social environment, and trait aggression in alcohol-related aggression', *Aggressive Behavior*, 33: 389–411.

Vitaro, F. and Brendgen, M (2005) 'Proactive and reactive aggression: a developmental perspective', in R. E. Tremblay, W. W. Hartup and J. Archer (eds), *Developmental Origins of Aggression*. New York: Guilford Press, pp. 447–64.

Wong, S., Audrey, G. and Gu, D. (2007) 'Assessment and treatment of violence-prone forensic clients: an integrated approach', *British Journal of Psychiatry*, 190: 66–74.

Chapter 5

Assessing the therapeutic needs of sexual offenders

Leigh Harkins and Anthony Beech

There are currently 7,446 sexual offenders in prison in the UK (from http://www.justice.gov.uk/docs/population-in-custody-jan08.pdf) and the recidivism rate typically is calculated to be 13.7 per cent (Hanson and Morton-Bourgon 2005), hence there is a pressing need for clinicians and workers in the field of sexual offender rehabilitation to assess the therapeutic needs of sexual offenders in order to offer potentially successful treatment. This is a field that is constantly being updated as new data becomes available. The aim of this chapter is to describe up-to-date thinking around the assessment of sexual offenders in terms of what needs to be addressed in treatment. Here, it should be noted that the approach taken to offender rehabilitation in the UK and North America is driven by the 'What Works' literature. The 'What Works' approach refers to the translation of research findings (generally from meta-analyses) into practice (Hollin, 1999). This approach is generally acknowledged as the current model of choice for many working with offenders in general (Ward *et al.* 2006). Brown (2005), for example, notes that most sexual offender programmes are offered in a manner consistent with the risk and need principles. Hence the aim of the chapter is to describe the assessment around this approach, where treatment is administered according to the level of an offender's risk, criminogenic needs and responsivity/intra-individual characteristics (e.g. motivation), which may influence treatment.

But before we consider the 'What Works' approach we would note that an important part of treatment is understanding what the offending means to the individual, hence the next section briefly describes functional assessment approaches in sexual offender assessment.

Functional assessment

Beech *et al.* (2003) note that any assessment of a sexual offender should include a detailed functional assessment to determine the underlying motives and functions for the offending behaviour. Functional assessment typically involves obtaining detailed information about the *antecedents*, the *behaviours* and the *consequences* of offending (the ABC model). Unfortunately this is not always a straightforward task with sex offenders due to them frequently being at some level of denial about aspects of the offence and therefore not willing to be completely truthful about the areas that the assessor needs to obtain information about. Currently the most useful framework is probably what is called a 'decision chain' (Ward *et al.* 1995). A decision chain is a sequence of choices leading to an offence. Each choice is characterised in terms of the situation it took place in, the thoughts that made sense of and responded to the situation, and the emotions and actions that arose from these thoughts. Decision chains have the advantage that they can describe offences that spring from negative emotional states and poor coping strategies (Wolf 1984) and those where more proactive motives are involved (Eldridge 1998; Laws 1999; Ward and Hudson 1996).

As for the assessment of why individuals commit, and carry on committing, sexual offences, Ward and Hudson (1998) suggest that there are distinct offence and relapse pathways, each associated with different psychological characteristics and clinical issues. These pathways are further defined by an individual offender's goal towards deviant sex (*approach* or *avoidance*). Approach goals involve a determination to sexually offend and concern the successful achievement of a particular state or situation regarding the successful commission of a sexual offence. For instance, someone with an approach goal may believe he is entitled to sex and therefore force sex on a non-consenting partner. Avoidant goals, on the other hand, involve a desire to avoid offending, aimed at the reduction of a particular state or situation (Cochran and Tesser 1996). A person with an avoidance goal may attempt to prevent themselves from committing sexual offences by using ineffective methods to distract themselves (Ward and Hudson 1998). Once an offence-related goal to offend has been established in approach or avoidant goal offenders the next stage in the process is the selection of strategies to achieve the desired goal. The decision to offend for the approach goal offender may involve the *active* use of strategies to bring about the desired state of offending. Or, alternatively, *automatic* strategies may be activated as a result of well-learned behaviours, or behavioural scripts, that will lead an offender to commit a sexual offence if activated. Assessment of approach/avoidant and active/passive strategies can be partly informed by the checklist developed by Bickley and Beech (2002), and/or by the system reported by Ward *et al.* (2004). See Figure 5.1 for a brief synopsis of how to assess these pathways.

We will now look in some detail at assessment-for-treatment based on the 'What Works' approach, starting with an overview of the 'What Works' approach itself.

The 'What Works' approach

The *psychology of criminal conduct* (PCC) is proposed as a theory discussing 'What Works' in offender rehabilitation (Andrews and Bonta 2006). This can be seen as a guide to the provision of effective treatment, and hence any assessment for treatment needs to take careful note of this approach. Andrews and Bonta (2003) advocate the use of risk/need/responsivity principles in determining the course of treatment for a particular individual.

The *risk principle* supports varying the intensity of treatment according to the risk level of the individual. In this way resources are most appropriately used to provide treatment to higher-risk offenders who can benefit from more intensive interventions than to lower-risk offenders who have a lower likelihood of reoffence. There is strong evidence that individuals at different risk levels have differential responses to treatment (Andrews and Dowden 2006; Friendship *et al.* 2003).

According to the *need principle*, treatment should be tailored to address the criminogenic needs, i.e. those psychological risk factors such as deviant sexual interests, pro-offending attitudes, socio-affective problems and emotional disregulation (Thornton 2002). There is evidence that these dynamic (changeable) risk factors are related to recidivism (e.g. Craig *et al.* 2007; Hanson and Harris 2000; Harkins 2008; Thornton 2002).

The *responsivity* principle dictates that treatment style should be tailored to meet the learning style and abilities of offenders (Andrews and Bonta 2003). Andrews and Bonta note that when correctional

Part 1: Passive versus Active Strategies

		Passive		Active
1	Degree of planning:	No awareness of any planning	0--1--2--3--4--5--6--7--8--9--10	Extensive and detailed overt planning
	Evidence for decision:			
2	Degree of thought before acting:	Very impulsive, little thought before acting	0--1--2--3--4--5--6--7--8--9--10	Fully considers consequences before acting
	Evidence for decision:			
3	Complexity of strategies used (*either* to offend *or* prevent offending):	Basic strategies, poor problem-solving abilities	0--1--2--3--4--5--6--7--8--9--10	Complex grooming or prevention strategies used
	Evidence for decision:			
4	Locus of control (victim stance):	Passive stance, events controlled externally	0--1--2--3--4--5--6--7--8--9--10	Sees self as in control of own behavior
	Evidence for decision:			
5	Ability to delay gratification:	Need for immediate gratification	0--1--2--3--4--5--6--7--8--9--10	Able to delay gratification for long-term gains, e.g. not getting caught
	Evidence for decision:			

Decision: Passive/Active/Don't Know (If 'Don't Know' please explain)

Part 2: Avoidant versus approach goals

		Avoidant		Approach
6	Reported desire to control/prevent offending:	Awareness of harm or fear of consequences, active restraint	0--1--2--3--4--5--6--7--8--9--10	No restraint
	Evidence for decision:			
7	Beliefs about children and sex (CDs):	Acknowledges abuse is harmful, few cognitive distortions	0--1--2--3--4--5--6--7--8--9--10	Sees no harm in sex with children, many cognitive distortions
	Evidence for decision:			
8	Degree of guilt/shame following offence:	Extreme guilt/ shame reported following offencd	0--1--2--3--4--5--6--7--8--9--10	No negative self-evaluation
	Evidence for decision:			
9	Level of pro-offending behaviours:	No explicit engagement in activities	0--1--2--3--4--5--6--7--8--9--10	Explicit activities supporting offending e.g. hobbies, clubs, child pornography, etc.
	Evidence for decision:			

Decision: Approach/Avoidance/Don't know (If 'Don't know' please explain)

Figure 5.1 Offence pathway checklist
Taken from Bickley and Beech (2002).

treatment adheres to all three of the risk, need and general responsivity principles, an effect size[1] (r) of only 0.02 is observed (Andrews and Bonta 2003). However, if two of the principles are adhered to the effect size (r) is 0.18 and if treatment is provided in a manner adhering to all three principles an effect size (r) 0.26 is observed (Andrews and Bonta 2003). If no treatment is offered or if none of the principles are followed, Andrews and Bonta (2003) report an effect size (r) of −0.02, demonstrating an *increase* in criminal recidivism. Even treatment driven by alternative theories recognises the utility of the principles of *risk*, *need* and *responsivity* (e.g. Ward and Stewart 2003). We will now examine each of these aspects in more detail, with the specific aim of how these should be assessed.

Assessment of risk I: actuarial

There is a general thrust and a growing body of research to suggest that treatment is most effective when administered according to the 'risk principle' (Andrews and Bonta 2003; Andrews and Dowden 2006). According to this principle, the most intensive treatment should be offered to the highest-risk offenders with little to no treatment being offered to lower-risk offenders because they are less likely to reoffend even without treatment. This is because it is easier to show a real treatment effect in high-risk offenders because their base rate of offending is so high, allowing more room for improvement as a result of treatment. Further to this, research has demonstrated, in the general offender literature, that reductions in recidivism among high-risk offenders only occur when high-intensity treatment is offered, while intensive treatment has a minimal or negative impact upon low-risk offenders (Andrews and Bonta 2003).

In order to ensure that treatment is offered at the intensity most appropriate for the risk level of the offender, accurate assessment of recidivism risk is necessary. This judgment can be arrived at in a number of ways, from structured actuarial measures to the use of unstructured clinical judgment for predicting sexual offence recidivism (Hanson *et al.* 2003). Actuarial measures of risk for recidivism, consisting of historical, unchangeable (i.e. static) variables, have generally been viewed as more accurate than empirically guided clinical judgment or unstructured clinical judgment (Hanson *et al.* 2003). A recent meta-analysis illustrated that actuarial measures developed empirically were more accurate than unstructured professional judgment ($d = 0.70$ and $d = 0.43$, respectively: Hanson and Morton-Bourgon 2007).

Actuarial measures that were developed on a conceptual basis rather than empirically were not found to be significantly more accurate ($d = 0.66$ and $d = 0.70$ respectively: Hanson and Morton-Bourgon 2007).

A number of actuarial methods have been developed to estimate the risk for recidivism among sexual offenders (Hanson *et al*. 2003). These instruments indicate which broad risk category (e.g. low, medium, high) the offender's risk score falls into. The reliability and validity of the most commonly used actuarial risk assessment instruments have now been reasonably well established (Hanson and Morton-Bourgon 2007; Langton *et al*. 2007; Sjöstedt and Långström 2001).

It is important to note that there is a divergence of opinion regarding the utility of actuarial measures. Hart *et al*. (2007) highlight problems with the precision of actuarial measures (i.e. the Violence Risk Appraisal Guide: Harris *et al*. 1993; and the Static-99: Hanson and Thornton 2000). They found there were quite large margins of error when making recidivism predictions for groups and even wider margins of error for predicting an individual's risk for recidivism, to the point that they claim the measures are 'virtually meaningless' at an individual level (p. 563) when trying to predict reoffence. However, they do acknowledge that these measures could still have utility in making administrative decisions about the frequency and intensity of risk management strategies.

In spite of these newly noted concerns, actuarial measures are currently in widespread use. Additionally, given the alternatives available (e.g. clinical judgment), these measures appear to be the better option (Hanson *et al*. 2003) than nothing at all. Given these noted concerns though, these measures should be used with caution and consideration of the points discussed. The following is a brief description of some of the recent risk predictors developed for adult male offenders.[2] To be able to use the scales the authors of each will need to be contacted to obtain all the necessary information and scoring guides. In some instances there is also a training requirement.

Static-99 (Hanson and Thornton 2000)

Static-99 consists of ten items that can be ascertained from an offender's history: prior sexual offences, prior sentencing occasions, convictions for non-contact sex offences, index non-sexual violence, prior non-sexual violence, unrelated victims, stranger victims, male victims, lack of a long-term intimate relationship and if the offender is aged under 25 on release (or now, if the offender is in the community). Hanson and Thornton reported Static-99 as having an average area under the curve (AUC) for the prediction of sexual recidivism in cross-validation samples of 0.71, and has subsequently been tested in at least fifteen diverse samples with an average predictive accuracy at least equivalent to that reported in Hanson and Thornton (Hanson *et al.* 2003). The revised scoring manual for the Static-99 is available from online from Public Safety Canada (http://ww2.ps-sp.gc.ca/publications/corrections/pdf/Static-99-coding-Rules_e.pdf).

Static-2002 (Hanson and Thornton 2003)

Static-2002 was developed to improve the consistency of the scoring criteria of Static-99 and increase its predictive validity. It consists of five content areas – age at release, persistence of sexual offending, deviant sexual interests, relationship to victims and general criminality – and thirteen items – age at release, number of sentencing occasions for sexual offences, any arrest as a juvenile for a sexual offence along with a conviction as an adult for a separate offence, high rate of sexual offending, any conviction for non-contact sex offences, any male victims, two or more victims under twelve-years of age, one unrelated, any unrelated victims, any stranger victims, number of prior arrest/sentencing occasions, any breach of conditional release, number of years free prior to index offence, and any convictions for non-sexual violence. Total scores can range from zero to fourteen. Several studies have provided support for the predictive validity of Static-2002 (Haag 2005; Hanson and Thornton 2003; Langton, Barbaree, Hansen *et al.* 2007; Langton, Barbaree, Seto *et al.* 2007) with values ranging from 0.71 to 0.76. The scoring manual for the Static-2002 is available from online from Public Safety Canada (http://ww2.ps-sp.gc.ca/publications/corrections/200301_Static_2002_e.asp).

Risk Matrix 2000 (RM2000: Thornton et al. 2003)

RM2000 has separate indicators for risk of sexual recidivism, non-sexual assault and overall violence. The prison, probation and police services in England and Wales have adopted the scale nationally. The first stage involves three static items: age at commencement of risk, sexual appearances and total criminal appearances. Points are awarded and the offender placed in one of four categories (low, medium, high or very high). The second stage of RM2000 contains four aggravating factors: male victim, stranger victim, non-contact sexual offences and lack of a long-term intimate relationship. If two aggravating factors are present the risk category is raised one level and if all four are present the risk is raised two levels. Thornton *et al.* report cross-validation on two UK samples. AUC coefficients varied from 0.74 to 0.81. The scoring manual for RM2000 is available online from the University of Birmingham's Centre for Forensic and Family Psychology at: (http://psg275.bham.ac.uk/forensic_centre/External%20Documents/SCORING%20GUIDE%20FOR%20RISK%20MATRIX(ver-Feb%202007).pdf).

Sex Offence Risk Appraisal Guide (SORAG: Quinsey et al. 1998)

The SORAG was developed in Canada. It was designed to predict violence committed by sexual offenders. SORAG has fourteen items which cover: living with both biological parents until age sixteen, school maladjustment, alcohol problems, evidence of a sustained intimate relationship, non-violent criminality, violent criminality, previous sexual contact convictions, convictions against girls under fourteen only, failure on prior conditional release, age at index offence, evidence of personality disorder, schizophrenia, evidence of deviant sexual preferences and psychopathy (as defined by the Psychopathy Checklist – revised: Hare 2003). Hanson *et al.* (2003), averaging five findings, reported that this scale had an average predictive accuracy a little better than the Rapid Risk Assessment of Sex Offender Recidivism (RRASOR: Hanson 1997), which is a four-item measure of risk for sexual recidivism that is included in the Static-99, and a little worse than Static-99. The scale may, however, have particular advantages in samples where personality disorder and strong deviant sexual preferences vary independently of prior sexual convictions.

Assessment of risk II: need/dynamic risk

Given the need for clinicians to accurately report an offender's risk for reoffence, it is important that, in addition to the valuable information that static measures of risk provide, dynamic factors are also examined. Hanson and Harris (2000, 2001) have identified two types of dynamic risk predictors – stable and acute risk factors. Stable dynamic risk factors have the potential to change but are relatively steady over time (e.g. sexual interest or belief systems). Acute dynamic risk factors are those that can be seen as readily fluctuating or 'panic now' factors, for example mood state, indicating more immediate risk for reoffence.

Thornton (2002) and Hanson and Harris (2000, 2001) suggest that stable dynamic risk factors can be encompassed within four overarching domains: (1) sexual interests/sexual self-regulation; (2) distorted attitudes/attitudes tolerant of sexual offending; (3) socio-affective functioning/intimacy deficits; and (4) self-management/self-regulation problems. Thornton (2002) identified high levels of problems in Domains 2, 3 and 4 as distinguishing between repeat offenders and those with only one conviction. Similarly Hanson and Harris (2000) identified problems that fall into these four risk domains as differentiating recidivists from non-recidivists. The overall level of dynamic risk has been found to be related to recidivism. A large project completed across Canada and in parts of the US followed 997 sexual offenders on community supervision for a period of 41 months (Hanson *et al.* 2007). They found that examining both dynamic risk variables and static variables was better at predicting sexual recidivism than static risk alone. Craig *et al.* (2007) also found that a Psychological Deviance Index, comprised of the four risk domains outlined by Thornton (2002), predicted sexual recidivism independent of static risk.

The following is a brief description of several measures of dynamic risk being used in the UK and North America. To be able to use the scales the authors of each will need to be contacted to obtain all the necessary information and scoring guides. In some instances there is also a training requirement.

Deviancy Classification (Beech 1998)

The deviancy construct was developed by Beech (1998) from the Sex Offender Treatment Evaluation Project (STEP: Barker and Morgan 1993; Beckett *et al.* 1994; Beech *et al.* 1999; Beech *et al.* 2005) test battery. The STEP research involved a series of evaluations of prison and probation treatment programmes for sex offenders across the UK. The deviancy construct was developed by Beech (1998) who classified child abusers according to their levels of problems on a battery of psychometric measures, assessing problems in child abusers in Domain 1 (strengths of deviant sexual interests), Domain 2 (distorted attitudes/beliefs) and Domain 3 (inadequate emotional congruence, intimacy deficits and self-esteem problems). Two main types of child abusers were identified using this system in terms of their psychometric profiles. These were termed high and low deviancy in terms of the differences between the groups and non-offenders on a number of psychometric measures (Fisher *et al.* 1999).

Here deviancy equates to the degree of deviation of scores from non-offender means rather than deviancy being used in a pejorative sense. Specifically, high deviancy men were found to have significantly higher levels of distorted attitudes about children and sex than low deviancy men and show significantly poorer empathy for victims of sexual abuse than non-offenders. Other significant differences between high deviancy and non-offending men indicate that they reported difficulty in forming intimate adult attachments, while perceiving their emotional needs could be better met by interacting with children than adults. The high deviancy group were also found to be significantly more under-assertive and to have significantly lower levels of self-esteem than non-offenders. In contrast, low deviancy offenders did not show globalised cognitive distortions about children nor did they show the high levels of emotional identification with children seen in high deviancy offenders. The low deviancy group also showed significantly higher levels of social adequacy problems than non-offenders, although this was not as marked as in the high deviancy group. This system is used in the UK probation service to assign individuals to longer or shorter treatment.

Structured Assessment of Risk and Need (SARN: Webster et al. 2006)

The SARN was developed by Her Majesty's Prison Service in the UK. It is a clinical framework used to assess sexual offenders' risk, need and progress in treatment (Webster *et al.* 2006). It is used primarily as a treatment planning tool. Within this measure, actuarial risk is first measured using the RM2000. The SARN uses clinical ratings to assess sixteen items that measure Thornton's (2002) four dynamic risk domains discussed in detail above: (1) sexual interest (i.e. sexual preoccupation, sexual preference for children, sexualised violence, other offence-related sexual interest); (2) distorted attitudes (i.e. adversarial sexual attitudes, sexual entitlement, child abuse supportive beliefs, rape supportive beliefs, women are deceitful beliefs); (3) social competence problems (i.e. inadequacy, distorted intimacy balance, grievance thinking, lack of emotional intimacy); and (4) self-management difficulties (i.e. lifestyle impulsiveness, poor problem- solving, poor emotional control). SARN uses a scoring protocol that determines the relevance of the particular factor both as a proximal factor leading up to the offence, and as a factor in the individual's life in general. Factors are scored either 0 (not present), 1 (present but not a central characteristic) or 2 (a central characteristic). Webster *et al.* (2006) provide support for the high inter-rater reliability of the SARN.

STABLE 2007 (Hanson et al. 2007)

Hanson and Harris developed a system with both stable and acute risk factors. Originally called SONAR, then STABLE and ACUTE 2000, this system has now been renamed in two parts STABLE and ACUTE 2007 (see later) (Hanson *et al.* 2007). STABLE 2007 assesses thirteen stable dynamic items: significant social influences, capacity for relationship stability, emotional identification with children, hostility toward women, general social rejection, lack of concern for others, impulsivity, poor problem-solving skills, negative emotionality, sex drive/sex preoccupation, sex as coping, deviant sexual preference and cooperation with supervision. These items are scored, 0, 1 or 2 to produce scale where those scoring 0 to 3 are considered low risk (n = 184), those scoring 4 to 11 as moderate risk (n = 449) and those scoring 12+ as high risk (n = 159) (Hanson *et al.* 2007). The scale has been evaluated in a prospective study called the Dynamic Supervision Project (Hanson *et al.* 2007). The inter-rater reliability of an earlier version of STABLE 2007 (i.e. STABLE 2000) has been reported by Hanson (2005) as very good (ICC = 0.89). Hanson and colleagues (2007) report the predictive accuracy for STABLE 2007 on its own to be reasonable (AUC = 0.67) for a sexual offence, and slightly better (AUC = 0.69) for any sexual offence or breach. When combined with the Static-99 the AUC values improve for both sexual recidivism (AUC = 0.76) and any sexual recidivism or breach (AUC = 0.73)

ACUTE 2007 (Hanson et al. 2007)

Hanson and Harris have also developed ACUTE 2007 (Hanson *et al.* 2007), which is the acute counterpart of STABLE 2007, which assesses the risk for both sex/violent recidivism and a total score for risk of general recidivism. It covers the following acute risk factors, with the first four contributing to the risk for sex/violent recidivism score, and all seven contributing to the risk for general recidivism score: victim access, hostility, sexual preoccupations, rejection of supervision, emotional collapse, collapse of social supports and substance abuse.

Hanson and Harris have examined the performance of the ACUTE 2007 variables in their Dynamic Supervision Project (Hanson 2005; Harris and Hanson 2003; Hanson *et al.* 2007). The results so far indicate good reliability between supervising officers scoring the earlier version of the ACUTE 2007 (i.e. ACUTE 2000) (median *ICC* = 0.90). Hanson and colleagues (2007) report a reasonable level of predictive accuracy for ACUTE 2007 for the sex/violence recidivism score (AUC = 0.74) for sexual offences and for the total score (AUC = 0.72).

Assessment of risk III: measures that combine static and dynamic factors

Sexual Violence Risk – 20 (SVR-20: Boer et al. 1997)

Developed in Canada, this scale is different to other risk predictors in that it does not use the final score to place an individual within a probability of reconviction range but rather leaves it to the assessor to make a judgment regarding risk level. It is therefore more of a 'judgment after review' instrument than a true actuarial risk predictor. The scale is intended to provide a list of items that have been shown by research to be indicative of reconviction. This allows the assessor to weight items in accordance with each individual situation. This of course means that the instrument's accuracy will vary depending on the judgment of the clinician applying it.

The SVR-20 has items which cover psychosocial adjustment, sexual offences and future plans. The twenty items are as follows: deviant sexual preference, victim of child abuse, level of psychopathy, major mental illness, substance abuse, suicidal or homicidal ideation, relationship problems, employment problems, violent non-sexual offences, general criminality, supervision failure, high frequency of sex offences, range of sex offenses, physical harm to victim, use of weapons, escalation in frequency or severity of sex offences, extreme denial or minimisation of sex offences, pro-offending attitudes, lack of realistic plans and negative attitude towards intervention. It also allows for the addition of three dynamic items: acute mental disorder, recent loss of social support network and frequent contact with potential victims.

Violence Risk Scale: Sex Offender Version (VRS:SO: Wong et al. 2003)

The VRS:SO is a measure, also developed in Canada, used to predict sexual recidivism and link treatment changes to sexual recidivism. It uses dynamic variables to identify treatment targets and allows for the measurement of change as a result of treatment. Change is measured by a modified version of the transtheoretical model of change (Olver et al. 2007; Prochaska et al. 1992). It is comprised of seven static and seventeen dynamic risk items and two responsivity factors. The static items are as follows: age at release, age at first sex offence, sex offender type, prior sex offences, unrelated victims, victim gender and prior sentencing dates. The dynamic items are: sexually deviant lifestyle, sexual compulsivity, offence planning, criminal personality, cognitive distortions, interpersonal aggression, emotional control, insight, substance abuse, community support, released to high-risk situations, sexual offending cycle, impulsivity, deviant sexual preference and intimacy deficits. The VRS:SO is comprised of three factors: sexual deviance (e.g. sexually deviant lifestyle, deviant sexual preference), criminality (e.g. impulsivity, interpersonal aggression) and treatment responsivity (e.g. insight, treatment compliance). Olver *et al.* (2007) report good levels of inter-rater reliability for the dynamic items at pre-treatment (ICC = 0.74) and post-treatment (ICC = 0.79). Olver *et al.* found overall AUC values of 0.71 and 0.72 at pre-treatment and post-treatment, respectively.

Assessment of intra-individual/responsivity characteristics

In addition to factors related to overall risk categories and criminogenic need, intra-individual characteristics also have an important impact on the effectiveness of treatment. Responsivity factors are those that are related to an individual's ability to benefit from treatment (Andrews and Bonta 2003). According to Andrews and Bonta (2003) treatment should be offered in a manner that is consistent with the learning style of the offender therefore these need to be considered prior to undertaking treatment. A number of potential responsivity factors have been proposed (e.g. intellectual functioning, offender type and hostility: Looman *et al.* 2005). However, because of space constraints, we have chosen to focus on psychopathy because of the negative impact someone scoring high in psychopathy can potentially have on a treatment group, and on motivation because of the importance placed on it in most treatment programmes.

Clinical psychopathy

Psychopathy has been widely studied among the general criminal population. It is possible that psychopathy presents an obstacle to therapy because men who score high in psychopathy are seen as more of a challenge to treat than non-psychopaths, but they may be treatable nonetheless (Caldwell *et al.* 1997; Langton *et al.* 2006; Looman *et al.* 2005). Therefore accurate assessment of psychopathy is important for ensuring that treatment is offered in a manner that will allow the individual to gain the most benefit from it.

The Psychopathy Checklist – Revised (PCL-R: Hare 2003) is the most common instrument for assessing psychopathy and is widely employed in both research and clinical settings. The PCL-R is a clinical assessment instrument developed to assess psychopathic personality traits. It is comprised of twenty items, rated on a three-point scale, that are scored on the basis of a semi-structured interview and file review. The PCL-R measures two factors (i.e. Factor 1: Interpersonal/ Affective and Factor 2: Social Deviance) which can each be broken down into two facets. The Interpersonal/Affective factor (Factor 1) is comprised of the following items for Facet 1 (Interpersonal): glibness/ superficial charm, grandiose sense of self-worth, pathological lying and conning manipulative. Facet 2 (Affective) is made up of the following items: lack of remorse or guilt, shallow affect, callous or lack of empathy and failure to accept responsibility for own actions. The Social Deviance factor (Factor 2) is made up of the following items for Facet 3 (Lifestyle): need for stimulation/proneness to boredom, parasitic lifestyle, lack of realistic long-term goals, impulsivity and irresponsibility. Facet 4 (Antisocial) is comprised of the following items: poor behavioural controls, early behaviour problems, juvenile delinquency, revocation of conditional release and criminal versatility. Two additional items (i.e. promiscuous sexual behaviour and many short-term marital relationships) contribute to the overall predictive validity of the PCL-R but do not fall into either of the factors. A score of 30 on the PCL-R is used as a cut-off to indicate psychopathy (Hare 2003). However, there is evidence to support the use of a lower cut-off of 25 in the UK in that the same level of psychopathy as observed in the US was found to be associated with lower scores on the PCL-R in the UK (Cooke and Michie 1999). It has been widely demonstrated to be a reliable and valid instrument with acceptable psychometric properties (Hare 2003; Salekin *et al.* 1996). Training on the PCL-R is required in order to conduct an assessment.

Motivation for treatment

Motivation for treatment has been discussed as a factor in successful treatment (Beech and Fisher 2002; Garland and Dougher 1991; Kear-Colwell and Pollock 1997; Looman *et al.* 2005; Miller and Rollnick 2002; Tierney and McCabe 2002). Motivation for treatment can be conceptualised and therefore assessed in a number of ways. For instance, it can range from acceptance of accountability for offending to willingness to attend treatment (Tierney and McCabe 2002).

Motivation for treatment in sex offenders has been considered in terms of Prochaska and DiClemente's (1982) transtheoretical model of change. This model specifies that individuals move through five stages of change: precomtemplation, contemplation, preparation, action and maintenance. The University of Rhode Island Change Assessment scale (URICA: McConnaughy *et al.* 1989; McConnaughy *et al.* 1983) is a common measure of motivation to change used in a wide range of populations.

The Multifactor Offender Readiness Model (MORM: Ward *et al.* 2004) has been suggested as a means of examining motivation in the wider context of treatment readiness. According to this model treatment readiness depends on a number of cognitive (e.g. beliefs about the treatment being offered), affective (e.g. guilt), volitional (e.g. patient's personal goals), behavioural (e.g. evaluations of their problem behaviour) and identity factors (e.g. core values) as well as external readiness conditions (e.g. therapeutic climate). Howells and Tennant (2007) suggest a number of questions that are useful in assessing level of treatment readiness such as: How does the patient perceive the therapeutic programme? Does the patient believe he or she is capable of change? Does the patient perceive coercion into treatment?

Up to this point we have described a number of commonly used current assessment approaches in determining the most appropriate treatment for sexual offenders. However, recent research and theory suggest that some newer approaches hold promise in terms of their ability to improve treatment effectiveness as well their intuitive appeal for the offender. The next section of the chapter will describe a more recent approach to the assessment, for treatment, of sexual offenders, as well as a more positive approach to treatment.

A collaborative approach to risk assessment

The movement towards more positive approaches to treatment (e.g. the Good Lives approach: Ward and Stewart 2003) have highlighted the value of viewing assessment as more of a collaborative process than in other approaches (see Beech 2001). Clinical psychology (e.g. Horvath and Greenberg 1994) and psychotherapy (e.g. Feasey 1999) have long recognised this as good therapist practice in that the client's best interests are served by this process. Shingler and Mann (2006) report using such an approach with sexual offenders, noting that the individuals being assessed invariably know themselves better than any assessor and that the assessment process must be approached in a genuine way.

Following from these ideas, Shingler and Mann (2006) suggest that the practice below should be followed in a collaborative approach to risk assessment:

1 Sensitively introduce and explain the assessment process, how the report based on the assessment will be used and how it can (potentially) benefit the client.

2 Listen to the client in an open minded way.

3 Deal sensitively with any initial negative reactions in the assessment process.

4 Discuss the results of static and dynamic assessments openly, with the client being asked to comment upon these results.

5 If the client shows an awareness of the highlighted problems they should be complimented; if not the assessment should be presented in such a way as to help the client understand how they ended up in their current situation. This approach is an important starting point for potential subsequent work on their treatment needs.

6 The subsequent report written on the basis of the previous points should be explained in such a way that the client understands the concepts outlined in the report.

7 The client should then be asked to comment upon the relevance of particular treatment needs identified in the report.

8 If the client disagrees with the identification of treatment needs they should be asked to explain why this is the case, and if their comments seem to be correct the report should be modified accordingly.

Along with this collaborative approach to assessing an individual's risk should also be an assessment of an individual's potential strengths. The Good Lives Model (GLM) is an approach that does so. The GLM focuses on promoting the welfare of the individual offender, instilling strengths in them and enhancing their capabilities to meet their needs in appropriate ways, in order to reduce their chances of committing further crimes (Ward and Stewart 2003). According to this theory, all human beings, including sex offenders, seek a set of primary 'goods' (Ward et al. 2006; Ward and Stewart 2003). A set of nine primary 'goods' have been identified as the following: life (including healthy living and functioning), knowledge, excellence in play and work (including mastery experiences), excellence in agency (i.e. autonomy and self-directedness), inner peace (i.e. freedom from emotional turmoil and stress), friendship (including intimate, romantic and family relationships), community, spirituality (i.e. finding meaning and purpose in life), happiness and creativity (Ward and Stewart 2003). Sexual offending arises as a result of an attempt to obtain these goods in a manner that is inappropriate (Ward *et al.* 2006; Ward and Stewart 2003).

In line with the GLM, Ward *et al.* (2006) suggest that for each human good, individuals should be asked questions around the following key points:

1 What does the (good) mean to you?
2 How important is this to you? Has your view of its importance changed over time?
3 How have you gone about achieving this (good) in your life? What strategies have worked best or worst?
4 Would you like to have more of this in your life?
5 What do you think has prevented you achieving this (good) in your life?
6 Where do you see yourself in one year five years/ten years time?

It is suggested that these questions allow the assessor to determine what each individual sees as a good life, and provides an understanding of what the individual's strategies have been in the past and what they can be in the future. Furthermore, these questions allow an assessment to be made about the scope of the individual's desire for human goods, the extent to which these goods have been pursued through inappropriate means in the past, whether there are conflicting goals in operation and the individual's current ability to formulate and implement their plans.

An additional area that has recently received attention for its ability to influence treatment effectiveness is the group process within treatment groups. Assessment of process issues, such as the therapeutic climate of the group will be discussed next.

Process issues

In the area of group psychotherapy, *process* refers to nature of the interactions between the members of the group (Yalom 1995). Process issues are those that are likely to have an influence on the quality of the interactions (e.g. therapist's characteristics or group cohesion) between the group members. Although this area has been neglected until relatively recently as it relates to sex offender treatment (see work by Beech and colleagues, e.g. Beech and Fordham 1997, and Marshall and colleagues, e.g. Marshall *et al.* 2003, for exceptions), its significance to the outcome of treatment has been highlighted in the general psychotherapy literature (e.g. Krupnick *et al.* 1996; Martin *et al.* 2000).

The therapeutic climate of a group is an important aspect of the group process to assess as studies have found a relationship between the therapeutic climate of a group, measured using the Group Environment Scale (GES: Moos 2002) and positive treatment outcome in sex offenders (Beech and Fordham 1997; Beech and Hamilton-Giachritsis 2005; Harkins and Beech 2008). MacKenzie and Livesley (1986) recommend that in studying process variables, it is helpful to use measures that deal with the group as an entire system (e.g. GES: Moos 2002).

Group Environment Scale (Moos 2002)

The GES is a 90-item measure containing scales that examine the overall therapeutic climate of different groups along three dimensions: relationships, personal growth or goal orientation, and system maintenance and change. It contains ten subscales:

1 *Cohesion* measures the member's group involvement in and commitment to the group and the concern and friendship they show for one another.
2 *Leader support* measures the amount of help, concern and friendship the leader shows for the members.
3 *Expressiveness* measures how much freedom of action and expression of feelings are encouraged in the group.
4 *Independence* measures how much the group encourages independent action and expression among members.
5 *Task orientation* assesses how much emphasis is placed on completing concrete, practical tasks and on decision-making and training.
6 *Self-discovery* measures how much the group encourages members' discussions of personal problems.
7 *Anger and aggression* measures the extent to which there is open expression of anger and disagreement in the group.

8 *Order and organisation* measures the formality and structure of the group and the explicitness of rules and sanctions.
9 *Leader control* measures the extent to which the leader directs the group, makes decisions and enforces rules.
10 *Innovation* measures how much the group promotes diversity and change in its own functions and activities.

These scales have been standardised on a large number of groups, allowing for the interpretation of group profiles. There is evidence for the internal consistency and the test–retest reliability (Moos 2002).

It is important to note that most of the work on assessment/risk predictors in sex offenders discussed above relates to adult males. As yet, there are no specific tools for female sex offenders and only a few for adolescents, although the research base – particularly for adolescent offenders – is growing. Although common sense would suggest that many of the static and dynamic factors would be relevant, caution is required when applying any of the systems outlined above to other populations. We will now briefly look at assessment in other populations.

Assessment in other groups

Assessing risk in adolescents

There are only two empirically based risk assessment scales currently available for juvenile sexual offenders and neither has been properly cross-validated as yet: the Juvenile Sex Offender Assessment Protocol (JSOAP: Prentky *et al.* 2000); and the Estimate of Risk of Adolescent Sexual Offender Recidivism (ERASOR: Worling and Curwen, in Calder 2001). Items in the JSOAP cover four factors. The first factor, *sexual drive/preoccupation,* contains items such as prior charges for sexual offences, duration of sexual offence history, evidence of sexual preoccupations/obsession, degree of planning and gratuitous sexual exploitation of the victim. The second factor, *impulsive/antisocial behaviour,* contains items such as caregiver consistency, history of expressed anger, school behaviour problems, school suspensions or expulsions, conduct disorder, antisocial behaviour, arrests before the age of sixteen, multiple types of offences, impulsivity, substance abuse and history of parental alcohol abuse. The third factor, *intervention,* contains items such as accepting responsibility for offending, internal motivation to change, understanding of sexual assault cycle and relapse prevention, evidence of empathy, remorse and guilt, and absence of cognitive distortions. The final factor, *community stability/ adjustment* contains items such as evidence of poorly managed anger in the community, stability of current living situation, stability of school, evidence of support systems and quality of peer relationships.

The ERASOR is designed to assess risk in twelve- to eighteen-year-old sexual offenders. This scale, like the JSOAP is still in the early stages of development. Items assess static variables related to past sexual offences and again the dynamic domains of sexual interests, pro-offending attitudes, socio-affective problems and self-management. Extra items related to family environment, problematic relationships with parents and lack of parental support are also included. With adolescents and children who have acted in a sexually inappropriate manner there is very real possibility that they are themselves the victims of sexual abuse and are behaving in a sexually reactive way. Assessments of the family are therefore extremely important. It is beyond the scope of this chapter to outline such assessments, but in terms of adolescent assessment several books (Barbaree *et al.* 1993; Calder 2001; O'Reilly *et al.* 2004) make a useful starting point in a consideration of the assessment of adolescents.

With assessment of young people there are limitations on the types of assessment that can be used or that may be appropriate to use. Consideration must be given to the ethics and appropriateness of any methods used on an individual basis. The use of information from external sources and family assessment are particularly pertinent.

Assessment of Internet offenders

There are likely to be characteristics that are unique to Internet offenders, although overlap between those who commit hands-on offences and those who engage in inappropriate sexual behaviour online is also expected. In Scotland, England and Wales Internet sex offenders are currently risk assessed using RM2000 and the Risk of Sexual Violence Protocol (RSVP: Hart *et al.* 2003), although it is acknowledged that work needs to be done to develop a measure specifically intended to assess risk in Internet offenders (Davidson 2007).

Factors that may not be directly related to Internet offending (e.g. sexual/psychosocial history, personality assessments, depression inventories) should be assessed because these may be related to why individuals choose the Internet as the medium for pursuing their sexual interests (Delmonico and Griffin 2008). Middleton *et al.*

117

(2006) report that Internet offenders generally tend to follow either an intimacy deficit (assessed using the UCLA Emotional Loneliness Scale: Russell *et al.* 1980) or emotional disregulation (assessed using the Interpersonal Reactivity Inventory – Personal Distress Scale: Davis 1980) pathway to offending which highlights the need to assess these areas. In assessing sexual interest among Internet offenders, measures such as the Abel Screen (Abel *et al.* 1998) and the Affinity Measure of Sexual Interest (Glasgow *et al.* 2003) are recommended (Delmonico and Griffin 2008). The Internet Sex Screening Test (Delmonico 1999) is a validated measure which can be used to assess an individual's problematic use of the Internet in a number of areas such as online sexual compulsivity and illegal sexual use of the computer (available online from http://www.internetbehavior.com/sexualdeviance). There is also preliminary support for the validity of the Internet Behaviour and Attitudes Questionnaire (IBAQ: O'Brien and Webster 2007). The IBAQ was developed in the UK to measure attitudes and behaviour of men who have been convicted of Internet child pornography-related offences.

Several assessment interviews have also been developed for Internet offenders. Delmonico and Griffin (2005) provide two structured assessment interviews (i.e. Internet Assessment Quickscreen and Internet Assessment) which are available online (http://www. internetbehavior.com/sexualdeviance). In addition, Quayle and Taylor (2002) have developed semi-structured interview guidelines to be used in assessing Internet offenders.

Assessing risk in female sexual offenders

It is likely that female sexual offenders have some risk factors and criminogenic needs that are unique to women, but there is also likely some overlap with factors that have been identified in men (Hollin and Palmer 2006). Assessments of female offenders have thus far tended to follow the same ideas as used for male offenders. How valid it is to do this is not known at the present time. Williams and Nicholaichuk (2001) report using the RRASOR (Hanson 1997) with female sexual offenders but this is on a very small sample (N = 11). The Level of Service Inventory – Revised (LSI-R), which is a measure of risk and need in the general offender population (Andrews and Bonta 1995), has been examined in women in the UK (Palmer and Hollin 2007) and Canada (Coulson *et al.* 1996). Although none of the women in these studies were reported to be sex offenders, the LSI-R did have good psychometric properties and was predictive of recidivism.

In terms of dynamic risk, there has also been some preliminary work to develop a female equivalent of the STEP test battery and the assessment of pro-offending attitudes (Beech *et al.* in press). In addition, there is an adult female form available for the Multiphasic Sex Inventory–II (MSI-II: Nichols and Molinder 1994). With female sex offenders it is known that a number of them will have co-offended with, and have been coerced by, male partners (e.g. Williams and Nicholaichuk 2001) and it is therefore important to assess them as individuals and their ability to resist pressure from such partners in the future. However, it is also important to note that in a review of the literature on female sex offenders, only three of the thirteen studies examined reported that the women had co-offenders (Johansson-Love and Fremouw 2006) so women's ability to commit sexual offences on their own must not be underestimated. What further complicates the assessment with many female offenders is that they may be primary caregivers to children and again this is an area that needs careful assessment. Ford and Cortoni (2008) recommend several important considerations in assessing female sexual offenders:

- the woman's previous sexual experiences, her feelings about these and how they might motivate her sexually deviant behaviour;
- her relationships and the social supports she has available to her;
- her coping style;
- any mental health difficulties;
- the nature and context of the offending behaviour;
- the role of sexual interests/arousal;
- her motivation for treatment.

Assessing risk in developmentally disabled sexual offenders

There is evidence to suggest that the 'What Works' approach to offender treatment is also appropriate in developmentally disabled sex offenders (Keeling *et al.* 2007). In terms of assessing risk, Tough (2001) found that the RRASOR, but not the Static-99, provided a good estimate of risk in those with an intellectual disability. However, Keeling *et al.* (2007) note that the risk level of individuals with an intellectual disability may be an underestimate. Such individuals are commonly not charged for their inappropriate sexual behaviour which may be treated as challenging behaviour rather than behaviour warranting criminal charges (Doyle 2004).

Given the noted challenges associated with assessing static risk, it is suggested that accurate assessment of dynamic risk/criminogenic need might be particularly important (Keeling *et al.* 2007). The

Dynamic Risk Assessment and Management System (DRAMS: Lindsay *et al.* 2004) is currently the only dynamic risk assessment measure specifically for individuals with an intellectual disability. It is designed to measure factors present before an aggressive (non-sexual) incident. An assessor scores the DRAMS on a continuum from 'no problem' to 'extreme problem' using simply worded questions which are supplemented with pictorial analogies for risk to help the client understand the process. The authors of this measure note that due to its limitations, the measure should be used as a clinical tool rather than a formal risk assessment (Lindsay *et al.* 2004). Other methods used to assess various aspects of dynamic risk in sexual offenders with intellectual disabilities include the use of a limited number of existing measures, adaptation of existing measures to increase ease of comprehension or the development of new measures specifically for use in offenders with intellectual disabilities (Keeling *et al.* 2007). See Keeling *et al.* (2007) for a review of appropriate measures for assessing each of the dynamic domains.

Several responsivity factors are particularly relevant in those with intellectual disabilities. Specifically, Keeling *et al.* (2007) suggest that intellectual functioning adaptive functioning, and literacy and comprehension be assessed. The Wechsler Adult Intelligence Scale–III (WAIS-III: Wechsler 1997) is the most current measure commonly used to assess intellectual functioning. Keeling and colleagues recommend the use of the Vineland Adaptive Behavior Scale (Sparrow *et al.* 1984), the Adaptive Behavior Scale – Residential and Community (2nd edition: Nihira *et al.* 1993), and the Supports Intensity Scale (American Association on Mental Retardation 2004) for assessing adaptive functioning. The Schonell Graded Reading Test (Schonell and Goodachre 1974) is recommended as a measure of literacy and comprehension (Clare and Gudjonsson 1992).

Assessing risk in mentally ill sex offenders

Assessment of mentally ill sex offenders can only take place when the individual's mental state has stabilised. They can then be assessed in the same way as non-mentally ill sex offenders. It may be that there are some offenders who only commit offences when mentally ill, either due to disinhibition or responding to delusional ideation. However, it is likely that some would commit offences regardless of their mental state and it is therefore important to assess the pro-offending attitudes and beliefs and sexual preferences of all mentally ill sex offenders. Two instruments are more relevant for mentally ill sexual offenders, the SVR-20 and the SORAG. The latter is a true actuarial instrument while the former is probably of more assistance in treatment planning.

The treatment of sexual offenders with mental health problems is discussed by Lockmuller *et al.* (2008). They note that an important issue to take into consideration in mentally ill offenders is that they may solely attribute their offending to their illness and thus have little insight into other contributory factors. A functional analysis and detailed clinical assessment will assist in developing a formulation of the individual's offending behaviour. In addition to other psychometrics that can be used to assess adult sex offenders (see the STEP psychometric test battery: Barker and Morgan 1993; Beckett *et al.* 1994; Beech *et al.* 1999; Beech *et al.* 2005), Lockmuller and colleagues (2008) also suggest that it is useful to include measures that allow the assessor to make the distinction between implicit beliefs (Ward 2000) and psychotic beliefs. To assist in making this distinction, measures such as Young's Schema Questionnaire (Young and Brown 1990) and subscales of both the Millon Clinical Multi-Axial Inventory (Millon 1997) and Personality Assessment Inventory (Morey 1991) are recommended.

Conclusions: putting the assessment process together

The exact assessment process will depend on a number of factors such as the characteristics of the offender, the purposes of the assessment and the information potentially available to the assessor (Beech *et al.* 2003). In allocating offenders to treatment, assessment of static risk level (e.g. RM2000) is useful for determining the appropriate treatment services. In line with the risk principle, those who are highest risk should be allocated to the highest-intensity treatment and the lowest-risk offenders should have little to no treatment resources directed to them. Assessment of static risk is also useful in making decisions about supervision. Static risk assessment measures are useful as they do not require the cooperation of the offender because they use items that can be obtained largely from police records and because the evidence base for the static actuarial scales is so much larger. Those measures that require more resources to complete (e.g. SORAG and SVR-20) are beneficial where intensive treatment is involved for a population that may contain individuals with multiple diagnoses (e.g. substance dependent, personality disordered and those with paraphilias).

In determining an individual's overall treatment needs, static actuarial assessments should be combined with functional analysis and assessment of stable-dynamic factors. Considering stable dynamic factors provides an indication of the individual's criminogenic need areas that should be addressed in treatment. In addition to influencing treatment allocation, examining dynamic factors can assist in determining whether the risk level has changed because they allow the assessor to judge: (1) whether an intervention has been relevant to the offender's needs; and (2) which areas of current behaviour are potentially significant as indications of the continuing operation of long-term risk factors.

In addition to the assessment of risk, responsivity factors should also be considered as these will play a role in how effective any particular treatment programme will be for an individual. For instance, those who are assessed as scoring high on measures such as the PCL-R will likely benefit more from a programme specifically designed with consideration of the features of such individuals.

These different assessment procedures can be sensibly combined so that the results of earlier processes can guide decisions about the use of additional procedures. For example, where an offender is identified as high or medium-high risk on a static risk instrument, it is then more worthwhile investing resources in a careful assessment of stable-dynamic and responsivity factors. For those demonstrating high levels of static and/or stable dynamic risk factors, regular measurement of acute risk factors using something like ACUTE 2007 is recommended for offenders under supervision in the community.

Notes

1 An effect size (r) of 0.1 represents a small difference 0.24 a medium difference and 0.37 a large difference (Coe 2002; Cohen 1988).
2 There is a copy of most of these in Prentky and Burgess (2000).

References

Abel, G.G., Huffman, J., Warberg, B.W. and Holland, R. (1998) 'Visual reaction time and plethysmography as measures of sexual interest in child molesters', *Sexual Abuse: A Journal of Research and Treatment*, 10: 317–35.
American Association on Mental Retardation (2004) *Supports Intensity Scale*. Washington, DC: American Association of Mental Retardation (see http://www.siswebsite.org).

Andrews, D.A. and Bonta, J. (1995) *LSI-R: The Level of Service Inventory – Revised*. Toronto, ON: Multi-Health Systems.

Andrews, D.A. and Bonta, J. (2003) *The Psychology of Criminal Conduct*, 3rd edn. Cincinnati, OH: Anderson.

Andrews, D.A. and Dowden, C. (2006) 'Risk principle of case classification in correctional treatment', *International Journal of Offender Therapy and Comparative Criminology*, 50: 88–100.

Barbaree, H.E., Marshall, W.L. and Hudson, S.M. (1993) *The Juvenile Sex Offender*. New York: Guilford Press.

Barker, M. and Morgan, R. (1993) *Sex Offenders: A Framework for the Evaluation of Community-Based Treatment*, Home Office Occasional Report. London: Home Office.

Beckett, R.C., Beech, A., Fisher, D. and Fordham, A.S. (1994) *Community-Based Treatment for Sex Offenders: An Evaluation of Seven Treatment Programmes*. London: Home Office Publications Unit.

Beech, A.R. (1998) 'A psychometric typology of child abusers', *International Journal of Offender Therapy and Comparative Criminology*, 42: 319–39.

Beech, A.R. (2001) 'Case material and interview', in C. Hollin (ed.), *Handbook of Offender Assessment and Treatment*. Chichester: Wiley, pp. 123–38.

Beech, A. and Fisher, D. (2002) 'The rehabilitation of child sex offenders', *Australian Psychologist*, 37: 206–15.

Beech, A. and Fordham, A.S. (1997) 'Therapeutic climate of sexual offender treatment programs', *Sexual Abuse: A Journal of Research and Treatment*, 9: 219–37.

Beech, A.R. and Hamilton-Giachritsis, C.E. (2005) 'Relationship between therapeutic climate and treatment outcome in a group-based sexual offender program', *Sexual Abuse: A Journal of Research and Treatment*, 17: 127–40.

Beech, A., Fisher, D. and Beckett, R. (1999) *STEP 3: An evaluation of the Prison Sex Offender Treatment Programme*, Home Office Occasional Report. Home Office Publications Unit. Available online at: http://www.homeoffice.gov.uk/rds/pdfs/occ-step3.pdf.

Beech, A.R. and Fisher, D.D. and Thornton, D. (2003) 'Risk assessment of sex offenders', *Professional Psychology: Research and Practice*, 34: 339–52.

Beech, A., Oliver, C., Fisher, D. and Beckett, R.C. (2005) *STEP 4: The Sex Offender Treatment Programme in Prison: Addressing the Needs of Rapists and Sexual Murderers*. Available online at: http://www.hmprisonservice.gov.uk/assets/documents/100013DBStep_4_SOTP_report_2005.pdf.

Beech, A.R., Parrett, H., Fisher, D. and Ward, T. (in press) 'Assessing female offenders' motivations and cognitions: an exploratory study', *Psychology, Crime and Law*.

Bickley, J.A. and Beech, A.R. (2002) 'An investigation of the Ward and Hudson pathways model of the sexual offense process with child abusers', *Journal of Interpersonal Violence*, 17: 371–93.

Boer, D.P., Hart, S.J., Kropp, P.R. and Webster, C.D. (1997) *Manual for the Sexual Violence Risk – 20: Professional Guidelines for Assessing Risk of Sexual Violence*. Vancouver, BC: Institute Against Family Violence.

Brown, S. (2005) *Treating Sex Offenders: An Introduction to Sex Offender Treatment Programmes*. Cullompton: Willan.

Calder, M.C. (2001) *Juveniles and Children Who Sexually Abuse: Frameworks for Assessment*. Lyme Regis: Russell House.

Caldwell, M.F., McCormick, D.J., Umstead, D. and Van Rybroek, G.J. (2007) 'Evidence of treatment progress and therapeutic outcomes among adolescents with psychopathic features', *Criminal Justice and Behavior*, 34: 573–87.

Clare, I.C.H. and Gudjonsson, G.H. (1992) *Devising and Piloting an Experimental Version of the 'Notice to Detained Persons'*, Royal Commission on Criminal Justice Research, Study No. 7. London: HMSO.

Cochran, W. and Tesser, A. (1996) 'The "what-the-hell effect": some effects of goal proximity and goal framing on performance', in L.L. Martin and A. Tesser (eds), *Striving and Feeling: Interactions Among Goals, Affect and Self-Regulation*. Mahwah, NJ: Erlbaum, pp. 99–120.

Coe, R. (2002) *It's the Effect Size, Stupid: What Effect Size Is and Why It Is Important*. Paper presented at the Annual Conference of the British Educational Research Association, Exeter, UK.

Cohen, J. (1988) *Statistical Power Analysis for the Behavioral Sciences*, 2nd edn. Hillsdale, NJ: Lawrence Erlbaum Associates.

Cooke, D.J. and Michie, C. (1999) 'Psychopathy across cultures: North America and Scotland compared', *Journal of Abnormal Psychology*, 108: 58–68.

Coulson, G., Ilacqua, G., Nutbrown, V., Giulekas, D. and Cudjoe, F. (1996) 'Predictive Utility of the LSI for Incarcerated Female Offenders', *Criminal Justice and Behavior*, 23: 427–39.

Craig, L.A., Thornton, D., Beech, A. and Browne, K.D. (2007) 'The relationship between statistical and psychological risk markers to sexual recidivism', *Criminal Justice and Behavior*, 34: 314–29.

D'Silva, K., Duggan, C. and McCarthy, L. (2004) 'Does treatment really make psychopaths worse? A review of the evidence', *Journal of Personality Disorders*, 18: 163–77.

Davidson, J. (2007) *Current Practice and Research into Internet Sex Offending*. Paisley: Risk Management Authority.

Davis, M.H. (1980) 'A multi-dimensional approach to individual differences in empathy', *JSAS Catalogue of Selected Documents in Psychology*, 10: 85.

Delmonico, D.L. (1999) *Internet Sex Screening Test*. Online at: http://www.internetbehavior.com/sexual deviance.

Delmonico, D.L. and Griffin, E.J. (2005) 'Internet Assessment: A Structured Interview for Assessing Online Problematic Sexual Behaviour'. Unpublished instrument, Internet Behavior Consulting.

Delmonico, D.L. and Griffin, E.J. (2008) 'Online sex offending: assessment and treatment', in D.R. Laws and W.T. O'Donohue (eds), *Sexual Deviance:*

Theory, Assessment and Treatment, 2nd edn. London: Guilford Press, pp. 459–85.

Doyle, D.M. (2004) 'The difference between sex offending and challenging behaviour in people with an intellectual disability', *Journal of Intellectual and Developmental Disability*, 29: 107–18.

Eldridge, H. (1998) *Therapist Guide for Maintaining Change: Relapse Prevention for Adult Perpetrators of Child Sexual Abuse*. Thousand Oaks, CA: Sage.

Feasey, D. (1999) *Good Practice in Psychotherapy and Counselling*. London: Whurr Brunner Routledge.

Fisher, D., Beech, A.R. and Browne, K.D. (1999) 'Comparison of sex offenders to non-offenders on selected psychological measures', *International Journal of Offender Therapy and Comparative Criminology*, 43: 473–91.

Ford, H. and Cortoni, F. (2008) 'Sexual deviance in females: assessment and treatment', in D.R. Laws and W.T. O'Donohue (eds), *Sexual Deviance: Theory, Assessment and Treatment*, 2nd edn. London: Guilford Press, pp. 508–26.

Friendship, C., Mann, R.E. and Beech, A.R. (2003) 'Evaluation of a national prison-based treatment program for sexual offenders in England and Wales', *Journal of Interpersonal Violence*, 18: 744–59.

Garland, R.J. and Dougher, M.J. (1991) 'Motivation intervention in the treatment of sex offenders', in W. Miller and S. Rollnick (eds), *Motivational Interviewing: Preparing People to Change Addictive Behavior*. New York: Guilford Press, pp. 303–13.

Glasgow, D.V., Osborne, A. and Croxen, J. (2003) 'An assessment tool for investigating paedophile sexual interest using viewing time: an application of single case research methodology', *British Journal of Learning Disability*, 31: 96–102.

Haag, A.M. (2000) 'Do Psychological Interventions Impact on Actuarial Measures: An Analysis of the Predictive Validity of the Static-99 and the Static-2002 on a Reconviction Measure of Sexual Recidivism'. Unpublished doctoral dissertation, University of Calgary, Alberta.

Hanson, R.K. (1997) *The Development of a Brief Actuarial Risk Scale for Sexual Offense Recidivism*, User Report 1997-04. Ottawa, ON: Department of the Solicitor General of Canada.

Hanson, R.K. (2005) 'Stability and change: dynamic risk factors for sexual offenders', in G. Serran, W.L. Marshall, Y. Fernandez and L. Marshall (eds), *Sexual Offender Treatment: Controversial Issues*. Chichester: Wiley, pp. 17–32.

Hanson, R.K. and Harris, A.J.R. (2000) 'Where should we intervene? Dynamic predictors of sexual offence recidivism', *Criminal Justice and Behavior*, 27: 6–35.

Hanson, R.K. and Harris, A.J.R. (2001) 'A structured approach to evaluating change among sexual offenders', *Sexual Abuse: A Journal of Research and Treatment*, 13: 105–22.

Hanson, R.K. and Morton-Bourgon, K. (2005) 'The characteristics of persistent sexual offenders: a meta-analysis of recidivism studies', *Journal of Consulting and Clinical Psychology*, 73: 1154–63.

Hanson, R.K. and Morton-Bourgon, K.E. (2007) *The Accuracy of Recidivism Risk Assessment for Sexual Offenders: A Meta-analysis*. Ottawa, ON: Corrections Research, Public Safety and Emergency Preparedness Canada. Available from: http://www.publicsafety.gc.ca/res/cor/rep/_fl/crp2007-01-en.pdf.

Hanson, R.K. and Thornton, D. (2000) 'Improving risk assessment for sex offenders: a comparison of three actuarial scales', *Law and Human Behavior*, 24: 119–36.

Hanson, R.K. and Thornton, D. (2003) *Notes on the Development of a Static-2002*. Available online from: http://ww2.psepc-sppcc.gc.ca/publications/corrections/200301_Static_2002_e.asp.

Hanson, R.K., Morton, K.E. and Harris, A.J.R. (2003) 'Sexual offender recidivism risk: what we know and what we need to know', in R.A. Prentky, E.S. Janus and M.C. Seto (eds), 'Sexually Coercive Behavior: Understanding and Management', *Annals of the New York Academy of Sciences*, 989: 154–66.

Hanson, R.K. Harris, A.J.R., Scott, T. and Helmus, L. (2007) *Assessing the Risk for Sexual Offenders on Community Supervision: The Dynamic Supervision Project*. Ottawa, ON: Corrections Research, Public Safety and Emergency Preparedness Canada. Available online at: http://www.publicsafety.gc.ca/res/cor/rep/_fl/crp2007-05-en.pdf.

Hare, R.D. (1996) 'Psychopathy: a clinical construct whose time has come', *Criminal Justice and Behavior*, 23: 25–54.

Hare, R.D. (2003) *The Hare Psychopathy Checklist – Revised (PCL-R)*, 2nd edn. Toronto, ON: Multi-Health Systems.

Hare, R.D., Clarke, D., Grann, M. and Thornton, D. (2000) 'Psychopathy and the predictive validity of the PCL-R: an international perspective', *Behavioral Sciences and the Law*, 18: 623–45.

Harkins, L. (2008) 'Sex Offender Treatment Effectiveness: Risk, Need, Responsivity and Process Issues'. Unpublished doctoral thesis, University of Birmingham, UK.

Harkins, L. and Beech, A.R. (2008) 'Examining the impact of mixing child molesters and rapists in group-based cognitive-behavioral treatment for sexual offenders', *International Journal of Offender Therapy and Comparative Criminology*, 52: 31–45.

Harris, A. and Hanson, R.K. (2003) 'The Dynamic Supervision Project: improving community supervision of sex offenders', *Corrections Today*, August: 60–4.

Harris, A., Phenix, A., Hanson, R.K. and Thornton, D. (2003) *Static-99 Coding Rule – Revised*. Available online at: http://ww2.psepc-sppcc.gc.ca/publications/corrections/pdf/Static-99-coding-Rules_e.pdf#.

Harris, G.T., Rice, M.E. and Quinsey, V.L. (1993) 'Violent recidivism of mentally disordered offenders: the development of a statistical prediction instrument', *Criminal Justice and Behavior*, 20: 315–35.

Hart, S.D., Michie, C. and Cooke, D.J. (2007) 'Precision of actuarial risk assessment instruments', *British Journal of Psychiatry*, 190: 60–5.

Hobson, J., Shine, J. and Roberts, R. (2000) 'How do psychopaths behave in a prison therapeutic community?', *Psychology, Crime and the Law*, 6: 139–54.

Hollin, C.R. (1999) 'Treatment programmes for offenders: meta-analysis, "what works," and beyond', *International Journal of Law and Psychiatry*, 22: 361–72.

Hollin, C.R. and Palmer, E.J. (2006) 'Criminogenic need and women offenders: a critique of the literature', *Legal and Criminological Psychology*, 11: 179–95.

Horvath, A.O. and Greenberg, L.S. (1994) *The Working Alliance: Theory, Research and Practice*. New York: Wiley.

Howells, K. and Tennant, A. (2007) 'Ready or not, they are coming: dangerous and severe personality disorder and treatment engagement', *Issues in Forensic Psychology*, 7: 11–20.

Johansson-Love, J. and Fremouw, W. (2006) 'A critique of the female sexual perpetrator research', *Aggression and Violent Behavior*, 11: 12–26.

Kear-Colwell, J. and Pollock, P. (1997) 'Motivation or confrontation: which approach to the child sex offender?', *Criminal Justice and Behavior*, 24: 20–33.

Keeling, J.A., Beech, A.R. and Rose, J.L. (2007) 'Assessment of intellectually disabled sexual offenders: the current position', *Aggression and Violent Behavior*, 12: 229–41.

Krupnick, J.L., Stotsky, S.M., Simmens, S., Moyer, J., Elkin, I., Watkins, J. and Plikonis, P.L. (1996) 'The role of the therapeutic alliance in psychotherapy and pharmacotherapy outcome: findings in the National Institute of Mental Health Treatment of Depression Collaborative Research Project', *Journal of Consulting and Clinical Psychology*, 64: 532–9.

Langton, C.M., Barbaree, H.E., Harkins, L. and Peacock, E. (2006) 'Sex offenders' response to treatment and its association with recidivism as a function of psychopathy', *Sexual Abuse: A Journal of Research and Treatment*, 18: 99–120.

Langton, C.M., Barbaree, H.E., Seto, M., Hansen, K.T., Harkins, L. and Peacock, E.J. (2007) 'Reliability and validity of the Static-2002 among adult sex offenders with reference to treatment status', *Criminal Justice and Behavior*, 34: 616–40.

Laws, D.R. (1999) 'Relapse prevention: the state of the art', *Journal of Interpersonal Violence*, 14: 285–302.

Lindsay, W.R., Murphy, L., Smith, G., Murphy, D., Edwards, Z., Chittock, C. et al. (2004) 'The Dynamic Risk Assessment and Management System: an assessment of immediate risk of violence with offending and challenging behavior', *Journal of Applied Research with Intellectual Disabilities*, 17: 267–74.

Lockmuller, M., Beech, A. and Fisher, D. (2008) 'Sexual offenders with mental health problems: Epidemiology, assessment and treatment', in K. Soothill, P. Rogers and M. Dolan (eds), *Handbook of Forensic Mental Health*. Cullompton: Willan, pp. 442–75.

Looman, J., Dickie, I. and Abracen, J. (2005) 'Responsivity in the treatment of sexual offenders', *Trauma, Violence, and Abuse*, 6: 330–53.

Loving, J.L. (2002) 'Treatment planning with the Psychopathy Checklist – Revised (PCL-R)', *International Journal of Offender Therapy and Comparative Criminology*, 46: 281–93.

McConnaughy, E.A., Prochaska, J.O. and Velicer, W.F. (1983) 'Stages of change in psychotherapy: measurement and sample profiles', *Psychotherapy: Theory, Research and Practice*, 20: 368–75.

McConnaughy, E.A., DiClemente, C.C., Prochaska, J.O. and Velicer, W.F. (1989) 'Stages of change in psychotherapy: a follow-up report', *Psychotherapy*, 26: 494–503.

MacKenzie, H.R. and Livesley, W.J. (1986) 'Outcome and process measures in brief group psychotherapy', *Psychiatric Annals*, 16: 715–20.

Mann, R.E., O'Brien, M., Rallings, M., Thornton, D. and Webster, S. (unpublished) 'Manual for the Structured Assessment of Risk and Need for Sex Offender (SARN-SO)'. Available from the Sex Offender Treatment Programme Team, Offending Behaviour Programmes Unit, HM Prison Service, Room 725 Abel House, John Islip Street, London SW1 4LH.

Marshall, W.L., Fernandez, Y.M., Serran, G.A., Mulloy, R., Thornton, D., Mann, R.E. and Anderson, D. (2003) 'Process variables in the treatment of sexual offenders: a review of the relevant literature', *Aggression and Violent Behavior*, 8: 205–34.

Martin, D.J., Garske, J.P. and Davis, M.K. (2000) 'Relation of the therapeutic alliance with outcome and other variables: a meta-analytic review', *Journal of Consulting and Clinical Psychology*, 68: 438–50.

Middleton, D., Elliot, I.A., Mandeville-Norden, R. and Beech, A.R. (2006) 'An investigation into the applicability of the Ward and Siegert Pathways Model of child sexual abuse with internet offenders', *Psychology, Crime and Law*, 12: 589–603.

Miller, W.R. and Rollnick, S. (2002) *Motivational Interviewing: Preparing People for Change*, 2nd edn. New York: Guilford Press.

Millon, T. (1997) *Millon Clinical Multiaxial Inventory – III Manual*, 2nd edn. Minneapolis, MN: National Computer Systems.

Moos, R.H. (2002) *Group Environment Scale Manual*, 3rd edn. Palo Alto, CA: Consulting Psychologists Press.

Morey, L.C. (1991) *The Personality Assessment Inventory Professional Manual*. Available from Psychological Assessment Resources, Inc. 16204, North Florida Avenue, Lutz, Florida 33549.

Nichols, H. and Molinder, I. (1994) *The Multiphasic Sex Inventory II – Adult Female Form*. Fircrest, WA: Nichols & Molinder Assessments.

Nihira, K., Leland, H. and Lambert, N. (1993) *Adaptive Behavior Scale – Residential and Community*. Austin, TX: Pro-ed (see http://www.proedinc.com).

O'Brien, M.D. and Webster, S.D. (2007) 'The construction and preliminary validation of the Internet Behaviours and Attitudes Questionnaire (IBAQ)', *Sexual Abuse: A Journal of Research and Treatment*, 19: 237–56.

O'Reilly, G., Marshall, W.L. and Carr, A. (2004) *The Handbook of Clinical Intervention with Juvenile Sexual Offenders*. New York: Routledge.

Olver, M.E., Wong, S., Nicholaichuk, T. and Gordon, A. (2007) 'The validity and reliability of the Violence Risk Assessment Scale – Sex Offender version: assessing sex offender risk and evaluating therapeutic change', *Psychological Assessment*, 19: 318–29.

Palmer, E.J. and Hollin, C.R. (2007) 'The Level of Service Inventory Revised with English women prisoners: a needs and reconviction analysis', *Criminal Justice and Behavior*, 34: 971–84.

Prentky, R.A. and Burgess, A. (2000) *Forensic Management of Sexual Offenders*. New York: Springer.

Prentky, R.A., Harris, B., Frizzell, K. and Righthand, S. (2000) 'An actuarial procedure for assessing risk with juvenile sex offenders', *Sexual Abuse: A Journal of Research and Treatment*, 12: 71–93.

Prochaska, J.O. and DiClemente, C.C. (1982) 'Transtheoretical therapy: toward a more integrative model of change', *Psychotherapy: Theory, Research and Practice*, 19: 276–88.

Prochaska, J.O., DiClemente, C.C. and Norcross, J. (1992) 'In search of how people change: applications to the addictive behaviors', *American Psychologist*, 47: 1102–14.

Quayle, E. and Taylor, M. (2002) 'Paedophiles, pornography and the Internet: assessment issues', *British Journal of Social Work*, 32: 863–75.

Quinsey, V.L., Harris, G.T., Rice, M.E. and Cormier, C. (1998) *Violent Offenders: Appraising and Managing Risk*. Washington, DC: American Psychological Association.

Russell, D., Peplau, L.A. and Cutrona, C.A. (1980) 'The Revised UCLA loneliness scale: concurrent and discriminant validity evidence', reproduced in the *Journal of Personality and Social Psychology*, 39: 472–80.

Salekin, R.T. (2002) 'Psychopathy and therapeutic pessimism: clinical lore or clinical reality?', *Clinical Psychology Review*, 22: 79–112.

Salekin, R.T., Rogers, R. and Sewell, K.W. (1996) 'A review and meta-analysis of the Psychopathy Checklist and the Psychopathy Checklist – Revised: predictive validity of dangerousness', *Clinical Psychology: Science and Practice*, 3: 203–15.

Schonell, F.J. and Goodacre, E.J. (1974) *The Psychology and Teaching of Reading*, 5th edn. Harlow: Oliver & Boyd/Longmans.

Shingler, J. and Mann, R.E. (2006) 'Collaboration in clinical work with sexual offenders: treatment and risk assessment', in G. Serran, W.L. Marshall, Y. Fernandez and L. Marshall (eds), *Sexual Offender Treatment: Controversial Issues*. Chichester: Wiley, pp. 225–39.

Sjöstedt, G. and Långström, N. (2001) 'Actuarial assessment of sex offender recidivism risk: a cross-validation of the RRASOR and the Static-99 in Sweden', *Law and Human Behavior*, 25: 629–45.

Sparrow, S.S., Balla, D.A. and Cicchetti, D.V. (1984) *Vineland Adaptive Behavior Scales*. Circle Pines, MN: American Guidance Service, Inc.

Stalans, L.J. (2005) 'Adult sex offenders on community supervision: a review of recent assessment strategies and treatment', *Criminal Justice and Behavior*, 31: 564–608.

Thornton, D. (2002) 'Constructing and testing a framework for dynamic risk assessment', *Sexual Abuse: A Journal of Research and Treatment*, 141: 139–53.

Thornton, D., Mann, R., Webster, S., Blud, L., Travers, R., Friendship, C. and Erickson, M. (2003) 'Distinguishing between and combining risks for sexual and violent recidivism', in R.A. Prentky, E.S. Janus and M.C. Seto (eds), 'Sexually Coercive Behavior: Understanding and Management', *Annals of the New York Academy of Sciences*, 989: 223–35.

Tierney D.W. and McCabe, M.P. (2002) 'Motivation for behavior change among sex offenders: a review of the literature', *Clinical Psychology Review*, 22, 113–29.

Tough, S.E. (2001) 'Validation of Two Standard Risk Assessments (RRASOR, 1997; STATIC-99, 1999) on a Sample of Adult Males Who Are Developmentally Delayed with Significant Cognitive Deficits'. Unpublished Masters thesis, University of Toronto, Canada.

Ward, T.W. (2000) 'Sexual offenders' cognitive distortions as implicit theories', *Aggression and Violent Behaviour*, 20 (10): 1–24.

Ward, T. and Hudson, S.M. (1996) 'Relapse prevention: a critical analysis', *Sexual Abuse: A Journal of Research and Treatment*, 8: 177–200.

Ward, T. and Hudson, S.M. (1998) 'A model of the relapse process in sexual offenders', *Journal of Interpersonal Violence*, 13: 700–25.

Ward, T. and Stewart, C.A. (2003) 'The treatment of sex offenders: risk management and the good lives model', *Professional Psychology: Research and Practice*, 34, 353–60.

Ward, T., Polaschek, D., Beech, A.R. (2006) *Theories of Sexual Offending*. Chichester: Wiley.

Ward, T., Louden, K., Hudson, S. and Marshall, W.L. (1995) 'A descriptive model of the offence chain in child molesters', *Journal of Interpersonal Violence*, 10: 453–73.

Ward, T., Bickley, J., Webster, S., Fisher, D., Beech, A. and Eldridge, H. (2004) *The Self-Regulation Model of the Offense and Relapse Process*. Victoria, BC: Pacific Psychological Associate Corporation.

Webster, S.D., Mann, R.E., Thornton, D. and Wakeling, H.C. (2007) 'Further validation of the short self-esteem scale with sexual offenders', *Legal and Criminological Psychology*, 12: 207–16.

Webster, S., Mann, R., Carter, A., Long, J., Milner, R., O'Brien, M., Wakeling, H. and Ray, N. (2006) 'Inter-rater reliability of dynamic risk assessment with sexual offenders', *Psychology, Crime and Law*, 12: 439–52.

Wechsler, D. (1997) *WAIS-III Administration and Scoring Manual*. San Antonio, TX: Psychological Corporation (see http://www.harcourtassessment.com).

Williams, S.M. and Nicholaichuk, T. (2001) *Assessing Static Risk Factors in Adult Female Sex Offenders under Federal Jurisdiction*. Paper presented at the 21st Research and Treatment Conference of the Association for the Treatment of Sexual Abusers, San Antonio, TX.

Wolf, S.C. (1984) *A Multifactorial Model of Deviant Sexuality*. Paper presented at the Third International Conference of Victimology, Lisbon, Portugal.

Wong, S. (2000) 'Psychopathic offenders', in S. Hodgins and R. Muller-Isberner (eds), *Violence, Crime and Mentally Disordered Offenders*. Chichester: Wiley, pp. 87–112.

Wong, S., Olver, M.E., Nicholaichuk, T.P. and Gordon, A. (2003) *The Violence Risk Scale – Sexual Offender Version (VRS-SO)*. Saskatoon, Saskatchewan: Regional Psychiatric Centre and University of Saskatchewan.

Worling, J.R. and Curwen, T. (2001) 'The "ERASOR" Estimate of Risk of Adolescent Sexual Offense Recidivism', in M.C. Calder (ed.), *Juveniles and Children Who Sexually Abuse: Frameworks for Assessment*. Lyme Regis: Russell House, pp. 372–97.

Yalom, I.D. (1995) *The Theory and Practice of Group Psychotherapy*, 4th edn. New York: Basic Books.

Young, J.E. and Brown, G. (1990) *Young Schema Questionnaire*. New York: Cognitive Therapy Center of New York.

Chapter 6

Assessing the clinical needs for stalking and domestic violence

Werner Tschan

Healthcare professionals offering treatment in stalking and/or domestic violence cases require two different approaches – one is the traditional therapeutic intervention, the other is ongoing risk assessment. The duty to protect third parties may overrule the duty of confidentiality; this implies a balancing of rights, based on the level of evidence of an increased risk of violence and/or suicidal attempts. Both strategies go hand in hand and incorporate techniques derived from *threat management*. Therapeutic approaches in these cases always face the 'intervention dilemma', which outlines the possibility that the intervention can increase the risk of violent outbursts dramatically. Sometimes no intervention is, therefore, the best approach. Defensive intervention strategies focus on the victim's side; whereas offensive strategies focus on the offender's side (e.g. police interventions, legal measurements and therapeutic interventions). The aim of any clinical intervention is to help affected victims, but also to stop the violence and to help offenders to find other coping strategies.

The clinical needs for stalking and domestic violence are primarily defined by the fact that the goal of the clinical work is always directed towards the clients. Clinical interventions should help contribute to stopping any form of violence (primary prevention). They should also help prevent violent outbursts and minimise any collateral effect of the violence experienced on health conditions and quality of life (secondary prevention). Threat management is often difficult to define, both in terms of the magnitude of violence that is to be expected and how individuals will be affected by this. There is considerable variability among the population and how they cope with traumatic experiences. To illustrate the clinical difficulties we must consider the situation of having a person in treatment who complains about the suicidal tendencies of a partner and the threats he or she has made. Shall we be more on the safe side and expect an extended suicide to occur, or are we more on the optimistic side, where we assume that things will not develop so dramatically? The decision-making process often follows a fine line where we can overreact or where we can fail due to an underestimation of the threat and its manifestations. The current chapter will underline how important it is to constantly question one's assumptions and to act based on given facts – whether you like them or not should not matter.

The underlying basics

Victim treatment can be considered a form of intervention in violence cases, as outlined in the ensuing paragraph. But before discussing the particular aspects for handling the clinical assessment in violent cases, some underlying basics have to be clarified. The most important aspect in clinical approaches to the subject is that professionals are prepared to think the 'unthinkable' and to openly discuss all possible scenarios, even the most bizarre and beyond one's worst imagination. This is certainly not an easy task and it challenges normal human reactions, in which one usually avoids thinking about such things. Furthermore, professionals have to be trained in dealing with the various scenarios. This can be compared with the training of fire-fighters. Their training prepares them for all kind of occurrences and how to react to them. For professionals involved in threat management the same rationale applies.

When working with victims, it is essential that professionals are able to give hope to their clients; however, this must always be addressed in a realistic and goal-oriented manner. In most cases, affected clients feel deeply disturbed when confronted with violent experiences: they have often faced life-threatening experiences and they do not understand their bodily and emotional reactions. They often feel as though they are still in the same situation, haunted by their past experiences. As well as therapeutic knowledge professionals require a profound understanding of attachment theory, psychotraumatology and neurodevelopment psychology when counselling and treating those affected. Human violence is always committed by persons and takes place within human relationships. It therefore affects the attachment system (Meloy 1992). Futhermore, these experiences lead to hard-wired brain connections as part of the fear network and determine stress reactions, where the hippocampus serves as a cognitive map of threatening experiences (Le Doux 1996). This is part of the human survival mechanism.

Professional training and knowledge in domestic violence, including intimate partner violence, is essential (Dutton 2006). Due to a lack of curricular integration of violence and its effects on the health condition and risk assessment, most healthcare professionals are not adequately prepared for this task (Krug *et al.* 2002; Zonana *et al.* 1999). Training significantly increases the handling of these issues (Hibbard and Zollinger 1990). To understand the impact of violence professionals need to understand the framework provided by attachment theory (Meloy 1992) as well as psychotraumatology.

Information management is another crucial aspect. The assessment should always consider all possible collateral information. When something doesn't fit into the puzzle, it should not be omitted but rather used as a stimulus to consider the entire picture again. A recent dramatic case from Switzerland illustrates the devastating effect of when the information-gathering process is inadequately performed. In this case, a 53-year-old man was released from a psychiatric ward after a local court decision. A psychiatrist evaluated the man and provided a risk assessment without considering collateral information. The man was involuntarily admitted to a psychiatric ward due to his threatening behaviour on 1 September 2007. A judge released the man from the psychiatric ward, based on the professional's assessment, on 7 September 2007. The judge neither consulted the physician who had admitted the man to the psychiatric ward, nor did he consult with the psychiatrists of the ward who knew the man quite well from previous hospitalisations, nor did the judge consult the police registry. On 16 September 2007 the man killed a cab-driver by stabbing him with a knife (NZZ 2007).

Unfortunately, this is not a unique case. We have seen similar deficits in the information management process, for example in Germany in a stalking case, where a man killed his ex-wife. This man had also been admitted to a psychiatric ward, but was then released by the physicians who did not realise how dangerous he was. Two days later, in the morning, he stabbed his former wife at her workplace. The physicians did not consider collateral information, and the essential message was not transmitted from one police force to the other. The murderer had told another man what he was about to do and this man had reported this to the police.

As well as information management, an interdisciplinary approach and close cooperation between the involved disciplines are *sine qua non* conditions. This is another challenge for the training of professionals, who are usually trained in their own domain only, thus creating a 'single disciplinary ghetto' effect. This can become a considerable hurdle in clinical risk assessment.

Also important to acknowledge is that clinical assessment is not a single event, rather it is an ongoing process. Neither stalking nor violence is a static phenomenon. Whenever new elements occur during the case management this should lead to a revision of the assessment and the strategy. The following case vignette illustrates the clinical situation.

A man in his forties contacted a psychiatrist for a threat evaluation. He and his intimate female partner had become the victim of a stalker. The stalker was her ex-husband, and they have two children together. She left him due to his violent behaviour (mainly verbal, occasionally physical, attacks), and she often felt very frightened during their marriage. After eight years the marriage was annulled, the children aged seven and five stayed under her care and he saw them every two weeks. She had a few short relationships, nothing very serious, until she met her current partner. After a few weeks into their relationship her ex-partner started to phone her and then him, in order to complain about their relationship, and he became verbally threatening. He sent text messages demanding that the new partner should finish the relationship. The victim tried to talk to him several times on the phone, but only encountered further derogatory and harassing remarks.

The ex-husband refused to see the children any longer. Finally, after he started stalking the woman's parents, they reported him to the police. After this, the verbal attacks increased even more, and he often called 40–50 times a day. One day he slashed all four tyres of the woman's car, after having made around ten phone calls letting them know what he was about to do. He also rang the doorbell several times unexpectedly, and demanded to see his children. When one of the children then opened the door, he entered the apartment and behaved as though he were at home.

The new partner then contacted the psychiatrist with problems sleeping, nightmares and a constant feeling of being threatened. Among his first questions were: 'How dangerous is this man?

How far will he go?' Both he and his partner were desperate. They made various attempts to call the police who declared that it was a private matter and did not intervene, except after he slashed the tyres. The ex-husband was fined for property damages, nothing else. The woman arranged a restraining order and involved the social services for helping in the handling of the children. It was settled that the father could see the children only when accompanied by a social worker.

How do you respond to this client? A clinical assessment is always based on the available information, and one of the conclusions is often that there is an urgent need for further information that must be gathered piece by piece. Four standard questions must be answered as immediately as possible:

1 Does the stalker own a weapon (e.g. handgun)?
2 Has he ever become physically violent in the past (e.g. convictions, including severe traffic violations)?
3 Does he consume alcohol or other drugs?
4 Does he express suicidal intentions?

The client could not answer all these questions for sure at the first interview, but he then talked with his partner who had known the stalker for years and was able to answer the questions with a high degree of certainty. It is important to note that for the stalker any form of violence is a coping strategy – when you intervene, you may challenge this approach and force the stalker to develop dramatic escalations.

The client was also told how to cope with the stalker and to avoid any direct contact, especially not to answer phone calls or text messages. For the handling of the children, social services should still be involved. The stalking stopped, and after a couple of months the client learned that the stalker had a new relationship and that he was undergoing psychotherapeutic treatment. The children refused initially to see their father, and the social services involved notified him about this. After several months, with the help of social services, the father was able to visit and see the children and would later invite them to come to his home.

The risk assessment was performed as an ongoing process according to the available information. In this case, the defensive strategy led to an acceptable outcome and the stalking behaviour finally stopped. The client and his partner were no longer worried. The risk assessment in interpersonal violence is based on three elements: the victim's perspective, the situational factors and the dynamic factors. With regard to each:

Risk assessment from the victim's perspective should include:

- collecting facts;
- victim's own risk prediction;
- goals of the victim;
- any ongoing interaction between victim and offender.

Situational (static) factors should include:

- location;
- whether children are involved;
- whether friends and relatives are available;
- whether there is an ongoing social relationship between victim and offender.

Dynamic factors should include:

- manifestations of personality traits;
- mental disorders;
- any evidence of dramatic moments (such as frustrations, etc.);
- any interventions.

A clinician always faces two duties when doing an assessment in stalking and violent cases. One is the *ongoing risk assessment* per se; the other one is the *duty to protect potential victims*. In the clinical situation these two aspects have to be dealt with simultaneously during the intervention process. The clinician has an obligation to warn third parties, according to the Tarasoff Doctrine (Anfang *et al.* 1996). This duty is explicitly given when those threatened are identified by the offender, e.g. by stating: 'I will attack this person.' Although the 'Tarasoff duty to warn' philosophy was coined by an American court it is now applicable worldwide, as a recent European Court on Human Rights' decision clearly indicates (Gavaghan 2007). Professionals can no longer claim confidentiality; rather they have to balance the rights involved when security aspects of third parties are concerned.

Challenging the intervention dilemma

Any form of intervention may increase the risk for further escalation. This dilemma is referred to as the 'intervention dilemma' (White and Cawood 1998). Two strategies are possible, one is more defensive and is based on interventions on the victims' side. In most cases, offenders are not aware of this type of intervention which does not therefore contribute to further escalation. The offensive strategy aims to intervene directly with the offender, either through the police or by legal means, such as restraining orders. The treatment of offenders is another form of direct intervention.

Therapeutic interventions and psycho-educative training for victims help them overcome any ambivalent feelings and attitudes towards the offenders. Especially in stalking cases the main strategy is to make the victim 'as invisible' as possible by avoiding any form of reaction, e.g. not answering phone calls, no self-defence, not sending back presents, etc. In case of litigation, solicitors must follow the same strategy by addressing issues from a legal perspective and not addressing the claim from a victim's perspective. To illustrate this: solicitors should not claim that the victim feels threatened by the behaviour; rather they should simply say that this behaviour is against the law and therefore unacceptable. Using this strategy solicitors avoid putting the victim in the centre of the attention.

Treatment approaches for offenders must cover a wide range of behaviour patterns, ranging from mild stalking to severe forms of violence. As the motivation for stalkers and violent offenders to undergo treatment is often non-existent, only mandatory treatment is possible (Tschan 2006).

Effective intervention strategies aim to bring the stalking and violent behaviour to an end. We prefer a pragmatic approach, e.g. when defensive strategies are effective, we do not recommend any additional offensive strategy, although this may often be contrary to what victims demand.

Interdisciplinary cooperation

Information management in clinical risk assessment is crucial, as illustrated in both previous case examples. A clinical risk assessment should never be performed alone; rather it should be based on a team decision whereby the various professionals all contribute from their different perspectives and experiences. Gathering information is also crucial, with the following representing key elements of this process:

- direct interview with affected person(s);
- documents, such as letters, e-mails, text-messages, etc.;
- contact with relatives or co-workers;
- contact with involved third parties;
- existing records, former police reports, court reports, etc.

The integration of various information sources is essential in the interdisciplinary approach. It is important to note that only medical professionals have access to medical records, and that only the police have access to police reports. Legal obligations related to individual data protection and confidentiality issues are often a considerable hurdle in the information gathering process.

For contact with the offender the following aspects should be considered:

- Use clear and directive language.
- Be goal-oriented.
- Be behaviour-oriented (i.e. no moral judgement).
- Use 'if – then' conditions (i.e. negotiating).
- No outlining menacing consequences.

It is important to note that in about 60–80 per cent of all cases simple police interventions will stop the interpersonal violence.

When discussing the causes and underlying problems of violent offenders, we must consider that this behavior is not a disease (Tschan 2006). According to a study by Kamphuis *et al.* (2004) over 80 per cent of all offenders seemed to have no psychiatric disorder at the time when the stalking occurred. About half of all stalking cases develop from an intimate relationship. Not surprisingly, there are many overlaps with domestic violence.

According to the literature about 80 per cent of offenders in severe stalking are men. Most stalkers seem to have great difficulties accepting a simple 'no'. Stalkers intend to impose power over another person. They want to control a person to behave in the way that they desire. Several studies have clearly indicated that many stalkers suffer from attachment problems in their life (Lewis *et al.* 2001; Dye and Keith 2003; Kamphuis *et al.* 2004). This offers an understanding of the stalking and violent behaviour in many cases. Interpersonal violence is always a relational offence – you cannot stalk without another person, for example.

There are a dozen stalking typologies; however, as a static concept, they are not very useful in describing the offender–victim dynamic over time (Voss 2004). Today the best available approach for offender intervention is the RECON typology (RElationship and CONtext-based: Mohandie *et al.* 2006) based on the relationship between offender and victim. There are also various theories for sexual offending (Ward *et al.* 2006). Typologies and theories of offending are helpful in understanding the underlying causes. However, the clinical risk assessment is based on given facts, not on theoretical models.

Risk assessment from a clinical perspective

Any thorough clinical risk assessment is based on data derived from past experiences and should provide a forecast for future developments. In general, the accuracy of predicting violent behaviour is considerably high for the following 24 to 48 hours but becomes very unsure for the long-term prognosis. As noted earlier, the risk assessment is not a single event; rather it is work in progress depending on the individual case. Experience is an important part of clinical risk assessment. However, it may be that twenty years of risk assessment experiences are based on false assumptions, therefore we recommend an interdisciplinary approach – the more discussions during the decision-making process, the better the result. You should never feel too secure when performing a risk assessment.

Clinical risk assessment is covered in detail in early chapters of this book but the core principles on which it is based include: (1) static factors; (2) dynamic factors; and (3) protective factors. With regard to each:

Static risk factors are:

- age;
- gender;
- origin;
- socio-economic background;
- educational level;
- own biographic experiences (e.g. violence);
- cultural situation;
- role models;

The static risk factors consist of what someone brings with them to a situation, whereas the dynamic risk factors describe how someone reacts in a given situation. These can include:

• psychiatric disorders and impairment in executive functions (depression, schizophrenia, substance abuse, sleep disturbances, physical illness);
• impulse control disturbances;
• problematic life conditions;
• feeling that there is no future;
• having access to weapons (primarily handguns).

And, finally, the protective factors can serve as a balance against static and dynamic risk factors, and can incorporate:

• personal resources;
• a social network;
• familial network and support;
• spirituality;
• cultural background.

However, in some cases the spiritual and cultural background can also be a risk factor. Therefore, the assessment must always be based on the individual situation.

Figure 6.1 illustrates the accuracy of the risk prediction, where the sensitivity gives us an answer to how good a certain prognostic element is and how much it can discriminate between effective violence and no violence at all. Risk prediction is always a balance between accuracy (sensitivity) and experience (specificity).

		Prediction		
		Yes	No	
Effective	Yes		False negative	Sensitivity
Violence	No	False positive		
		Specificity		

Figure 6.1 Risk prediction

Therapeutic strategies

Therapeutic strategies in stalking and violent cases are goal oriented and behaviour focused. They are not primarily based on underlying disorders and problems, i.e. 'Traditionally, most areas of psychiatry have focused on disorder of mental function, with behaviour regarded as a mere epiphenomenon' (Mullen 2007: vii). Figure 6.2 illustrates the different approaches and underlying problems which have to be focused on in the therapeutic approach.

Offence-focused treatment is based on a semi-structured cognitive-behavioural treatment approach, added by psycho-educative aspects. It can be divided into offence focused aspects and personality focused aspects as follows:

Offence focused:

- offence reconstruction;
- cognitive distortions;
- underlying causes;
- impulse control (internal–external);
- offence-related personality aspects;
- victim empathy;
- improving impulse control;
- openness;
- intimacy and emotionality;
- responsibility;
- work – life balance;
- crisis management.

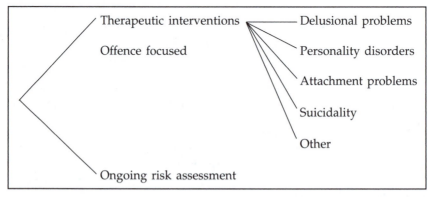

Figure 6.2 The therapeutic approach

Personality focused:

- anger management;
- power and powerlessness;
- own victimisation;
- social skills;
- fear reduction;
- substance abuse;
- eating problems;
- identity and self-esteem;
- nature and ecology;
- ethical concerns;
- personal perspectives;
- spirituality.

In most cases the first goal is to stop the stalking and/or violent behavior and then to solve any underlying problems. In cases of escalation it is also of primary importance to prevent any violent outbursts, often only achievable in close cooperation with other disciplines, especially law enforcement authorities. After the offence-focused approach we consider the specific therapeutic challenges related to the individual case.

The offence-focused treatment is illustrated in the Figure 6.3. It is also important to acknowledge the importance of using different therapeutic approaches depending on the underlying causes as indicated in Figure 6.3. With regards to each:

Delusional problems

As clinicians in stalking cases we can be confronted with delusional disorders (297.1 DSM-IV, F 22.0 ICD-10). The diagnostic criteria for this include as follows (DSM-IV 2000):

A   Nonbizarre delusions of at least one month's duration.
B   Criterion A for Schizophrenia[1] has never been met.
C   Apart from the impact of the delusion(s) or its ramifications, functioning is not markedly impaired and behavior is not obviously odd or bizarre.
D   If mood episodes have occurred concurrently with delusions, their total duration has been brief relative to the duration of the delusional periods.
E   The disturbance is not due to the direct physiological effects of a substance or a general medical condition.

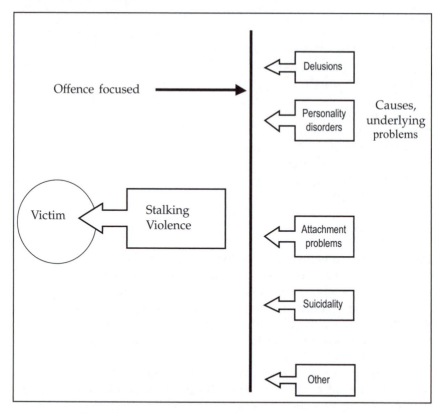

Figure 6.3 The offence-focused approach

Specific types include: Erotomanic type: delusions that another person, usually higher in status, is in love with the individual (see DSM-IV for other examples).

In clinical practice the delusional disorder is the duty of the treating psychiatrist 'to judge what is right and what is wrong, what is true and what is not' (Musalek 2003: 156). The disorder undermines the social judgment and functioning of the affected person, especially in erotomania: 'The patient suffering from delusional ideas is no longer able to decide what he or she wants to do: the delusional convictions move the patient' (Musalek 2003: 157). In the therapeutic process, a reliable working situation must be established, where affected individuals feel able to communicate their difficulties and perspectives. Cognitive restructuring combined with neuroleptic treatment is the preferred method of choice. For the treating therapist it is important to note that delusional disorders are much more prevalent in daily practice than described by clinical-based research.

Personality disorders

Personality disorders are described as an enduring pattern of inner experience and behaviour that deviates markedly from the expectations of the individual's culture. It is pervasive and inflexible, has an onset in adolescence or early childhood, is stable over time, and leads to distress or impairment. The DSM-IV lists ten different types of personality disorders, based on the predominant personality aspects (301.0 – 301.9 DSM IV, F60-62 ICD-10). The diagnostic criteria for a personality disorder according to the DSM-IV are:

A   An enduring pattern of inner experience and behaviour that deviates markedly from the expectations of the individual's culture. This pattern is manifested in two (or more) of the following areas: (1) cognition (2) affectivity (3) interpersonal functioning (4) impulse control

B   The enduring pattern is inflexible and pervasive across a broad range of personal and social situations.

C   The enduring pattern leads to clinically significant distress or impairment in social, occupational, or other important areas of functioning.

D   The pattern is stable and of long duration, and its onset can be traced back at least to adolescence or early adulthood.

E   The enduring pattern is not better accounted for as a manifestation or consequence of another mental disorder.

F   The enduring pattern is not due to the direct physiological effects of a substance or a general medical condition.

This categorical perspective is enlarged by the dimensional perspective that personality disorders represent maladaptive variants of personality traits that merge imperceptibly into normality and into one another.

In accordance with Fiedler (2001), the diagnosis of a personality disorder can only be made: (1) when someone suffers under his/her personality traits, (2) when they are relevant for the development of another psychiatric disorder (e.g. affective disorder, suicidality, etc.); and (3) if the person due to his/her personality problems faces social difficulties (e.g. ethical or legal conflicts). The treatment itself is goal-oriented and focused on individual needs, but also considers resources and positive aspects.

Attachment problems

Attachment difficulties, especially in adulthood, are not yet included into the categorical diagnostic systems in psychiatry. In the DSM-IV they are addressed as relational problems, without receiving the professional attention that they deserve. There is a diagnosis 313.89 *Reactive Attachment Disorder of Infancy or Early Childhood*, but for adults no diagnostic entity exists. This raises critical philosophical questions about the approaches and concepts of current psychiatry, the keyword being: the neglect of attachment. As interpersonal violence is always a relational problem, there is an urgent need to reconsider the understanding of psychiatric problems from a perspective of attachment theory. For the treatment of violent offenders this approach opens a wide range of intervention strategies, as in many cases the attachment problems play a crucial role in its development.

Attachment interventions are based on a comprehensive understanding of adult inner working models, and their modification through corrective attachment therapy (Levy and Orlans 2000). In many cases, past traumatic experiences have a deep impact on the development of inner working models (Bowlby 1988), self-esteem (Fonagy *et al.* 2002) and adult relationships (Levy and Orlans 1998). However, attachment problems can never be an excuse for an unacceptable dissocial behaviour.

Suicidality

Psychiatrists must have a comprehensive understanding of treating suicidal patients. In stalking and violent cases, a suicidal person can become extremely dangerous. She or he no longer fears any consequences, either for him or herself or for others. A thorough suicidal risk assessment is a sine qua non requirement (Simon and Hales 2006), and always requires a risk assessment of extended suicide as well. Approximately one in four stalkers shows suicidal ideations (Mohandie *et al.* 2006).

Other

A wide range of other problems can be identified as determinants for violent behaviour, for example courting behaviour, revenge and poor social skills, to name but a few. There exists a variety of possible treatment approaches which will help to improve someone's abilities, e.g. social skills training to overcome dating problems.

The offence-focused approach avoids endless debates about the underlying causes, the theoretical foundations of the different hypotheses and the school-specific treatment modalities. Stalking and violence are considered an unacceptable complex social interaction between an offender and their victim. Treatment first aims to stop the violent behaviour; solving underlying problems is the second step. Of course, the two steps go hand in hand, and their division here is only for didactic purposes. When violent offenders realise that the treatment is aimed to help them, their motivation to participate increases significantly. To bring them into treatment, use of specific legislation may be necessary as their insight and motivation is often not present. There is a therapeutic bias, when the motivation is considered as a precondition for a successful treatment (Miller and Rollnick 1991). Rather, building motivation should be part of the treatment process.

Conclusions

Stalking and domestic violence are relational offences, where human attachment behaviour plays a crucial role. The dynamic between offender and victim illustrates how attitudes about acceptable behaviour contribute to the escalation in violent acts towards others. Any clinical risk assessment is always based on past experiences and predicts further developments. The short-term accuracy is generally high and decreases over time. Interactions are defensive when offenders are not directly involved and become offensive the more offenders are in the focus. The intervention dilemma describes the phenomenon that any form of intervention can contribute to an escalation. Defensive strategies carry lower risk than offensive strategies. Therefore, defensive strategies should be considered first and foremost.

A clinical risk assessment always goes hand in hand with case management. The information management process is also crucial and requires ongoing contact. It is also important to remember how the risk assessment is a process, not a single event, which integrates new developments. Finally, interpersonal violence is characterised by a range of different behaviour patterns, e.g. domestic violence, sexual violence, stalking. There is considerable overlap across these various forms, and there always exists a path to violent escalations where interventions are possible.

Note

1 Diagnostic criteria for Schizophrenia, A. Characteristic symptoms: two (or more) of the following, each present for a significant portion of time during a 1-month period (or less if successfully treated): (1) delusions (2) hallucinations (3) disorganized speech (4) grossly disorganized or catatonic behaviour (5) negative symptoms. Note: Only one Criterion A symptom is required if delusions are bizarre or hallucinations consists of a voice keeping up a running commentary on the person's behaviour or thoughts, or two or more voices conversing with each other (DSM-IV 2000: 312).

References

Anfang, S.A. and Appelbaum, P.S. (1996) 'Twenty years after Tarasoff: reviewing the duty to protect' *Harvard Review of Psychiatry*, 4: 67–76.

Bowlby, J. (1988) *A Secure Base*. London: Routledge.

Dutton, D.G. (2006) *Rethinking Domestic Violence*. Vancouver, BC: University of British Columbia Press.

Dye, M.L. and Keith, E.D. (2003) 'Stalking and psychosocial abuse: common factors and relationship-specific characteristics', *Violence and Victims*, 18: 163–80.

Fiedler, P. (2001) *Persönlichkeitsstörungen*. Weinheim: Psychologie Verlags Union, p. 5.

Fonagy, P., György, G., Jurist, E.L. and Target, M. (eds) (2002) *Affect Regulation, Mentalization, and the Development of the Self*. New York: Other Press.

Gavaghan, C. (2007) 'A Tarasoff for Europe? A European human rights perspective on the duty to protect', *International Journal of Law and Psychiatry*, 30: 255–67.

Hibbard, R.A. and Zollinger, T.W. (1990) 'Patterns of child sexual abuse knowledge among professionals', *Child Abuse and Neglect*, 14: 347–55.

Kamphuis, J.H., Emmelkamp, P.M.G. and de Vries, V. (2004) 'Informant personality descriptions of post intimate stalkers using the five factor profile', *Journal of Personality Assessment*, 82: 169–78.

Krug, E.G., Dahlberg, L.L., Mercy, J.A., Zwi, A.B. and Lozano, R. (2002) *World Report on Violence and Health*. Geneva: World Health Organisation.

Le Doux, J. (1996) *The Emotional Brain: The Mysterious Underpinnings of Emotional Life*. New York: Simon & Schuster.

Leong, G.B. (1994) 'De Clérambault Syndrome (erotomania) in the criminal justice system: another look at this recurring problem', *Journal of Forensic Science*, 39: 378–85.

Levy, T.M. and Orlans, M. (1998) *Attachment, Trauma, and Healing. Understanding and Treating Attachment Disorder in Children and Families*. Washington, DC: CWLA.

Levy, T.M. and Orlans, M. (2000) 'Attachment disorder as an antecedent to violence and antisocial patterns in children', in T.M. Levy (ed.), *Handbook of Attachment Interventions*. San Diego, CA: Academic Press.

Lewis, S.F., Fremouw, W.J., Del Ben, K. and Farr, C. (2001) 'An investigation of the psychological characteristics of stalkers: empathy, problem-solving, attachment and borderline personality features', *Journal of Forensic Science*, 46: 80–4.

Meloy, R.J. (1992) *Violent Attachments*. Northvale, NJ: Jason Aronson.

Miller, W.R. and Rollnick, S. (1991) *Motivational Interviewing: Preparing People to Change Addictive Behaviour*. New York: Guilford.

Mohandie, K., Meloy R.J., McGowan, M.G. and Williams, J. (2006) 'The RECON typology of stalking: reliability and validity based upon a large sample of North American stalkers', *Journal of Forensic Sciences*, 51: 147–55.

Mullen, P.E. (2007) 'Foreword', in D.A. Pinals (ed.), *Stalking: Psychiatric Perspectives and Practical Approaches*. Oxford: Oxford University Press, pp. vii–x.

Musalek, M (2003) 'Meaning and causes of delusions', in B. Fulford, K. Morris, J. Sadler and G. Stanghellini (eds), *Nature and Narrative. An Introduction to the New Philosophy of Psychiatry*. Oxford: Oxford University Press, pp. 155–69.

NZZ (2007) 'Weitere Versämnisse vor dem Totungsdelikt?', *Neue Zürcher Zetitung*, 232.

Simon, R.I. and Hales, R.E. (2006) *Textbook of Suicide Assessment and Management*. Washington, DC: American Psychiatric Publishing.

Tschan, W. (2006) 'Deliktfokussierte Behandlung von Stalkern', in J. Hoffmann and H.G.W. Voss (eds), *Psychologie des Stalking*. Frankfurt: Verlag für Polizeiwissenschaften, pp. 213–34.

Voss, H.-G.W. (2004) 'Zur Psychologie des Stalkings', in J. Bettermann and M. Feenders (eds), *Stalking. Möglichkeiten und Grenzen der Intervention*. Frankfurt: Verlag für Polizeiwissenschaft.

Ward, T., Polaschek, D.L.L. and Beech, A.R. (2006) *Theories of Sexual Offending*. Chichester: Wiley.

White, S.G. and Cawood, J.S. (1998) 'Threat management of stalking cases', in J. Reid Meloy (ed.), *The Psychology of Stalking*. San Diego, CA: Academic Press, pp. 295–315.

Zonana, H., Abel, G., Bradford, J., Hoge, S.K., Metzner, J., Becker, J., Bonnie, R., Fitch, L. and Hughes, L. (1999) 'Preface', in *Dangerous Sex Offenders: A Task Force Report of the American Psychiatric Association*. Washington, DC: American Psychiatric Association, p. vii.

Part 2

Treatment

Chapter 7

Treatment approaches for violence and aggression: essential content components

Jane L. Ireland

The current chapter aims to provide an outline of recommended content for violence/aggression therapy. It aims to provide a review rather than detailed analysis of the core approaches required for effective treatment. Points will be illustrated where possible using elements of a recently developed and revised violence treatment programme (Life Minus Violence: see Ireland 2007, and Chapter 4, this volume). Focus will be on the concept of habitual aggression (i.e. repeated aggression), since it is habitual aggressors who are most likely to come into contact with professional services for aggression management.

Regardless of the exact nature or emphasis of therapy for violence and aggression there are five domains that treatment should have in common if they are to begin to reflect the treatment needs of habitual aggressors. These are the areas of:

1 information processing;
2 emotional acceptance, reactivity and regulation;
3 developmental changes (including learning history);
4 aggression motivation; and
5 relapse prevention.

These five areas are integral to the core aggression literature, particularly the first four, with relapse prevention more commonly found in the antisocial literature base. Researchers and clinicians who concern themselves solely with the antisocial literature base, however, are at risk of neglecting the importance and influence of information processing, emotions, developmental changes and aggression motivation in particular. As discussed in Chapter 4, there is overlap between the aggression and antisocial literature (Ireland 2007; Tremblay and Côté 2005), but an over-focus on the latter will lead to the neglect of core aggression theory and literature, as appears to have happened with some 'violence' treatment approaches (e.g. Violence Reduction Programme: Wong *et al.* 2007) which arguably are more *antisocial* management programmes than *aggression* management.

The importance of accounting for developmental changes and aggression motivation (areas 3 and 4) are covered in detail in Chapter 4, and readers are thus referred there for a comprehensive discussion of the importance of these two topics. Focus in the current chapter will be on the importance of incorporating the three areas of information processing, emotions and relapse prevention. What will become apparent as the chapter progresses is the complex interplay between information processing and emotion. This highlights how separating these two areas clinically is artificial and that both also feature in relapse prevention which, like information processing and emotions, has to form a core component of therapy.

Treatment content I: information processing

Information processing theory, specifically social information processing, should underpin all attempts to understand and treat aggressive behaviour. This is because it is recognised as a primary theory underpinning the development and maintenance of aggression (e.g. Fontaine 2006; Huesmann 1998). Although a number of information processing models exist, only a small number have had focused application to human behaviour, with a number of models originally developed to explain computer processing and artificial intelligence. One of the most popular models applied to human behaviour was that of Dodge (1986). This conceptualised an individual's behavioural responses to a social situation to follow a series of information processing steps. The steps, in order, include:

(a) encoding social cues in the environment;
(b) forming a mental representation and interpretation of these cues;
(c) searching for a possible behavioural response;
(d) deciding on a response;
(e) enacting the chosen response.

In a reformulation of this model, Crick and Dodge (1994) proposed that information processing should not be viewed as rigidly sequential, and that the processing of information at each step should be seen as occurring in simultaneous parallel paths. Crick and Dodge (1994) argued that in reality individuals will be engaged in multiple social information-processing activities at the same time. Dodge (1986) also argued that biases or deficits within any of the processing steps could lead to an aggressive behavioural response.

A later model by Huesmann (first proposed in 1988 but updated in 1998) attempted to take these models one step further, by integrating the previous information processing models into one 'Unified Model of Information Processing'. This model incorporated the importance of:

- Social scripts, namely 'guides to social actions'. Scripts basically represent behavioural scripts which can be enacted following the presentation of a stimulus such as a triggering event.
- Normative beliefs, i.e. the beliefs an individual holds which they believe others hold, and which endorse acceptability of violence in some situations. An example of which may be 'It's OK to hit someone who hits you'.
- Emotions and the way in which these can impact on processing ability, belief activation and script choice.
- Perception-errors, namely 'hostile attribution biases' where an aggressive individual will demonstrate a bias towards misinterpreting the actions of others and, specifically, see hostility in ambiguous or neutral situations (Huesmann 1998).

All four concepts – emotions, normative beliefs, scripts and hostile attribution biases – are important to explore and/or challenge during therapy since their amendment, alteration and/or management is likely to lead to a reduction in aggression expression. The unified model also favoured a true *processing* approach to understanding aggression as opposed to a 'problem-solving' approach. Earlier models such as those of Dodge (1986) and Crick and Dodge (1994) based their models on the premise that certain social interactions are labelled as a problem by the individual involved when this may not be the case. Indeed, the unified model is not presented as a deficiency model where it is automatically assumed that aggression is a product of a skills deficit. Rather, it is accepted that aggression can have an adaptive function and be representative of skill. This is not to say, however, that aggression is acceptable: at a prosocial level clearly it is not. However, there does need to be at least an acceptance that aggression, in some instances, can represent an adaptive and effective method by which to deal with conflict.

Adopting an information-processing approach to understanding and managing aggression is important as it allows for a focus on the processes (i.e. decisions) involved (Rubin and Krasnor 1986), particularly with regard to interpersonal aggression (Hastings 2000). It is also in keeping with research emphasising social cognition and social cognitive influences in offending behaviour (Bennett *et al.* 2005). One of the most important elements of the information processing approach is the aforementioned concept of a cognitive 'script'. Scripts represent a sequence of actions that correspond to a familiar situation. Once an individual enters a script, the scripted behaviours then proceed relatively automatically (Rubin and Krasnor 1986).

Scripts

The concept of a script is important when discussing how strategies are accessed and selected by an individual. Strategy retrieval can either be scripted and automatic or a conscious and deliberate process. However, all strategies must already exist in the individual's repertoire. To illustrate an example of a basic social script, consider the task of ordering food in a restaurant. A common script would proceed as follows:

1 Enter the restaurant.
2 Ask to be seated.
3 Request a menu.
4 Consider the menu.
5 Ask the waiter if you can order.
6 Order.

For individuals who have ordered in a restaurant previously, steps 2 to 6 would be triggered automatically upon entering the restaurant.

Strategy repertoires may vary in size, complexity and perceived acceptability and effectiveness (Rubin and Krasnor 1986), and they tend to increase with age (Crick and Dodge 1994). Once a strategy has been implemented and is viewed as successful, the social problem-solving process ends, with information about the success of this strategy retained by the individual, affecting where in future the strategy will fall in the individual's hierarchy of possible responses.

This results in the solution being accessed and implemented sooner in ensuing situations (Rubin and Krasnor 1986). Thus an individual who has used aggression to resolve conflict, who considers this to have been a successful strategy, is likely to store this response as a 'script' and access it sooner in future conflict.

Response generation

Research has also explored the response generation elements of problem-solving during conflict situations among aggressive children (e.g. steps (c) to (e) of Dodge's 1986 model), with research indicating that aggressive children tend to generate fewer solutions to social problems than non-aggressive children, and to produce initial solutions that are effective but *further* solutions that are likely to be ineffective (Richard and Dodge 1982). These aggressive individuals are felt to lack a *range* of effective solutions. Similarly, Pierce and Cohen (1995) argued that aggressive children not only produce fewer possible responses to conflict situations, but that they also produce more hostile responses than non-aggressive children and evaluate these (hostile) responses more favourably as they value the expected outcome of them. Perry *et al.* (1986) found that aggressive children were also more assured of their ability to utilise aggression in order to obtain their desired reward. From this, it is suggested that the aggressive child has learnt to value what can be achieved through aggression, and thus they are more likely than non-aggressive children to resort to aggression to attain what they want. The aggressive child formulates strong beliefs concerning the positive consequences of the use of aggression for the self, and attaches less value to its negative consequences (Pierce and Cohen 1995). There has also been confirmation of these findings within adult forensic samples, namely prisoners (e.g. Ireland 2001; Ireland and Archer 2002).

One of the advantages of social information *processing* models is their focus on individual cognitions and behaviours that are based on individual learning experiences and an individual's ability to retrieve solutions to actual or potential conflict. In this way they emphasise *individual* differences. A further advantage of both the unified and the reformulated models is their focus on parallel and not sequential processing: classic models such as that proposed by Dodge (1986) outlined a stage-by-stage process (i.e. one stage is completed before another), whereas it is more accepted now that stages can occur simultaneously (i.e. connectionist models of cognitive processing).

Treatment programmes for violence and aggression should, therefore, emphasise the simultaneous approach to social information processing, removing the focus on stage-by-stage approaches and encouraging offenders to consider their behaviour as something that occurred within a context of parallel processing, i.e. a behaviour that was influenced by past environmental elements (e.g. socialisation, learning and developmental experiences, cognitions), current situational elements (i.e. triggers or cues for aggression), affect (e.g. emotions) and cognitive processes simultaneously.

More recent aggression treatment programmes have attempted to incorporate information processing explicitly within treatment delivery. One illustrative example is the Life Minus Violence – Enhanced (LMV-E) programme where the parallel nature of processing is examined by breaking aggressive incidents down into a series of 'choice steps' or 'links' using an approach known as 'Aggression Choice Chains' (ACCs) and 'Non-Aggression Choice Chains' (NACCs). The former explores an aggressive incident and the latter how the aggressive incident could have been converted into a non-aggressive incident though a challenging of normative beliefs and cognitions, by widening the non-aggressive scripts available and by encouraging more reflection on the negative consequences of choosing an aggressive response.

To reflect the notion of simultaneous processing, each individual 'choice step' is depicted in a circular fashion with beliefs, cognitions ('fleeting thoughts') and emotions integrated into the information processing elements required to make a choice, i.e. identifying the situation; determining the available choices; evaluating these possible choices; making and enacting a choice; and evaluating the consequences of this choice. Offenders complete between six and eight choices or 'links' for each aggressive incident. An example of a blank choice step and a completed choice step for one link from an aggression choice chain are represented in Figures 7.1 and 7.2.

What is evident from Figures 7.1 and 7.2 is the integration of emotion around all elements of processing. Emotion is not conceptualised as a separate stage but as a fully incorporated element. Although emotions are clearly embedded into information processing models they are such a significantly important area to include that they require separate discussion.

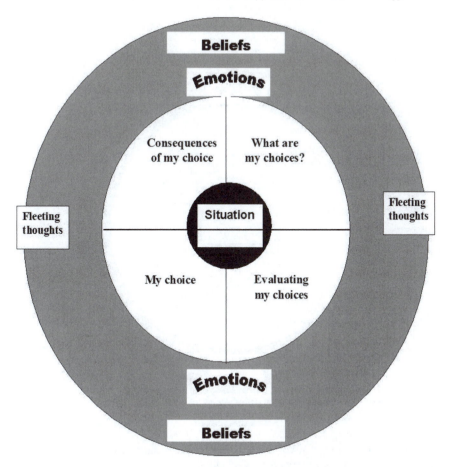

Figure 7.1 Example of a blank link from an Aggression Choice Chain
© *Life Minus Violence Programme – Enhanced*.

Treatment content II: emotional regulation, acceptance and reactivity

The concept of emotions is an important one to include within aggression management programmes. This is captured well by Steffgen and Gollwitzer (2007) who state: 'Emotions are not merely epiphenomena of aggression; they can be triggers, amplifiers, moderators, even ultimate goals of aggressive behaviour' (p. iii). Indeed, Steffgen and Gollwitzer reflect on the importance of understanding the functional link between emotions and aggression, highlighting its value not only

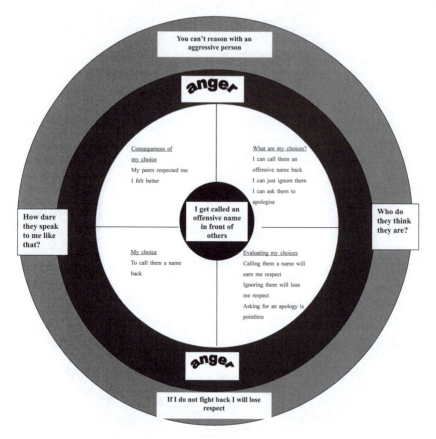

Figure 7.2 Example of a completed link from an aggression choice chain.
© *Life Minus Violence Programme – Enhanced.*

for a theoretical understanding of violence but also for its efficient control, prevention and amelioration.

Despite an acknowledged link between aggression and emotion there remains few writings which have focused on this concept jointly (Steffgen and Gollwitzer 2007). There has also been an over-focus on emotion as a 'static' concept, and on the role of anger alone. With regard to the former issue, it is important also to acknowledge a strong developmental aspect to the actual experiencing of emotion. This is an often neglected finding; for example, the older the client the longer it may take for them to become emotionally aroused to a stimulus, particularly in more advanced age, but once aroused their emotions may be experienced more intensely (Schulz 1985), depending on the circumstances and mood state (Kunzmann and Grühn 2005). Recognising the importance of developmental changes is vital since treatment cannot presuppose that individuals have generic needs; their individual development needs to be accounted for, with a recognition that change in presentation will inevitably occur over time (see also Chapter 4 on developmental changes in aggression).

With regard to the link between anger and aggression, this has been studied extensively, often with anger conceptualised as an antecedent (e.g. Davey *et al.* 2005; Baumeister and Bushman 2007). It is certainly the case that the subjective experience of anger is closely related to the expression of aggression, although the importance of not overstating the association is noted, with various mediating factors known to increase or decrease the potential for aggression in an individual experiencing anger (Baumeister and Bushman 2007). It is also recognised that there is a range of further emotions important to account for in any understanding of aggression, such as fear, anxiety, pain, shame, guilt, jealousy, envy, excitement, pleasure, frustration, rejection and humiliation (Baumeister and Bushman 2007; Ireland 2007; Montada 2007), to name but a few. Shame in particular has been related to increased aggression as has pain, whereas guilt is reported to have an inhibitory effect (Montada 2007). All emotions are important, however, in that all are associated with physiological arousal, either high or low arousal, which in turn can interfere with an individual's ability to process information (Huesmann 1998).

The emotion of anger does appear to have dominated aggression treatment programmes as a treatment target, with the full range of emotions rarely considered. There is also a tendency to explore the concept of 'stress' separately and not to reflect on the integration of this concept with emotion (Verona *et al.* 2007). Stress, for example, is equally related to emotions aside from anger, for example frustration and anxiety. Indeed, it may be the *combination* of negative emotion and an individual's perception that this is stressful which can produce an aggressive response. This highlights the importance of integrating stress formally into emotion-component modules of aggression programmes, as opposed to considering 'stress management' as a separate isolated treatment target. Thus although the current section may use the emotion of anger to illustrate learning points this is in no way an attempt to exclude the importance of other emotions.

Regardless of the emotion under study, however, there remains a core truism: emotion is a subjective experience often accompanied by a physiological reaction and an individual's evaluation or rather *cognitive appraisal* of this (Baumeister and Bushman 2007; Montada 2007). Appraisal represents the cognitive component of interpretation, and explains why emotion features explicitly in more recent information processing models (e.g. Huesmann's 1998 Unified Model). Emotions can also be conceptualised as helpful and unhelpful. For example, the experience of fear can drive a protective avoidance reaction in the face of a threat, with the emotion of pain a method by which continued harm can be reduced. Unhelpful components of emotion can include chronic experiences of emotion which lead to a maladaptive response such as non-adaptive aggression.

It is not sufficient to simply refer to 'emotional management', however, as the target for treatment. The concept of emotional management is more complex and comprises three elements; acceptance, regulation and reactivity. *Acceptance* refers to the importance of not trying to inhibit or suppress emotion, and particularly the cognitions underpinning this (a point that will be addressed later). *Regulation* describes the strategies an individual employs consciously or subconsciously to manage emotion, either cognitive strategies and/or behavioural. *Reactivity* is the extent to which an individual reacts to a negative or positive event (e.g. Kunzmann and Grühn 2005), with this often coexisting with emotional acceptance. Aggression treatment programmes need to cover all three areas – acceptance, regulation and reactivity – when addressing emotional management strategies with aggressors. The focus clinically has tended to be on the regulation component alone, perhaps because it represents the most overt and tangible approach to convey to clients.

Somewhat integral to the areas of emotions and aggression is the concept of under- and over-controlled aggression. This was originally proposed as a rather simplistic dichotomous approach describing how emotion, specifically anger, can relate to expressions of aggression (Megargee 1966). The original conceptualisation described over-controlled aggressors as those for whom a strategy for ignoring emotions had developed, resulting in emotions only being identified when they become overwhelming. Thus these were the classic non-acceptors of emotion. Under-controlled aggressors, by contrast, over-attend to emotion, resulting in an inability to manage even minor emotional fluctuations. Their aggression fits more, therefore, within the reactivity component of emotion management. To illustrate, examples of an under-controlled and an over-controlled aggressor are depicted in Figure 7.3.

- **Over-controlled**

Tony is convicted of a serious assault towards his ex-wife's new partner. He talks about a 'red mist descending' prior to the assault. He does not have a history of previous aggression and there are no reports of frequent anger loss. His victim sustained 25 stab wounds, leading to a punctured lung.

- **Under-controlled**

Mark has been on the ward for five months. In this time he averages four incidents of verbal aggression a week, with eight counts of physical aggression. He reports feeling that he has to protect himself against other patients and thus 'attacks first'. He reports that his verbal aggression is always motivated by anger whereas his physical aggression is sometimes motivated by a wish to leave a situation as he feels unsafe.

Figure 7.3 Examples of under- and over-controlled aggression

In clinical practice the over-controlled aggressor can present as more severe since the act of their aggression appears to far outweigh the reported antecedents. Conversely, the under-controlled aggressor presents as an individual seemingly reacting to all actual and perceived provocations. It is, however, more appropriate to consider under- and over-controlled as representing the opposing ends of a continuum. Those placed more towards the under-controlled end of the spectrum present with treatment needs focused more on the control of emotion (i.e. the classic emotional regulation component) and those towards the over-controlled end with treatment needs focused more on emotional acceptance. For example, with a client who finds it challenging to accept emotion, treatment would focus on recognising and restructuring the emotional experience and associated cognitions, as opposed to simply ignoring the emotion. In clinical practice, however, it is often more complicated than a case of simply placing someone on a single continuum of under- or over-controlled. Individuals are more complex and it can be unrealistic to view their behaviour in a polarised fashion: often they will present with components of both under- and over-control depending on the circumstances and the specific emotion under study.

A comment on the structuring of cognitions is, however, important at this point. What should *not* be recommended as part of treatment is the suppression of cognitions since this can have the opposite effect, increasing the existence of the cognitions (and raising physiological arousal). Encouraging thought suppression or thought inhibition (e.g. 'Just try and stop having those angry thoughts') may make logical sense to some clinicians but it is counter-productive; the very act of thought suppression produces an eliciting and cyclic effect. It either raises the perception of emotional stress which can serve to promote an aggressive reaction or it encourages cognition rumination and/ or rehearsal (fantasy). This issue of thought suppression has been reflected on extensively in the cognitive literature, and it has been applied to aggression (e.g. Davey *et al.* 2005). It has been referred to as the 'white bear effect' following the anecdote provided by Tolstoy where he had reportedly challenged his brother to stand in a corner of a room until he could no longer think of white bears (Wegner 1989), the consequence of which being that the brother stood for some considerable time. The point from this is simply that the more we try to suppress a thought the more intrusive it becomes.

Wegner (1989) argued that it is the very act of thought suppression that makes a thought more intrusive. Nagtegaal and Rassin (2003) applied this to violence, supporting their assertion that intrusive thoughts and thought suppression were positively related to aggression. Thought suppression also ties in well with information processing models where frequently imagined violence is considered a form of elaborate rehearsal. Such rehearsal reinforces schemata or existing emotional memories which then drive how an individual perceives an event and acts on it. Indeed, repetitive violent thoughts are considered to activate aggressive scripts and schemata, making them more accessible for the aggressor (Nagtegaal and Rassin 2003).

Thought suppression is an important point to note for clinical as well as research purposes. There is a risk that over-controlled aggressors, through the act of encouraging them to accept their emotions, could be at risk of developing intrusive cognitions if this is not carefully managed. Conversely, with over-controlled aggressors what is not advised is the suppression of the frequently experienced cognitions (e.g. angry thoughts) that are causing them difficulty. Rather, from a clinical perspective, the focus should be on restructuring cognitions by increasing challenging cognitions or counter-cognitions (e.g. instead of angry thoughts habitualising 'cool' or calming thoughts), and by the use of behavioural distraction (e.g. teaching engagement in an absorbing activity), and *not* instructing the suppression of aggressive thoughts.

In view of the interplay between cognitions and emotion in aggression expression it is important to digress slightly at this point to the method by which emotions can be engendered in a controlled fashion during therapy. Identifying the existence of true aggressive cognitions can be challenging if clients are requested to volunteer these in conditions of 'cold cognition', i.e. when they are not emotionally aroused. If a memory of an aggressive incident is to be accessed, and it is accepted that emotion is a core component of how this incident has been processed and stored in memory, then emotions needs to be accessed in order to reach cognition.

Thus a condition of 'hot cognition' (i.e. a state of arousal) needs to be induced in a controlled fashion; once in this condition a client is then required to access the relevant cognitions. Put simply, if someone committed an act of aggression when in a state of anger arousal then inducing a controlled form of that arousal can be helpful in accessing the true angry cognitions that they experienced, cognitions which can then be restructured. This is a concept that has been referred by some as 'remember what you feel' (Laird *et al.* 1982).

This is not, however, an issue of creating the same level of arousal; rather the aim is to *mimic* the emotional state. There are controlled methods available for inducing mood although most have been applied to experimental research paradigms. The Life Minus Violence – Enhanced (LMV-E) programme, for example, utilises Mood Induction Procedures (MIPs: see Burkitt and Barnett 2006, and Kliegel *et al.* 2007), since these have clinical application and have been used in a controlled fashion successfully. The specific MIPs used in LMV-E focus on accessing autobiographical memory since this is one of the easiest induction procedures to introduce, control and manage. Offenders are asked to recall an event that they have experienced relevant to the mood that is being induced. They are asked to focus on:

1 Where they were.
2 When it occurred.
3 Who was involved.
4 What happened.
5 What in particular had induced the mood.

There are a number of steps which accompany this mood induction procedure which are outside the scope of the current chapter. However, once the mood is induced, or rather mimicked, offenders are then invited to access relevant cognitions. Not only are such techniques used to access emotional memory for specific aggressive incidents of interest, but they are also used to access emotional memory for non-aggressive incidents to access already existing non-aggressive cognitions. MIPs are also utilised to demonstrate to offenders learning points concerning the impact of emotion on processing, and in particular the influence of emotion on script choice and schema activation.

To return now briefly to the concept of under- and over-controlled aggression. As noted earlier, this has had most application to the emotion of anger when in fact its application could easily be extended to other subjective emotions and experiences (e.g. shame, guilt, stress, etc.). Similarly, the classic 'over-under' controlled continuum, although certainly of value, does little to explain the function of expressed aggressive behaviour and the functional link between emotion and aggression. For this a complete functional assessment is required (see Chapter 4).

There have also been attempts to try and refine the classification system of Megargee. Blackburn (1993), for example, has suggested the separation of over-controlled aggressors into two types: a conforming type and an inhibiting type. Put simply, the former refers to an individual who denies their emotions (e.g. 'I never get angry') whereas the inhibiting type is someone who does not deny their emotions but who is unable to inform others of them (e.g. 'I feel angry but I am scared to tell anyone'). Conforming types are thought to be socially skilled whereas the inhibiting type are more socially avoidant. The inclusion of these two types is of use in that they demonstrate the true complexity of individual behaviour.

For example, the conforming type could be described as an individual who does not engage in rumination or have aggressive-supporting cognitions to the same extent as other aggressors (Davey *et al*. 2005). They would fit more with the concept of an individual failing to *accept* emotions in their entirety. The function of their emotional denial may be one of wishing to maintain an outward presentation of control. In short they could represent the aggressor who has total non-acceptance of emotion. The inhibiting type, however, is thought to be characterised by cognitive rumination and rehearsal (Blackburn 1993), and thus would fit more with the *reactivity* element of emotion, i.e. reacting to experiences via rumination and rehearsal as opposed to non-acceptance. This illustration simply highlights the importance of being clear of a client's presenting emotional management difficulty, i.e. is it emotional non-acceptance or is it emotional reactivity? The decision on this point will help to determine a more individualised treatment pathway.

What this section has aimed to illustrate is the importance of considering emotion and its link to aggression expression in detail. The *functional* link between aggression and emotion and how an individual has *appraised* their experience is essential to understand in each individual case. Simply focusing on the subjective name that is given to the emotion (e.g. 'anger', 'fear', 'shame'), does little to drive a treatment approach. The label a client provides to their own emotion is a subjective one. Thus treating the label is too simplistic. Rather the focus has to be on how the individual has cognitively appraised their emotional experience. Similarly, the focus of aggression treatment has to include an individual's ability to *accept* and *regulate* their emotions, coupled with a detailed understanding of the maladaptive *reactive* strategies that they may have employed. Thus there are five essential components that need to be considered in any treatment approach – function, cognitive appraisal, acceptance, regulation and reactivity. These components should then automatically inform individualised relapse prevention plans designed to reduce expressions of aggression.

Treatment content III: relapse prevention

Relapse prevention is a core element of overall treatment provision and should have a significant proportion of treatment time allocated to it. It should not be considered an afterthought or confused with maintenance or booster elements of treatment. Relapse prevention has had application to a range of problematic presentations including addictive behaviour (Marlatt and Donovan 2005), mental illness (Hewitt and Birchwood 2002) and offending behaviour, most notably sex offending (Ward and Brown 2004; Laws *et al.* 2001). It covers the identification of triggers and cues that occur prior to lapses or relapses, and helps in developing strategies for managing this via adaptive coping skills (Meuser 2004) with a focus on behavioural practice (e.g. role-play rehearsal). The procedures employed as part of relapse prevention focus on enhancing a client's self-management skills to maintain the change already begun by therapy. In essence, it is the component in which further consolidation of learning can be achieved.

Although there are a number of models of relapse prevention in existence (e.g. Martlatt and Gordon 1985, applied to substance misuse; Pithers *et al.* 1988, and Laws *et al.* 2001, applied to sex offending), criticisms have been levelled on conceptual and empirical grounds

(Ward 2000). Ward (2000) proposed a comprehensive model of relapse prevention termed the Self-Regulation Model of the Relapse Process (SRM-RP), which accounted for the criticisms of previous models.

This model arguably has strong application to violence treatment: it is comprehensive, and accounts for a number of pathways towards relapse that take into account different types of goals, varying emotional states and different types of planning. It accounts also for the dynamic nature of offending, the influence of background factors, distal (distant) vulnerability factors, decision-making and how this contributed to high-risk situations, initial lapses, the offence itself and the impact of the offence on subsequent offending. In many ways this model shares similarities with the unified information processing model described earlier, although the two have, unfortunately, not been brought together in the literature. Similarities between the two models should be acknowledged, however, and can be noted as follows:

- Both include attention to the importance and integration of emotion.
- Planning in the SRM-RP equates to script selection.
- Goals and decision-making in the SRM-RP equates to script selection and evaluation.
- 'Offence' equates to script enactment.
- 'Impact of offence' equates to script evaluation.

The Self-Regulation Model also accounts for the psychological mechanisms that drive or inhibit the process of relapse (Ward 2000). It outlines how individuals can experience three major problems with self-regulation.

1 A failure to control their behaviour and emotions, acting in a disinhibited way. For example, repeatedly failing to control feelings of humiliation leading to overt expressions of displeasure such as shouting (i.e. under-controlled aggression). Or, over-inhibiting emotional responses leading to an over-controlled expression of aggression which could, seemingly, be to a minor provocation.

2 Use of ineffective strategies to achieve goals that fail and result in a loss of control (e.g. wanting to be liked by peers resulting in going to extreme lengths to try and gain admiration, such as drinking to excess, becoming inebriated and consequently losing control). This would equate to the notion of selecting scripts that are not going to produce success (i.e. information processing models).

3 Having initial goals that are unhelpful and/or that are associated with offence-supportive values and beliefs (e.g. feeling that the only way to obtain respect from others is to demonstrate your physical prowess through acts of aggression. This is likely linked to a normative belief concerning the acceptability of physical aggression, and again parallels with information processing models).

The Self-Regulation Model comprises nine phases and, in keeping with information processing models, emphasises the importance of parallel processing and how the phases can appear non-sequential for an individual (Ward 2000). Although the application of this model has been applied to understanding sex offending, its comprehensive nature and reformulation of previous models ensures its value to aggression as a whole is enhanced. The stages, taken from Ward (2000) are:

- *Phase 1 - Life event.* An event occurs which is appraised by an individual in a way likely to initiate the activation of a goal or behaviour that may bring them closer to offending (e.g. accessing an aggressive script).

- *Phase 2 – Desire for a 'deviant' act.* The emergence of a desire to engage in maladaptive activity. This desire is likely to be triggered by an individual's learning history (e.g. a learned or normative belief that aggression has positive consequences).

- *Phase 3 – Offence-related goals established.* The desire to engage in a maladaptive behaviour results in the establishment of an offence-related goal. At this point an offender will begin to consider how acceptable the desire is and what, if anything, should be done about it. Thus an aggressive script is selected, evaluated and a behavioural plan of enactment considered. Two goals come into play here – avoidance (i.e. not to aggress) and approach (i.e. planning to aggress), with avoidance goals potentially more difficult to employ, particularly if a high emotional state/psychological distress is evident.

- *Phase 4 – Strategy selected.* The selection of a strategy to reach a goal, whether this is a desire to avoid offending or not. Four pathways are outlined: *avoidance-passive* where an individual desires to avoid offending but actively fails to do so; *avoidance-active* where an individual makes an active attempt to avoid offending; *approach-automatic* where an individual automatically follows an over-learned behavioural aggressive script designed to lead to an offence; *approach-explicit* where there is a conscious and well planned strategy developed to commit an offence.

- *Phase 5 – High-risk situation entered.* For example, contact with a high-risk victim group, the outcome of which will be based on the strategy selected at Phase 4.

- *Phase 6 - Lapse.* The immediate precursors to an offence, e.g. possibly obtaining a weapon and walking towards a victim. In essence this is the phase where an offender has lapsed and is intending to commit an offence and becomes preoccupied with the positive consequences that they associate with the aggression.

- *Phase 7 – Offence.* The aggression is committed, accompanied either by positive or negative emotional states depending on the nature of the goal (see phase 4). For example:
  - *Approach goals* may be accompanied by a positive emotional state such as excitement, where an offender has actively planned and then commits an offence.
  - *Avoidance goals* may be accompanied by negative emotional states such as anger which an offender feels unable to control, despite their desire to avoid committing an offence.

- *Phase 8 – Post-offence evaluation.* Evaluation of the aggression. For example, offenders following avoidant pathways may evaluate themselves negatively and feel guilt or shame; those following the approach pathways are hypothesised to experience more positive affect (e.g. pride, feelings of success).

- *Phase 9 – Attitudes towards future offending.* The impact of the offence on future intentions and expectations and, in essence, an evaluation of goals. For example, those following the *approach-automatic* pathway are thought likely to have their behavioural scripts associated with offending reinforced because they evaluate the behaviour as a 'successful' one, i.e. one with positive gain; those using the *approach-explicit* pathway are expected to continue to refine and develop their abusive strategies, in essence to learn what worked and what did not (to increase success or to raise the level of positive emotion experienced).

Figure 7.4 presents an illustration of how these phases may present in a case example. Underlying this self-regulation model is the importance of assessing the goals which an offender presents with. For example, are their goals inhibiting a prosocial response? Are there normative beliefs evident serving to make an act of aggression 'OK'?

The goal of relapse prevention is to maintain awareness of what contributes to a lapse and a relapse, with a focus on the identification and management of high-risk situations. Thus, in treatment, the stages indicated in the Self-Regulation Model would be explored with an offender with a view to challenging and preventing the entering of a high-risk situation and a lapse.

Relapse prevention would achieve this by enhancing progress in other areas of functioning (e.g. social relationships, health, vocation), as opposed to simply focusing on the offending behaviour pattern. It is this latter element which should have a particular focus for violence treatment and where a model known as the 'Good Lives Model' (GLM: e.g. Ward and Brown 2004) becomes of particular significance to offender rehabilitation. Whereas the Self-Regulation Model outlines to offenders the *process* of relapse, the GLM provides more potential guidance for treatment and therapy in terms of understanding what are serving as *motivators* for individuals, namely what they are aiming to achieve and how this has changed over their life. The inclusion of this approach therefore brings in a further developmental aspect to treatment.

The GLM is a product of increased interest in 'positive psychology'. This approach argues for a focus on client strength as opposed to client weakness. The GLM has a strong basis in self-determination theory (Seligman 2002). It is thus certainly not a new theory, even though some areas of practice appear to market it as such. Rather, GLM is an application of existing founding psychological theory developed to understand individual motivation. It is an approach which aims to understand individual presentation by focusing on what are termed innate psychological needs (e.g. inherent/intrinsic needs) that form the basis for motivation and personality integration and the conditions required to foster this positive process. In essence it outlines the competences required for positive growth and integration, and for positive self-development and personal well-being (i.e. need to feel competent, need to feel connected with others and need for autonomy), while at the same time accounting for environmental factors serving to prevent or undermine self-motivation, social functioning and personal well-being (Ryan and Deci 2000). The GLM focuses specifically on the application of self-determination theory to offenders.

171

Phase	
Life event	Simon presents with a history of resentment to authority, a fear of being controlled and a tendency to over-attend to emotion. He has a history of using weapons during conflict situations. Simon's landlord sends him a letter telling him to clean his flat or he will be evicted. Simon feels that this is unfair and controlling, leading him to experience emotions of anger and humiliation.
Desire for a deviant act	Simon wishes to 'get back' at his landlord. He feels that the only way he can gain respect is to show his landlord that he cannot be controlled. Simon holds the belief that 'Aggression is a way of earning respect'. Simon feels that when he (Simon) has retaliated to attempts by others to control him, this has seemed effective.
Offence-related goal established	Simon feels highly aroused with regard to anger and humiliation which makes a goal of avoidance more difficult. He begins to ruminate on his landlord's perceived behaviour and plans how to 'get back' at him (i.e. *approach goal*).
Strategy selected	Simon plans to wait outside for his landlord when he comes to collect the rent as he knows he always does this on his own. Simon plans to threaten him and 'scare him off', and to 'show him who is in charge'. Simon plans to leave the flat with a flick-knife in his pocket (i.e. *approach-explicit strategy*).
High-risk situation entered	Simon waits for the landlord outside the flat.
Lapse	Simon goes up to the landlord when he arrives and tells him that he wants to speak to him. He checks that his knife is still in his back pocket as he wants to resolve this situation quickly. Simon is assured that using a weapon will get his point across more effectively.
Offence	Simon threatens the landlord with violence and holds the knife to his neck. Simon feels exhilarated and in control (i.e. an *approach goal* has been chosen and thus positive emotion is more likely).

Post- offence evaluation	Simon feels proud of himself, namely that he has handled the situation well and that the landlord will now leave him alone (i.e. an approach pathway chosen leading to the experiencing of positive affect).
Attitudes towards future offending	Simon evaluates the events again and decides that if the landlord does threaten him in the future he will need to clearer with his threats and perhaps involve his peers to help him threaten the landlord as well (i.e. an *approach-explicit* pathway linked in with the continued development of the aggressive strategy to promote further perceived success).

Figure 7.4 An application of the Ward (2000) self-regulation model to aggression

In its application to offending, the GLM focuses on enhancing an offender's capabilities in order to achieve their primary human good, instilling strengths in the individual as opposed to simply identifying deficits (Aspinwall and Staudinger 2003). Ward and Gannon (2006) identify the following ten primary goods which, in the literature, are identified as important for increasing psychological well-being. These are as follows:

- life, including healthy living and functioning;
- knowledge;
- excellence in work and play, including success experiences;
- excellence in agency, i.e. autonomy and self-directedness;
- inner peace, i.e. freedom from emotional turmoil and stress;
- friendship, including intimate, romantic and family relationships;
- community;
- spirituality, in the broad sense of finding meaning and 'purpose' in life;
- happiness;
- creativity.

It is important, not only when planning for change but throughout the course of the therapy, to focus on these goods and an individual's efforts to achieve them. The primary aim of treatment is to identify where the difficulties in securing the goods lie, and to help provide the individual with the knowledge, skills and competencies to achieve these goods in a successful and appropriate manner (Ward and

Gannon 2006). This model argues that by enhancing an offender's ability to secure their 'primary human goods' this should then reduce their chances of committing offences in an inappropriate attempt to secure such goods. For example, in the case study of Simon illustrated in Figure 7.4, Simon is arguably trying to reach the primary good of 'inner peace' (i.e. effective management of stress and the emotions of anger and humiliation) using aggression. Relapse prevention for Simon would therefore focus on ways of reaching this primary good without resorting to aggression.

The GLM is focused on helping aggressors to 'live better lives' (Ward 2002: 521) by helping them to achieve the same primary goods as non-aggressors. Through an application of the Good Lives Model treatment aims to further enhance the individualised element of therapy, with personalising therapy a key element of relapse prevention work (Hewitt and Birchwood 2002).

Conclusions

The current chapter has attempted to demonstrate the core content requirements required for aggression therapy, with a focus on information processing, emotional management and relapse prevention. It highlights the integration between information processing and emotion, arguing strongly for the inclusion of both in aggression treatment programmes. Neither can be omitted from treatment although there is a tendency for some treatment approaches to perhaps adopt a narrow focus, either by concentrating on antisocial behaviour and missing core aggression theory and/or by over-focusing on subjective emotion, usually anger. The current chapter has also tried to illustrate the importance of integrating relapse prevention into treatment, highlighting how relapse prevention models are also influenced by information processing and emotional management. Since the ultimate aim of therapy is to develop insight into previous behaviour and to build on existing strengths to prevent a reoccurrence, relapse prevention therefore becomes a core element.

The current chapter has tried to demonstrate the problems with adopting a narrow approach to the development of violence and aggression therapy, and arguing for a more individualised approached to treating aggression. Individualised does not automatically mean individual therapy, however. There are certainly positives with individual therapy, particularly as a precursor to future work or for clients for whom their learning styles are not conducive to group therapy (e.g. significant cognitive impairment). However, group therapy approaches are preferred where possible. The reason for this is simple – processing and the interpretation of emotion which leads to aggression does not occur in a vacuum; it occurs in a context, involving environmental antecedents and the evaluations of the behaviour of others. Treating aggression therefore in the absence of social context becomes problematic.

There is sometimes a misperception that group therapy fails to account for individual differences. Whereas this may be true for some group therapy programmes dealing with very prescriptive behaviour it is certainly not true for them all (e.g. Life Minus Violence – Enhanced as one example). Group therapy can, and should, be individualised by the use of focused client-led pre-assessments (see Chapter 4) and the tailoring of discussions and treatment targets to fit the specific clients in the group. For violence and aggression intervention the role of a peer group should never be underestimated since these form part of the context in which aggression occurs.

Importantly, therapy also occurs not just in the *content* of the approach but also in the *process*. Critiques of group therapy tend to focus on the content and not the importance of group process. The current chapter has demonstrated, for example, the role of *normative* beliefs in information processing, the importance of the *subjective* interpretation of emotion and *realistic planning and goal-setting* for managing high-risk situations (i.e. relapse prevention). The presence of a peer group with whom a client is able to identify (i.e. who have source credibility) can be an effective method of bringing about change in attitudes and perception. The literature on persuasion, for example, suggests it can be improved if the source is credible and similar. Arguably, normative beliefs cannot be fully dealt with in the absence of reference to a credible source or one that is considered similar (i.e. other habitual aggressors). Subjective interpretations of emotions benefit from challenging by a credible and similar source, with the feasibility of relapse prevention plans profiting by input from similar peers. Individual therapy will only achieve these goals in part.

What the current chapter has attempted to illustrate as its core message is the importance of not losing individuality as a treatment target. There may be similarities between habitual aggressors but there are also unique differences. Although information processing, emotional management and relapse prevention are essential content, all of these areas have individuality as a core doctrine. It remains vital therefore that individuality is not lost in either the development or the delivery of treatment approaches for violence.

Acknowledgements

Thanks are expressed to Fiona Wilks-Riley for reviewing and commenting on an earlier version of this chapter, and in particular for her comments on the integration of information processing theory.

References

Aspinwall, L.G. and Staudinger, U.M. (2003) *A Psychology of Human Strengths: Fundamental Questions and Future Directions for a Positive Psychology*. Washington, DC: American Psychological Association.

Baumeister, R.F. and Bushman, B.J. (2007) 'Angry emotions and aggressive behaviours', in G. Steffgen and M. Gollwitzer (ed.), *Emotions and Aggressive Behavior*. Ashland, OH: Hogrefe & Huber, pp. 61–75.

Bennett, S., Farrington, D. and Huesmann, R. (2005) 'Explaining gender differences in crime and violence: the importance of social cognitive skills', *Aggression and Violent Behavior*, 10: 263–88.

Blackburn, R. (1993) *The Psychology of Criminal Conduct: Theory, Research and Practice*. New York: Wiley & Sons.

Burkitt, E. and Barnett, N. (2006) 'The effects of brief and elaborate mood induction procedures on the size of young children's drawings', *Educational Psychology*, 26: 93–108.

Crick, N.R. and Dodge, K.A. (1994) 'A review and reformulation of social information processing mechanisms in children's social adjustment', *Psychological Bulletin*, 115: 74–101.

Davey, L., Day, A. and Howells, K. (2005) 'Anger, over-control and serious violent offending', *Aggression and Violent Behavior*, 10: 624–35.

Dodge, K.A. (1986) 'A social information processing model of social competence in children', in M. Perlmutter (ed.), *Minnesota Symposia on Child Psychology*. Hillsdale, NJ: Lawrence Erlbaum Associates, Vol. 18, pp. 77–125.

Fontaine, R.G. (2006) 'Applying systems principles to models of social information processing and aggressive behaviour in youth', *Aggressive and Violent Behavior*, 11: 64–76.

Hastings, B.M. (2000) 'Social information processing and the verbal and physical abuse of women', *Journal of Interpersonal Violence*, 15: 650–64.

Hewitt, L. and Birchwood, M. (2002) 'Preventing relapse of psychotic illness: role of self-monitoring of prodomal symptoms', *Disease Management and Health Outcomes*, 10: 395–407.

Huesmann, L.R. (1998) 'The role of social information processing and cognitive schema in the acquisition and maintenance of habitual aggressive behavior', in R.G. Geen and E. Donnerstein (eds), *Human Aggression: Theories, Research, and Implications for Social Policy*. San Diego, CA: Academic Press, pp. 73–109.

Ireland, J.L. (2001) 'The relationship between social problem solving and bullying among male and female adult prisoners', *Aggressive Behaviour*, 27: 297–312.

Ireland, J.L. (2007) 'Introducing a new violence treatment programme: Life Minus Violence', *Forensic Update*, July. Leicester.

Ireland, J.L. and Archer, J. (2002) 'The perceived consequences of responding to bullying with aggression: a study of male and female adult prisoners', *Aggressive Behavior*, 28: 257–72.

Kliegel, M., Jäger, J. and Phillips, L.H. (2007) 'Emotional development across adulthood: Differential age-related emotional reactivity and emotional regulation in a negative mood induction procedure', *International Journal of Aging and Human Development*, 63: 217–44.

Kunzmann, U., and Grühn, D. (2005) 'Age differences in emotional reactivity: the sample case of sadness', *Psychology and Aging*, 20: 47–59.

Laird, J.D., Wagener, J.J., Halal, M. and Szegda, M. (1982) 'Remembering what you feel: effects of emotion on memory', *Journal of Personality and Social Psychology*, 42: 646–57.

Laws, R.D., Hudson, S.M. and Ward, T. (2001) *Remaking Relapse Prevention With Sex Offenders: A Sourcebook*. Thousand Oaks, CA: Sage.

Marlatt, G.A. and Donovan, D.M. (2005) *Relapse Prevention: Maintenance Strategies in the Treatment of Addictive Behaviours*, 2nd edn. London: Guilford Press.

Marlatt, G.A. and Gordon, J.R. (1985) *Relapse Prevention: Maintenance Strategies in the Treatment of Addictive Behaviours*. London: Guilford Press.

Megargee, E. (1966) 'Undercontrolled and overcontrolled personality types in extreme anti-social aggression', *Psychological Monographs*, 80: 1–611.

Meuser, K.T. (2004) 'Clinical interventions for severe mental illness and co-occurring substance use disorder', *Acta Neuropsychiatrica*, 16: 26–35.

Montada, L. (2007) 'Emotion-based aggression motivates', in G. Steffgen and M. Gollwitzer (eds), *Emotions and Aggressive Behavior*. Ashland, OH: Hogrefe & Huber, pp. 19–37.

Nagtegaal, M.H. and Rassin, E. (2003) 'The usefulness of the thought suppression paradigm in explaining impulsivity and aggression', *Personality and Individual Differences*, 37: 1233–44.

Perry, D.G., Perry, L.C. and Rasmussen, P. (1986) 'Cognitive and social learning mediators of aggression', *Child Development*, 45: 55–62.

Pierce, K.A. and Cohen, R. (1995) 'Aggressors and their victims: towards a contextual framework for understanding children's aggressor-victims relationships', *Developmental Review*, 15: 292–310.

Pithers, W.D., Kashima, K.M., Cumming, G.F. and Beal, L.S. (1988) 'Relapse prevention: a method of enhancing maintenance change in sex offenders', in A.C. Salter (ed.), *Treating Child Sex Offenders and Victims: A Practical Guide*. Newbury Park, CA: Sage.

Richard, B.A. and Dodge, K.A. (1982) 'Social maladjustment and problem solving ability in school aged children', *Journal of Consulting and Clinical Psychology*, 50: 226–33.

Rubin, K.H. and Krasnor, L.R. (1986) 'Social cognitive and social behavioral perspectives on problem solving', in M. Perlmutter (ed.), *Minnesota Symposia on Child Psychology*. Hillsdale, NJ: Erlbaum, Vol. 18, pp. 1–68.

Ryan, R.M. and Deci, E.L. (2000) 'Self-determination theory and the facilitation of intrinsic motivation, social development and well-being', *American Psychologist*, 55: 68–78.

Schulz, R. (1985) 'Emotion and affect', in J.E. Birren and K.W. Schaie (eds), *Handbook of the Psychology of Aging*, 2nd edn. New York: Van Nostrand Reinhold, pp. 531–43.

Seligman, M.E.P. (2002) 'Positive psychology, positive prevention and positive therapy', in C.R. Snyder and S.L. Lopez (eds), *Handbook of Positive Psychology*. New York: Oxford University Press, pp. 3–9.

Steffgen, G. and Gollwitzer, M. (eds) (2007) *Emotions and Aggressive Behavior*. Ashland, OH: Hogrefe & Huber.

Tremblay, R.E. and Côté, S. (2005) 'The developmental origins of aggression: where are we going?', in R.E. Tremblay, W.W. Hartup and J. Archer (eds), *Developmental Origins of Aggression*. New York: Guilford Press, pp. 447–64.

Verona, E., Reed, A., Curtin, J.J. and Pole, M. (2007) 'Gender differences in emotional and overt/covert aggressive response to stress', *Aggressive Behavior*, 33: 261–71.

Ward, T. (2000) 'Relapse prevention: critique and reformulation', *Journal of Sexual Aggression*, 5: 118–33.

Ward, T. (2002) 'Good lives and the rehabilitation of offenders: promises and problems', *Aggression and Violent Behaviour*, 7: 513–28.

Ward, T. and Brown, M. (2004) 'The good lives model and conceptual issues in offender rehabilitation', *Psychology, Crime and Law*, 10: 243–57.

Ward, T. and Gannon, T. (2006) 'Rehabilitation, etiology and self-regulation: the Good Lives Model of sexual offender treatment', *Aggression and Violent Behavior*, 11: 77–94.

Wegner, D.M. (1989) *White Bears and Other Unwanted Thoughts: Supression, Obsession and the Psychology of Mental Control*. New York: Penguin Books.

Wong, S., Audrey, G. and Gu, D. (2007) 'Assessment and treatment of violence-prone forensic clients: an integrated approach', *British Journal of Psychiatry*, 190: s66–s74.

Chapter 8

Treatment approaches for sexual violence

Carol A. Ireland and Rachel Worthington

Theories relating to an understanding of sexual violence, including individual motivations and functions, have greatly developed over recent years. Most of these models continue to focus on child sexual abuse, and make a number of efforts to extrapolate to other types of sexual violence. It can be difficult to make reference to theories of sexual violence, without referring to one of the founding theories, namely Finkelhor's pre-condition model of child sexual abuse (Finkelhor 1984). Finkelhor's model was the first to move away from single-factor models of sexual violence to look at a more holistic approach, with the recognition that offending behaviour was complex. The model argued the need to examine a range of factors relating to sexual violence, looking at internal and external factors as well as offering a framework upon which to base clinical interventions (Ward and Hudson 2001; Ward *et al.* 2006).

Finkelhor's model, although groundbreaking at its development in the 1980s, has now been superseded by other models of sexual violence. While Finkelhor's precondition model attempted to combine a variety of psychological approaches, such as psychoanalytical, attributional and learning theories (Ward and Hudson 2001), it could be argued that such combined strategies can lead to confusion in understanding as to the development of sexual violence. Furthermore, Finkelhor's model does not clearly consider the function of sexual violence. The model begins at the point where the motivation to sexually offend is already present, with little consideration as to how such motivations may have originated (Ward and Hudson 2001). Developmental factors now feature within the more current models of sexual violence.

One of the more developed and influential models, and one which first began to explore developmental factors, is Marshall and Barbaree's integrated theory of child sexual abuse (Marshall and Barbaree 1990), later revised by Marshall *et al.* (1999). This model attempted to make use of the key factors identified in both Finkelhor's precondition model and other models of sexual violence, as well as offer a more detailed understanding as to the development and maintenance of sexual violence. Indeed, it is this model, which is used more predominantly in therapies addressing sexual violence in the UK. In a more enhanced development from previous models of sexual violence, Marshall *et al.* (1999) address sexual violence as emanating from certain developmental vulnerability factors. They identify a number of such developmental vulnerability factors that can exacerbate and increase a risk of sexual violence (Ward *et al.* 2006). One of these factors can include insecure attachments, such as a child being exposed to poor parenting. This can lead to a potential failure to explore and to take risks, leading to a development of mistrust in others as the child develops into adolescence and later adulthood (Marshall and Barbaree 1990; Marshall *et al.* 1999). Such insecure attachments have also been linked to poor mood management and problem-solving, low self-esteem and poor self-worth (Ward *et al.* 2006), ultimately leading to a potential fear of disclosing feelings and emotions during adulthood, such as seeing the world as a hostile place (Marshall and Barbaree 1990; Marshall *et al.* 1999; Ward *et al.* 2006). Additional developmental vulnerability factors can also include inappropriate role modelling (Marshall and Barbaree 1990; Marshall *et al.* 1999). For example, if a child is sexually abused and, as a result of grooming and coercion, perceives this abuse to be rewarding in some way, then there is the argument that beliefs that sex with children is appropriate could potentially be fostered (Marshall and Barbaree 1990; Marshall *et al.* 1999).

Within Marshall and Barbaree's integrated theory of child sexual abuse, the transition from childhood to adolescence is regarded as a crucial stage. For example, puberty is regarded as critical for the development of sexual scripts, where a child moving toward adolescence is able to identify what are appropriate and non-appropriate sexual activities and beliefs. It is further argued that poor childhood experiences can negatively affect the necessary social skills that are required to develop and maintain intimate relationships with others. Consequently, efforts to achieve intimate relationships can be met with rejection, and a deficit in social skills can lead an individual to, among other factors, regard children as being more sexually viable, as they are less likely to reject them (Marshall and Barbaree 1990; Marshall *et al.* 1999).

In a similar fashion to Finkelhor's precondition model, Marshall and Barbaree also examine situational factors that may increase vulnerabilities towards sexual violence. Within their model, such factors include stress, intoxication and sexual stimuli (such as the presence of a victim). What is unique to Marshall and Barbaree's integrated model is that they argue any individual can be at risk of committing sexual violence, but the greater the level of vulnerability possessed, the more chance of a sexual offence occurring (Marshall and Barbaree 1990). Indeed, a key factor within the model is the view that vulnerable individuals meet a number of psychological needs through sexual activity (Ward *et al.* 2006).

While Marshall and Barbaree offer a comprehensive theory of sexual violence, their theory/model still looks at sexual offending in very general terms, and does not allow for specific differences within groups, such as different types of child abusers. Although this model does offer different offence pathways, these are not always clearly visible within the model, and do require understanding on the part of the clinician to identify and formulate them. This is where a more recent model, Ward and Siegert's pathways model (2002), attempted to 'knit together' the effective aspects of all the sexual offender models that came before, including Marshall and Barbaree's. This model is presented in detail in Chapter 10. Yet, Marshall and Barbaree's model does demonstrate that sexual violence can be regarded as resulting from a contribution of factors that are interactional in nature, introducing the idea of vulnerability factors and further looking at the origin of sexual violence. Importantly, it helps to identify workable treatment areas, such as self-esteem, coping and intimacy deficits.

Current approaches to treatment for sexual violence

The challenge for sexual violence treatment is to apply the theories of sexual violence in a helpful way, which helps to understand, formulate and manage an individual's treatment needs. The current approaches for the treatment of sexual violence are predominantly cognitive behavioural, with the emphasis on cognitive and behavioural varying in accordance with the needs of the individual. The treatment format for offenders who have committed sexual violence takes a stage approach which mirrors the assessment format. The first stage involves the assessment of the risk and needs of the individual in order to assess the suitable dosage of treatment that the individual requires. Based on these assessments, the individual is then assigned to an appropriate treatment programme. Throughout this treatment their risk and needs are further assessed and evaluated so that treatment within that programme can be modified to meet their needs. Upon completion of treatment, a report of the individual's progress is compiled, focusing on the progress that they have made in each of the identified areas of risk and need. The suitability of outstanding and further treatment would also be identified.

The most utilised approaches of treatment for offenders who are convicted of sexual violence in the UK is the nationally accredited family of Sex Offender Treatment Programmes (SOTP). These are run in a variety of forensic settings such as forensic hospitals and community forensic services, but predominantly in HM Prison Service. As an illustration, HM Prison Service will be emphasised, although such therapies are conducted in a range of secure and non-secure forensic settings.

HM Prison Service currently offers a range of therapies to match the treatment needs of individual offenders. The Core (or 'mainstream') SOTP is designed for male sex offenders who are assessed as being medium to very high risk of engaging in sexual violence, in that they present with a wide range of treatment needs; it is cognitive-behavioural in nature. This risk is assessed through the Risk Matrix 2000 (Sexual Offending version: HM Prison Service) and the Structured Assessment of Risk and Need (SARN: HM Prison Service). The aim of the programme is to assist the individual to identify factors which took them closer towards offending. These factors are based on current literature about sexual offending. The Core SOTP also aims to explore offence-related attitudes and beliefs which sexual offenders/group members may have held in the build up to offending and/or in their lives generally, and which would be regarded as vulnerability factors to their risk. The programme assists the individual to adopt strategies, such as the use of victim empathy, for reducing offence-related thoughts, feelings and behaviours. The primary focus of the programme is to identify goals that help group members move away from offending, towards an offence-free life. There is emphasis on practising the skills needed to achieve these new goals. The Core SOTP consists of 86 group sessions and lasts approximately six months.

The Adapted SOTP targets the same treatment needs as the Core SOTP, but it has been adapted for individuals who have social and/ or cognitive impairments. The aims of the programme are to increase sexual knowledge, to modify offence-justifying thinking, to develop an ability to recognise feelings in themselves and others, to gain an understanding of victim harm and to develop relapse prevention skills (Williams *et al.* 2007). The programme is approximately 95 sessions long and runs for approximately eight months.

Based on the risk-need responsivity principle, the Extended SOTP was designed to address the needs of those individuals whose needs are not sufficiently met by the Core SOTP. Thus the programme is suitable for those who are assessed as being high or very high risk, and who have successfully completed the Core SOTP. The Extended SOTP is more schema-focused based, and is aimed at exploring underlying core beliefs about the self, world and others which may have taken the individual closer towards offending. The programme covers three main treatment need areas: problematic thinking styles, emotion management and intimacy skills. It is 73 sessions long and takes approximately six months to complete.

The most recent addition to the HM Prison Service family of sexual offending treatments is the Healthy Sexual Functioning programme (HSF). This is aimed at individuals who are assessed as being at high risk of reoffending and who have offence-related sexual interests. Again, the duration of the programme may vary according to the needs of the individual but is based on four modules, looking at developing a more healthy sexuality, assessment and learning to manage patterns in sexual arousal, relapse prevention and motivational engagement.

The Rolling SOTP programme takes a different approach to the others, and is so called because of the way in which group members may be 'rolled on' and 'rolled off' at different times, making it effectively an 'open group'. The programme is designed for lower-risk male sexual offenders, such as those with less treatment needs than medium and higher-risk offenders, and is similar to the Core SOTP programme but with a greater emphasis on attachment styles and relationships. The length of the programme and the between-session work allocated to the individual vary according to their treatment needs. Thus the dosage of treatment can range from 45 to 60 sessions.

The Better Lives Booster SOTP is designed to 'boost' the skills that a client has developed through the other SOTPs above. Thus the focus of the programme is to engage in skills practice to consolidate learning and to take the individual away from offending. The group is heavily based on the 'Good Lives Model' of offender rehabilitation which will be discussed later in this chapter, and seeks to encourage group members to develop healthy, prosocial, balanced lives. Unlike the other programmes, the Better Lives Booster may be delivered in a range of formats, such as differing session lengths, and has also been adapted for individuals with social and/or cognitive difficulties. The programme may be delivered as a high-intensity treatment programme for offenders who are within twelve months of release, delivered at three or four sessions per week. The low-intensity version targets individuals who have completed their main treatment but have a considerable amount of time to serve before release, running for around one session per week. Thus the low-intensity version is designed to assist in the maintenance of change.

The Good Lives Model of Offender Rehabilitation

The current predominant model used to address offending and problematic behaviour has been the 'risk-need approach' of the Good Lives Model of Offender Rehabilitation (Ward 2002; see also Chapters 5 and 4, this volume). This approach focuses on decreasing the likelihood that individuals will engage in offending and problematic behaviour. Historically, this was done by identifying and managing dynamic risk factors. Dynamic risk factors are regarded as those factors that can be changed in an individual, such as attitudes and beliefs, as opposed to static risk factors such as the age of the offender when they committed their first offence. It is hoped that the management of dynamic risk factors will reduce offence-related behaviours. Dynamic risk factors could include antisocial attitudes (e.g. beliefs that offending does not cause any harm, or that the victim enjoyed the offence), inappropriate ways of coping with emotions (e.g. becoming violent when angry or using self-harm to cope with negative feelings) and poor self-management (not being able to solve problems or generate alternative ways of doing things). However, the primary criticism of this approach is that while, correctly, focus is given to reducing and managing risk, enhancement of the quality of life is neglected (Ward 2002). Ward and Stewart (2003a) propose that this has led to the inadequate replacement of inappropriate behaviours and skills, where these inadequate behaviours are removed and not replaced, and therefore this has hindered the degree to which risk is managed.

The introduction of 'Positive Psychology', which seeks to explore ways in which human potential for fulfilment can be maximised (Linley and Joseph 2004), has made two significant contributions to the consideration of what can constitute a 'Good Life'. Firstly it asserts that a person does not have to be absent of psychopathology (mental illness or personality disorder) in order to have a Good Life. Secondly, as a result of the introduction of Positive Psychology, definitions surrounding factors that assist in the developing of a Good Life have been defined.

The 'Good Lives' approach asserts that happiness and well-being do not come from the attainment of wealth and the purchasing and acquisition of goods (extrinsic goals). Rather, psychological well-being is developed through satisfying basic psychological needs (intrinsic goals). Research from a variety of fields, including psychological and social science (Cummins 1996), evolutionary theory (Arnhart 1998), practical ethics (Murphy 2001) and anthropology (Nussbaum 2000), has contributed to a consensus regarding what these basic human needs are in Western culture. Murphy (2001) summarises these as follows:

1 *Healthy living* – this involves healthy physical living in terms of both physical and sexual health.
2 *Knowledge* – having an area of knowledge that you feel is varied and important to you.
3 *Excellence in work and play* – feeling that you have mastered something or that there is something that you excel in.
4 *Excellence in agency* – feeling that you have some self-direction and independence or self-sufficiency.
5 *Inner peace* – freedom from emotional turmoil and stress.
6 *Relatedness* – this includes intimate, romantic, family and community relationships.
7 *Spirituality* – finding meaning and purpose in life.
8 *Happiness* – engaging in activities that make you personally happy.
9 *Creativity* – engaging in creative ways of thinking or behaving and increasing/developing ways in which you engage with the world.

Emmons (1996) proposes that a contented and fulfilling life should seek to fulfil each of these primary needs and have a balance of achievement in each. For example, it is argued by Emmons (1996) that, if a person focuses on achieving all of their primary needs through excellence in work and play, this could lead to deficits in their ability to meet their primary need for 'relatedness' or 'creativity'. In addition, Ward *et al.* (2007) propose that psychological, social and lifestyle problems emerge when these nine goods are not achieved appropriately, are too limited and not evenly distributed, or when there is conflict between achieving different goods and when the individual lacks the capacity to adjust to changing circumstances.

Research by Kasser (2002) has demonstrated that people may attempt to use inappropriately orientated activities, such as offending, in order to achieve these needs through unhelpful behaviours. Examples of these include substance misuse, self-harm, inappropriate sexual behaviour, excessive alcohol use, over-eating and irresponsible spending resulting in debt. Ward and Stewart (2003b) propose that a 'Good Life' becomes possible 'when an individual possesses the necessary conditions for achieving primary goods' (p. 26). Furthermore, they suggest that 'Good Lives' are always context-dependent, but that these contexts should provide varied and realistic possible ways of living which take into account an individual's capabilities, temperament, interests, skills, commitments and support networks. Rapp (1998) suggests that activities should enable a person to develop a sense of *purpose* and *dignity*.

Sagiv and Schwartz (2000) emphasised the importance of the environment in achieving well-being and 'Good Lives'. They suggested that environments which are congruent with a person's goals and values and which provide opportunities for achieving those goals are more likely to provide experiences of a positive sense of well-being. In addition, when social support is linked with such an environment there are better conditions for increased well-being.

However, when the environment in which a person is placed holds values and goals which contradict their own, this can cause conflict. In this situation it is recommended that a period of *acculturation* is facilitated (Gill and Vega 1996), whereby the person is given time to adjust to their new culture. It is argued by the authors that this socialisation enables individuals to adopt *values* and *goals* which are more congruent with their environment. Of most significance is the proposition by Rapp (1998) that: 'The psychological, vocational, and social aspects of rehabilitation should be integrated within a coherent multifaceted treatment plan, rather than be considered separately.'

The benefits of developing 'Good Lives'

Ward and Stewart (2003b) argue that the best way of addressing offending behaviour is by adopting a holistic approach to rehabilitation, focusing on balancing the management of risk with the development of 'Good Lives'. In addition, the Good Lives Model (GLM) provides a flexible person-centred approach to rehabilitation.

Historically the risk-need model has primarily focused on acculturating individuals, in terms of changing their values, but little attention has been given to developing alternative, replacement goals in order to take the individual not only away from offending, but towards a better life. The Good Lives Model (GLM) of rehabilitation incorporates this facet.

Ward and Stewart (2003b) suggest that rehabilitation effectively links 'Good Lives' with treatment interventions, providing the balance between the two factors. Furthermore, numerous research has demonstrated the effectiveness of the Good Lives Model. For example, Ryan and Deci (2000) found that those who had focused on developing a 'Good Life' had lower levels of anxiety. Marshall et al. (1999) has also found that targeting self-esteem (linked to the good of 'Inner Peace') was associated with reductions in deviant sexual arousal. All of these are treatment needs in offending behaviour.

Maruna (2001) has also provided evidence that being able to obtain all the important human goods in socially acceptable and rewarding ways is linked with successfully desisting from offending behaviour. Proeve (2003) also proposes that external factors, such as institutional or community settings, are equally important in effective rehabilitation.

In addition, the Good Lives Model takes into account the ways in which Offence Parallel Behaviours (OPBs) can be managed. OPB (Jones 2000) is behaviour that is demonstrated some time after the offence and that is related to the behaviours that emerge at any point before or after an offence. For example, the risk-need model may focus on illicit drug use as a risk factor. The GLM takes into account how the environment may restrict access to such substances but how this human need fulfilment may be replaced. For example, a person may seek to attain 'Inner Peace' through drug use in the community but replace this with excessive caffeine consumption or misuse of medication. The GLM enables a more appropriate understanding of how the human need for 'Inner Peace' may be fulfilled in a more appropriate way.

Perhaps of most value, the GLM validates vocational activities in their own right, such as work placements in forensic settings, as something which is an essential part of rehabilitating an individual on to a 'good life'. These are indeed treated as an integral part of recovery/coping with the future. This is helpful in terms of how staff providing rehabilitation are able to frame the work they are engaged in.

It has been demonstrated that rehabilitation is most effective when there is a balance between risk management and developing good lives to replace the function of this risk (Ward and Stewart 2003a). Furthermore, the development of a 'Good Life' should be closely linked with goals that take the person further away from offending and unhelpful patterns of behaviour.

Motivational theory and its application to assessment and treatment

In order to maximise the potential for treatment success when addressing sexual violence, it is paramount to refer to theories of motivation so as to understand what motivates individuals and how behaviour change may be encouraged, implemented and maximised. When attempting to understand motivation and its links towards maximising treatment success, it is important to consider the individuality of motivation and its dynamic nature. Motivation can help to predict behaviour, and it is important to consider that levels of motivation may vary within individuals, with one person demonstrating high motivation in one area yet lower motivation in another. There are a number of key theories when addressing human motivation – two of these are self-determination theory (Ryan and Deci 2000) and goal-setting theory (Locke 1996).

The self-determination theory of human motivation offers a more integrated approach toward understanding what motivates and engages individuals. It is a broad theory of human motivation and assumes individuals have an innate drive towards their own development and psychological growth (Ryan and Deci 2000). Thus it would argue that an individual is driven to manage ongoing challenges, using such challenges to develop themselves as individuals. Yet this drive is not an automatic one but requires continual support from the social environment. Ultimately, the social environment can either maximise or hinder an individual's ability to master their ongoing challenges (Ryan and Deci 2000). As such, the social environment in which sexual violence treatment work takes place is of paramount importance and therapy itself is not sufficient on its own. As such, self-determination theory would argue for the importance of maximising a social environment that encourages an individual to manage their ongoing challenges, in this instance their sexual violence and/or desire to sexually offend.

Ryan and Deci (2000) identified three basic needs, which are important aspects of human motivation. These are competence, relatedness and autonomy. Ryan and Deci (2000) argue that these needs must be satisfied across the lifespan for an individual to experience an ongoing sense of integrity and well-being (Ryan and Frederick 1997; Ryan and Deci 2000). It is argued that competence, relatedness and autonomy increase intrinsic motivation. Intrinsically motivated activities are those that individuals find interesting, and which they would complete in the absence of operationally separable consequences, based on individuals' needs to feel competent and self-determined (Ryan and Deci 2000). Indeed, intrinsic motivation can be regarded as a key factor in promoting change.

Competence refers to the need to feel skilled in some areas. It includes the desire to receive positive feedback that signifies the effectiveness, and therefore competence, of themselves as individuals. As such, competence is important in enhancing intrinsic motivation (Ryan and Deci 2000). With regard to treatment interventions addressing sexual violence, self-determination theory would identify the importance of positive and specific feedback. This would include reinforcement that encourages individuals to feel competent in their non-offending behaviours and activities. Such feedback and reinforcement would enhance individuals' intrinsic motivation and willingness to change.

Relatedness, namely the relationships between individuals, is argued to have a powerful influence on intrinsic motivation (Ryan and Deci 2000). Self-determination theory would hypothesise that, across the lifespan, intrinsic motivation is more likely to flourish in situations where relationships are secure (Ryan and Deci 2000). Yet, and importantly, such a sense of relatedness is not required to be something the individual experiences closely themselves, but simply the presence of secure relationships within the individual's social environment is the minimal requirement.

The final need is that of autonomy. This is an important need, where an individual feels that the activities that they engage in are done so naturally and spontaneously, where they feel free to follow their inner interest (Ryan and Deci 2000). This is an important application with regard to treatment interventions of sexual violence, where it is important to instil in individuals the sense of autonomy and freedom of choice in order to maximise their motivation and willingness to engage. As such, Ryan and Deci (2000) argue that individuals work at their best and happiest when they feel they have some level of control over their daily lives. It is therefore of paramount importance to consider this need to have a level of control in the choices made when engaging with individuals, such as attempting to change unhelpful, offence-related behaviours.

While self-determination theory can offer a background to understanding human motivation, there are other theories that can offer more of a practical application, such as goal-setting theory (Locke 1996). Goal-setting theory identifies an individual's conscious goals with regard to tasks and behaviours that they engage in. The emphasis is on individuals being motivated by clear goals and appropriate feedback, with the working towards a goal providing a major source of motivation (Locke 1996).

Using a human motivation and goal achievement perspective, Locke (1996) argues that the more difficult the goal, the greater the achievement. Also, the more specific the goal, the more focused the individual is on achieving this goal. It is further argued that specific and challenging goals can create the highest performance. Locke (1996) argues that a commitment to goals, and hence a genuine determination, is crucial if these goals are challenging for the individual. This is particularly important when engaging in therapy or intervention related to sexual violence, where the goals identified to be modified and changed are often challenging. In some instances, the unhelpful behaviours that need to be modified may have been occurring over a period of years. Nonetheless, Locke (1996) argues that an individual could be committed, or at least make some effort, to achieve goals that they view as important for themselves and achievable. This indicates that, in intervention work with sexual violence, it would be of benefit if goals were important for the client, challenging, yet also achievable.

Self-efficacy is also regarded as an important factor with regard to human motivation and goal-setting theory. As such, Locke (1996) argues that individuals that are high in self-efficacy are more likely to set high goals, accept and commit themselves to difficult goals, respond to setbacks positively and discover successful strategies to the task in hand (Locke 1996). Similarly, in intervention work for sexual violence, increasing the self-efficacy can be an important factor in maintaining engagement and maximising progress.

Managing resistance and denial

The concept of denial originates from Freud's work, where it was regarded as a defence mechanism for coping with guilt, anxiety and other disturbing emotions aroused by reality. Cohen (2001) argued that denial is 'a mode of defence which consists in a subject's refusing to recognise the reality of a traumatic perception'. While Freud's work on denial was very much in its infancy to what we understand now, it was nonetheless groundbreaking in its acknowledgement of the concept. It also encouraged a theoretical discussion about denial, beginning to look at why an individual may deny distressing situations.

Cohen (2001) identified a number of types of denial, namely literal, interpretive and implicatory denial. With regard to literal denial, it is argued that the individual asserts that something simply did not happen or is simply not true, such as a perpetrator of sexual violence reporting that they did not rape their victim. Such a refusal to acknowledge facts may be a genuine ignorance or deliberate aversion to acknowledging the truth, as this may be too difficult to bear (Cohen 2001). In interpretive denial the basic facts are not denied but are interpreted in a different way. For example, the partner of a perpetrator of sexual violence could remark that 'they couldn't have raped them, it must have been consenting, they must have wanted it'. Such denial can be a genuine inability to grasp what the facts can mean to others (Cohen 2001). Finally, implicatory denial is where there is no attempt to deny the facts or to distort them in any way, but one chooses to disregard the moral, psychological or political implications of having to recognise the importance of such facts (Cohen 2001). In the case of the partner whose boyfriend is the perpetrator of sexual violence on someone else, the partner could report 'I know that he raped her, but to be fair she should not have told him she was going to have sex with him, and then change her mind, she was asking for it really'. Yet, with regard to implicatory denial, it must be acknowledged that in some cases the rationalisations may appear fair, such as the incident where an individual comes across a physical assault but makes the decision not to prevent this through fear of retribution. The difference here is when the individual knows what needs to be done, does have the means to do something about it and there is no risk involved, but chooses not to become involved (Cohen 2001). Unlike the other types of denial, it is not about the knowledge of the fact being the issue, but rather what the individual chooses to do with this fact (Cohen 2001).

When working with an individual who presents in denial of all or some aspects of their sexual violence, it is important to be collaborative. It is important to work together in order to encourage exploration of the barriers that are leading to this denial, with a confrontational approach producing twice the resistance (Miller *et al.* 1993). Further, when working with denial, it is important to attempt to elicit information rather than teach it. It is important to re-refer to self-determination theory in relation to this, where it is of value for an individual to feel a sense of autonomy over the choices that they make, in this instance whether they choose to acknowledge some or all aspects of their sexual violence.

Another important factor when working with denial is to look for signs of ambivalence, no matter how small. Ambivalence, namely uncertainty as to where they are now and where they wish to be in the future (with regard to change and/or treatment needs), indicates a potential for change, where 'ambivalence is a signal that change may be on the horizon' (Clark 2006). Once ambivalence has been identified, it is important to try and increase it, as well as resolve the ambivalence by creating a discrepancy between where the individual is currently in their life and where they wish to be with regard to their needs, wants and goals. As such, the larger the discrepancy, the greater the desire to change (Clark 2006).

Part of denial may further be that of 'resistance', where a client works in opposition to their clinician (Newman 1994). While in some instances resistance can be regarded as a barrier towards change, it is important to recognise resistance, not as a difficulty, but as an opportunity to gather information and to encourage behavioural change (Newman 1994). Client resistance with regard to sexual violence intervention work can take a variety of forms. Examples of these could include finding it difficult to answer questions as part of the assessment process, not completing between-session work, appearing slow to complete work within the intervention or appearing to lack detail in relation to this, not wishing to engage in either assessment or therapy, finding it difficult to recognise improvements made or feeling they are unable to change.

When considering client resistance, it is important to recognise that, for these individuals, the prospect of change can be difficult and uncomfortable. In some instances it may be perceived as frightening by the client (Newman 1994), as they may be asked to change and modify aspects of their lives that have been fundamental for a number of years. One could thus reasonably expect some level of resistance. Newman (1994) would argue that such information can indeed strengthen the therapeutic relationship, help the clinician understand the origins of such resistance and consequently help to develop an intervention that may assist the client in increasing their motivation to change their unhelpful behaviours. Newman (1994) emphasises the importance of clinicians developing a detailed formulation of resistance, demonstrating further empathy towards the client (in accordance with self-determination theory) and identifying interventions that are right for each client's needs.

When assessing the basis of such resistance, it is key to be detailed and specific. For example, while it can be useful to state that 'the client did not complete the between-session work as they lacked the confidence and have low self-esteem', it is more helpful to determine exactly in what way they lack the confidence and have low self-esteem, how this is developed, what aspects of between-session work heightened or highlighted this, and how strong this is in relation to the negative consequences they feel they may suffer by *not* completing the work (Newman 1994). As such, Newman (1994) identified eight questions that are important to be considered when assessing resistance. These are as follows.

1 *What is the function of the client's resistant behaviour?* The emphasis here is to focus on the reasons for the client not wishing to engage in the assessment, therapy or intervention work. It is useful to identify if the resistance is occurring within a certain area and if there was anything about the client's behaviour during these times that can be reflected on and discussed as part of the assessment process. It is further useful to determine if the resistance is a function of any beliefs that they hold, such as feelings that the clinician may be attempting to control them, and so to accept and appear compliant would potentially make them feel worthless. Similarly, to enter in conflict may make them feel they have a sense of control and freedom of choice, in line with self-determination theory. It is also important here to consider if the clients are indeed making efforts to defend their autonomy in some way, even if in an unhelpful way.

2 *How does this current resistance fit with their historical pattern of resistance?* It is important here to explore when, and under what circumstances, the client has declined to engage in the past, and if there are any previous relationships that parallel the current relationship between clinician and client. It is further useful here to explore how the current situation is similar to or different from

previous occasions where the client had declined to engage or resisted change, and to explore these in some detail.

3 *What may be some of the client's beliefs that may be fuelling this resistance?* It is important here to consider how the client personally is interpreting the current situation, and indeed if any of their beliefs exacerbate this. It is important here for the clinician to explore thoughts and feelings that precede or accompany any negative statements that demonstrate a resistance to change, to gather a detailed level of information.

4 *What might the client feel will happen if they comply?* Newman (1994) argues that a client may potentially feel that a current situation, such as engaging in sexually violent behaviours, is actually one which is familiar and safe for them as individuals. As such, they may be fearful that, if they look to change, they are venturing into the unknown. They could perceive this as uncomfortable, disorientating and, in some situations, frightening (Young 1990). As a result, they may feel that to change creates more complications in their lives, and may fear that they will lose their sense of identity. As such, resistance can be self-preserving, as they can perceive change as changing totally who they are (Mahoney 1991).

5 *How might the client be misinterpreting or misunderstanding the therapist's suggestions, methods and intentions?* It is important to consider that there may simply be a misunderstanding between client and clinician. Similarly, there may be belief systems that may lead to consistently misconstruing interpersonal situations, such as when a person uses hostile attributional biases in their interactions with others.

6 *What skills does the client lack that might make it difficult at this moment in time to be collaborative?* It is important to consider the possibility that the individual is struggling in terms of skills, as opposed to resistance per se. For example, do they have difficulty in problem-solving skills that are preventing their learning in this area? Do they have difficulty in negotiating and communicating effectively, as well as asserting themselves and demonstrating perspective taking? If it is felt that they do, it is then important to explore the impact this may have on their interactions and, consequently, resistance.

7 *What factors in the client's environment may not be supporting a readiness for change?* It is important to consider that any positive

changes made during a therapy or assessment session may not be positively reinforced by others in their external environment. As such, Newman (1994) argues for the importance of reviewing the client's environment to determine if it supports and encourages change, and if not, how this may then impact upon the individual's demonstrated resistance.

8 *What, as a therapist, do I need to revise? Is there anything about this client I need to understand more of?* Newman (1994) argues that, if a client asserts that you have not understood them sufficiently as a clinician, it is important not to disregard this possibility outright, as indeed there may be evidence to support that this is indeed the case.

Conclusions

It is hoped that this chapter has reflected the complexity with regard to understanding the nature and function of sexual offending, and yet with such complexity comes heightened understanding. Models of rehabilitation, such as the Good Lives Model, have been invaluable in forging the link between theory and practice, offering some clear considerations for maximising engagement with clients. In particular, such models have been influential in reminding professionals as to the scientific theories of rehabilitation. This includes offender rehabilitation, drawing from a wide range of established approaches from anthropology to sociology. There can be many opportunities for working successfully with forensic clients, and it is hoped that this chapter has portrayed the key factors with regard to human motivation, as well as strategies for working with the numerous barriers that may be presented. As such, the challenges that can sometimes be seen from clients can be regarded as a real opportunity to understand and to help them develop and grow as individuals.

Acknowledgements

Thanks are extended to Sharon Xuereb for her helpful and considered comments on an earlier draft of this chapter.

References

Arnhart, L. (1998) *Darwinian Natural Right: The Biological Ethics of Human Nature*. Albany, NY: State University of New York Press.

Clark, M.D. (2006) 'Entering the business of behavior change: motivational interviewing for probation staff', *Journal of the American Probation and Parole Association*, 30 (1): 3845.

Cohen, S. (2001) *States of Denial: Knowing about Atrocities and Suffering*. Cambridge: Wiley.

Cummins, R.A. (1996) 'The domains of life satisfaction: an attempt to order chaos', *Social Indicators Research*, 38: 303–28.

Emmons, R.A. (1996) 'Striving and feeling: personal goals and subjective wellbeing', in P.M. Gollwitzer and J.A. Bargh (eds), *The Psychology of Action: Linking Cognition and Motivation to Behavior*. New York: Guilford Press.

Finkelhor, D. (1984) *Child Sexual Abuse: New Theory and Research*. New York: Free Press.

Gill, A.G. and Vega, W.A. (1996) 'Two different worlds: acculturation stress and adaptation among Cuban and Nicaraguan families', *Journal of Social and Personal Relationships*, 13: 435–56.

HM Prison Service (n.d.) 'Risk Matrix 2000 (Sexual Offending Version)'. Unpublished.

HM Prison Service (n.d.) 'Structured Assessment of Risk and Need (SARN)'. Unpublished.

Jones, L. (2000) *Identifying and Working with Clinically Relevant Offence Paralleling Behaviour*. Paper presented at the Division of Clinical Psychology, Forensic Special Interest group, Nottinghamshire.

Kasser, T. (2002) *The High Price of Materialism*. Cambridge, MA: MIT Press.

Linley, P. A. and Joseph, S. (2004) *Positive Psychology in Practice*. Hoboken, NJ: Wiley & Sons.

Locke, E.A. (1996) 'Motivation through conscious goal setting', *Applied and Preventative Psychology*, 5: 117–24.

Mahoney, M. (1991) *Human Change Processes*. New York: Basic Books.

Marshall, W.L. and Barbaree, H.E. (1990) 'An integrated theory of sexual offending', in W.L. Marshall, D.R. Laws and H.E. Barbaree (eds), *Handbook of Sexual Assault: Issues, Theories, and Treatment of the Offender*. New York: Plenum Press.

Marshall, W.L., Anderson, D. and Fernandez, Y. (1999) *Cognitive Behavioural Treatment of Sexual Offenders*. Chichester: Wiley.

Maruna, S. (2001) *Making Good: How Ex-Convicts Reform and Rebuild Their Lives*. Washington, DC: American Psychological Association.

Miller, W.R., Benefield, R.G. and Tonigan, J.S. (1993) 'Enhancing motivation for change in problem drinking: a controlled comparison of two therapist styles', *Journal of Consulting and Clinical Psychology*, 61: 455–61.

Murphy, M.C. (2001) *Natural Law and Practical Rationality*. New York: Cambridge University Press.

Newman, C.F. (1994) 'Understanding client resistance: methods for enhancing motivation to change', *Cognitive and Behavioral Practice*, 1: 47–69.

Nussbaum, M.C. (2000) *Women and Human Development: The CAPABILITIES Approach*. New York: Cambridge University Press.

Proeve, M.J. (2003) 'Responsivity factors in sexual offender treatment', in T. Ward, D.R. Laws and S.M. Hudson (eds), *Sexual Deviance: Issues and Controversies*. London: Sage.

Rapp, C.A. (1998) *The Strengths Model: Case Management with People Suffering from Severe and Persistent Mental Illness*. New York: Oxford University Press.

Ryan, R.M. and Deci, E.L. (2000) 'Intrinsic and extrinsic motivations: classic definitions and new directions', *Contemporary Educational Psychology*, 25: 54–67.

Ryan, R.M. and Frederick, C.M. (1997) 'On energy, personality and health: subjective vitality as a dynamic reflection of well-being', *Journal of Personality*, 65: 529–65.

Sagiv, L. and Schwartz, S.H. (2000) 'Values priorities and subjective well-being: direct relations and congruity effects', *European Journal of Social Psychology*, 30: 177–98.

Ward, T. (2002) 'Good Lives and the rehabilitation of offenders: promises and problems', *Aggression and Violent Behaviour*, 7: 513–28.

Ward, T. and Hudson, S.M. (2001) 'A critique of Hall and Hirschman's quadripartite model of child sexual abuse', *Psychology, Crime and Law*, 7: 333–50.

Ward, T. and Siegert, R.J. (2002) 'Toward a comprehensive theory of child sexual abuse: a theory knitting perspective', *Crime and Law*, 8: 319–51.

Ward, T. and Stewart, C.A. (2003a) 'The treatment of sex offenders: risk management and Good Lives', *Professional Psychology: Research and Practice*, 34: 353–60.

Ward, T. and Stewart, C.A. (2003b) 'Good Lives and the rehabilitation of sexual offenders', in T. Ward, D.R. Laws and S.M. Hudson (eds), *Sexual Deviance: Issues and Controversies*. London: Sage.

Ward, T., Mann, R. and Gannon, T. (2007) 'The Good Lives model of offender rehabilitation: clinical implications', *Aggression and Violent Behavior*, 12 (1): 87–107.

Ward, T., Polaschek, D. and Beech, T. (2006) *Theories of Sex Offending*. Chichester: Wiley.

Williams, F., Wakeling, H. and Webster, S. (2007) 'A psychometric study of six self-report measures for use with sexual offenders with cognitive and social functioning deficits', *Psychology, Crime and Law*, 13 (5): 505–22.

Young, J.E. (1990) *Cognitive Therapy for Personality Disorders: A Schema-focused Approach*. Sarasota, FL: Professional Resource Exchange.

Chapter 9

Treatment approaches for interpersonal violence: domestic violence and stalking

Nicola Graham-Kevan and Stefanie Ashton Wigman

This chapter discusses the academic and clinical (where available) literature on intimate partner violence (IPV) and stalking. It begins by defining terms and explaining the use of *domestic violence* terminology adopted in this chapter. The traditional approach to treating domestic violence between romantic partners will then be discussed in relation to both the studies on treatment efficacy as well as the literature on risk factors associated with this type of family violence. Five specific topics related to treating IPV will then be discussed: substance use, culture, therapeutic alliance, personality and couples counselling. Ex-partner stalking will then be explored starting with descriptions and definitions of stalking. Four specific topics relating to stalking of ex-partners will then be discussed: attachment, psychopathology, substance abuse and criminality. The chapter concludes with six key points to consider when assigning and treating intimate partner aggression and harassment.

Terms and definitions

Probably the most widely used term to describe violence between romantic partners is *domestic violence*. This term, however, lacks specificity as it has been used to describe all forms of violent and/ or potentially abusive behaviour carried out by one or more family member towards other family members. Terms such as *woman abuse* or *wife battering* are, conversely, too narrow in focus, as they concern only behaviours towards female victims. Additionally the use of adjectives such as *battering* are unhelpful as they connote severe chronic violence, which in reality only constitutes a minority of cases. Finally, terms such as *abuse* imply that a behaviour is both inherently unwelcome and morally unjustified. Although this may seem straight-forward it is not. All behaviours occur within a relationship context and it is not possible to deduce motivations, consequences, legality or morality of actions without first exploring the contextual basis of them. Therefore this chapter will use term *intimate partner violence* (IPV) to describe the use of physically aggressive acts towards romantic partners (e.g. wives, husbands, girlfriends, boyfriends). The term IPV does not encompass verbal aggression or acts of controlling behaviour such as isolation, economic abuse or emotionally abusive behaviour; neither does it include child or elder abuse.

Traditional approaches to understanding and treating IPV

Traditional approaches to understanding and treating IPV are based upon the simple and superficially logical theoretical framework of feminist political theory. Applying this theory to IPV leads to the assumption that IPV is male aggression towards women, which men use to dominate and control female partners. Such behaviour is explained as the result of society's socialisation of men and women to accept and conform to patriarchal ideology (e.g. Dobash and Dobash 1979; Pagelow 1984). Extending this logic leads to the presumption that treatment of IPV perpetrators should involve men only and should aim to re-educate the offending men by challenging their negative views about women and their beliefs in their rights as men to control women. The most widely used and influential of feminist perpetrator programme is based on the Duluth model (http://www.duluth-model.org/). The Duluth model has not risen to worldwide dominance because of an impressive literature supporting its theoretical and practical utility, however, it appears instead that Duluth's success is due to the work of feminist activists and the willingness of practitioners and policy-makers to accept both feminist conceptualisation of, and solutions to, the problem of IPV. Indeed there is a lack of support for both the theoretical and therapeutic aspects of Duluth-based perpetrator programmes (e.g. Babcock *et al.* 2004; Dutton and Corvo 2007).

Historically there is evidence that a patriarchal culture may have predominated within western society (e.g. Dobash and Dobash 1979; George 1994) and recent meta-analysis suggests that cross-culturally women's empowerment is related to their victimisation and the perpetration of IPV (Archer 2006). However, there is little evidence that such a system prevails in the West currently (for example, see Archer 2006, for gender empowerment figures for European nations), and even where it is found on an individual basis it may actually act to protect women from violent attacks from men (Felson 2002; Kantor *et al.* 1994; Sorensen and Telles 1991).

There is scant empirical support in the academic literature for adopting this type of feminist-informed programme. On a theoretical level there is little support for a relationship between a man's patriarchal views and his assaultative behaviour towards his partner (Sugarman and Frankel 1996). Neither does traditional sex-role ideology emerge as the sole or most important predictor of men's IPV (Stith *et al.* 2004). Indeed when it is possible to control for pre-existing antisociality (Capaldi *et al.* 2001) longitudinal data suggests that hostile attitudes towards women do not prospectively predict men's IPV. Empirical evaluations of clinical outcome studies also fail to find any support for Duluth-type programmes. A recent meta-analytic review of perpetrator programme efficacy found that current treatment programmes have a minimal impact on post-treatment recidivism at best (Babcock *et al.* 2004). Babcock compared the effect sizes of the different treatments (effect size here refers to a standardised measure of effect). Cohen (1992) indicated that an effect size of 0.2 is indicative of a small effect, 0.5 a medium and 0.8 a large effect size. Babcock *et al.* (2004) found that the treatment effect size for Duluth-type programmes (which was small at around $d = 0.20$) was no better than cognitive-behaviour therapy (CBT-type programmes) and significantly worse than those found for a sixteen-week group therapy and a twelve-week relationship enhancement skills training group, which showed quite large effect sizes. Even evaluations of the Duluth programme found on the Duluth website (http://www.duluth-model.org/) do not offer any more concrete support for this model's application to treatment.

Where effects are found for Duluth these are typically differences between those who complete a Duluth programme and those who drop out (for example, we calculated an effect size of $d = 0.21$ from the Novak and Galaway 1983, evaluation). Such a comparison is confounded by the individual differences likely to be found between the two groups. This is illustrated in the second study listed on the Duluth website conducted by Shepard (1992). The treatment effect referred to disappeared when background and intervention variables (such as duration of assault prior to the programme, court-ordered chemical dependency evaluation, received chemical dependency treatment, child abuse victimisation history and previous convictions for non-assault crimes) were controlled for: '[T]he extent to which men participated in the [Duluth treatment programme] did not determine whether or not they would recidivate' (Shepard 1992: 2). In an attempt to ascertain whether Duluth-type programmes actually reduced recidivism, the US Department of Justice commissioned a study to evaluate the efficacy of batterer intervention programmes (Ashcroft *et al.* 2003). Unlike many previous studies that lacked scientific rigour, the two studies carried out made an attempt to use random allocation to treatment or control. They found that one of the studies had no effect and the second had little effect on reoffending behaviour. Even the small effect found for the second programme could be attributed to the differences between offenders who complete a programme and those that do not. Ashcroft *et al.* (2003) comment:

> [B]oth programs have low response rates and high dropout rates – characteristics that can lead to overtly positive estimates of program effects. Those who continue to batter are not likely to participate in intervention programs; if they participate in the beginning, they are likely to dropout. Hence it is not clear if the result found in the Brooklyn [the second study] evaluation is the result of attrition or a true program or a monitoring effect.

Studies have found that dropouts have higher risk profiles (such as being younger, less educated, unemployed, higher exposure to violence as a child, severe psychopathology, history of non-domestic violence prior arrests, clinical levels of problems with alcohol) when compared to completers. This would strongly suggest greater pre-existing risk factors (see Daly *et al.* 2001; Snow, Jones and Gondolf 2001). It would be most usual if two groups were created whereby one had 'high risk' men and the other had 'low risk' men, which were then compared on rates of reoffending and no difference was found. The presence of risk factors presupposes greater recidivism because risk factors have been identified due to their association with increased risk (Scott and Resnick, in press).

Risk factors for IPV and treatment implications

Contrary to a feminist conceptualisation of IPV, perpetrator gender is not a risk factor. Women and men are equally likely to use IPV.

Archer (2000) found that women were actually slightly more likely to report using IPV and to use it more frequently (although this effect size was small). Examining injury prevalence, the evidence from Archer's (2000) meta-analysis suggests that men are more likely to inflict injury with 62 per cent of those injured being women. This tells us that although men and women are both using physical aggression, women are more likely to be injured, which is consistent with the difference in size and strength of men and women. Physical size is a strong predictor of fighting ability and it is for this reason that boxing-weight classes are used. Even small weight differences (typically 3 kg) result in fighters being placed in different classes (International Boxing Federation 2006). Therefore, the disparity in injury rates does not necessarily mean that men's domestic violence is intentionally more severe than women's, only that they are more likely to cause injury even if the same acts of aggression are used.

In order to investigate risk or predisposing factors that are predictive of later use of physical aggression towards a partner it is necessary to consult longitudinal studies. The risk factors that have been identified in the literature for later aggressive behaviour are generally shared by both girls and boys. Interestingly these risk factors appear to predict both general and partner aggression (Moffitt *et al.* 2000; Tremblay *et al.* 2004). Risk factors that have been identified include low intelligence, impulsivity, fearlessness, a general lack of empathy and negative emotionality. Those who use aggression as adults (both men and women) are extremely likely to have a long history of oppositional and aggressive behaviour beginning very early in life (Hay 2005).

Connolly *et al.* (2000a, 2000b) studied boys and girls and found that children who used negative and controlling interaction styles in friendships, who were identified as being school bullies and who showed poor conflict resolution skills went on to interact with romantic partners in a similar negative and controlling manner. Ehrensaft, Cohen and Johnson (2006) used a longitudinal design to explore the causal relationship between personality disorder traits and domestic violence and found that these predicted both women's and men's risk of partner violence ten years later. As Ehrensaft, Cohen and Johnson (2006) comment, this suggests that '... individuals who go on to perpetrate partner violence are more stably impulsive, angry, self-centered and experience greater affective instability' (p. 480). This research suggests that men and women have similar personality predictors of their own use of IPV.

Individual differences such as emotional regulation (Linder and Collins 2005), low stress tolerance (Frye and Karney 2006), histories of childhood abuse and family violence (O'Leary *et al.* 1994; Linder and Collins 2005) and antisocial behaviours during childhood and adolescence (Capaldi and Clark 1998; Moffitt *et al.* 2001) similarly predict later domestic violence perpetration for both men and women. Further there is evidence of 'assortative mating'. This is a term used to describe the tendency for people to pair up with others who have similar personalities and interpersonal styles to themselves (Brown 2004; Kim and Capaldi 2004; Moffitt *et al.* 2001). Therefore aggressive antisocial men may marry/cohabit with aggressive antisocial women – this explains why most IPV involves mutual aggression (e.g. Graham *et al.* 2004: Straus 2005).

The 'What Works' literature tells us that evidence-based interventions work best and that ideologically based ones are likely to be ineffective (McGuire 2002). The research studies reviewed above are some of the most scientifically rigorous presently available and their findings suggest that IPV interventions must address psychological risk factors such as negative emotionality and impulsivity, interpersonal styles that are coercive and bullying, as well as poor conflict resolution skills, to successfully treat IPV. At present, models are based upon feminist ideology rather than empirically supported risk factors. Existing violence programmes developed for non-domestic violence offenders could be explored with a view to adapting those practices that are found to be effective with general violence groups for use with domestic violence perpetrators.

Substance use and IPV treatment

Both alcohol and some drugs (e.g. diazepam) are associated with an increased risk of reactive or 'emotionally driven' aggression (Blair 2001). Alcohol is also related to both men's and women's IPV perpetration and victimisation (O'Farrell and Murphy 1995; O'Farrell *et al.* 2004) and may be associated with increased severity of violence, anger and fear (Graham *et al.* 2004). Additionally alcohol and drug-related problems have been found to have detrimental effects on both the functioning of children of substance-using parents (Burstein *et al.* 2006) and intergenerationally on the children's own substance use and parenting styles (Locke and Newcomb 2004). The relationship between substance use and IPV is itself complex. Individualised assessment of co-morbidity of IPV and alcohol and/or drug use is critical to understanding the relationship (if any) between substance use and an offender's use of IPV. For some offenders this relationship may be direct while for others unconnected. Potter-Efron (2007) lists several potential relationships between IPV and substance use:

1 Any mood altering substance is capable of promoting anger and/ or aggression, but this is not inevitable.
2 Many individuals with anger and aggression problems also have substance use problems.
3 There may be a causal relationship between IPV and substance use, and this may go either way.
4 Both IPV and substance use may be caused by a third condition such as major mood disorder.
5 Short- and long-term reactions to substances create many different types of problems related to aggression (intoxication, withdrawal and substance-induced paranoia).

Therefore substance use can be: unrelated to IPV; used to rationalise IPV use; a direct cause of IPV; an additive effect to already existing predispositions; synergistic, by interacting with risk factors; a neutraliser which reduces the likelihood of IPV. Treatment for substance use and IPV will depend upon the relationship between them. Therefore different treatment approaches would need to be utilised where substance use is used to alter mood compared to where substances are used to enable the offender to 'defy authority', e.g. his/her partner (White 2004). Dutton (2003b), for example, found that alcohol use was associated with borderline personality (BP) traits, e.g. 'an intense fear of being "abandoned" and "left" by others, going to great lengths to prevent this, with extreme reactions within relationships, including impulsivity and extreme displays of emotions' (DSM-IV), and suggested that those with borderline personality organisation may use alcohol to manage their negative emotions. Intervention in this case may be concentrated on helping the client to manage their emotions in a more constructive way. In contrast, where a client is using alcohol to assert him or herself, assertiveness training may be of more utility.

Research suggests that treatment for alcohol may be more effective than many IPV treatment programmes at reducing IPV perpetration and victimisation (O'Farrell and Murphy et al. 1995; O'Farrell et al. 2004). O'Farrell and colleagues found that behavioural couples therapy was effective by improving relationship functioning which led to a reduction in problem drinking which in turn resulted in lower levels of IPV. It is not clear, however, whether the success was due to the alcohol treatment per se or the couples element of the therapy. There also appears to be an interaction between client antisocial personality disorder (ASPD) (e.g. 'Deceitful and persistent lying, impulsivity, poor planning for the future, aggressive, and lacking in remorse, recklessly disregarding themselves and others', DSM-IV), alcohol and IPV. Fals-Stewart et al. (2005) found that although alcohol increased non-ASPD men's minor aggression it did not increase ASPD men's. Additionally alcohol was a factor in both groups of men's use of severe IPV, but more strongly for ASPD than non-ASPD men. Therefore treatment for substance use may have differential effects, but appears to be important for perpetrators who use severe IPV. Treatment for alcohol may also enhance the efficacy of traditional IPV treatment programmes (Gondolf 1999). Bednar (2003) suggests that treatment for substance use may facilitate treatment for IPV and vice versa. Where one problem is recognised while the other denied by the client, goal setting for the accepted problem may precede an exploration (and hopefully later acceptance) of how the denied problem creates barriers to reaching the clients' desired goals. Helping the client to understand how IPV negatively impacts upon his or her situation is an important step in creating a motivated and engaged client.

Culture and IPV treatment

Culture can be conceptualised in a similar way to alcohol (White 2004). It can be: unrelated to IPV; used to rationalise IPV use; a direct cause of IPV; an additive effect to already existing predispositions; synergistic, by interacting with risk factors; a neutraliser which reduce the likelihood of IPV. It is therefore important to understand the role culture plays (if any) in an individual's IPV perpetration and/ or victimisation. For example, Latino culture can be both protective against IPV perpetration (e.g. machismo culture can encourage protective attitudes towards women) or alternatively be interpreted as supporting IPV towards women by creating expectations of domineering 'hot-blooded' masculinity (Kantor et al. 1994; Prospero 2008; Sorensen and Telles 1991). Patriarchy may encourage violent oppression of women (e.g. Egypt, where the vast majority of men and women agreed that a man was justified in beating his wife in some circumstances: El-Zanty et al. 1995), or alternatively encourage societies to adopt a paternal attitude towards women that extols chivalry, which may actually protect women from male violence (Felson 2002).

Religious belief may also be used to rationalise or neutralise aggressive tendencies. Cullen *et al.* (2007) suggest that religion may insulate against criminal involvement. Faith-based programmes may also have a positive effect on prisoner adjustment and offender recidivism (e.g. Baier and Wright 2001; Clear and Sumter 2002; DiIulio 2001a; Johnson 2004; Johnson *et al.* 2001; Johnson *et al.* 1997; O'Connor and Perreyclear 2002; Zimmer 2004–5). In inner cities, religion can act as a buffer against a criminogenic environment, with the church being seen to offer both faith and social services to its members (Jang and Johnson 2001; Johnson *et al.* 2000). There is evidence, however, that religious belief can also be used to support IPV (e.g. 'honour killings'). When working with IPV perpetrators and victims it is important to differentiate religious custom and criminal law. Cultural beliefs are no defence to criminal behaviour and those who reside within a nation are subject to its laws. Therefore, although successful treatment may depend upon a level of cultural awareness and sensitivity, the therapist needs to be clear that IPV perpetration is illegal and will not be condoned.

The culture of the therapeutic environment is also potentially an important aspect of the treatment of IPV. For clients who are incarcerated in secure sites, the prison or hospital culture is an important element in understanding prisoner behaviour and the potential effects of any prison-based intervention (Dvoskin and Spiers 2004). It is therefore important that, as far as possible, all staff who come into contact with prisoners/patients are aware of how the site's culture can help or hinder rehabilitation efforts. Both community-based and custody based interventions should ensure that staff and clients are treated with respect at all times. Modelling of good behaviour is important but does not end when therapy ends. A firm, fair and respectful demeanour is important to maintain at all times when dealing with clients.

Therapeutic alliance and IPV treatment

The therapeutic alliance is an important predictor of post-treatment recidivism (Brown and O'Leary 2000; Taft *et al.* 2003). Duluth approaches have been described as overly confrontational (Taft *et al.* 2003) and based upon 'shaming techniques' (Corvo and Johnson 2003) which are likely to be 'anti-therapeutic'. A shame-inducing approach is unlikely to be effective (McGuire 2002) and is particularly problematic when working with clients with borderline personality traits who are likely to represent a significant proportion of IPV perpetrators (Dutton 2003a, 2003b – see discussion below). However, others have argued that process factors are more important in explaining outcome variance than are treatment factors (Taft *et al.* 2003) with client factors being more important than therapist factors or the specific techniques employed (Lambert 1978). It is likely that both treatment approaches and client factors are important and that the two interact. Research on client reactance suggests that approaches that are perceived as reducing freedom to make choices are particularly counterproductive with clients who show a defensive, dominant, autonomous and non-affiliative personality style, such as those with ASPD or psychopathy (e.g. lack of a conscience or sense of guilt, lack of empathy, egocentricity, pathological lying, repeated violations of social norms, disregard for the law, shallow emotions and a history of victimising others). Silvia's (2006) work suggests that although it may not be possible to readily reduce reactance that is driven by negative interpersonal styles such as those described above, by being less threatening it is possible to reduce situationally driven reactance. For those dispositionally predisposed to resist interventions, paradoxical interventions may be more effective (Dowd and Wallbrown 1993). *Paradoxical interventions* are injunctions and directives that 'essentially attempt to induce change by discouraging it' (Shqham-Salomon *et al.* 1989: 590).

Personality and IPV treatment

Research suggests that a majority of court-mandated IPV perpetrators, and a significant minority of IPV perpetrators found in general populations, have a disorder of their personality, with the prominent disorders being borderline and antisocial personality disorders (Dixon and Browne 2003; Hamberger and Hastings 1986; Holtzworth-Munroe *et al.* 2000; Waltz *et al.* 2000). Holtzworth-Munroe and Stuart (1994) identified a subgroup of batterers they termed dysphoric/borderline. These were men who were insecurely attached to their partner, likely to experience depression and borderline personality (BP) traits and likely to have a criminal record for non-violent offences and substance use problems. Dutton (2003) found that BP traits were common among men in treatment for IPV. He also found that men who scored highest on BP traits also used the most physical aggression and controlling and emotionally abusive behaviours (as reported by their wives). The high levels of abusive behaviours used by BP clients are believed to be the result of a process by which early experiences of childhood abuse, separations, losses and disruptions lead to poor adult emotional regulation and a fragile sense of self. This combination results in BP clients having problems recognising and managing their emotions as well as a tendency to use interpersonal relationships to maintain their sense of self. Support at the neurocognitive level has recently been provided by Blair (2001). He discusses the reactive threat-response system which initiates a violent response when triggered by sufficient threat. What is sufficient threat is an individual difference variable which is likely to be influenced by experience (particularly early experience) as well as genetic vulnerabilities. Once the threshold for action is reached and flight is not an option then aggression will follow. What is apparent in people who use reactive aggression is that their resting threat level is likely to be higher than non-aggressive individuals and so they take less stimuli to reach the threshold for aggression. Coupled with a distrustful personality and unstable self-image (see Table 9.1 below) it is easy to see why BP clients are prone to frequent aggressive outbursts.

Holtzworth-Munroe and Stuart (1994) identified a subgroup of male batterers who displayed antisocial/psychopathic traits, although emerging research suggests that these subgroups may also be found among female perpetrators (e.g. Babcock *et al.* 2003). These men were described as presenting with antisocial personality disorder or psychopathy, were highly likely to have substance abuse problems and be impulsive, were unlikely to suffer from depression, would be moderately likely to have problems with anger and would have a dismissing attachment style. Although there is a general antipathy

Table 9.1 Borderline thinking errors

- **Dichotomous (black and white) thinking**
  Splitting of intimate other; splitting self-concept

- **Personalisation**
  The tendency to excessively relate external occurrences to the self
  Includes self-blame

- **Catastrophising**
  Inability to differentiate others' wishes from demands

Source: Dutton (2003)

towards such clients, research on IPV treatment suggests that they can benefit from treatment (e.g. Gondolf and White 2001). Such individuals may benefit from a treatment approach that focuses on enlightened self-interest (Dryden *et al.* 1999). Additionally, the use of motivational interviewing techniques to increase client readiness to change and hence improve the client–therapist relationship may also be very beneficial with IPV perpetrators who show antisocial or psychopathic traits (Taft *et al.* 2004).

Dutton (2008) provides a useful summary of the IPV perpetrator categories as summarised in Table 9.2.

Couples therapy for IPV

Although couples work is often regarded as not appropriate for IPV perpetrators, this assumption is based upon the feminist conceptualisation of IPV and is not supported by either the empirically supported aetiology of IPV or outcome studies of couple therapy. Couples therapy would appear to be a sensible option for relationships involving mutual violence. Mutuality is the rule rather than the exception in IPV (Capaldi *et al.* 2007; Capaldi *et al.* 2003; Straus 2005; Stets and Straus 1990) and, contrary to Johnson's (1995) theory, mutuality is not confined to relationships where only minor and infrequent IPV is used (Capaldi and Owen 2002; Graham-Kevan and Archer 2003). Neither is women's involvement in mutually assaultative relationships always (or even usually) confined to self-defensive or reactive aggression. Additionally, much more of men's IPV appears to be in response to women's initiation than vice versa (Capaldi *et al.* 2007; Graham-Kevan and Archer 2008; Straus 2005) and women's initiation is as strong a predictor of men's future use of IPV as men's own past IPV use (Capaldi *et al.* 2003). Mutual aggression is associated with increased injury for both sexes but especially for women who initiate the violence. Therefore, where mutual IPV is present, work with both partners is essential.

Even after an official response to IPV by a male partner, most IPV relationships remain intact (Bouchard and Lee 1999; Harris 2003). It is likely that some of these relationships do so because the victim and/ or perpetrator do not have the means (emotional or economic) to leave; however, others remain intact due to the desire by the partners to stay together. In such cases couples therapy may be an appropriate treatment option. Research on couples therapy suggests that it is at least as effective as single-sex groupwork and does not place victims

Table 9.2 IPV perpetrator categories

Over-controlled aggression	Under-controlled aggression	Cyclical
Flat affect or constantly cheerful persona	Violent inside and outside home	Cyclical 'phases'
Attempts to ingratiate therapist	History of antisocial behaviour (car theft, burglary, violence)	High levels of jealousy
Tries to *avoid* conflict	High acceptance of violence	Violence predominantly/exclusively in intimate relationship
High masked dependency	Negative attitudes to women (macho)	Attachment: fearful/angry
Attachment: preoccupied	Attachment: dismissing	High levels of depression, dysphoria, anxiety-based rage
High social desirability scores	Usually victimised by extreme physical abuse as a child	Ambivalence to wife/partner
Overlap of violence and alcohol use	Low empathy	MCMI: borderline
Some drunk driving arrests	Associations with criminal/ marginal subculture	
Lists 'irritations' in anger diary	MCMI: antisocial PD aggressive-sadistic PD	
Chronic resentment		
MCMI: avoidant/dependent/ passive-aggressive		

Source: Dutton (2008).

at increased risk of harm (Stith *et al.* 2003) with multi-couple groups appearing to be most effective (Stith *et al.* 2004). Additionally, as other family members are frequently also victimised and/or perpetrators of physical aggression family therapy may also be necessary. Hamel (2005) suggests clinicians assess the use of IPV by both partners regardless of the size and strength of the parties. It is also necessary to assess aggression directed towards other family members such as children and elderly relatives, as well as sibling violence and child-to-parent aggression. Once the family has been assessed, ideally where families are intending to remain intact, '[T]reat all members of the family, using individual, couples, family, and group therapy as needed, but adopt a family systems perspective and strive to avoid rigid distinctions between perpetrators and victims' (p. 109).

Stalking and IPV

Where relationships involving partner violence discontinue there is a risk of ex-partner stalking. A main risk factor for former-intimate stalking is intimate partner violence. IPV may be an antecedent and hence a risk factor for future stalking, or may occur simultaneously with stalking while the relationship is intact or after a relationship break-up (e.g., Coleman 1997; Douglas and Dutton 2001; Kienlen *et al.* 1997; Mechanic *et al.* 2000; Tjaden and Thoennes 2000). Stalking has been proposed to be a variant of IPV (e.g. Logan *et al.* 2000) which shares the same underlying mechanism, such as difficulty in dealing with real or perceived threats of abandonment or rejection. It is important to assess the function of the stalking behaviour as similar behaviours may serve different functions for different individuals, or even for the same individual over different periods of time. For example, stalking and aggression may be perpetrated in response to separation and function to re-establish emotional proximity (see below); alternatively the same behaviour may instead be a reaction to the 'humiliation' of rejection and function to reassert a sense of power in the perpetrator (Douglas and Dutton 2001).

Descriptions and definitions of stalking

Stalking has been described as a 'contemporary challenge for forensic and clinical psychiatry' (Kamphuis and Emmelkamp 2000: 206). A clinical definition of stalking is 'an abnormal long-term pattern of threat or harassment directed toward a specific individual' (Meloy and Gothard 1995: 248). Former-intimate stalkers are reported to be the most common and most dangerous type (e.g. Mullen *et al.* 2000), making them important to understand, manage and treat. However, although intimate-partner stalkers in forensic populations are frequently found to have used the most violence, this is not the case in non-forensic samples. This implies that lower order stalking by an ex-partner may not be regarded as requiring outside interventions (either by the victim or by the criminal justice system) and may be seen as more normative than acquaintance or stranger stalkers using similar behaviours. Therefore ex-partner stalkers may not be any more 'dangerous' than other types of stalkers if figures are based upon the proportion within each category rather than across categories.

Much of the research that has investigated stalking does use the term 'stalkers'. This is obviously labelling: that a person may engage in stalking behaviour is not likely to necessarily define the individual as a whole. There has been a move away from these types of labels in clinical practice, and thus it may be more appropriate for clinicians to avoid the 'stalker' label and instead refer to an individual with behaviours indicative of stalking. This chapter does refer to the somewhat labelling term of 'stalkers'; this is because the bulk of the literature on the topic of stalking also does this. The clinical and risk assessment of those who engage in stalking has been considered elsewhere in the text. Here, a brief summary of the key risk factors for stalking is considered. Specifically, five of the most common risk factors, and potentially the most suitable for treatment, will be considered: (1) intimate partner violence; (2) attachment; (3) personality disorders (PDs); (4) substance abuse; and (5) prior criminal history. This is followed by a discussion of how these risk factors can inform and assist treatment initiatives and interventions.

Risk factors for stalking

Attachment

Stalking has been proposed as a pathology of attachment (Meloy 1992, 1996). This has been specifically related to erotomania: a delusional disorder whereby the sufferer believes they can gain the love and affection of their target with persistence and by proving themselves 'worthy'. More generally, Meloy (1992, 1996) suggested that childhood attachment problems develop from inconsistent or disrupted parenting (including separation from a carer), and are subsequently carried into adult relationships, resulting in a poor relationship with the intimate partner (Kienlen *et al.* 1997; Kienlen 1998). The perception of imminent or actual loss in adulthood such as infidelity or relationship break-up, which can be experienced by many stalkers just prior to their stalking actions (Kienlen *et al.* 1997), can activate intense feelings in the perpetrator such as separation anxiety. Separation anxiety is a negative reaction to separation, involving 'proximity-seeking' behaviours (Hazan and Shaver 1987; Kienlen 1998; Borochowitz and Eisikovits 2002). These behaviours are aimed at becoming physically or emotionally close to the attachment figure, and in cases of stalking may involve following, or persistently contacting the former partner in person or via other means.

Insecure attachments are characteristic of stalkers (e.g. Meloy 1992; Douglas and Dutton 2001; Tonin 2004; Dutton and Winstead 2007; Wigman *et al.* in press); in particular preoccupied attachment, which is characterised by a positive view of others and a negative view of self. This pattern means that the preoccupied individual needs validation and approval from those who they hold in high regard. This type of attachment is linked with the unstable emotions and borderline personality traits as well as obsessional thoughts which are frequently evident in stalkers (Meloy 1996; Douglas and Dutton 2001). Stalkers have been found to be significantly more insecure in attachment than matched groups of community and forensic samples (Tonin 2004). Further, such preoccupied individuals have particular difficulty in adjusting to a relationship break-up (Barbara and Dion 2000). Stalkers with one victim were more preoccupied than those who targeted more than one victim (Tonin 2004). Although research remains in its infancy, attachment theory may notably assist in the development of treatment strategies for such offenders.

Delusional and personality disorders

Cluster B personality disorders (PDs) are most common in stalkers, particularly borderline personality disorder (BPD) and narcissistic disorders (Harmon, Rosner, and Owens 1995; Meloy and Gothard 1995; Kienlen *et al.* 1997; Meloy 1999; Kamphuis and Emmelkamp 2000; Douglas and Dutton 2001; Purcell *et al.* 2001; Sfiligoj 2003), although *not* antisocial PD (Douglas and Dutton 2001). Generally, these disorders are represented by a lack of identity or sense of self (Zona *et al.* 1998). BPD is specifically characterised by intense unreciprocated attachment to a partner, abandonment or rejection concerns and unstable, angry behaviour. Douglas and Dutton (2001) suggested stalkers were conceptually similar to batterers with borderline personality organisation, reinforcing the link between IPV and stalking.

Narcissistic PD is generally characterised by a desire for attention and power, by an individual's exploitative nature, jealous tendencies, lack of empathy and a sense of entitlement (DSM-IV 1994). Narcissistic individuals are prone to stalking, and may be particularly likely to stalk former-partners. Meloy (1999) suggested that this is because the characteristics of those who are narcissistic, such as their jealousy, grandiosity and sense of entitlement, may be manifested when they are rejected or abandoned by the intimate partner from whom they seek attention. This rejection may generate shame, rage and/or envy. Meloy (1999) suggested that the experience of these emotions in narcissists can result in behavioural pursuit or stalking in order to regain control over the ex-partner or to seek revenge. Narcissists react destructively, sometimes aggressively, to social rejection and have low levels of empathy and caring (Twenge and Campbell 2003; Baumeister et al. 1996). Kernberg (1998) reported that malignant narcissism is characterised by narcissistic PD, antisocial and paranoid facets and aggression, and can be accompanied by a lack of conscience, a need for power and a grandiose sense of self-worth. Kernberg saw malignant narcissism as the middle point on a spectrum of pathology ranging from narcissistic PD at the low end to psychopathy at the high end of narcissistic pathology.

Antisocial personality disorder (ASPD) is the only Cluster B disorder considered less likely to be associated with stalking. From an attachment perspective, those with ASPD are emotionally dismissive and so are less likely to engage in the intense relationships that can lead to former-intimate stalking (Meloy and Gothard 1995; Kienlen et al. 1997; Meloy 1998; Douglas and Dutton 2001). However, Zona et al. (1998) suggested that ASPD may be characteristic of stalkers who were abusive during their intimate relationship. In their college sample, Spitzberg and Veksler (2007) identified that threatening and aggressive forms of unwanted intrusions in particular were associated with attributions of ASPD of the pursuer. It may be that stalking behaviour by those with ASPD results from chance encounters with the target where the stalker feels their reputation is threatened by the target, rather than the result of deliberate attempts to make contact.

Dependent personality disorder is characterised by a need to be cared for and a fear of abandonment or separation (Sfiligoj 2003), and has been associated with stalking behaviours (Meloy and Gothard

1995; Kienlen *et al.* 1997; Purcell *et al.* 2001; Sfiligoj 2003) in both a non-psychotic (Kienlen *et al.* 1997) and a female stalker sample (Purcell *et al.* 2001). Dependent PD stalkers are particularly likely to stalk when an intimate relationship is under threat or has been terminated (Zona *et al.* 1998). Overall, given that the characteristic symptoms of personality disorders are 'relatively recognisable' and are likely to be 'identifiable early in a person's manifest relationship behaviour' then this 'suggests the possibility for far better personal assessments of risk than previously available' (Spitzberg and Veksler 2007: 286).

Substance abuse

Alcohol and drug abuse are risk factors for former-intimate stalking, although the number of stalkers engaging in substance abuse varies across samples and categories from just 2 per cent in some studies (e.g. Harmon *et al.* 1995) to 70 per cent in others (Meloy and Gothard 1995). Mullen *et al.* (1999) found that almost a third of a group they termed 'rejected' stalkers (who were mainly rejected by an intimate partner) had abused substances. Of the Axis I disorders, substance abuse is the most common type in stalkers (Douglas and Dutton 2001). Consideration of this would be useful for treatment initiatives, as the substance abuse may serve to reduce a stalker's inhibitions and/or increase impulsivity, potentially resulting in increased engagement in stalking behaviours or escalation of the severity of these behaviours. As discussed earlier, the role that substance abuse plays in stalking behaviours requires individual assessment before its role can be more clearly established.

Prior criminal history

Stalking is not generally a crime committed by otherwise law-abiding citizens. Many stalkers have prior criminal records (e.g. Mullen *et al.* 1999) and former-intimate stalkers in particular have been found to be likely to have violent criminal histories (Mohandie *et al.* 2006). Mullen *et al.* (1999) found that 36 per cent of their sample of 145 stalking cases referred to a psychiatric clinic were rejected stalkers; 79 per cent of this sub-sample had had a prior intimate relationship with the victim. Of the rejected stalkers, over half had previous criminal convictions. In such cases, stalking may represent a continuation of IPV and/or controlling behaviours used previously while the relationship was still intact (e.g. Kropp *et al.* 2002a). Consistent with risk factors identified for other criminal behaviours, stalkers have

215

been found to be impulsive toward the victim (e.g. Meloy 2007) and emotionally volatile (Douglas and Dutton 2001). Sheridan and Boon (2002) identified ex-partner harassers to be motivated by anger and impulsivity. They stated that management of these stalkers should consider this impulsivity factor, the high risk of violence and other types of aggression and that any threats should be taken seriously. Contact between stalker and victim should be reduced, and preferably stopped altogether. This would serve to remove reinforcements, as suggested by Westrup (1998, 2000) and may end stalking by ASPD individuals (see above).

Existing interventions

The functional analytic approach to stalker treatment involves understanding, predicting and managing behaviour by identifying associated variables that may affect such behaviour (Westrup 2000). This approach aims to identify key environmental factors or potential triggers (i.e. antecedents) that may relate to subsequent feelings and behaviour (and later, consequences), such that the 'frequency of a behaviour could be controlled by manipulating environmental variables' (Westrup 1998: 281). Stalking behaviours can be strengthened through positive (gaining something desired: e.g. the victim's time or attention) or negative (avoiding something aversive: e.g. the loneliness felt after an intimate relationship break-up) reinforcement, and can be reduced or terminated by punishment or by removing reinforcement when the stalking behaviour occurs. This approach is based on operant conditioning theory, which uses consequences to modify voluntary behaviour (Skinner 1953). All aspects of the stalking behaviour should be considered, e.g. the type, duration and severity. This may also include consideration of the risk factors identified in this chapter. Westrup (1998, 2000) stated that both intervention and treatment strategies can be supported using the information provided by the functional analytic approach. Others (Tschan 2006), suggest this approach may be too narrow and more detailed cognitive-behavioural approaches may be more beneficial. Stressful experiences such as relationship break-up can 'trigger' negative and pervasive thoughts, and for stalkers, these may be related to issues of rejection and 'betrayal' by the ex-partner. Cognitive behavioural therapy focuses on tackling these negative beliefs and cognitions, and facilitates the development and reinforcement of new thought processes surrounding the individual problems or issues

(Babcock 2002). Mullen *et al.* (1999, 2000) have proposed such an approach.

For treatment, Mullen *et al.* (1999) suggested an emphasis on the factors maintaining stalking behaviour such as denial, justification or minimisation of this behaviour, and on the negative effects of the stalking for the stalker themselves (enlightened self-interest, as detailed earlier in the chapter). However, an acceptance that 'personal change is necessary' is not always evident (Babcock 2002: 133); therefore, treatment initiatives should be 'robust enough to accommodate [this] denial' (p. 133). As in cases of sex-offender treatment, encouraging victim empathy may assist in some stalker treatment. In individual therapy this could include role-play and a consideration of the wishes of others and of the impact of stalking (Mullen *et al.* 2000). Mullen *et al.* (1999) identified strategies for working with these clients, including an appropriate balance of therapeutic and legal interventions which may vary according to the type of stalking offender. According to the researchers, rejected stalkers are responsive to police or judicial interventions, such as fines or prospective imprisonment. This intervention is less likely to be successful if the stalker is morbidly jealous, or if they are involved in a child custody battle with their victim. Additionally, as many stalkers have some form of psychopathology, psychotherapy to improve interpersonal skills and improve insight into the function that stalking serves the client may also be beneficial. Mullen *et al.* (2000) highlighted that stalkers, like many other types of offenders, typically experience very difficult personal lives (frequently due to mental health problems) and lack the social skills necessary to engage in situationally appropriate conduct. Thus they require long-term therapy as well as community support upon release. Pharmacological interventions may also be helpful; for example, depressive disorders associated with obsession and impulsivity can be assisted by serotonin selective re-uptake inhibitors (SSRIs) and clomipramine (Mullen *et al.* 2000). A consideration of personal problems (such as improving the social networks and skills required to interact effectively with others) could be employed as a 'lever to alter their behaviour' (Mullen *et al.* 2000: 279). Multidimensional interventions are frequently required to alleviate or terminate the desire to stalk a victim.

Babcock (2002) and Tschan (2006) reported that biological deficits should be considered before any other treatment is utilised. Tschan also argued that an offence-focused treatment approach addressing the stalker's behaviours rather than his or her personality factors may be preferable. As discussed above, personality factors need to be considered when deciding on the appropriate therapeutic style to be adopted and interventions need to be responsive to individual characteristics such as these. Intervention should be designed around the results of a thorough assessment of a range of factors in order to be able to deliver an effective treatment plan. These include a violence risk assessment, recidivism risk, motivation to change and background information such as prior criminal history and psychological variables such as attachment styles (Tschan 2006).

In their review of the literature Kamphuis and Emmelkamp (2000) grouped stalkers into erotomanic/delusional stalkers, secondary erotomanic stalkers (both characterised by Axis I psychotic disorders) and rejected stalkers (characterised by Axis II personality disorders). They provided different treatment recommendations for each group whereby the underlying psychopathological problems are assessed and treated/managed as appropriate. Tailored treatment has been recommended by other researchers (Mullen *et al.* 2000; Kropp *et al.* 2002b; Tschan 2006; Kuenher *et al.* 2007) and is consistent with the 'What Works' literature (McGuire 2002). Rejected stalkers who are most likely to be former-intimates of the victim are most likely to benefit from psychotherapeutic interventions that target their personality pathology, along with legal and judicial sanctions. However, according to Kamphuis and Emmelkamp (2000), those with erotomania or other psychoses are the most resilient and difficult stalkers to treat. As such, legal interventions would be necessary to attempt to deter the stalker from engaging in further stalking actions. Such interventions should be used with care. In some instances legal sanctions such as restraining or trespassing orders can anger and further motivate the perpetrator to engage in increasingly severe stalking. Alternatively, other types of stalkers may view these sanctions as the 'price of love', and so part of the process of achieving their desired relationship with the target. This reaction is particularly characteristic of intimacy seeking stalkers (Mullen *et al.* 1999), who aim to establish a relationship with the victim and who usually have erotomania or some other delusional disorder.

In addition to erotomania, whereby the patient holds the delusional belief that another person is in love with him/her, secondary erotomania is this delusional belief accompanied by a broader psychotic illness (Lloyd-Goldstein 1998), such as schizophrenia. Secondary erotomania is easier to treat, usually using neuroleptic drug treatment and focusing on the underlying psychotic illness. However, psychotherapy is not likely to be an effective treatment for either erotomanics or those with secondary erotomania (Kamphuis and Emmelkamp 2000).

One of the main considerations when treating stalkers is that many research studies have utilised clinical/forensic samples (e.g. Zona *et al.* 1993; Harmon *et al.* 1995; Purcell *et al.* 2001), which are likely to consist of more severe types of stalkers and stalking behaviour. Only a small number of those who perpetrate stalking are investigated further, charged or convicted of stalking (e.g. Harris 2000), yet we know that stalking has co-morbidity with other crimes, particularly aggressive crimes. Therefore forensic mental health practitioners, and those who work with offenders, will potentially interact with stalkers in treatment settings more frequently than they are aware and should be alert to reports that indicate stalking may have been an element in an offence even if it was not identified as such. Although severe stalkers are more likely to be identified as such to authorities, the less severe or 'new' stalkers frequently remain unnoticed or this element of their offending is missed, yet they may be more responsive and acquiescent to treatment (Westrup 2000).

Treatment initiatives are often involuntary for stalkers and so stalkers frequently manifest low or non-existent motivation to change (Kamphuis and Emmelkamp 2000). Some researchers suggest that to enhance motivation treatment approaches require a clearly defined legal framework which includes disciplinary procedures for non-attendance (Tschan 2006).

Case management

Kropp *et al.* (2002b) applied the principles of risk management of stalkers using a multi-agency, multi-disciplinary perspective. Their main intervention objective was to prevent further aggressive behaviour rather than assuage the symptoms, stating that their intervention was 'preventative rather than rehabilitative' (p. 147). Kropp *et al.* (2002b) used the term 'case management' rather than 'treatment' because of clients' typical lack of cooperation with treatment. The researchers identified six key principles of case management:

1 Focus on 'identifying, assessing and containing' risk (p. 147). This will include consideration and management of the risk factors for stalking detailed earlier.

2 A diverse, multidisciplinary team (including law enforcement, legal agencies, healthcare workers, etc.) to evaluate the evidence

and draw a considered opinion as to whether the case constitutes stalking. This team will go on to recommend strategies for the investigation and management of a stalking case.

3 Deliver comprehensive and integrated services: each service should have a clear role, and awareness of the policies and procedures of the other services.

4 Improve psychosocial adjustment: including treatment of personality disorders, and substance abuse, which are both related to impulsivity. Treatment may include anti-psychotic drugs, group or individual therapy, anger management, vocational skills training and educational programmes to assist in changing attitudes to violence. This is important, considering relationship aggression is a strong risk factor for stalking.

5 Limit risk with high supervision: usually undertaken by police, legal or security professionals to deter or make it difficult for the stalker to contact or pursue the victim. The supervisor will monitor the stalker, and be in contact with the victim and other relevant parties (e.g. counsellors, healthcare workers, family members); supervision should always accompany any treatments that are imposed.

6 Improve victims' security resources: a process that aims to minimise the physical and psychological impact of stalking, should it continue regardless of the presence of supervision and treatment. It is helpful that the authors emphasise the importance of working with victims and view victims' 'safety planning' as an essential aspect of case management, as this is an area that is often neglected. Sheridan and Boon (2002) and Westrup (2000) also emphasise the importance of victim welfare during treatment of the stalker.

Suggested improvements and future research

Research on the treatment of stalking offenders is in its infancy. Often, the treatment initiatives used for violent and sex offenders are applied to stalking offenders, and aspects of these treatments may be beneficial. However, stalking may be fundamentally different to other crimes (see Kropp *et al.* 2002a, for examples of this when assessing risk of violent and stalking offenders). Therefore, as documented above, researchers have attempted to identify treatments and interventions specific to stalkers.

Future research should systematically consider the effectiveness of drug and psychotherapeutic interventions for stalkers (Kamphuis and Emmelkamp 2000). The role of legal sanctions in the 'treatment' or prevention of future stalking actions should be considered as a function of the type of stalker: certain treatments or strategies will be more effective in reducing the stalking for some perpetrators than for others. Research should work towards consensus and clarity of guidelines for practitioners who are treating stalking offenders. Suggestions in the literature do share some common elements. Most researchers would agree that treatment should consider: (1) the underlying disorders of stalking offenders; (2) utilising a multi-disciplinary team to assess and treat stalkers – for example, former-intimate stalkers are likely to require treatment for their involvement in 'domestic violence' as well as stalking; and (3) balancing law enforcement initiatives and interventions (this may include recommendations from the functional analytic approach, such as removing reinforcements and introducing punishments for the stalking actions) with psychotherapeutic treatment strategies – this 'balance' will differ for the various types of stalker.

In recent years, useful and detailed typologies of stalkers have emerged (e.g. Mullen *et al.* 1999; Sheridan and Boon 2002) which have developed understanding of the different treatment needs relevant to various types of stalking offenders. However, consensus on a typology of stalkers would have clear beneficial implications for treatment. In 2000, Kamphuis and Emmelkamp reported that there were 'no clear guidelines' (p. 208) for the treatment of stalkers, and we are just beginning to see some suggestions emerging.

Overall conclusions

This chapter discussed the academic and clinical literature on IPV and stalking. Both types of offence share common elements with criminal behaviour in general. However, there are also unique elements that require further empirical and clinical investigation. To summarise, six key points are presented below to guide assessment and treatment. These are as follows:

1 Clinicians should resist simplistic explanations of IPV and stalking.

2 IPV is perpetrated by men and women and is frequently mutual in nature.

3 IPV perpetrators and stalkers share many of the same risk factors and psychopathological problems that other offenders have.

4 The literature on IPV and stalking suggests that a range of treatment needs are likely to be present.

5 Individualised assessment of a wide range of potential risk factors is required to match client need with treatment targets.

6 Client variables such as psychopathology are important when designing and delivering treatment, and that treatment should to be responsive to the individual needs.

References

Archer, J. (2000) 'Sex differences in aggression between heterosexual partners: a meta-analytic review', *Psychological Bulletin*, 126: 651–80.

Archer, J. (2006) 'Cross-cultural differences in physical aggression between partners: a social-role analysis', *Personality and Social Psychology Review*, 10: 133–53.

Ashcroft, J., Daniels, D.J. and Hart, C.V. (2003) *Batterer Intervention Programmes: Where Do We Go from Here?* Office of Justice Programs, National Institute of Justice, US Department of Justice. (See: http://www.ojp.usdoj.gov/nij.)

Babcock, J.C., Green, C.E. and Robie, C. (2004) 'Does batterers' treatment work? A meta-analytic review of domestic violence treatment', *Clinical Psychology Review*, 23: 1023–53.

Babcock, J.C., Miller, S. and Siard, C. (2003) 'Toward a typology of abusive women: differences between partner-only and generally violent women in the use of violence', *Psychology of Women Quarterly*, 13: 46–59.

Babcock, R. (2002) 'Psychopathology and treatment of stalking', in J. Boon and L. Sheridan, *Stalking and Psychosexual Obsession*. New York: Wiley & Sons, pp. 125–39.

Baier, C. and Wright, B. (2001) '"If you love me, keep my commandments": a meta-analysis of the effect of religion on crime', *Journal of Research in Crime and Delinquency*, 38: 3–21.

Barbara, A.M. and Dion, K.L. (2000) 'Breaking up is hard to do, especially for preoccupied lovers', *Journal of Personal and Interpersonal Loss*, 5: 315–42.

Baumeister, R.F., Smart, L. and Boden, J.M. (1996) 'Relation of threatened egotism to violence and aggression: the dark side of high self-esteem', *Psychological Review*, 103: 5–33.

Bednar, S.G. (2003) 'Substance abuse and woman abuse: a proposal for integrated treatment', *Health and Mental Health Treatment and Prevention*, 67: 52–7.

Blair, R. (2001) 'Neurocognitive models of aggression, the antisocial personality disorders, and psychopathy', *Journal of Neurology, Neurosurgery and Psychiatry*, 71: 727–31.

Borochowitz, D.Y. and Eisikovits, Z. (2002) 'To love violently', *Violence Against Women*, 8: 476–94.

Bouchard, G.P. and Lee, C.M. (1999) 'Violence against the spouse: are couple treatments appropriate?', *Canadian Psychology*, 40: 328–42.

Brown, J. (2004) 'Shame and domestic violence: treatment perspectives for perpetrators from self psychology and affect theory', *Sexual and Relationship Therapy*, 19: 39–56.

Brown, P.D. and O'Leary, K.D. (2000) 'Therapeutic alliance: predicting continuance and success in group treatment for spouse abuse', *Journal of Consulting and Clinical Psychology*, 68: 340–5.

Burstein, M., Stanger, C., Kamon, J. and Dumenci, L. (2006) 'Parent psychopathology, parenting, and child internalizing problems in substance-abusing families', *Psychology of Addictive Behaviors*, 20 (2): 97–106.

Capaldi, D.M. and Clark, S. (1998) 'Prospective family predictors of aggression toward female partners for at-risk young men', *Developmental Psychology*, 34: 1175–88.

Capaldi, D.M., Kim, H.K. and Shortt, J.W. (2004) 'Women's involvement in aggression in young adult romantic relationships', in M. Putallaz and K.L. Bierman (ed.), *Aggression, Antisocial Behavior, and Violence Among Girls*. New York: Guilford Press.

Capaldi, D.M., Kim, H. and Shortt, J. (2007) 'Observed initiation and reciprocity of physical aggression in young, at-risk couples', *Journal of Family Violence*, 22: 101–11.

Capaldi, D.M., Shortt, J.W. and Crosby, L. (2003) 'Physical and psychological aggression in at-risk young couples: stability and change in young adulthood', *Merrill-Palmer Quarterly*, 49 (1): 1–27.

Capaldi, D. M., Dishion, T. J., Stoolmiller, M. and Yoerger, K. (2001) 'Aggression toward female partners by at-risk young men: the contribution of male adolescent friendships', *Developmental Psychology*, 37 (1): 61–73.

Capaldi, D.M., Stoolmiller, M., Clark, S. and Owen, L. (2002) 'Heterosexual risk behaviors in at-risk young men from early adolescence to young adulthood: prevalence, prediction, and association with STI contraction', *Developmental Psychology*, 38: 394–406.

Clear, T.R. and Sumter, M.T. (2002) 'Prisoners, prison, and religion: religion and adjustment to prison', *Journal of Offender Rehabilitation*, 35: 127–59.

Cohen, J. (1992) 'A power primer', *Psychological Bulletin*, 112: 155–9.

Coleman, J. R. (1997) 'Stalking behaviour and the cycle of domestic violence', *Journal of Interpersonal Violence*, 12: 420–32.

Connolly, J., Furman, W. and Konarski, R. (2000a) 'The role of peers in the emergence of heterosexual romantic relationships in adolescence', *Child Development*, 71: 1395–408.

Violent and Sexual Offenders

Connolly, J., Pepler, D., Craig, W. and Taradash, A. (2000b) 'Dating experiences of bullies in early adolescence', *Child Maltreatment*, 5: 299–310.

Corvo, K. and Johnson, P. (2003) 'Vilification of the "batterer": how blame shapes domestic violence policy and interventions', *Aggression and Violent Behavior*, 8: 259–82.

Cullen, F.T., Pealer, J.A., Santana, S.A., Fisher, B.S., Applegate, B.K. and Blevins, K.R. (2007) 'Public support for faith-based correctional programs: should sacred places serve civic purposes?', *Journal of Offender Rehabilitation*, 45: 29–46.

Daly, J.E., Power, T.G. and Gondolf, E.W. (2001) 'Predictors of batterer program attendance', *Journal of Interpersonal Violence*, 16: 971–91.

DiIulio, J.J. Jr (2001a) 'Not by faith alone: religion, crime, and substance abuse', in E.J. Dionne Jr and M.H. Chen (eds), *Sacred Places, Civic Purposes: Should Government Help Faith-Based Charity?* Washington, DC: Brookings Institution Press, pp. 77–93.

DiIulio, J.J. Jr (2001b) 'Compassion in truth and action: what Washington can not do to help', in E.J. Dionne Jr and M.H. Chen (eds), *Sacred Places, Civic Purposes: Should Government Help Faith-Based Charity?* Washington, DC: Brookings Institution Press, pp. 273–86.

Dixon, L. and Browne, K. (2003) 'The heterogeneity of spouse abuse: a review', *Aggression and Violent Behavior*, 8: 107–30.

Dobash, R.P. and Dobash, R.E. (1979) *Violence Against Wives: A Case Against Patriarchy*. New York: Free Press.

Dobash, R.P. and Dobash, R.E. (2004) 'Women's violence to men in intimate relationships: working on a puzzle', *British Journal of Criminology*, 44: 324–49.

Douglas, K.S. and Dutton, D.G. (2001) 'Assessing the link between stalking and domestic violence', *Aggression and Violent Behavior*, 6: 519–46.

Dowd, E.T. and Wallbrown, F. (1993) 'Motivational components of client reactance', *Journal of Counselling and Development*, 71 (5): 533–8.

Dryden, W., Neenan, M. and Yankura, J. (1999) *Counselling Individuals: A Rational Emotive Behavioural Handbook*, 3rd edn. Philadelphia, PA: Whurr Publishers.

DSM-IV (1994) *Diagnostic and Statistical Manual: Text Version*, 4th edn. Washington, DC: American Psychological Association.

Dutton, D.G. (2003a) 'Theoretical approaches to the treatment of intimate violence perpetrators', *Journal of Aggression, Maltreatment and Trauma*, 7: 7–23.

Dutton, D.G. (2003b) *The Abusive Personality*. New York: Guilford Press.

Dutton, D.G. (2008) *Domestic Violence*. Annual Conference of the Division of Forensic Psychology, British Psychological Society, Edinburgh.

Dutton, D.G. (in press) 'Transforming a flawed policy: a call to revive psychology and science in domestic violence research and practice', *Aggression and Violent Behavior*.

224

Dutton, D.G. and Corvo, K. (2007) 'The Duluth model: a data-impervious paradigm and a failed strategy', *Aggression and Violent Behavior*, 12 (6): 658–67.

Dutton, L.B. and Winstead, B.A. (2007) 'Predicting unwanted pursuit: attachment, relationship satisfaction, relationship alternatives, and break-up distress', *Journal of Social and Personal Relationships*, 23: 565–86.

Dvoskin, J. and Spiers, E. (2004) 'On the role of correctional officers in prison mental health', *Psychiatric Quarterly*, 75: 41–59.

Ehrensaft, M.K., Cohen, P. and Johnson, J.G. (2006) 'Development of personality disorder symptoms and the risk for partner violence', *Journal of Abnormal Behavior*, 115: 474–83.

Ehrensaft, M.K., Moffitt, T.E. and Caspi, A. (2006) 'Is domestic violence followed by an increased risk of psychiatric disorders among women but not men? A longitudinal cohort study', *American Journal of Psychiatry*, 163: 885–93.

El-Zanty, F., Hussein, E.M., Shawky, G.A., Way, A.A. and Kishor, S. (1995) *Egypt Demographic and Health Survey 1995*. Cairo: National Population Council.

Fals-Stewart, W., Leonard, K. and Birchler, G. (2005) 'The occurrence of male-to-female intimate partner violence on days of men's drinking: the moderating effects of antisocial personality disorder', *Journal of Consulting and Clinical Psychology*, 73: 239–48.

Feder, L. and Wilson, D. (2005) 'A meta-analytic review of court-mandated batterer intervention programs: can courts affect abusers' behavior?', *Journal of Experimental Criminology*, 1 (2): 239–62.

Felson, R.B. (2002) *Violence and Gender Reexamined*. Washington, DC: American Psychological Association.

Frye, N.E. and Karney, B.R. (2006) 'The context of aggressive behavior in marriage: a longitudinal study of newlyweds', *Journal of Family Psychology*, 20 (1): 12–20.

George, M.J. (1994) 'Riding the donkey backwards: men as victims of un-acceptable victims of marital violence', *Journal of Men's Studies*, 3: 137–59.

Gilchrist, E., Johnson, R., Takriti, R., Weston, S., Beech, T. and Kebbell, M. (2003) *Domestic Violence Offender: Characteristics and Offending-Related Needs*, Home Office Research Findings No. 217. London: Home Office.

Gondolf, E. (1999) 'A comparison of four batterer intervention systems: do court referral, program length, and services matter?', *Journal of Interpersonal Violence*, 14: 41–61.

Gondolf, E. and Russell, D. (1986) 'The case against anger control treatment programs for batterers', *Response to the Victimization of Women and Children*, 9: 2–5.

Gondolf, E. and White, R.J. (2001) 'Batterer program participants who repeatedly reassault: psychopathic tendencies and other disorders', *Journal of Interpersonal Violence*, 16 (4): 361–80.

Graham, K., Plant, M. and Plant, M. (2004) 'Alcohol, gender and partner aggression: a general population study of British adults', *Addiction Research and Theory*, 12: 385–401.

Graham-Kevan, N. and Archer, J. (2003) 'Patriarchal terrorism and common couple violence: a test of Johnson's predictions in four British samples', *Journal of Interpersonal Violence*, 18: 1247–70.

Graham-Kevan, N. and Archer, J. (2005) 'Investigating three explanations of women's relationship aggression', *Psychology of Women Quarterly*, 29: 270–7.

Graham-Kevan, N. and Archer J. (in press) 'Does controlling behaviour predict physical aggression and violence towards partners?', *Journal of Family Violence*.

Hamberger, L.K. and Hastings, J.E. (1986) 'Personality correlates of men who batter and nonviolent men: some continuities and discontinuities', *Journal of Family Violence*, 6: 131–47.

Hamel, J. (2005) *Gender Inclusive Treatment of Intimate Partner Abuse: A Comprehensive Approach*. New York: Springer.

Harmon, R. B., Rosner, R. and Owens, H. (1995) 'Obsessional harassment and erotomania in a criminal court population', *Journal of Forensic Sciences*, 40: 188–96.

Harris, G. (2006) 'Conjoint therapy and domestic violence: treating the individuals and the relationship', *Counselling Psychology Quarterly*, 19 (4): 373–9.

Harris, J. (2000) *The Protection from Harassment Act 1997 – An Evaluation of Its Use and Effectiveness*, Home Office Research, Development and Statistics Directorate Research Findings No. 130. London: Home Office.

Hay, D.F. (2005) 'The beginnings of aggression in infancy', in R.E. Tremblay, W.W. Hartup and J. Archer (eds), *Developmental Origins of Aggression*. New York: Guilford Press, pp. 107–32.

Hazan, C. and Shaver, P.R. (1987) 'Romantic love conceptualized as an attachment process', *Journal of Personality and Social Psychology*, 52: 511–24.

Holtzworth-Munroe, A. and Stuart, G.L. (1994) 'Typologies of male batterers: three subtypes and the differences among them', *Psychological Bulletin*, 116: 476–97.

Holtzworth-Munroe, A., Stuart, G.L., Meehan, J.C., Herron, K. and Rehman, U. (2000) 'Testing the Holtzworth-Munroe and Stuart (1994) batterer typology', *Journal of Consulting and Clinical Psychology*, 68: 1000–19.

International Boxing Federation (2006) *Rules Governing Championship Contests effective September 1, 2006*. Accessed on 21 February 2008 at: http://www.ibf-usba-boxing.com/index.php?pg=20.

Jang, S.J. and Johnson, B.R. (2001) 'Neighborhood disorder, individual religiosity, and adolescent use of illicit drugs: a test of multilevel hypotheses', *Criminology*, 39: 109–43.

Johnson, B.R. (2004) 'Religious programs and recidivism among former inmates in Prison Fellowship programs: a long-term follow-up study', *Justice Quarterly*, 21: 329–54.

Johnson, B.R., Larson, D.B. and Pitts, T.C. (1997) 'Religious programs, institutional adjustment, and recidivism among former inmates of Prison Fellowship programs', *Justice Quarterly*, 14: 145–66.

Johnson, B.R., Jang, S.J., De Li, S. and Larson, D.B. (2000) 'The "invisible institution" and black youth crime: the church as an agency of local social control', *Journal of Youth and Adolescence*, 29: 479–98.

Johnson, B.R., Jang, S.J., Larson, D.B. and De Li, S. (2001) 'Does adolescent religious commitment matter? A reexamination of the effects of religiosity on delinquency', *Journal of Research in Crime and Delinquency*, 38: 22–44.

Johnson, M.P. (1995) 'Patriarchal terrorism and common couple violence: two forms of violence against women', *Journal of Marriage and the Family*, 57: 283–94.

Kamphuis, J.H. and Emmelkamp, P.M.G. (2000) 'Stalking – a contemporary challenge for forensic and clinical psychiatry', *British Journal of Psychiatry*, 176: 206–9.

Kamphuis, J.H., Emmelkamp, P.M.G. and de Vries, V. (2004) 'Informant personality descriptions of postintimate stalkers using the five factor profile', *Journal of Personality Assessment*, 82: 169–78.

Kantor, K., Jasnski, J.L. and Aldarondo, E. (1994) 'Sociocultural status and incidence of marital violence in Hispanic families', *Violence and Victims*, 9: 207–22.

Kenny, M. (2007) 'Review of women who perpetrate relationship violence: moving beyond political correctness', *Child Abuse and Neglect*, 31: 596–7.

Kernberg, O.F. (1998) 'The psychotherapeutic management of psychopathic, narcissistic, and paranoid transferences', in T. Millon, E. Simonson, M. Birket-Smith and R.D. Davis (eds), *Psychopathy: Antisocial, Criminal, and Violent Behavior*. New York: Guilford Press, pp. 372–92.

Kienlen, K.K. (1998) 'Developmental and social antecedents of stalking', in J.R. Meloy (ed.), *The Psychology of Stalking: Clinical and Forensic Perspectives*. London: Academic Press, pp. 52–65.

Kienlen, K.K., Birmingham, D.L., Solberg, K.B., O'Regan, J.T. and Meloy, J.R. (1997) 'A comparative study of psychotic and non-psychotic stalking', *Journal of the American Academy Psychiatry and the Law*, 25: 317–34.

Kim, H.K. and Capaldi, D.M. (2004) 'The association of antisocial behavior and depressive symptoms between partners and risk for aggression in romantic relationships', *Journal of Family Psychology*, 18 (1): 82–96.

Kropp, P.R., Hart, S.D. and Lyon, D.R. (2002a) 'Risk assessment of stalkers: some problems and possible solutions', *Criminal Justice and Behavior*, 29: 590–616.

Kropp, P.R., Hart, S.D., Lyon, D.R. and LePard, D.A. (2002b) 'Managing stalkers: coordinating treatment and supervision', in J. Boon and

L. Sheridan (eds), *Stalking and Psychosexual Obsession*. New York: Wiley & Sons, pp. 141–63.

Kuehner, C., Gass, P. and Dressing, H. (2007) 'Increased risk of mental disorders among lifetime victims of stalking – findings from a community study', *European Psychiatry*, 22: 142–5.

Lambert, M.J. and Bergin, A.E. (1994) 'The effectiveness of psychotherapy', in A.E. Bergin and S.L. Garfield (eds), *Handbook of Psychotherapy and Behavior Change*, 4th edn. New York: Wiley, pp. 143–89.

Linder, J.R. and Collins, W.A. (2005) 'Parent and peer predictors of physical aggression and conflict management in romantic relationships in early adulthood', *Journal of Family Psychology*, 19 (2): 252–62.

Lloyd-Goldstein, R. (1998) 'De Clérambault on-line: a survey of erotomania and stalking from the old world to the world wide web', in J.R. Meloy (ed.), *The Psychology of Stalking*. London: American Press, pp. 195–211.

Locke, T.F. and Newcomb, M.D. (2004) 'Child maltreatment, parent alcohol- and drug-related problems, polydrug problems, and parenting practices: a test of gender differences and four theoretical perspectives', *Journal of Family Psychology*, 18: 120–34.

Logan, T.K., Leukefeld, C. and Walker, R. (2000) 'Stalking as a variant of intimate violence: implications from a young adult sample', *Violence and Victims*, 15: 91–111.

Lundeberg, K. and Carlton, R.P. (2000) 'The intergenerational transmission of spouse abuse: a meta-analysis', *Journal of Marriage and the Family*, 62: 640–54.

McGuire, J. (2002) 'Criminal sanctions versus psychologically-based interventions with offenders: a comparative empirical analysis', *Psychology, Crime and Law*, 8 (2): 183–208.

McGuire, J. and Priestley, P. (2000) 'Reviewing "what works": past, present and future in J. McGuire (ed.), *What Works: Reducing Reoffending? Guidelines from Research and Practice*. Chichester: John Wiley & Sons.

Mechanic, M.B., Uhlmansiek, M.H., Weaver, T.L. and Resick, P.A. (2000) 'The impact of severe stalking experienced by acutely battered women: a examination of violence, psychological symptoms and strategic responding', *Violence and Victims*, 15: 443–58.

Meloy, J.R. (1992) *Violent Attachments*. Northvale, NJ: Jason Aronson.

Meloy, J.R. (1996) 'Stalking (obsessional following): a review of some preliminary studies', *Aggression and Violent Behavior*, 1: 147–62.

Meloy, J.R. (1998) 'The psychology of stalking', in J.R. Meloy (ed.), *The Psychology of Stalking: Clinical and Forensic Perspectives*. London: Academic Press, pp. 2–21.

Meloy, J.R. (1999) 'Stalking: an old behavior, a new crime', *Forensic Psychiatry*, 22: 85–99.

Meloy, J.R. (2007) 'Stalking: the state of the science', *Criminal Behaviour and Mental Health*, 17: 1–7.

Meloy, J.R. and Gothard, S. (1995) 'Demographic and clinical comparison of obsessional followers and offenders with mental disorders', *American Journal of Psychiatry*, 152: 258–63.

Mirrlees-Black, C., Mayhew, P. and Percy, A. (1996) *The 1996 British Crime Survey: England and Wales*, Home Office Research Bulletin No. 19. London: Home Office Research and Statistics Department.

Moffitt, T.E., Caspi, A., Rutter, M. and Silva, P.A. (2001) *Sex Differences in Antisocial Behaviour: Conduct Disorder, Delinquency, and Violence in the Dunedin Longitudinal Study*. Cambridge: Cambridge University Press.

Moffitt, T.E., Caspi, A., Rutter, M. and Silva, P.A. (2001) *Sex Differences in Antisocial Behaviour: Conduct Disorder, Delinquency, and Violence in the Dunedin Longitudinal Study*. Cambridge: Cambridge University Press.

Moffitt, T.E., Krueger, R.F., Caspi, A. and Fagan, J. (2000) 'Partner abuse and general crime: how are they the same? how are they different?', *Criminology*, 38: 199–232.

Mohandie, K., Meloy, J.R., McGowan, M.G. and Williams, J. (2006) 'The RECON typology of stalking: reliability and validity based upon a large sample of North American students', *Journal of Forensic Sciences*, 51: 147–55.

Mullen, P.E., Pathé, M. and Purcell, R. (2000) *Stalkers and Their Victims*. Cambridge: Cambridge University Press.

Mullen, P.E., Pathé, M., Purcell, R. and Stuart, G.W. (1999) 'Study of stalkers', *American Journal of Psychiatry*, 156: 1244–9.

Murphy, C. and Dienemann, J. (1999) 'Informing the research agenda on domestic abuser intervention through practitioner-researcher dialogues', *Journal of Interpersonal Violence*, 14 (12): 1314–26.

Novak, S. and Galaway, B. (1983) *Domestic Abuse Intervention Project Final Report*. Duluth MN: Domestic Abuse Intervention Project. Accessed on 30 June 2006 on: http://www.duluth-model.org/.

O'Connor, T.P. and Perreyclear, M. (2002) 'Prison religion in action and its influence on offender rehabilitation', *Journal of Offender Rehabilitation*, 35: 11–33.

O'Leary, K.D., Malone, J. and Tyree, A. (1994) 'Physical aggression in early marriage: prerelationship and relationship effects', *Journal of Consulting and Clinical Psychology*, 62 (3): 594–602.

O'Leary, K.D., Barling, J., Arias, I. and Rosenbaum, A. (1989) 'Prevalence and stability of physical aggression between spouses: a longitudinal analysis', *Journal of Consulting and Clinical Psychology*, 57: 263–8.

O'Farrell, T. and Murphy, C. (1995) 'Marital violence before and after alcoholism treatment', *Journal of Consulting and Clinical Psychology*, 63 (2): 256–62.

O'Farrell, T., Murphy, C., Stephan, S., Fals-Stewart, W. and Murphy, M. (2004) 'Partner violence before and after couples-based alcoholism treatment for male alcoholic patients: the role of treatment involvement and abstinence', *Journal of Consulting and Clinical Psychology*, 72 (2): 202–17.

Pagelow, M.D. (1984) *Family Violence.* New York: Praeger.

Potter-Efron, R.T. (2007) 'Anger, aggression, domestic violence and substance use', in J. Hamel and T. Nichols (eds), *Family Interventions in Domestic Violence: A Handbook of Gender-Inclusive Theory and Treatment.* New York: Springer.

Prospero, M. (2008) *Domestic Violence in Ethnic Minority Populations.* Paper presented at the 'From Ideology to Inclusion: Evidence-Based Policy and Intervention in Domestic Violence' Conference, 15–16 February, Sacramento, California.

Purcell, R., Pathé, M. and Mullen, P.E. (2001) 'A study of women who stalk', *American Journal of Psychiatry,* 158: 2056–60.

Rivett, M. (2006) 'Editorial: treatment for perpetrators of domestic violence: controversy in policy and practice', *Criminal Behaviour and Mental Health,* 16 (4): 205–10.

Rooney, J. and Hanson, R. (2001) 'Predicting attrition from treatment programs for abusive men', *Journal of Family Violence,* 16 (2): 131–49.

Rothschild, B., Dimson, C., Storaasli, R. and Clapp, L. (1997) 'Personality profiles of veterans entering treatment for domestic violence', *Journal of Family Violence,* 12 (3): 259–74.

Scott, C.L. and Resnick, P.J. (in press) 'Violent risk assessment in persons with mental illness', *Aggression and Violent Behavior.*

Serbin, L., Stack, D., De Genna, N., Grunzeweig, N., Temcheff, C.E., Schwartzmann, A.E. *et al.* (2004) 'When aggressive girls become mothers', in M. Putallaz and K. L. Bierman (ed.), *Aggression, Antisocial Behavior, and Violence Among Girls.* New York: Guilford Press.

Sfiligoj, T.M. (2003) 'A comparison of stalkers and domestic violence batterers', *Journal of Psychological Practice,* 8: 20–45.

Shepard, M. (1992) 'Predicting batterer recidivism five years after community intervention', *Journal of Family Violence,* 7 (3): 167–78.

Sheridan, L. and Boon, J. (2002) 'Stalker typologies: implications for law enforcement', in J. Boon and L. Sheridan, *Stalking and Psychosexual Obsession.* New York: Wiley & Sons, pp. 63–82.

Shqham-Salomon, V., Avner, R. and Neeman, R. (1989) *'You're* changed if *you* do and changed if *you* don't: mechanisms underlying paradoxical interventions', *Journal of Consulting and Clinical Psychology,* 57: 590–8.

Skinner, B.F. (1953) *Science and Human Behavior.* New York: Free Press

Snow Jones, A. and Gondolf, E.W. (2001) 'Time-varying risk factors for reassault among batterer program participants', *Journal of Family Violence,* 16 (4): 345–59.

Sorenson, S.B. and Telles, C.A. (1991) 'Self-reports of spousal violence in a Mexican-American and non-Hispanic white population', *Violence and Victims,* 6: 3–15.

Spitzberg, B.H. and Veksler, A.E. (2007) 'The personality of pursuit: personality attributions of unwanted pursuers and stalkers', *Violence and Victims,* 22: 275–89.

Stets, J. and Straus, M.A. (1990) 'Gender differences in reporting marital violence and its medical and psychological consequences', in M. A. Straus and R. Gelles (eds), *Physical Violence in American Families*. New Brunswick, NJ: Transaction Press.

Stith, S.M., Smith, D.B., Penn, C.E., Ward, D.B. and Tritt, D. (2004) 'Intimate partner physical abuse perpetration and victimization risk factors: a meta-analytic review', *Aggression and Violent Behavior*, 10: 65–98.

Straus, M.A. (2005) 'Women's violence towards men is a serious social problem', in D.R. Loseke, R.J. Gelles and M.M. Cavanaugh (eds), *Current Controversies on Family Violence*, 2nd edn. Newbury Park, CA: Sage, pp. 55–77. Free download from: http://pubpages.unh.edu/~mas2/VB33R%20Women%27s%20Violence%20Toward%20Men.pdf.

Sugarman, D.B. and Frankel, S.L. (1996) 'Patriarchal ideology and wife-assault: a meta-analytic review', *Journal of Family Violence*, 11: 13–40.

Taft, C., Murphy, C.M., Elliott, J.D. and Keaser, M.C. (2001) 'Race and demographic factors in treatment attendance for domestically abusive men', *Journal of Family Violence*, 6: 385–400.

Taft, C., Murphy, C., Elliott, J. and Morrel, T. (2001) 'Attendance-enhancing procedures in group counseling for domestic abusers', *Journal of Counseling Psychology*, 48 (1): 51–60.

Taft, C., Murphy, C., Musser, P., and Remington, N. (2004) 'Personality, interpersonal, and motivational predictors of the working alliance in group cognitive-behavioral therapy for partner violent men', *Journal of Consulting and Clinical Psychology*, 72 (2): 349–54.

Taft, C., Murphy, C., King, D., Musser, P. and DeDeyn, J. (2003) 'Process and treatment adherence factors in group cognitive-behavioral therapy for partner violent men', *Journal of Consulting and Clinical Psychology*, 71 (4): 812–20.

Titterington, V. and Harper, L. (2005) 'Women as the aggressors in intimate partner homicide in Houston, 1980s to 1990s', *Journal of Offender Rehabilitation*, 41 (4): 83–98.

Tjaden, P. and Thoennes, N. (2000) 'The role of stalking in domestic violence crime reports generated by the Colorado Springs police department', *Violence and Victims*, 15: 427–41.

Tonin, E. (2004) 'The attachment styles of stalkers', *Journal of Forensic Psychiatry and Psychology*, 15: 584–90.

Tremblay, T.E., Nagin, D.S., Séguin, J.R., Zoccolillo, M., Zelazo, P.D., Boivin, M., Pérusse, D. and Japel, C. (2004) 'Physical aggression during early childhood: trajectories and predictors', *Pediatrics*, 114: 43–50.

Tschan, W. (2006) *Stalking: A Treatment Approach for Offenders*. Paper presented at 159th American Psychiatric Annual Meeting, 24 May, Toronto, Canada.

Twenge, J.M. and Campbell, W.K. (2003) '"Isn't it fun to get the respect that we're going to deserve?" Narcissism, social rejection, and aggression', *Personality and Social Psychology Bulletin*, 29: 261–72.

Westrup, D. (1998) 'Applying functional analysis to stalking behavior', in J.R. Meloy (ed.), *The Psychology of Stalking*. London: Academic Press.

Westrup, D. (2000) *Stalking in the US: Time to Focus on Treatment*. Paper presented at the 'Stalking: Criminal Justice Responses' Conference, Sydney, Australia.

White, W. (2004) 'Substance use and violence: understanding the nuances of the relationship', *Addiction Professional*, 13–19.

Wigman, S.J.A., Graham-Kevan, N. and Archer, J. (in press) 'Investigating sub-groups of stalkers: the roles of attachment, dependency, jealousy and aggression', *Journal of Family Violence*.

Worley, K., Walsh, S. and Lewis, K. (2004) 'An examination of parenting experiences in male perpetrators of domestic violence: a qualitative study', *Psychology and Psychotherapy: Theory, Research and Practice*, 77 (1): 35–54.

Zimmer, B. (2004–5) 'The effect of faith-based programs in reducing recidivism and substance abuse of ex-offenders', *Journal of Community Corrections*, 14: 7–19.

Zona, M.A., Palarea, R.E. and Lane, J.C. (1998) 'Psychiatric diagnosis and the offender-victim typology of stalking', in J.R. Meloy (ed.), *The Psychology of Stalking*. San Diego, CA: Academic Press, pp. 69–84.

Zona, M.A., Sharma, K.K. and Lane, J. (1993) 'A comparative study of erotomanic and obsessional subjects in a forensic sample', *Journal of Forensic Science*, 38: 894–903.

Part 3

Management

Chapter 10

When thinking leads to doing: the relationship between fantasy and reality in sexual offending

Tim Jones and David Wilson

Immersing ourselves in our 'own world' provides an opportunity to escape from the restraint, confines and persecution of reality – albeit the persecution we impose upon ourselves. This highly personal place enables us to dwell on thoughts, aspirations and dreams, and unless such thoughts are verbalised or acted upon they remain purely in a psychological space. Naturally, some thoughts are shared. Individuals, for example, might think about winning the National Lottery and will dream (both personally and verbally) about how a substantial win would change their life and how they would spend their new found wealth. Such thoughts, however, are of limited interest, and the very fact they are verbalised represents their social acceptability. But what about those thoughts that represent our deepest, darkest and most erotic desires – sexual fantasies? Such thoughts are unlikely to be verbalised and when they are, they are likely to be shared between consenting adults and only ever acted out in part. The likelihood of two individuals sharing exactly the same sexual fantasy is limited because fantasies are a complex interaction of experience, thought and arousal highly personal to the individual.

Sexual fantasies are not temporally constrained. Their fluidity enables them to be recalled, rehearsed, manipulated and abandoned as the individual chooses. Neither are they constrained by ethnicity, age, gender, duration or frequency. Sexual fantasies may form nothing more than a fleeting thought, or may represent a longer period of reflection where certain acts are mentally replayed, in part to increase an individual's level of physiological arousal. Doskoch (1995), for example, suggests that on average men fantasise about sex 7.2 times per day and women 4.5 times per day. Sexual fantasies, by their very nature therefore, truly represent 'our own world' and for the majority of individuals this is where they reside. For some individuals, however, the satisfaction of mental recall is insufficient and sexual fantasies are projected into the physical or 'real' world. As fantasies enter the realm of physicality they cross the barrier between 'thinking' and 'doing', and for some this partnership is so intrinsically linked that thinking almost always leads to doing. For consenting adults, such behaviour, although sometimes on the boundaries of acceptability and extremity, is mutually enjoyed without the fear of reprimand and serves to satisfy the fantasies of those individuals. Such fantasies are likely to be rehearsed both during the act and in the future, but they are not static and will also be updated as a result of the fantasy being acted upon in the physical environment. For those individuals who are unable to consent, who are physically and psychologically vulnerable, forcing 'our own world' upon them is permanently damaging and illegal. Exploring the link between 'thinking' and 'doing' is a critically important step in understanding the transition of sexual fantasies into reality, and in understanding why for some individuals such a transition involves offending yet for others it does not.

Sexual fantasy

Sexual fantasies perhaps best represent our most uninhibited thoughts, aspirations and desires where criticism, taboo and embarrassment are invited only by the self, and not imposed by others. Such secret 'erotic' desires serve to sexually arouse and excite, but where sharing and acting upon those desires would be deemed inappropriate. There are of course situations where sexual fantasies are shared and physically acted out, either through self-masturbation or between consenting, like-minded adults in relatively safe and confined environments. The infiltration of reality can occur in both a non-invasive and ubiquitous manner through adult-themed retail environments such as Ann Summers and Sh! Such commercially popular environments reflect our desires to share (albeit in a limited form), discuss and reflect upon our sexual fantasies in a 'normalised' environment. Ann Summers for example tussles for dominance alongside more traditional retail outlets in shopping centres and high-streets throughout the United Kingdom, providing a 'safe' retail environment where both men and women are welcomed and shop alongside each other for often sexually explicit and fantasy-provoking material. On the whole, such normalisation is acceptable, and the image of the 'traditional sex shop' has drastically changed from an environment predominately aimed and frequented by men complete with concealed windows and warnings of explicit material on display, to one of smart facades with eye-catching windows seeking to invite as many couples and single women through their doors as men. This challenges the convention that such stores (and to some extent fantasies) are male domains (Malina and Schmidt 1997). This of course is notwithstanding the differences between 'traditional' and the new 'normalised' environments, where the former is more likely to sell sexually graphic pornographic material and the latter underwear and sex 'aids'. Both, however, seek to serve the same purpose – the reflection of fantasy into reality.

The transition between fantasy and reality can move beyond the accepting retail environments described previously to other arguably 'darker' and more seductive environments including swinging parties, sex clubs, dogging sites, saunas and holiday sex resorts. In such environments fantasies are projected into reality with gusto and expectation, but not always without fear of reprimand. Male adult members of a Manchester-based sadomasochistic club, for example, were arrested in September 1989 for violating the Offences Against the Person Act 1861, even though mutual genital manipulation acts (based on the member's sexual fantasies) were consensual (Thomas 2000; Green 2001). This draws into question the issue of social acceptability and level of normalisation we are prepared to grant sexual fantasies. On the one hand it is publicly acceptable to promote 'soft' fantasy on the high street, but on the other it is unacceptable when fantasies turn 'harder', even if they remain largely 'hidden' from the voyeuristic eyes of society. Fantasy and reality are so inextricably linked that without each other there would be no place for Ann Summers or sadomasochistic clubs to exist. Indeed, we suggest that fantasies are influencing and shaping our environment to such an extent that Ann Summers now reports in excess of 140 UK-based stores (Ann Summers 2008).

Fantasies, however, originate as part of our 'own world' and to some extent this is where they remain as internalised secret desires. The very phrase 'fantasy' suggests mental imagery coupled with sounds, expectations and physiological response that may last no longer than a fleeting thought of some sexual activity, or may take the form of a more elaborate story but both with the same aim of sexual arousal (Hicks and Leitenberg 2001). Therefore it is sensible to suggest that once a fantasy has occurred and therefore sexual arousal has taken place, the progression of the fantasy into some form of reality forms part of this sequential progression. Naturally, there are occasions and times where acting upon sexual fantasies would be deemed wholly inappropriate and, for the majority of individuals, sexual arousal is balanced and controlled by the norms, attitudes and values of social acceptability. The 'fantasy space', however, is an important part of our 'own world' as this space enables individuals to be relatively free to indulge their lusts and impulses in ways that might be unacceptable in reality (Wilson 1997). Fantasies, therefore, afford the individual with a 'space' where highly personal and sexually arousing thoughts can be reflected upon, updated and manipulated without the transition into the real world due to such societal constraints.

For the majority, it appears that sexual fantasies are relatively tame with many conventional fantasies focusing around present partners and bedroom scenes. For those that move beyond the confines of the bedroom, Doskoch (1995) suggests three 'primary' types of sexual fantasies: forbidden imagery, sexual irresistibility and dominance and submission fantasies. Forbidden imagery refers to those thoughts focusing upon images of unusual partners (possibly celebrities and unobtainable others, e.g. married friends) and positions. Sexual irresistibility is concerned with issues of seductiveness and multiple partners, while dominance and submission allows the individual to reflect upon rape and bondage-based fantasies. Within the realm of fantasy any of these types are both plausible and carry no penalty either psychologically or socially – they are simply fantasies: hypothetical constructs blending eroticism and knowledge of the real world (locations, people or situations) to create arousal. Even when elements of Doskoch's fantasy types transit into the real world they too carry no penalty (many individuals may experiment with light bondage and seductiveness), and some are even supported and promoted by physical environments such as sex clubs.

The link between fantasy and reality (albeit selected parts of a fantasy) is clear, although the link between simply 'thinking' and 'doing' is significantly more controversial, particularly when considering offending behaviour. Quayle and Taylor (2003) observe that, 'there appears to be little support for the allegation of a direct causal link between viewing pornography and subsequent offending behaviour'. Therefore, if an individual views pornography with a rape-based scenario, Quayle and Taylor (2003) suggest this is insufficient to suggest the individual will move on to commit a rape-based offence. However, what happens if the individual's fantasy is also taken into consideration? If the individual also holds a rape-based fantasy (which is highly plausible following Doskoch's reasoning) which is strengthened, changed or viewed in a different way following viewing pornography, does this highly personal thought process supported by eroticism and arousal now lead to offending? There is a distinct difference between passively viewing imagery and imagery that actively results in the creation or support of a pre-existing fantasy, so to some extent 'thinking' can lead to 'doing' when such thinking is also supported by arousal – *fantasy*.

If we hold a fantasy about rape, however, are we likely to take it to the extreme of actual physical rape, or do we 'play out' this fantasy in a less extreme and more accepting form such as persuading our partner to play the role of the victim and to say no during intercourse – a form in itself legally and ethically problematic? The next question is what happens once an element of a fantasy has been 'played-out' (but not in its entire or original form)? Do we update the fantasy with what has happened in reality, and thus prevent a state of cognitive dissonance? Or do we seek to push the boundaries of the original fantasy, continuing to act out more and more, seeking to finally and fully fulfil the original fantasy?

Such questions, particularly the latter ones, are only of interest and therefore importance if thinking does lead to behaviour that is unwanted, non-consensual, damaging and ultimately illegal. Even in the case of rape-based fantasy, some may question both the level of acceptability (even within the remit that fantasies reside within highly personal spaces) and the notion of 'harm'. Is it psychologically harmful to erotically think about rape, particularly when such thoughts are coupled with a strong, reinforcing arousal response? Further, if fantasising about rape results in self-masturbation the transition from fantasy to reality has clearly occurred (complete with a physical and psychological response), then this may serve to strengthen and reinforce the fantasy to such an extent that the individual moves onto a new or stronger fantasy. If fantasising about members of an individual's own family, rape or other forms of sexual violence result in illegal and disturbing acts then the link between thinking and doing is a critical one. For example, the *Guardian* (2006) reported the trial of Graham Coutts, who was convicted of murder (and is currently awaiting a re-trial following a successful appeal in 2006 – see report in the *Guardian*, 20 July 2006), for fulfilling his fantasy of asphyxiation and hanging by strangling a teacher to death. Likewise, if an individual fantasies about performing sexual acts on a child and conducts such acts in the real world then the link between thinking and doing is one worthy of further exploration and challenge.

Spaces

Thus far two 'spaces' have been considered – psychological space (where fantasies are created, reflected upon, manipulated and abandoned), and physical space (where fantasies are either acted out or where socially acceptable places are chosen to explore such fantasies further). There is, however, a third space, a hybrid pseudo-real space where the boundaries between acceptability and convention are blurred to such an extent that disentangling them is almost an impossible task – the virtual space. The virtual space is where elements of fantasy are perfectly blended with reality to create images, sounds and video reflective of the other two spaces, and crucially feed into the psychological (or fantasy) space. It is a space where new ideas emerge and existing ones can be 'tried out' through sheer voyeurism: there is no requirement on the individual to fully engage within the space but the newly afforded ability to choose the level to which one immerses balances tentatively between thinking and doing.

Pornography is an exemplar of pseudo-reality and therefore of this third 'virtual space', where images of fantasy are coupled with reality but where acting out does not *physically* involve us as individuals, but instead invites us as voyeurs. Research supports the link between offenders viewing inappropriate images of children to generate and reinforce sexual fantasy which is later (physically) reinforced through masturbation (Wyre 1992).

While pornography has been widely available since the mid-1800s, originally touted as 'erotica', it is since the advent of the Internet into mainstream society during the technological explosion of the mid-1990s that pornography has become more widely and freely accessible. Both the variety and intensity of pornography has also increased ranging from soft pornographic imagery to hardcore anime images. It is worthy to note that anime, originating from Japan, takes the form of cartoon-based characters following the tradition of Manga and is truly fantasy-based in every sense. It is interesting, therefore, that those characters designed to reflect other elements of fantasy are now being utilised in a sexual way. King (1999) argues that more research into internet use and human sexuality is required as more people have access to types of materials that were previously unavailable, or available only at great personal risk. Pornographic images of children are an example where the Internet has transformed the access to images that were once difficult and risky to locate (for a general introduction to crime, deviance and the Internet, see Williams

2006). Even in its more advanced stages, the use of the Internet by sexual offenders has largely been unexplored (Taylor *et al.* 2001), which is particularly surprising considering both the wide use of the Internet and the thousands of pornographic images of children available (Quayle and Taylor 2003). Furthermore, Middleton (2007) suggests that research data into the evaluation of assessment and treatment outcomes of problematic Internet use has trailed behind the rapid growth of inappropriate use in this area.

Silverman and Wilson (2002) reported that in 2005 the Obscene Publications Unit of Greater Manchester Police seized about a dozen images of child pornography during the whole year, but in 1999 the unit recovered 41,000 images and by 2001 so many images were being recovered that they stopped counting. The number of convictions for offences in relation to possession, creation and distribution of indecent images of children has increased by almost 500 per cent between 1999 and 2004 (Home Office 2006; Middleton 2007). The number of pornographic images and the number of individuals accessing them is likely to increase in an upward trend reflecting the increase in the number of households with Internet access. In 2002 the number of households in Great Britain with Internet access was approximately 45 per cent rising to 61 per cent (15 million households) in 2007 (National Statistics 2007).

The extent to which the virtual space can fuel fantasies and may play an important role in catalysing the relationship between thinking and doing is highlighted by studies suggesting that the Internet provides an attractive alternative to an unhappy or mundane life (Morahan-Martin and Schumacher 2000) and that prolonged Internet activity can be associated with mood changes (Kennedy-Souza 1998). This isn't to suggest, however, that only those individuals who are deemed to lead a mundane or unhappy life are prolific Internet users, nor that they access online pornography. However, it does suggest that some individuals may be more predisposed to Internet use particularly when other environmental stimulation is lacking. Hills and Argyle (2003) further suggest that individuals frequently change their original intentions when accessing the Internet to involve themselves in something more interesting and gratifying – recall of sexual fantasies coupled with arousal is likely to be more interesting and gratifying in many cases than the original intentions of Internet use. Such studies clearly demonstrate the psychological allure of the Internet and how pornographic images (as exemplars of virtual spaces) – even those that are illegal – may be accessed to provide alleviation from the mundane.

The virtual space therefore provides a third tier between fantasy and reality. This pseudo-real space is a potent combination of pure fantasy and reality, where individuals are able to blend, update and further manipulate their original erotic thoughts and desires. Furthermore, it is a space catalysing thinking into doing just as high-street retail stores catalyse fantasy into reality. The virtual space provides individuals with the opportunity to view, experience and dwell upon images, sounds and videos of others partaking in their fantasy and, in turn, affords them with the opportunity to update their original fantasies, act them out or abandon them. With the exception of the ethical and manipulation issues associated with legal pornography, the extent to which such material is problematic is questionable, particularly with the origins of erotica dating back thousands of years. However, when material 'normalises' behaviour, particularly when that behaviour is deviant, non-consensual and illegal, a problem does exist. Virtual spaces promoting the use of sexual violence, rape, incest and abuse seek to titillate those with a pre-disposition for such scenarios, in doing so, however, they both demonstrate the acceptability of such behaviour (through the relative ease of access to both material and like-minded individuals), and provide an even greater opportunity for individuals to voyeur upon and experience such sexual behaviour. With increased normalisation and the 'barrier' of social acceptability (encompassing norms, attitudes and values) coming under threat, the fragile link between thinking and doing is further weakened. This third space, however, is under-researched and lacks understanding. Many individuals will hold fantasies relating to forbidden imagery, dominance and rape (Doskoch 1995), but never access online pornography. Similarly, many individuals who access such material will never go on to abuse, but in the minority of individuals whose fantasies are so extreme and their arousal so high, the opportunity to further fuel their fantasies through access to pornographic material is so strong that they are already thinking and doing – the question is not one of does thinking lead to doing, but *when* will thinking lead to doing?

Offending spaces

In the 'psychological space' of the offender, fantasies are places where offences may initially take place, actual offences are recalled or existing ones are manipulated and updated. Those individuals whose fantasies incorporate offending against children are likely to initially develop their fantasies prior to actual offending here in the psychological space. The offending space model (see Figure 10.1 – and Wilson and Jones 2008) takes into consideration the role of each of the three previously outlined spaces and, crucially, the interaction between them and the permeable barrier of social acceptability and normalisation. In particular, the offending space model accounts for the transition between thinking (fantasy) and doing (committing offences) in convicted paedophiles. The reason for choosing this group of offenders to help inform the design of the model and to help further our understanding of sexual offenders is twofold. First, the link between sexual fantasy and 'doing' is reflective of behaviour that is non-consensual, harmful and illegal, therefore demonstrating the highly negative transition from psychological thought to physical behaviour. Secondly, paedophiles are a 'hard to reach group' unlikely to discuss their fantasies (and in particular their intentions) prior to conviction, but for whom such extreme sexual behaviour is of interest to themselves, therapists and society. The US postal survey reports that only one in every three people convicted of downloading child pornography had actually committed an offence against a child, which suggests a more casual link than the one we are arguing for here, and one which is not necessarily clear but certainly warrants more investigation (Silverman and Wilson 2002; Wilson 2007). If committing an offence against a child doesn't follow from a sexual fantasy about children, it can be argued that such a link is not causal as the offence has happened without the preceding context of 'thinking'. However, by virtue of downloading child pornography from the Internet, the individual doing this is actually performing a behaviour (albeit a voyeuristic one), and one which is likely to result in some form of arousal and is therefore fantasy based. It is also reasonable to argue that since a child (who is unable to provide consent) has been photographed or videoed either naked or as part of a sexual act, the child has been violated and through downloading such material the individual is further performing an offence against that child. The model, however, does acknowledge that even when access, opportunity and motivation are coupled together with the three spaces, lack of congruency or consistency between fantasy and reality, or norms and values, may be sufficient to prevent offending from occurring.

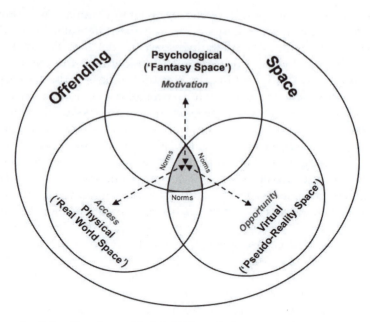

Figure 1 Offending Space Model (Wilson & Jones, 2008)

The offending space model (Wilson and Jones 2008) was developed based on case-study data from a convicted paedophile serving his sentence at HMP Grendon. HMP Grendon is unique in the penal system of England and Wales in that it operates as a therapeutic community (see Genders and Player 1995, for a general introduction to the prison, and Wilson and Jones 2008, for a review of the methods adopted to help inform development of the model). Case-study data with a paedophile named 'James' (not his real name but one adopted to provide anonymity) was crucial in developing an understanding of the link between thinking and doing and the transition of fantasy into reality. The proposed model is also unique in that it takes into consideration the fluidity of sexual fantasies and the relationship of the third tier of 'virtual space'.

While retaining important differences, the offending space model does incorporate some theoretical elements of Ward and Siegert's (2002) pathways model, a model itself incorporating theoretical perspectives and features while addressing the limitations of the following frameworks: Marshall and Barbaree's (1990) description of the effects of developmental adversities; Hall and Hirschman's (1992) typology discussions; and Finkelhor's (1984) multi-factorial pathways model addressing the psychological vulnerabilities involved in child sexual abuse. The pathways model (Ward and Siegert 2002) proposes five potential pathways with four of the five pathways reflecting a primary causal 'mechanism' that can result in sexually abusive behaviour. Ward and Siegert define a mechanism as follows:

> ... a mechanism is what makes things work or function and a dysfunctional mechanism is one that fails to work as intended or designed. Examples of dysfunctional mechanisms include impaired cognitive or behavioural skills and mental states such as maladaptive beliefs and desires. Psychological mechanisms generating child sexual abuse constitute *vulnerability* factors. (Ward and Siegert 2002: 332)

The offending space model recognises the notion of dysfunctionality in self-regulation and social acceptability (defined as a combination of attitudes, beliefs, values and norms) as a crucial component that may lead to offending behaviour. The model suggests that even when motivation, access and opportunity afford the individual with the opportunity to offend, offending may not occur if self-regulation and social acceptability remain functional. The offending space model both recognises the high permeability of this barrier but also the importance of congruency between fantasy, pseudo-reality (afforded by the virtual space) and the physical environment. If a level of discongruency between fantasy and reality exists, even with dysregulation of social acceptability and self-regulation, offending may not occur. The strength of 'sexual fantasies' and the extent to which other environments provide congruency is in part due to the physiological level of arousal coupled with fantasies.

The pathways model (Ward and Siegert 2002) proposes the following five pathways to child sex offending:

1 *Intimacy and social skills deficits.* Sexual abuse arises from dysfunctionality with intimacy and social skills. Insecure attachment styles with parents or caregivers and abuse and neglect in childhood results in poor relationships characterised by lack of self-esteem, emotional loneliness and isolation.

2 *Deviant sexual scripts.* Distorted sexual scripts and dysfunctional attachment styles may result in sexual abuse as interpersonal contact is only achieved via sexual contact. Individuals are likely to demonstrate deviant patterns of sexual arousal, intimacy deficits, inappropriate emotional experience and inappropriate cognitive distortions.

3 *Emotional dysregulation.* Individuals may have 'normal' sexual scripts and do not face the same issues as individuals with deviant sexual scripts; however, they have difficulties in the self-regulation of their emotions (Thomson 1994). Individuals are likely to experience becoming overwhelmed and sexually inhibited by their emotional state or adopt sexual behaviour to help soothe their emotional dysregulation.

4 *Anti-social cognitions.* Individuals with anti-social cognitions do not experience deviance in sexual scripts but have a general tendency towards deviance and criminality. Individuals are more likely to experience difficulties with impulsivity and engage in behaviours consistent with conduct disorder from an early age.

5 *Multiple dysfunctional mechanisms.* Individuals hold both deviant sexual scripts which coincide with dysfunctions on all of the other psychological mechanisms.

Arguably, all of the mechanisms involved in the pathways model are of interest. However, in relation to the offending space model, deviance with sexual scripts and emotional dysregulation are of most importance. As fantasies are largely uninhibited due to their high degree of personalisation they afford the perfect opportunity for deviance. Individuals do not have to constrain their thoughts and do not fear reprimand because the 'psychological space' is regulated by the 'self' and not by others. The model does acknowledge that interactions with other individuals may influence (both positively and negatively) some aspects of fantasies; however, they are predominately regulated by the self. In contrast to the pathways model, the offending space model suggests that deviant sexual scripts or deviant fantasies are in fact coupled with emotional dysregulation, which in turn can lead to contact offending. Emotions are in part likely to be difficult to regulate because of the strong arousal tendency of sexual fantasies which are further reinforced through behavioural outputs such as masturbation. We propose that to see the mechanisms in isolation, albeit with the recognition of a 'catch-all' fifth mechanism, is too simplistic due to the rich interrelations between deviant fantasies, dysregulation of emotions, dysregulation of social acceptability and lack of control.

Psychological space

The psychological space best represents the pure 'fantasy space' and provides the motivation for offending. Without fantasy and thinking about a sexual fantasy there is no motivation, and without motivation it is highly unlikely an offence will occur. The psychological space enables fantasies to be initiated and replayed and mental 'fantasy' imagery to be constructed. This space is both dynamic and is heavily influenced by both the physical and virtual spaces. If aspects of the virtual space lack consistency or congruency with the psychological space they may be abandoned or incorporated into an 'updated fantasy space'. For James the psychological space is deeply entwined with fantasy rehearsal and mentally 'acting out' and replaying fantasies, demonstrating the active nature of this space, particularly in contrast to the more passive 'virtual space'. Sexual fantasies occur most vividly at the onset of puberty, although this is not to suggest that such fantasies do not occur at an earlier age, nor that they lack intensity prior to puberty. In reflecting upon his fantasies at puberty, James states the following: 'I can't remember much at 12, but at 13/14 I started thinking about it. I don't actually think it took up a full fantasy until probably 14/15. I started to think about children in a sexual way ... children I'd seen ...'

This statement is reflective of the onset of vivid sexual fantasies and also demonstrates how James's fantasies were created and updated through influence with other spaces (either virtual or physical), highlighting the link between the three spaces. James comments on his fantasies by stating the following: 'I guess fantasy is where I want it to go, what I can do for getting aroused to that thought.'

'Where I want it to go' – arguably this suggests James's desire to move his thoughts and his fantasies about children from the psychological space and into the physical space. This doesn't indicate offending per se as fantasies could be played out through self-masturbation – an act itself requiring a combination of physicality and fantasy replay, but in the absence of any offending behaviour. However, it does suggest an important link between 'thinking' and 'doing' – the transition from fantasy to reality.

In the psychological space fantasies are dynamic and transient, and are inextricably linked to physical and virtual spaces. As a convicted paedophile, James alludes to having committed offences on approximately twelve (female) children prior to his incarceration, and that his offences played an important role in the development of his fantasies. Thus as the fantasies developed so did his offending behaviour:

> I think as my fantasies grew my offending grew ... the actual curiosity to touch her [names family member] obviously made me touch her and I guess from then on as my fantasies grew the more I actually involved doing it to a child.

> I think your fantasies stay with what you've done and you revisit.

> So the abuse that I've carried out in the past has gone on to fantasise about doing it to a real person.

> Yes, it could be part of my fantasy (giving pleasure as a way of helping) ... I can believe that the victim enjoyed it because it felt good.

James makes reference to both the revisiting aspect of the psychological space and the dynamic interaction between the psychological space and physical space. Motivation is contained within the psychological space and without motivation to move the fantasy into reality, the fantasy is likely to remain within the psychological space. James comments on how his 'curiosity' to touch a family member motivated him to follow out the action and actually begin touching that family member. In a cyclical relationship his fantasies fuelled his offending behaviour and his offending behaviour helped to update, redefine and shape his fantasies. An important part of James's fantasies was the integration of pleasure and enjoyment for the victim and to deny that the victim was in any way distressed. Even though distress was inevitable, to acknowledge this would have led to incongruency between the fantasy and reality and therefore manifest itself as cognitive dissonance. Although James was in a position of power and dominance over his victim, this did not manifest itself in his fantasy in the same way as, say, an individual with a sadomasochistic fantasy, but James psychologically challenged his fantasy and changed this relationship into one of enjoyment and approval:

> I always seek approval of people through what I do. I feel that I am being helpful and I feel that they're liking it then I'll be more helpful to them

> [*If the child was upset or unhappy how did that affect your ...?*]
> It didn't go into my fantasy.

Arguably this may have been an attempt by James to introduce the norms of sexual behaviour into his fantasies – in other words, sex should not occur without consent and that pleasure follows sexual gratification. However, this demonstrates how fantasies are developed following interaction with the physical space. The following example shows that the psychological space is not limited by spatio-temporal constraints, and the dynamic nature of fantasies:

> Because although I abused a child I didn't necessarily masturbate over it that night or fantasise on it, but it may come again. It may not be that I'm fantasising doing it with that child but it may mean that the actual abuse I've done with that child goes into a fantasy about another child that I may have captured, that I might have seen the other week or a picture in the paper.

The relationship between thought and action is also clear as James incorporates memories of previous offending into his fantasies, and may recall a fantasy about offending but not necessarily immediately following an offence. The psychological space enables James to replay his fantasies in a space and time that suits, and either play out these thoughts mentally or physically through self-masturbation or further abuse. Interestingly, James uses the word 'captured' when referring to his fantasy of another child suggesting a more dominant, controlling and violent aspect to his fantasy, rather than the 'pleasurable' and 'helpful' perception previously conveyed.

Physical space

The strength of the relationship between the psychological space and physical space is unequivocal because to be 'played out' – to be truly satisfied – fantasies need to transcend into the physical 'real world'. The physical space affords a crucial element for offending through the provision of access. After all, without access the sexual offender may have motivation but is unable to act out their fantasies (and is therefore unable to reincorporate their offences into subsequent fantasies), and the fantasy remains in the psychological space. The physical space is also a space in which non-offending behaviour – such as masturbation occurs, and is therefore viewed as the space in which all behavioural outcomes take place.

Furthermore, the physical space may play an important role in preventing offending from occurring (not only through lack of access opportunities), but also through lack of congruency. If, for example, an individual has a fantasy located within a particular environment and an offence takes place in that environment, the fantasy and environment remain congruent and therefore the fantasy is positively reinforced. If the environment changes, it may of course prevent access, but is also now incongruent with the original fantasy and may prevent offending from occurring. It would be too simplistic to suggest that in order to prevent offending paedophiles are moved to new environments as within time their fantasies are likely to adjust and incorporate their new environment. However, in the shorter term a lack of congruency may prevent an offence from taking place. James's offences (primarily) took place within a UK context and with people he knew or 'acquaintances':

> Most of them had been people I'd know. [Names an individual] she lived next door and I abused her ... there were [names a group] across the street that knew me when I was growing up with my mum ... I took advantage of the fact that she knew me growing up with my mum.

For James the physical locality of his home environment and immediate surroundings afforded him the opportunity to offend and provided the necessary access. His subsequent early abuse fantasies were also in relation to this physical environment. When James spent time working abroad he states that while he still had fantasies about children and the motivation remained to commit offences, the lack of access and, as we have argued, the incongruency between original offending environment and new context may have prevented him from offending:

> Obviously [names a country] was the ideal place to fuel my fantasies. I didn't know people out there especially people with families – I think that was the only thing that kept me from offending because I didn't have access. I spent time on the beach and obviously seeing children undressing was part of the fantasy.

Initially access appears to be the most important factor; however, James was working in an English bar where opportunities to meet English-speaking families would have been high. James also comments that part of his 'access' to victims involved seeking approval from their family. Therefore some opportunities for access could have existed and the extent to which James is telling the truth can be questioned:

'I'd be friendly and gain the trust of the family, thinking this is a nice guy. I've used my personality to gain access.'

Virtual space

The virtual space blends fantasy and reality in a 'pseudo-real' environment, where opportunities to offend are provoked and fantasies can be created, replicated and updated from the rich tapestry of available sources and materials. As previously suggested, the Internet is perhaps the space that best affords and creates new opportunities for offending behaviour, where an offender's fantasies can be played out before their eyes, and where elements of previously unthought of or untapped offending potential can be incorporated into fantasies and then 'acted out' in the real world. The importance of the virtual space to the offending model is through its reinforcement of both fantasies and physical behaviours, where the offender can view other individuals offending in ways similar to what they have done or hope to do. It is a space where values and societal norms are not imposed, and in James's words:

The Internet is designed purely for sexual thoughts.

A male may be abusing the hell out of a child – using that as a fantasy – it's a totally different kind of image, it's almost the very best of the actual fantasy on the screen – in the book it's not the fantasy, you've got to make it a fantasy.

These poignant and indicative statements eloquently demonstrate the important role of the pseudo-real space in helping to create and re-evaluate fantasies within the psychological space. The fact that James can see someone 'abusing the hell out of a child' grounds his fantasies in a physical reality, the 'real world', and provides reinforcement to James that such behaviour is acceptable, exciting and – importantly – achievable. Through James's own admission the link between fantasy and behaviour (thinking and doing) is an inextricably linked one, where fantasy fuels offending and vice versa ('as my fantasies grew the more I actually involved doing it to a child'). Therefore what is the relationship between the virtual space, fantasies and offending behaviour?

I think it actually made me fantasise more, I don't think it made me offend more but I suppose it made me do different things in the offences, but I don't think it made me offend more. I don't think the actual Internet made the abuse more but definitely the fantasies were more frequent. I think – I spent hours.

This statement suggests that the Internet provides more opportunity to fantasise more. However, it also provides a dichotomy, because James suggests that fantasising more didn't lead to an increase in offending although, in his words, 'as my fantasies grew my offending grew' highlights the causal relationship between 'thinking' and 'doing'. If the Internet is fuelling fantasies both in frequency and complexity it is reasonable to assume that the fantasies may be later played out in the physical space as either offending behaviour or masturbation.

The virtual space provides the opportunity to blend elements of what is being perceived with the offender's fantasy, and if incongruencies exist between perception and fantasy the offender can choose to remove these incongruencies to ensure the 'pseudo-real' and fantasy remain consistent:

Obviously if there's a scene on the Internet and I see a male abusing a child I didn't then take that fantasy and watch them abuse. It just didn't come into my head – I never justified it because someone else was doing it would make it okay. The justification was given the fact that I saw the child and if they didn't seem too uncomfortable if you like – the story made the child seem that it was okay.

For James his fantasies didn't involve another individual abusing a child, and when such images were perceived in the virtual space they failed to be incorporated into his fantasies. Part of James's fantasies (as previously indicated) was the acceptance by the child that what was happening was 'pleasurable' or 'comfortable', and if incongruencies existed between the virtual and fantasy spaces James would ignore what was being perceived to ensure his fantasies remained consistent and congruent.

The importance of the virtual space in terms of reinforcement for the psychological space is particularly significant for James as he spent on average between six and seven hours an evening searching and looking at child pornography on the Internet: 'It's just so much – the longer you watch, the more you see and the more you see the further you want to go'.

Where did James want to go? The more James watched and became involved with the 'pseudo-real world' the further his fantasies would have been fuelled. James may have wished to have searched for longer, delving deeper into the Internet looking for extreme and titillating images to serve his sexual desires. The combination of fantasy and pseudo-reality may have been played out in either further 'surfing' behaviour, offending behaviour or self-masturbation behaviour: 'Occasionally I masturbate at the computer or just masturbate to what's on [the computer screen].'

The virtual space is not limited to the computer, but images of children in relatively benign contexts such as newspapers, television and even compact-disc covers can provide sufficient 'pseudo-real' material to fuel and combine with existing fantasies or help to create new ones:

> I still struggle to a certain degree with fantasies. I try not to masturbate with them now but they are still there – I can't hide away from the fact that they are still there and I have to monitor what I watch. I have to be careful that I don't watch a programme that I know is going to sexually arouse me.

> He [another prisoner] bought a CD and on the cover was images of children naked – they weren't photographs they were images but that was enough to fuel my excitement ... I booked the CD out just to see these children.

Conclusions

The immersion into 'our own world' provides the opportunity to purely fantasise about our most erotic desires, which for the majority are without malice, intentional hurt or damage. However, for a minority such fleeting thoughts are the gateway to offending behaviour. The offending space model attempts to map the contours between thinking and doing, and in doing so attempts to finally uncover the unique interrelationship between thought and behaviour. If fantasies remained purely in the psychological space then offending shouldn't occur, but underlying processes prevent fantasies from residing purely in the psychological space. A critical combination of dysregulation of behaviour and social acceptability combined with environmental congruency provides the unique opportunity for offending. The tendency for fantasies to transist into physicality is arguably more likely to occur than ever before because fantasies are supported by an ever growing space – *the virtual space*. It is the opportunity for normalisation of sexual fantasies by this 'third space' which is likely to catalyse fantasies into the realm of acceptability, and to enable individuals to further recall, dwell and manipulate their fantasies more than ever before. The normalisation of extreme sexual behaviours, even those that are damaging, illegal and derogatory, may result in the increasingly vulnerable and permeable layer of social acceptability being eroded even further. As fantasies become the 'norm' and creep further into reality, more extreme fantasies are likely to be created in the psychological space and in turn will find themselves being played out either in part or in full, in physical or virtual spaces.

Understanding the role of virtual spaces further is crucial in understanding the relationship between thinking and doing. It is acknowledged that the offending space model is in its infancy and requires further refinement, verification and evidence. However, it is an exploratory and to some extent unique model in that it incorporates a hybrid space. Further, the model does not suggest that every individual who has sexual fantasies will act upon those fantasies, nor that every deviant fantasy – such as rape-based scenarios (Doskoch 1995) – will transist into anything more than a fleeting thought or desire. The critically important role of social acceptability and regulation should not be underestimated in helping to prevent behaviour that is deemed inappropriate, unacceptable and damaging from occurring. Such societal 'rules', the conducts of behaviour and self-regulation prevent for the majority extreme fantasies ever being played out in the real world. However, if extreme behaviour is normalised the existing black-and-white areas of acceptability may be grayed.

The question therefore remains whether *thinking* does in fact lead to *doing*. However, one thing is certain, and that is that fantasies created in the realm of 'our own world' do not always reside there. Their creation is merely the first step of normalisation and because of their high level of personalisation and their ability to be recalled and acted out they represent an important area of future research. As James has stated in his own words, fantasies afford the opportunity for the creation of an individual's 'own world', even if that world is dysfunctionally skewed:

It was my own world. It was a place I felt safe in, I could get everything I wanted out of it and I didn't have to feel inadequate.

References

Ann Summers (2008) *Ann Summers Store Guide*. Available at: http://www.annsummers.com/storesList.asp (last accessed: 29 February 2008).

BBC News Online (2006) *BT Sounds Child Web Porn Warning*. Available at: http://news.bbc.co.uk/1/hi/uk/4687904.stm (last accessed: 25 April 2007).

Doskoch, P. (1995) 'The darker side of fantasies', *Psychology Today*, 33: 12.

Finkelhor, D. (1984) *Child Sexual Abuse*. New York: Free Press.

Genders, E. and Player, E. (1995) *Grendon: A Study of a Therapeutic Prison*. Oxford: Oxford University Press.

Green, R. (2001) '(Serious) sadomasochism: a protected right of privacy?', *Archives of Sexual Behaviour*, 30: 543–50.

Guardian (2006) 'Teacher's killer found guilty of sex murder on retrial', 20 July.

Hall, G.C.N. and Hirschman, R. (1992) 'Sexual aggression against children: a conceptual perspective on etiology', *Criminal Justice and Behaviour*, 19: 8–23.

Hicks, T.V. and Leitenberg, H. (2001) 'Sexual fantasies about one's partner versus someone else: gender differences in incidence and frequency', *Journal of Sex Research*, 38: 43–51.

Hills, P. and Argyle, M. (2003) 'Users of the Internet and their relationship with individual differences in personality', *Computers in Human Behaviour*, 19: 59–70.

Home Office (2006) *Sexual Offences*. Available at: http://www.homeoffice.gov.uk/crime-victims/reducing-crime/sexual-offences/ (last accessed: 21 April 2007).

Kennedy-Souza, B.L. (1998) 'Internet addiction disorder', *Interpersonal Computing and Technology*, 6: 1–2.

King, S.A. (1999) 'Internet gambling and pornography: illustrative examples of the psychological consequences of communication anarchy', *CyberPsychology and Behaviour*, 2: 175–93.

Malina, D. and Schmidt, R.A. (1997) 'It's business doing pleasure with you: Sh! A women's sex shop case', *Marketing Intelligence and Planning*, 15 (7): 352–60.

Marshall, W.L. and Barbaree, H.E. (1990) 'An integrated theory of the etiology of sexual offending', in W.L. Marshall, D.R. Laws and H.E. Barbaree (eds), *Handbook of Sexual Assault: Issues, Theories and Treatment of the Offender*. New York: Plenum.

Middleton, D. (2007) *Child Porn Offenders Similar to Paedophiles*. Paper presented to the Annual Residential Conference of Forensic Psychiatry, Prague, February.

Morahan-Martin, J. and Schumacher, P. (2000) 'Incidence and correlates of pathological internet use among college students', *Computers in Human Behaviour*, 16: 13–29.

255

National Statistics (2007) *Society: Internet Access*. Available at: http://www. statistics.gov.uk/CCI/nugget.asp?ID=8andPos=1andColRank=1andRank= 192 (last accessed: 26 February 2008).

Quayle, E. and Taylor, M. (2003) 'Model of problematic internet use in people with a sexual interest in children', *CyberPsychology and Behaviour*, 6 (1): 93–106.

Silverman, J. and Wilson, D. (2002) *Innocence Betrayed: Paedophiles, the Media and Society*. Cambridge: Polity Press.

Taylor, M., Holland, G. and Quayle, E. (2001) 'Typology of paedophile picture collections', *Police Journal*, 74: 97–107.

Thomas, T. (2000) *Sex Crime: Sex Offending and Society*. Cullompton: Willan.

Thomson, R. (1994) 'Emotion regulation: a theme in search of a definition', in N. Fox (ed.), *The Development of Emotion Regulation: Biological and Behavioural Considerations*, Monographs of the Society for Research in Child Development No. 59, pp. 225–52.

Ward, T. and Siegert, R.J. (2002) 'Towards a comprehensive theory of child sexual abuse: a theory knitting perspective', *Psychology, Crime and Law*, 8: 319–51.

Williams, M. (2006) *Virtually Criminal: Crime, Deviance and Regulation Online*. London: Routledge.

Wilson, D. (1997) 'Gender differences in sexual fantasy: an evolutionary analysis', *Personality and Individual Differences*, 22: 27–31.

Wilson, D. (2007) *Is Seeing Doing?* Available at: http://www.martinfrost.ws/ htmlfiles/feb2007/crimes_seedo.html (last accessed: 1 March 2007).

Wilson, D. and Jones, T. (2008) 'In my own world: a case study of a paedophile's thinking and doing and his use of the internet', *Howard Journal of Criminal Justice*, 47: 1–14.

Wilson, D. and McCabe, S. (2002) 'How HMP Grendon "works" in the words of those undergoing therapy', *Howard Journal of Criminal Justice*, 41: 279–91.

Wolak, J., Finkelhor, D. and Mitchell, K.J. (2005) *Child Pornography Possessors Arrested in Internet-Related Crimes: Findings from the National Juvenile Victimization Study*. Alexandria, VA: National Center for Missing and Exploited Children.

Wyre, R. (1992) 'Pornography and sexual violence: working with sex offenders', in C. Itzin (ed.), *Pornography: Women, Violence and Civil Liberties*. Oxford: Oxford University Press.

Chapter 11

Comparative analysis of the management of sexual offenders in the USA and UK

Bill Hebenton

> ... a democratic society, following popular views, will embody a form of risk aversion for low probability risks that might result in serious harm. The result will be in the direction of the Precautionary Principle. (Sunstein 2005: 26)

This chapter takes a comparative perspective on the development of controls on sexual offenders released into the community in the USA (state and federal levels) and UK (England and Wales). It provides both a socio-historical account of policy developments since the 1940s in the USA and the mid-1990s in the UK, and a critical analysis of the political and cultural contexts within which such developments have taken root. Key comparative questions addressed include deployment of symbol and substance in policy; utilisation of criminal and civil regulation; role of and for criminal justice agencies; modes of public involvement; and consideration of analytic frameworks. The chapter concludes with an assessment of likely future trends in the management of released sexual offenders on both sides of the Atlantic.

By examining policy interventions in respect of sexual offenders released into the community in the USA (state and federal levels) and UK (England and Wales), the current chapter, by necessity, is also a comparative excursion into public fears, the sense of democracy, the role of 'expertise' and the attempt to regulate in an apparently insecure world. I will, therefore, be moving between the policy realm and the search for explanation – between the 'what' and the 'why'. The study of the control of danger in any society is like gazing into a reflecting pool. The waters there reflect back to us the kinds of people we have become (see generally Douglas 1992; Garland 1990). Sexual crime has always fascinated. Socio-historical study of England and Wales suggests that each decade seems to produce a particular focus: in the 1950s it was concern about organised prostitution; the move towards a partial decriminalisation of homosexuality was arguably the focus of the 1960s; the new wave of the women's movement took rape as a major issue in the 1970s (vying with child physical maltreatment); child sexual abuse was recognised as a serious problem in the 1980s (see Soothill and Francis 2002). In the 1990s, the apogee of concern fell on the more general spectre of the 'sexual offender' at large. Giving voice to the sexual offender, as captured in the following extract from Tony Parker, now makes the late 1960s seem a very long time ago:

> ... it's like a malady come upon you and you don't know what to do ... But you couldn't expect other people to understand it, could you? They say, 'Well I don't feel like that, how can he?' They think it's disgusting, it's horrible, they wouldn't want to know about it even, or consider it. And you'd never know with someone, would you, if you wanted to talk to them, just how they'd react? They all think it's something else, you see; their mind springs on to something else. Because it says it, doesn't it, when they read out the charge: 'Indecent assault?' It's only natural for them, people think it means more than it does. They think it must mean actually raping a boy, or trying to, an actual sexual act of that kind, and that you're dirty and horrible and cruel. But even the police you know, they told my mother about it once; they said to her, 'Your son's not one of these sex maniacs, don't think that, it's just this weakness he's got for liking to fondle little boys.' That was something at least; however awful it is, that's something that could be said. (Parker 1969: 68)

From the perspective of 2008, exploring the richness of marginalised lives as Parker does seems somehow 'out of place', lacking a 'fit' with the contemporary landscape of fears, concerns and anxieties. To coin a phrase, we live now in more 'precise times'.[1] In what follows in this chapter, I take a comparative look at the background to these 'precise times' in both the UK (England and Wales) and USA, and at the development of controls on sexual offenders released into the community. I provide both a socio-historical account of policy developments since the 1940s in the USA and the mid-1990s in the UK (England and Wales), and a critical analysis of the political and cultural contexts within which such developments have taken root.

Legislative and policy developments in the USA

At the time of writing, all jurisdictions in the USA are working to implement, by July 2009, the mandatory minimum standards of the Adam Walsh Child Protection and Safety Act 2006. The Walsh Act, now the fulcrum for future developments in the USA at federal and state levels, can also be understood as the apogee of managing a problem first 'identified' in its present 'manifestation' in the 1990s. Writing about the USA, Mona Lynch notes:

> Sex offenders emerged as the ultimate dangerous criminal class in the 1990s: They appeared to be the criminal justice 'issue of the year' every year in that decade ... and as a category of offenders, they were (and continue to be) among the highest priority for the criminal justice system to manage and contain. (Lynch 2002: 529)

While we still await the definitive history, both Lawrence Friedman (1993) and Philip Jenkins (1998), each in their own way, provide us with socio-historical accounts of a century of US policy responses to sexual crime – a pattern characterised by several major peaks of panic and subsequent legal action which shaped recent American history. In what follows, I note that although the image of the sexual offender changes in official rhetoric, arguably the common thread across time periods is that the regulatory response can be characterised as both rapidly responding to the expressed needs of the populace and creatively borrowing legal forms from one area to solve problems in another.

Plugging the prevention gap – from the 1930s to the present

In the decades preceding what we may call the modern era in dealing with sexual offenders – in other words, prior to the late 1930s – biological notions of sexual degeneracy dominated thinking in the USA (Jenkins 1998); pessimism about the deterrent effects of incapacitation in institutions for sexual crimes per se yielded to another source of pessimism. This equally deep pessimism surrounded available treatment (and its lack) during confinement. By the late 1930s, however, a new clinical optimism in prediction and rehabilitation options, fostered by medical practitioners, ushered in the first wave of sexual psychopath laws. The state of Michigan enacted sexual psychopath legislation in 1937. To an extent, the demands of the medical profession, legal leaders and civic groups served as catalysts for this wave of sexual offender legislation. These groups were convinced that sexual offending was evidence of mental disorder and required (psychiatric) treatment rather than punishment (Hacker and Frym 1955). Yet in the same period of the 1930s there is also evidence that the public became more concerned about sexual offences, publicised in the emerging mass media – indeed, as Sutherland points out in his well-known assessment of the popular literature of the time, the legislation implicitly reflected the public's anxieties about these sexual crimes (Sutherland 1950a, 1950b). Although refuting the propositions as either false or unproven, he lists the 'facts': that serious sexual crime is on the increase; that it is committed by 'sexual psychopaths' who have little control over their behaviour and would continue to be a danger throughout their lives; that they could be identified before ever committing a sexual crime. Releasing them, therefore, after punishment was to put women and children in future danger. Confinement until 'cured' through psychiatric means was the only acceptable option. Psychopath laws of the period often explicitly reflected this two-tiered objective in their preamble – take the Illinois provisions – '(1) To protect society by sequestering the sexual psychopath so long as he [sic] remains a menace to others, (2) and to subject him [sic] to treatment to the end that he may recover from his psychopathic condition and be rehabilitated' (Grabowski 1988: 438).

By 1960 there were some 27 states and the District of Columbia with a version of a sexually dangerous person law. The basis of state authority for such laws rested on both a recognised general police power of the state and the doctrine of *parens patriae*. As Swanson noted, pursuant to the Tenth Amendment to the Constitution, states have the right to: 'Make, ordain and establish all manner of wholesome and reasonable laws, statutes and ordinances, either with penalties or without, not repugnant to the constitution, as they shall judge to be for the good and welfare of the commonwealth ...' (Swanson 1960: 215). Whereas every state had a civil procedure for committing persons as mentally ill, the smaller group of 27 states had a second civil procedure for persons charged as 'sexual psychopaths', 'sexually dangerous' or other similar labels. This trend from the late 1930s onwards to the early 1960s had emphasised the treatment of offenders through involuntary civil commitment procedures rather than punishment after conviction. Reasons for jurisdiction over such offenders varied among these 27 states: some states required conviction for some sexual crime prior to commitment, some needed only that the person be charged of such offences, and others only a showing that the person probably was a 'sexual psychopath'.

Beginning in the late 1950s and continuing for nearly two decades, there was an ebb in the panic over sex crimes, sexual deviance and sexual behaviour generally. This was accompanied by the easing of some of the restrictive and invasive intervention measures that had been previously adopted (Jenkins 1998). Some medical experts and academics advocated fewer criminal laws aimed at sexual deviants as the understanding of what even constituted sexual deviance entered a state of upheaval. Formal legal intervention was seen as counterproductive for offenders and even victims in some situations. Indeed, by the late 1980s almost half of the states with sexually dangerous persons legislation had revoked the statutes, principally because of the recognition that not all violent sexual offenders would respond to the same therapy, a growing awareness that such offenders were not mentally ill, a lack of proven treatment methods in reducing recidivism and the rising concern for civil rights. There was also a growing sensitivity in the courts and in academic circles about the racial disproportionality in sex crime prosecutions and punishments, and about the procedural rights of those suspected of, charged with and punished for all kinds of criminal offences (e.g. *Miranda* v. *Arizona* 1966). Thus, during this 'liberal era' (Jenkins 1998), both the definition of sexual deviance and the appropriateness of criminalising deviant sexual acts were pointedly questioned.

By the 1980s, social and legal concern with sexual offences resurged, with some reshaping of early incarnations of panic. At its root was the perceived need to 'plug the prevention gap', evident to everyone from the continuing, notorious and well-publicised cases of fatal sexual violence against women and children. The uniqueness of this period lies in the confluence of social and cultural forces that manufactured an aggressively preventive approach to the regulation of sexual offenders. A number of factors combined to create this perception of a prevention gap and turned public attention to regulatory mechanisms that would permit intervention in anticipation of offending, not just after the offence. Pratt (1997) points out that the duty of the state to protect its members from violence is now widely recognised in advanced western societies. In the USA, arguably two other trends overlaid this duty. The first trend was the gradual but dramatic move in the 1980s to the adoption of determinate criminal sentencing based on standardised guidelines and away from indeterminate sentencing (Tonry 1996). The change had a twofold effect. In keeping with other law-and-order changes, it put an end to the early release of prisoners who had convinced parole boards that they had been quickly rehabilitated. But there was another unintended consequence. By removing discretion, the change deprived states of their power to exercise long-term, flexible control over offenders deemed 'too dangerous' to release from prison. By the late 1980s and early 1990s, persons imprisoned under such determinate schemes became eligible for release. Since, by definition, determinate sentencing was tied to the gravity of the offence rather than the individual characteristics of the prisoner, even an inmate's evident dangerousness did not, in itself, provide a basis for extending their time in prison. This created a gap in the states' ability to protect against recidivist sexual violence.

The second trend was the thrust, due in part to feminist activism and scholarship, that brought the issue of rape and, later, pornography as uniquely damaging and subjugating for women and children to the forefront in political, legal and media realms (Dean 1996). American society's increased attention to sexual violence had produced a change in its perceived seriousness; social judgments about appropriate punishment for sexual offenders had changed. Existing penal sentences for violent, recidivist offenders were judged to be 'inadequate', too short to allow meaningful treatment in prison and inconsistent with supervised release after imprisonment (D'Emilio and Freedman 1997).

However construed in the past, in recent years it is clear that a 'discourse of disgust' has underlain the federal legislative agenda on these matters (see Lynch 2002, for an analysis of Congressional debates of the 1990s). The expanding level of involvement by the federal government in directing state approaches to the sexual offender problem has indeed been the single most significant regulatory development, an effort that began in earnest in 1994. At that time, a provision entitled the 'Jacob Wetterling Crimes Against Children and Sexually Violent Offender Registration Act' was included in the omnibus 1994 crime bill and required that federal crime-fighting dollars (Byrne grants) be withheld from states that did not have sex offender registration systems in place. As a result of this provision, 49 states had established such programmes by 1996. In 1996, the Wetterling Act was amended to allow for community notification ('Megan's Law'), which permitted law enforcement personnel to disclose registry information to neighbourhood residents about sex offenders who live in close proximity. The Wetterling Act is a federal law that provides guidelines to the states but is implemented and administered at the state level. Some states notify the public only about sex offenders who pose a high risk to the community, but other states employ broad notification practices and disseminate information about all registered sex offenders. In more recent years, the Wetterling Act has quickly spawned a set of proposed amendments and new legislation that both deepened the federal government's involvement in states' regulation of sex offenders (primarily through similar threats of fiscal withholding) and that increased direct federal involvement in the prosecution and punishment of sex offenders. Recent developments, culminating in the previously mentioned Adam Walsh Child Protection and Safety Act 2006, have included the mandate of state Internet websites listing convicted sex offenders and the establishment of a national online sex offender registry that allows a search beyond one's own state borders (see Appendix 10.1 for a chronological summary).

The legislative goals of sex offender registration and notification are to increase the public's awareness of sexual offenders and to help people protect themselves and their children from sexual crimes. Early community notification strategies commonly included press releases, flyers and door-to-door warnings about the presence of sex offenders (see Hebenton and Thomas 1996a). Since states are now federally mandated to post their sex offender registries online, however, the Internet appears to have become the primary source of information for the public about convicted sexual offenders (Levenson *et al.* 2006).

Post-release legislative and policy developments in the UK

As in the USA, a number of tragic cases in the 1990s in England and Wales have attracted widespread publicity, provoked public outcry and provided the impetus for legislative and organisational change. An examination of some of the most high-profile cases suggests a number of prominent themes – revelations about paedophile rings, child pornography and the vulnerability of children in environments traditionally considered secure such as homes, after-school/youth clubs and schools. The prevalence of 'stranger danger' cases specifically highlighted the dangers posed by convicted or suspected offenders living in the community and has been used as the basis for a media-led cry for a more punitive criminal justice response. As Greer (2003) has recently argued, media representations of sex crime give the public important cues about how they should perceive the nature and extent of sex crime, how they should think and feel about it, how they should respond to it and the measures that might be taken to reduce risk. The notion of the sexual offender as 'an observable enemy' can be seen in newspaper reports of the Robert Oliver case from the mid-1990s. Shortly after Oliver's release from prison a *Guardian* newspaper headline declared: 'Police Warn of Threat to Young Males: Town on Paedophile Alert' (15 October 1997: 2). Alongside a photograph of a semi-naked Oliver with bared teeth, the report noted how 'Schools and youth clubs in Brighton were yesterday put on high alert after it was revealed that the convicted paedophile killer Robert Oliver is staying in town'. The *Daily Mail* (15 October 1997: 10) also reported on Oliver's arrival in Brighton and included details of his homosexual relationship with fellow paedophile Sydney Cooke. It asked: 'Could these evil men be living next door to you?', and provided photographs and last known whereabouts.

The rape and murder of four girls in Belgium in 1995 by Marc Dutroux, a released sexual offender, amplified European media interest in the failure of authorities to punish such offenders (Rainer *et al.* 2003). In Britain, media interest in sexual offenders released from prison and allowed to live anonymously in the community was crystallised by the abduction and murder, in 2000, of seven-year-old Sarah Payne by a paedophile, Roy Whiting. Following Whiting's conviction, newspaper reports focused on the consensus view that Whiting, despite being a dangerous predator, had been allowed to roam freely and kill Sarah Payne. Whiting's conviction, therefore, gave British newspapers and 'advocacy' pressure groups, including the NSPCC, an opening to argue that there existed a public policy vacuum in which the authorities appeared uncertain – indeed incompetent – about how to deal with risks posed by sexual offenders released from prison into the community.

However, the newspapers' role in mediating between policy and public agendas is by no means relevant only to the issue of offenders in the community. In the context of public concern about risks posed by offenders, the 'circle of definers' temporarily extended to include sections of the news media that had sought to redefine risks to communities both from offenders but also those criminal justice professionals failing to protect communities from harm. In the case of Roy Whiting, for example, newspaper accounts criticised the probation service for failing to prevent Sarah Payne's death. This helped set in train processes that led policy-makers and professionals arguably to lose control of the sexual offender agenda (Kitzinger 1999). Moreover, the policy community faced a powerful newspaper agenda in which popular knowledge about 'obvious risks' posed by offenders impacted on public communication about management of these risks. This extension to the circuit of policy communication concerning management of offenders post-sentence resulted in the press agenda on offenders becoming pivotal. As Critcher puts it, 'It mediates between policy and public agendas, constructs the public agenda and seeks to influence policy agendas' (Critcher 2002: 530).

Since the 1990s, Britain's local newspapers have been concerned with the moral encoding of the allocation of risks surrounding the release of convicted sex offenders from prison. In particular, their concerns over the risk to local communities in which offenders have been rehoused have helped construct a powerful symbolic figure of 'the sexual offender' as the quintessential 'outsider' who has infiltrated the 'decent heart' of the community. This dominant perception of 'the offender' as existing beyond the community also underlines how popular knowledge of sexual offending spoke to 'collective experiences of fear, risk and anxiety in ways which clearly could not be calmed by appeals to the professional credentials of official agents (whether the police, the probation service or government ministers)' (Collier 2001: 235).

Arguably, the legislative isolation of sexual offenders in the contemporary period has its roots in the 1991 Criminal Justice Act which permitted 'longer than normal' custodial sentences for the protection of the public (section 2 [2]b, Criminal Justice Act 1991). The Act also introduced mandatory post-release supervision for all offenders who had served a sentence of imprisonment beyond twelve months. Further underpinning of the perceived gap in public protection came with the 1996 consultation document on the sentencing and supervision of sexual offenders (Home Office 1996), which advocated strengthening the arrangements for supervising convicted sexual offenders following their release from custody. These proposals were later embodied in a comprehensive range of measures founded on the basic premise that the best way to protect the community and potential victims is through increased restriction, surveillance and monitoring (see Appendix 10.2, and Hebenton and Thomas 1996b, for an analysis of our preoccupation with 'tracking' habitual offenders).

One of the key measures in the official response to concern over sex offenders was sexual offender registration. Registration, initially provided for by Part I of the Sex Offenders Act 1997, required certain categories of sex offender to notify the police of their name and address and any changes to these details within a specified period

(Cobley 2000: 323–32; Thomas 2000: 106–22). Following calls for reform, the original registration requirements in the 1997 Act were first tightened by the Criminal Justice and Courts Services Act 2000 and later replaced by Part 2 of the Sexual Offences Act 2003. For example, initial registration is now required in person within three days as is any subsequent registration of changes to the offender's personal details. A kind of iterative process was set in train, by which legislation to control sexual offenders in the community generated its own problems requiring 'further' responses.

A panoply of other control mechanisms were iteratively added – these have included sex offender orders and restraining orders, used to prohibit the offender from frequenting places where there are children such as parks and school playgrounds. Both of these orders have now been combined and replaced with a new expanded order – a sexual offences prevention order – under the Sexual Offences Act 2003. This Act also introduced a second new measure – the risk of sexual harm order – a new civil preventative order, designed to protect children from sexual harm. It can be used to prohibit specified behaviour, including the 'grooming' of children (Ost 2004).

The conditions attached to registration for the offender and the degree of notification (disclosure) permitted to the community vary depending on the assessed level of risk. In England and Wales there are now Multi-Agency Public Protection Arrangements (MAPPA) to carry out this task (Bryan and Doyle 2003). MAPPA were formally created by sections 67 and 68 of the Criminal Justice and Court Services Act 2000, legislation that provided statutory force to the local liaison and cooperation that had emerged throughout the 1990s to respond to child protection regimes specifically and sexual offending more generally. The Act placed a statutory duty upon police and probation to work jointly as 'Responsible Authorities', requiring them to establish arrangements for assessing and managing risks posed by sexual and violent offenders, to review and monitor these arrangements and to publish annual reports on their operation. The Criminal Justice Act 2003 added prisons as Responsible Authorities and introduced to agencies a 'duty to cooperate' with the arrangements, including local health authorities and trusts, housing authorities and registered social landlords, social services departments, Youth Offending Teams, local education authorities and indeed electronic monitoring providers. The rationale for such a duty is to maximise the operational performance of MAPPA by ensuring that all agencies with a part to play in the management of sexual (and violent) offenders make their contribution within a collective management plan. According to the official guidance, MAPPA operates at three levels of risk management:

1 *Ordinary risk management (level 1)* locates risk management within the agency responsible for the 'low to medium risk' offender and without significant involvement from other agencies.

2 *Local inter-agency risk management (level 2)* depends on the 'active involvement' of more than one agency in risk management because of a higher level of risk or complexity.

3 *The Multi-Agency Public Protection Panels (level 3)* operate to manage the 'critical few', drawing together key active partners who take joint responsibility for the community management of offenders. An offender referred to this level of management is defined as someone who: (a) is assessed under OASys (Offender Assessment System) as being a high or very high risk of causing serious harm; *and* (b) presents risks that can only be managed by a plan which requires close cooperation at a senior level due to the complexity of the case and/or because of the unusual resource commitments it requires; *or* (c) although not assessed as a high or very high risk, the case is exceptional because the likelihood of media scrutiny and/or public interest in the management of the case is very high and there is a need to ensure that public confidence in the criminal justice system is sustained (Home Office 2004).

As mentioned earlier, the issue of disclosure of information between agencies and to the public is now a matter for MAPPA. The law governing information exchange between authorities in public protection work is considered to be permissive, largely insulating agencies from liability (Power 1999 2003). In relation to disclosure to the public (that is, third parties), matters are far from clear. In the frenzy of legislation aimed at the regulation of sexual offenders over the last decade or so, what is especially noteworthy is the reluctance of Parliament to take the opportunity to resolve the vexed issue of disclosure of information to the public. Instead, the position is determined largely by case law, some statutory provisions related to child care proceedings and then secondary guidance by departmental circular from the Home Office (see Home Office 1997).

The present arrangements are opaque and complex and the field is now a crowded policy space with authorities recognising that disclosure is governed essentially by cases at common law and subject to interpretation via the Human Rights Act 1998 – where authorities must not act in breach of concerned parties' (including offenders) Convention rights. Helen Power, in her review of relevant cases concerning sexual offenders, concludes that in relation to disclosure 'the courts are a long way from lending their support to American-style community notification, not least because of their increasing sensitivity to offenders' privacy rights' (Power 2003: 86). Additionally, it is clear that current European Court's jurisprudence on this matter seeks to impose positive obligations on member states to prevent breach of privacy rights. Paradoxically, the same jurisprudence also gives rise to the possibility that public authorities, like MAPPA, may be held liable to victims, actual or potential, of decisions not to disclose (Starmer 2001). In other words, under the European Convention on Human Rights jurisprudence, positive obligations may require disclosure to third parties – including, arguably, by way of wider community notification.

Conclusion: convergence, divergence or convergent divergence?

Jenkins (1998) may be correct when he argued, a decade ago, that the institutionalisation and politicisation of sexual crime has now given contemporary conceptions of the sexual offender a durability that their predecessors lacked. Certainly, ten years on, the institutionalisation of the concept of 'protection from sexual violence' on both sides of the Atlantic has created a range of advocacy groups and claims-makers with a stake in the maintenance of concern about sexual violence in a way quite unlike earlier times where dissenting voices may have challenged defective legislative responses. Public health approaches to the issue of the management of sexual offenders in the community (for example, Laws 2000), at least in the real-world political sphere on both sides of the Atlantic, seem like straws in the wind (but see Kemshall and Wood 2007).

While the sexual offender has been constructed in both England and Wales and the USA in a broadly similar fashion in terms of public protection, it is in the ways in which the public (community) itself has been constructed in relation to the management of sexual offenders that is particularly instructive. Government in England and Wales, unlike the USA, has sought to keep the public at 'arm's length' and assumes the public as a potential source of risk to expert-led risk management strategies (as seen in public reactions to the release of Robert Oliver and Sydney Cooke mentioned earlier).

Public knowledge of sexual offender risk has become equated with vigilantism, and as a potential source of threat to government policy on 'effective' management. A 'Sarah's Law' (the UK equivalent of 'Megan's Law') was resisted by police and probation on the grounds that it would drive offenders underground and rules on disclosure remain opaque and legalistic. The public is viewed as irrational about 'risk' and prey to negative media influence. The *News of the World*'s 'name and shame' campaign (following the murder of Sarah Payne in the summer of 2000) fuelled public disorder and vigilante action (some against wrongly identified people) and highlighted the growing division between experts and the public.

While professional bodies such as the Association of Chief Officers of Probation, the Association of Chief Police Officers and NACRO all criticised the campaign as 'grossly irresponsible' and likely to drive offenders underground, sections of the media argued that 'common sense' should prevail and that parents had the 'right to know'. As Jones and Newburn (2004) point out, the overall campaign retained momentum and the bereaved parents met with the junior Home Office minister at the time to discuss public disclosure. They emerged from the meeting saying that they had been 'assured there will be a Sarah's Law' (*Guardian*, 13 September 2000). Paradoxically, the campaigns did not result in a 'Sarah's Law'.

The subsequent trial and conviction of Roy Whiting in December 2001, a registered sexual offender and known to agencies, rekindled calls for a Sarah's Law and challenged the expertise and professionalism of those agencies managing offenders in the community. Government ministers continued to argue for the 'unworkability' of a broad notification strategy, and that any attempt to do so would create more mobility among offenders. Arguably, these interactions did, however, contribute to the introduction of Multi-Agency Public Protection Arrangements, the appointment at a later stage of lay members to MAPPA and to harsher measures for sex offenders including life imprisonment for some categories of offence (Criminal Justice and Court Services Act 2000, Criminal Justice Act 2003).

As I concluded in an earlier piece:

While the symbolic elements of 'policy rhetoric' and 'style' appear to have been remarkably similar on both sides of the Atlantic, the degree to which this rhetoric has been played out in concrete changes on community protection policy has been strikingly different in England and Wales. This appears to be due, in large part, to the resistance of key players in the criminal justice policy 'network' to public notification schemes. (Hebenton 2008)

Indeed, in that earlier consideration, I went on:

> Both the National Probation Service and the Association of Chief Police Officers have, over the decade, opposed any direct 'Megan's Law'. The fact of this resistance, and the form that it took, speaks to at least a degree of difference between the extant cultures of control on the two sides of the Atlantic ... It also shows ... that institutional and political differences can mediate the practical impact of populist politics. Such differences, I would suggest, need also to include the culturally embedded issues of directly elected versus appointed criminal justice officials and the expectations coincident upon a society where direct democracy and cultural expectations of citizenship are rather different. (Hebenton 2008)

Indeed, the American cultural consensus is reflected in remarks by Roxanne Lieb, a Washington State policy analyst and long-time observer of developments in sexual offender management, opining that 'the notion that the government knows that a dangerous sex offender is moving into a neighbourhood and does not warn the community because of liability concerns, or because it is "police business", has become unacceptable to most US citizens' (Lieb 2000: 430).

It is clear that at the level of policy 'style' and 'rhetoric' on the management of sexual offenders there is broad convergence, but in terms of policy 'content' and 'outcomes' in the community, there is considerable divergence between the USA and England and Wales. In research terms, what is needed is a conceptual framework to help explain this. A contender for explanatory analysis may be Joachim Savelsberg's institutional approach which introduces the organisation of knowledge production and of political and legal decision-making as central concepts in understanding nation-specific differences in punishment levels (Savelsberg 1994).

Savelsberg uses the concept of 'knowledge' to mean ideas that guide social action: it encompasses analytical and normative ideas and beliefs that people assume to be true about, for example, the nature of crime, criminals and functions of punishment. He argues that such knowledge is produced and diffused by social institutions such as advocacy organisations, news media, public opinion polls and government. It is easy to see that these institutions are not shaped the same in different places and at different times (he compares the USA, the Federal Republic of Germany and the old 'GDR (German Democratic Republic)'). In short, he argues that while the insecurities of late modernity may not be as dramatic in Germany as they are in the United States, they have certainly affected everyday life. Yet imprisonment rates indicate that the social control reaction was very distinct. The reason for this difference in reaction, he argues, partly lies in the nation-specific institutional arrangements through which knowledge is produced and diffused, and in which legal and political decision-making is embedded. Institutions filter the impact global change has on policy outcomes in a given country to such a degree that global processes (modernisation, advances in information technology, media) produce distinct cultures of control in different national contexts.

The German system is based on a model of bureaucracy that ties decision-makers closely into the state apparatus while keeping them at arm's length from the populace. The American system, on the other hand, ties decision-makers more tightly to their constituents. This is obvious for the executive branch of government. Yet the point applies to the judicial and legislative branches as well. In the judicial branch American judges and prosecutors are elected officials in many jurisdictions while their German counterparts are life-tenured civil servants. The former have to be more sensitive when their constituents experience that 'sense of ontological uncertainty'. Thus, if people express this feeling through punitive attitudes, elected judicial officials are likely to be inclined to adapt their decisions accordingly. The difference holds further for the legislative branch, where American legislators are only loosely tied to their parties. Political parties may endorse candidates, but candidates have to win primaries; they are nominated by their constituents. German legislators, in contrast, are nominated by their highly organised and bureaucratised parties and tied to long-term party platforms. Faction discipline is almost mandatory in legislative voting. As a consequence of these differences, the attention of American legislators, as compared to their German counterparts, is much more attuned to public opinion polls and other measures of their constituents' opinions and anxieties. Again, the point is that anxieties identified as characteristic for late modernity do not uniformly translate into political and legal decision-making in all countries. They may well be present in many western countries. Yet, they pass through country-specific institutional filters before they produce cultures of control.

Interestingly, and borrowing again from the sociology of punishment literature, Barker (2006) develops the Savelsberg approach, using a more explicitly conceptual framework around 'local political cultures of control' and explaining historical differences in imprisonment rates in California, Washington State and New York State. She distinguishes between two dimensions of state power: variations in political authority (measured by the degree of centralisation) and variation in political practices (as measured by the degree of civic engagement). A similar analysis could be fruitfully applied to the policy area of sexual offender management.

In addition to the previously described registration, community notification and residence restrictions, at present in the USA at least seventeen states currently have statutes in place that authorise some form of electronic location tracking for sexual offenders on supervised release. Other states are exploring both legislative enactments or executive orders to implement such programs (Hobson 2006). Many programmes contain limits that restrict their application to specific classes of offenders, commonly violent sexual offenders or those convicted of sexual offences against children. But the use of location tracking has already expanded beyond simple regulation of sexual offenders on formal release. The current trend is to impose a requirement of lifetime monitoring of certain offenders, either through independent statutory mandate or as a condition of specially agreed mandatory lifetime supervision terms. Many of these statutes apply retroactively, so that an offender convicted years ago and long since disentangled from the criminal justice system must submit to supervision via an electronic device. These provisions tend to be drawn on broad categorical grounds that provide for no individualised determination of dangerousness or likely recidivism. They apply equally to the sexual offender in hospice care as to the one on the street.

In the summer of 2006, with the imprimatur of the then Home Secretary Dr John Reid, the Home Office launched a review of public protection arrangements for children, and in June 2007 the Home Office published its *Review of the Protection of Children from Sex Offenders* (Home Office 2007). The document talks of 'greater rights and information for the public', as well as a new process whereby certain people can register with the police their child protection interest in a named individual. Where this individual is a known child sex offender, there will be a duty on the police to consider disclosure. Furthermore, it recommends continuing to ensure residence restrictions, optimising use of the latest technology in the management of offenders, including trialling the use of mandatory polygraph tests (lie detectors) and reviewing the use of satellite tagging and tracking. All of this seems to signal a kind of convergent divergence towards US developments, especially when taken alongside the development of a 'most wanted' website by the Child Exploitation and Online Protection (CEOP) Centre (a list of high-risk child sex offenders who are not complying with their notification requirements and have gone missing. Offender details include photographs, names and aliases, dates of birth and other identifying information). The government argue that the profile of this website should be raised, so the public is aware of the most high-risk offenders who have absconded and are therefore not being managed by the authorities, and point to the fact that the website has already been shown to increase the likelihood of listed offenders being apprehended. To paraphrase the old Chinese proverb, we may be on the verge of even more 'interesting times'.

Appendix 10.1   Summary of legislative developments by the US federal government

1994 – Jacob Wetterling Crimes Against Children and Sexually Violent Offender Registration Act

Enacted as a part of the Omnibus Crime Bill of 1994, the Jacob Wetterling Crimes Against Children and Sexually Violent Offender Registration Act:

- established guidelines for states to track sex offenders;
- required states to track sex offenders by confirming their place of residence annually for ten years after their release into the community or quarterly for the rest of their life if the sex offender was convicted of a violent sex crime.

1996 – Megan's Law

During the mid-1990s every state and Washington, DC passed a 'Megan's Law'. In January of 1996 Congress enacted Megan's Law. The federal 'Megan's Law':

- provided for the public dissemination of information from states' sex offender registries;
- required state and local law enforcement agencies to release relevant information necessary to protect the public about persons

273

registered under a state registration programme established under the Jacob Wetterling Crimes Against Children and Sexually Violent Offender Registration Act;

- provided that information collected under state registration programmes could be disclosed for any purpose permitted under a state law.

1996 – The Pam Lyncher Sex Offender Tracking and Identification Act of 1996

This law required the Attorney General to establish a national database for the FBI to track the location of a certain category of sex offenders. The law also:

- mandated those sex offenders living in a state without a minimally sufficient programme to register with the FBI;
- required the FBI to periodically verify sex offender addresses;
- allowed for the dissemination of information necessary to protect the public to federal, state and local officials responsible for law enforcement activities or for running background checks pursuant to the National Child Protection Act;
- contained provisions relating to notification of the FBI and state agencies when a mandated sex offender moved to another state.

1997 – The Jacob Wetterling Improvements Act

Passed as part of the Appropriations Act of 1998, the Jacob Wetterling Improvements Act took several steps to amend provisions of the Jacob Wetterling Act. This law:

- required that state courts, or acceptable alternative procedures or legal standards, be used to make a determination about whether a convicted sex offender should be considered a sexually violent offender;
- required registered offenders who change their state of residence to register under the new state's laws;
- required registered offenders to register in the states where they worked or went to school if those states were different from their state of residence;
- directed states to participate in the national sex offender registry;
- extended sex offender registration requirements to sex offenders convicted in federal or military courts.

1998 – Protection of Children from Sexual Predators Act

This Act contained several provisions which:

- amended the federal criminal code making it illegal to use the mail or other means of interstate and foreign commerce to transmit materials used in the production of child pornography, to transmit specified personal information of minors with the intent to engage in illegal sexual activity, or to knowingly transmit obscene material to a child under the age of 16;

- increased penalties for several categories of federal crimes related to the sexual exploitation of children;

- required electronic communication service providers to report any knowledge of circumstances where a violation of a child pornography law was apparent to designated law enforcement agencies;

- freed electronic communication service providers from liability pursuant to their efforts to comply with this Act;

- directed the Bureau of Justice Assistance to carry out the Sex Offender Management Assistance (SOMA) programme to help eligible states to comply with registration requirements;

- directed the FBI to create an investigative centre, the Investigative Programs Critical Incident Response Group, to assist federal, state and local authorities in investigating child abductions, mysterious disappearances of children, child homicide and serial murder;

- prohibited federal funding to programmes that gave federal prisoners access to the Internet without supervision.

2000 – The Campus Sex Crimes Prevention Act

Passed as part of the Victims of Trafficking and Violence Protection Act, the Campus Sex Crimes Prevention Act:

- required any person who was required to register in a state's sex offender registry to notify the institution of higher education at which the sex offender worked or was a student of their status as a sex offender, and to notify the same institution if there was any change in their enrolment or employment status;

- required that the information collected as a result of this Act be reported promptly to local law enforcement and entered promptly into the appropriate state record systems;

- amended the Higher Education Act of 1965 to require institutions obligated to disclose campus security policy and campus crime statistics to also provide notice of how information concerning registered sex offenders could be obtained.

2003 – Prosecutorial Remedies and Other Tools to end the Exploitation of Children Today (PROTECT) Act

This Act:

- expanded supervised release provisions and increased penalties for some sex offences;

- created a pilot programme to run fingerprint checks on child service providers and volunteers to see if they had criminal records;

- authorised electronic surveillance for suspects of some sex crimes;

- eliminated a statute of limitations and pretrial release for selected sex crimes;

- required law enforcement agencies to report all missing persons up to the age of 21 to the National Crime Information Center;

- directed the Attorney General to appoint a national AMBER Alert Coordinator;

- directed the AMBER Alert Coordinator to establish standards for issuing alerts, the extent of alert dissemination and the appropriate geographic area for alerts, including the dissemination of information about the special needs of victims to appropriate public officials;

- authorised grant programmes to develop communications and notifications systems along highways and assist states in the development and enhancement of alert systems;

- authorised Secret Service agents, at the request of state or local law enforcement officials, to provide assistance in an investigation involving missing and exploited children;

- prohibited producing or distributing images, under specified conditions, that depict a minor engaging in sexual conduct, even if no minor was involved in the production;

- prohibited using or inducing a minor outside of the United States to engage in sexually explicit conduct for the propose of production of images for transportation to the United States;

- required states to maintain a website containing registry information;

- required the Department of Justice to maintain a website with links to each state website (the Dru Sjodin National Sex Offender Public Website);

- authorised appropriations to help defray state costs for compliance with new sex offender registration provisions.

2006 – Adam Walsh Child Protection and Safety Act

This Act:

- consistently requires registration of sex offenders in all jurisdictions in which they reside, are employed or attend school;

- broadens the range of offences covered from aggravated sex acts, such as rape, to include sex crimes with elements of sexual contact, even if they are not sex acts, and includes attempts or conspiracies to commit covered offences;

- adds crimes like possession of child pornography;

- extends registration requirements to juveniles at least fourteen years of age adjudicated delinquent for a crime comparable to or more severe than an aggravated sexual abuse crime as defined in federal legislation;

- establishes three tiers of offenders, based on the severity of the crime. States must establish minimum requirements for offenders in each tier: tier 1 are generally misdemeanor offenders serving less than a one-year sentence; tier 2 includes most felony sexual abuse and exploitation crimes, including those involving minors; and tier 3 is the most serious class of forcible felony sex crimes, as well as sexual contact crimes that involve victims under the age of thirteen. Duration of the registration requirement of sex offenders is set according to the tier levels;

- increased verification requirements to include an in-person appearance annually, semi-annually or quarterly, depending on the tier of the offender. The in-person verification also requires updated photos, as needed;

- requires many new pieces of information as part of each sex offender registration record, including a photo and physical description, fingerprint and palm prints, DNA sample, social security number, driver's licence and motor vehicle information, details of places where the offender works or attends school, criminal history and text of the offence leading to registration;

- seeks greater uniformity in public sex offender websites, providing that most/all appropriate information about the sex offender be available to the public via the web. It also makes requirements regarding search capabilities and participation in the National Sex Offender Registry;

- contains in addition provisions allowing juveniles and tier 1 offenders who have not committed new offences to have their period of required registration reduced. Adjudicated juveniles subject to lifetime registration may have that reduced to 25 years if they commit no new offences in 25 years. Tier 1 sex offenders can reduce required registration to ten years as a result of having no new offences in that time.

Appendix 10.2 Summary of legislative developments in England and Wales

1996 – Family Law Act

Introduced powers to make an abuser leave a given household when children were at risk (this was an amendment to the 1989 Children Act).

1997 – Sex Offenders Act (Part 1)

Introduced the UK sex offender register. Registration, initially provided for by Part 1 of the Sex Offenders Act 1997, required certain categories of sex offender to notify the police of their name and address and any changes to these details within a specified period.

1997 – Police Act

Part 5 of this Act introduced the concept of the Criminal Records Bureau as a centralised body to improve the pre-employment screening of workers with children and vulnerable adults. The Bureau started operating in 2002.

1998 – Crime and Disorder Act

Introduced the Sex Offender Order (SOO), that is a civil order placed upon those with a history of sexual offending who look likely to reoffend. The order require placement on the Sex Offender Register (if not already registered) and allow for the specification of 'negative' requirements that the person desist from certain behaviours. Breach of the order resulted in a criminal procedure.

1999 – Protection of Children Act

Allows the Department of Health and the Department of Education to compile a national list of those considered unsuitable to work with children and vulnerable adults – even if there has been no previous conviction.

2000 – Criminal Justice and Court Services Act

Introduced the Disqualification Order. This is made at the point of sentence for twelve months or more; it prevents the offender from working with children – thus even to apply for such work is a criminal offence. The Act also introduced the Multi-Agency Public Protection Panels – these are inter-agency arrangements (police, probation, local authority, private housing landlords and so on) which monitor and assess risk for violent and sexual offenders in their geographical area The Act also introduced Restraining Orders – these are made at the point of sentence to prevent offenders going near certain named people or certain places. The Act tightened registration procedure under the Sex Offenders Act.

2002 – Police Reform Act

Made it easier to obtain a Sex Offender Order and also introduced the emergency measure of the Interim Sex Offender Order.

2003 – Sexual Offences Act

Part 2 replaces registration arrangements under the 1997 Sex Offenders Act. Both the Sex Offender Order and the Restraining Order have now been combined and replaced with a new expanded order – a Sexual Offences Prevention Order. The Act also introduces the Risk of Sexual Harm Order – a new civil preventative order which has been designed to protect children from sexual harm. It can be used to prohibit specified behaviour, including the 'grooming' of children.

This term covers the situation where a potential offender will seek to make contact and become familiar with a child in order to prepare them for abuse either directly or, as is the case more recently, through Internet chat rooms. The term has recently found expression in section 15 of the Sexual Offences Act 2003, which makes it an offence to 'meet a child following sexual grooming'.

Acknowledgements

I wish to thank Terry Thomas (Leeds) and the Home Office and British Academy who funded our earlier collaborative research.

Note

1 Judge Danforth pronounces at the Salem witch trials: 'This is a sharp time, now, a precise time; we live no longer in the dusky afternoon when evil mixed itself with good and befuddled the world. Now, by God's grace, the shining sun is up, and them that fear not light will surely praise it' (*The Crucible*, Act III, by Arthur Miller 1953).

References

Barker, V. (2006) 'The politics of punishing: building a state governance theory of American imprisonment variation', *Punishment and Society*, 8: 5–32.

Bedarf, A. (1995) 'Examining sex offender community notification laws', *California Law Review*, 85: 885–939.

Bryan, T. and Doyle, P. (2003) 'Developing Multi-Agency Public Protection Arrangements', in A. Matravers (ed.), *Sex Offenders in the Community: Managing and Reducing the Risks*, Cambridge Criminal Justice Series. Cullompton: Willan, pp. 189–206.

Cobley, C. (2000/5) *Sex Offenders: Law, Policy and Practice*, 1st/2nd edn. Bristol: Jordans.

Collier, R. (2001) 'Dangerousness, popular knowledge and the criminal law: a case study of the paedophile as sociocultural phenomenon', in P. Alldridge and C. Brant (eds), *Personal Autonomy, the Private Sphere and the Criminal Law*. Oxford: Hart, pp. 223–43.

Critcher, C. (2002) 'Media, government and moral panic: the politics of pedophilia in Britain 2000–1', *Journalism Studies*, 3: 521–35.

D'Emilio, J. and Freedman, E.B. (1997) *Intimate Matters: A History of Sexuality in America*, 2nd edn. Chicago, IL: University of Chicago Press.

Dean, C. (1996) *Sexuality and Modern Western Culture*. New York: Twayne.

Douglas, M. (1992) *Risk and Blame: Essays in Cultural Theory*. London: Routledge.

Friedman, L. (1993) *Crime and Punishment in American History*. New York: Basic Books.

Garland, D. (1990) *Punishment and Modern Society*. Oxford: Oxford University Press.

Garland, D. (2003) 'The rise of risk', in R. V. Ericson and A. Doyle (eds), *Risk and Morality*. Toronto, ON: University of Toronto Press, pp. 48–86.

Grabowski, J.F. (1988) 'The Illinois Sexually Dangerous Persons Act', *Southern Illinois University Law Journal*, 12: 437–45.

Greer, C. (2003) *Sex Crime and the Media: Sex Offending and the Press in a Divided Society*. Cullompton: Willan.

Hacker, F.J. and Frym. M. (1955) 'The Sexual Psychopath Act in practice – a critical discussion', *California Law Review*, 43: 766–99.

Haggerty, K.D. (2003) 'From risk to precaution', in R.V. Ericson and A. Doyle (eds), *Risk and Morality*. Toronto, ON: University of Toronto Press, pp. 193–214.

Hebenton, B. (2008) 'Sexual offenders and public protection in an uncertain age', in G. Letherby, K. Williams, P. Birch and M. Cain (eds), *Sex as Crime*. Cullompton: Willan.

Hebenton, B. and Thomas, T. (1996a) 'Sexual offenders in the community: reflections on problems of law, community, and risk management in the USA, England, and Wales', *International Journal of the Sociology of Law*, 24: 427–43.

Hebenton, B. and Thomas, T. (1996b) 'Tracking sex offenders', *Howard Journal of Criminal Justice*, 35: 97–112.

Hobson, B.R. (2006) 'Banishing acts: how far may states go to keep convicted offenders away from children?', *Georgia Law Review*, 40: 961–4.

Home Office (1996) *Sentencing and Supervision of Sex Offenders: A Consultation Document*, Cm. 3304. London: HMSO.

Home Office (1997) *Sex Offenders Act*, Circular 39/97. London: Home Office.

Home Office (2004) *MAPPA Guidance (Version 2)*. London: Home Office.

Home Office (2007) *A Review of the Protection of Children from Sex Offenders*. London: Home Office.

Jenkins, P. (1998) *Moral Panic: Changing Concepts of the Child Molester in Modern America*. New Haven, CT: Yale University Press.

Jones, T. and Newburn, T. (2004) 'The convergence of US and UK crime control policy: exploring substance and process', in T. Newburn and R. Sparks (eds), *Criminal Justice and Political Cultures*. Cullompton: Willan, pp. 123–51.

Kemshall, H. and Wood, J. (2007) 'Beyond public protection: an examination of community protection and public health approaches to high-risk offenders', *Criminology and Criminal Justice*, 7: 203–22.

Kitzinger, J. (1999) 'The ultimate neighbour from hell? Stranger danger and the media framing of paedophiles', in B. Franklin (ed.), *Social Policy, the Media and Misrepresentation*. London: Routledge, pp. 207–21.

Laws, D.R. (2000) 'Sexual offending as a public health problem: a North American perspective', *Journal of Sexual Aggression*, 5: 30–44.

Levenson, J.S., D'Amora, D.A. and Hern, A. (2006) 'Megan's Law and its impact on community re-entry for sex offenders', *Behavioral Sciences and the Law*, 25: 587–602.

Lieb, R. (2000) 'Social policy and sexual offenders: contrasting United States' and European policies', *European Journal on Criminal Policy and Research*, 8: 423–40.

Lynch, M. (2002) 'Pedophiles and cyber-predators as contaminating forces: the language of disgust, pollution, and boundary invasions in federal debates on sex offender legislation', *Law and Social Inquiry*, 27: 529–66.

Ost, S. (2004) 'Getting to grips with sexual grooming? The new offence under the Sexual Offences Act 2003', *Journal of Social Welfare and Family Law*, 26: 147–59.

Parker, T. (1969) *The Twisting Lane: Some Sex Offenders*. London: Hutchinson.

Power, H. (1999) 'Sex offenders, privacy and the police', *Criminal Law Review*, 3: 16.

Power, H. (2003) 'Disclosing information on sex offenders: the human rights implications', in A. Matravers (ed.), *Sex Offenders in the Community: Managing and Reducing the Risks*, Cambridge Criminal Justice Series. Cullompton: Willan, pp. 72–101.

Pratt, J. (1997) *Governing the Dangerous*. Sydney: Federation Press.

Rainer, R., Livingstone., S. and Allen, J. (2003) 'From law and order to lynch mobs: crime news since the Second World War', in P. Mason (ed.), *Criminal Visions: Media Representations of Crime and Criminal Justice*. Cullompton: Willan, pp. 208–31.

Savelsberg, J. (1994) 'Knowledge, domination and criminal punishment', *American Journal of Sociology*, 97: 1346–81.

Soothill, K. and Francis, B. (2002) 'Moral panics and the aftermath: a study of incest. *Journal of Social Welfare and Family Law*, 24: 1–17.

Starmer, K. (2001) 'Positive obligations under the Convention', in J. Jowell and J. Cooper (eds), *Understanding Human Rights Law*. Oxford: Hart, pp. 139–59.

Sunstein, C.R. (2005) *Laws of Fear: Beyond the Precautionary Principle*. Cambridge: Cambridge University Press.

Sutherland, E. (1950a) 'The diffusion of sexual psychopath laws', *American Journal of Sociology*, 56: 142–8.

Sutherland, E. (1950b) 'The sexual psychopath laws', *Journal of Criminal Law and Criminology*, 40: 543–54.

Swanson, A.H. (1960) 'Sexual psychopath statutes: summary and analysis', *Journal of Criminal Law and Criminology*, 51: 215–20.

Thomas, T. (2000/5) *Sex Crime: Sex Offending and Society*, 1st/2nd edn. Cullompton: Willan.

Tonry, M. (1996) *Sentencing Matters*. New York: Oxford University Press.

Chapter 12

Challenges of managing the risk of violent and sexual offenders in the community

Thomas Considine and Philip Birch

On 13 November 2007 Andrew Bridges, HM Chief Inspector of Probation governing England and Wales, gave an address to an All-Party Parliamentary Committee on the following topic 'Dangerous Offenders – What Can Be Achieved?' (http://www.homeoffice.gov. uk). As the Chief Inspector of Probation one of his main tasks is to review the management of all offenders who, while under statutory supervision in the community, commit a serious further offence (which is referred to under the acronym SFO). A point to raise here is although the term/acronym is drawn from a UK perspective it taps into broader principles which have a universal relevance. Although it is, as Andrew Bridges acknowledges, a debatable point as to what actually counts as a 'serious' further offence it would be reasonable to say that the types of crimes under scrutiny would primarily involve those of a violent and/or sexual nature; this would be supported by the examples he cites in his address, e.g. Naomi Bryant, who was murdered by Anthony Rice in August 2008 while being supervised on a life licence by Hampshire Probation Service, and Anthony Monkton, who was a wealthy financier from London who was murdered in 2004 by Damien Hanson and Elliot White, both of whom were under the supervision of London Probation Service. Both of these cases were subject to inspectorate review by Andrew Bridges. In this address, which follows similar themes raised his annual report of the National Probation Service (2007), he raises several points which are of central concern to this chapter and are worth noting as a means of introducing the challenges of managing the risk of violent and sexual offenders in the community. Incidentally, for the sake of brevity, we will use the term 'dangerous offenders' from here on to cover both violent and sexual offences.

One recurring point Bridges makes is that, while every effort should be made to manage potential harm, the risk dangerous offenders pose can never be fully eradicated and risk of harm, in various forms and to various degrees, are a prevalent feature of our daily lives. In this regard Andrew Bridges offers a corrective to public and media expectations about what can be realistically achieved in the management of dangerous offenders: he is challenging a prevalent 'blame culture' ('heads on pikes' is the more colloquial metaphor used). This raises an important theme about the social and cultural context in which the perceptions of dangerous offenders are perceived and their subsequent management. This is something we will consider later in this chapter.

Another feature he raises is the difficulty of defining and identifying dangerous offenders. He locates this problem primarily in practical and statistical terms: the majority of those who commit SFOs were assessed as medium or low risk of harm (the majority of these assessments were, according to Bridges, correct), whereas those classed as high or very high risk account for around 20 per cent of SFOs. In other words the majority of those classed as high risk do not commit serious further offences and the majority who do commit further serious crimes were not judged to be a serious threat. The simple point is that it is not as immediately straightforward as it may seem to differentiate between dangerous and non-dangerous offenders. This raises important questions about the use and efficacy of predictive risk assessment tools and this is an area for consideration in this chapter.

One other key question Andrew Bridges addresses, which is, perhaps, the overarching consideration when looking at managing dangerous offenders in the community, is why actually bother with any form of community supervision at all and simply opt for incarceration? His response to this is threefold. First, it would have practical implications in terms of resources and costs as he estimates it could lead to an increase in the prison population by an additional fifteen thousand. Secondly, in connection with the problem of differentiating the dangerous and non-dangerous offenders, it would be difficult to know with confident accuracy who to indefinitely imprison, as those not assessed as high risk or more could still pose a threat. Lastly, incarceration would not actually answer the question he posed in his title. Although certain offences and certain offenders will attract permanent incarceration there are a significant number of dangerous offenders for whom, colloquially speaking, 'locking up and throwing away the key' would not apply which still leaves the question of their management.

In addressing this issue Andrew Bridges raises a number of points which we wish to explore further in this chapter. He notes how misplaced assumptions about community supervision may arise primarily through changes in terminology – 'being under supervision' has replaced 'being on probation' – which creates a sense that community supervision could and should mirror prison in terms of control and supervision. One aspect we will consider in this discussion is the significance of language in both defining and describing dangerous offenders, as this not only illuminates the challenges but provides possible solutions as well. Furthermore, he taps into an ongoing debate about the nature of community supervision and increasing community control measures and so, although Andrew Bridges is adamant that the prison and community controls are two distinctly separate entities, we will consider how these boundaries may be blurred in the pursuit of risk management. In this regard we will look at both operational and legislative measures in place to manage dangerous offenders, as well technical developments in the realm of public safety.

We indicated above that, in our study of managing dangerous offenders in the community, we wished to analyse it within a specific cultural and social framework. By way of a preliminary introduction to this particular analysis we should specify that when we are talking about managing dangerousness we are, inevitably perhaps, also talking about risk: discussions of dangerousness and risk in criminological discourses have become virtually synonymous (Nash 2006). We will not initially challenge this convergence of these two terms but we will consider another possible conception of risk, and the implications for managing dangerous offenders, later in this chapter.

Deconstructing risk

The debate on what to do with dangerous offenders is not a particularly new one – it appears to have been a perennial social concern for almost two centuries, if not more (e.g. Pratt 2000). However, what is new is the context in which these debates take place. Risk, as Mary Douglas (1992) argues, is not just a matter of technical or conceptual analysis but is also a product of specific social interactions and, as such, it reveals a great deal about the social environment in which it is created.

It seems well established to the point of becoming a cliché that the single defining feature of contemporary society is that of risk and the 'risk society' (Giddens 1990; Beck 1992). Risk has become the dominant theme within the broad spectrum of social sciences and especially criminal justice (see Kemshall 2003, 2006). The landscape of the 'risk society' has been very well mapped out (for example, see Loader and Sparks 2002, 2007 respectively, who use the adjective 'landscape' in their title) and, rather than resurvey the same terrain, so to speak, we will pick out the salient landmarks of the 'risk society' and the significance for the management of dangerous offenders. As well as using Anthony Giddens and Ulrich Beck as our key guides we will also draw extensively upon the ideas of David Garland (1995, 2001). These authors offer some clarity in what is a rather confusing and crowded terrain.

The first key point is that the 'risk society' can be described as the shift from modernity to post or late modernity. Modernity could be characterised as a belief in the utility and efficacy of scientific methodology. Modernity is underpinned by the empiricism, secularism and rational principles. This led to progressive developments within technical, medical and social sciences. It is a paradigm which is optimistic in nature. Garland cites the emergence of the modern criminal justice system from the end of the nineteenth century to the 1970s. He refers to this as the emergence of 'penal welfarism'; this is characterised by the use and application of 'scientific' knowledge to explain criminal behaviour (drawing upon biological, psychological and social science theories respectively); it is associated with the emergence of experts and a professional elite (e.g. probation officers: Vanstone 2007) and is underpinned by an underlying optimism that criminal behaviour, and by extension dangerous offenders, can be reformed. It reaches it apotheosis in the 'rehabilitative ideal' (Cavadino and Dignam 2005).

Late modernity is characterised as increasing ambivalence about the ubiquitous merits of progress; each new development also carries with it unintended threats. This can be characterised within the realm of criminal justice as a shift from rehabilitation to 'nothing works' (Martinson 1974). This may not be literally true (see Maguire 1995) but it captures the underpinning spirit of the last thirty years; trust in experts and the 'liberal elite' (Loader 2006) has been severely eroded and the belief in rehabilitation has been significantly diminished. There has been a shift from reform to risk management or 'actuarial justice' (Feely and Simon 1992). Actuarial risk assessment tools have their origins in the eighteenth century and are probability calculations assessing the likelihood of risk. They are not concerned with individual assessment per se but large groups and aggregate factors and can be used to develop preventative risk factors. These are alluded to by Andrew Bridges in his address cited above. As Garland (2001) points out, there is a shift from looking at people and causes of crime to looking at places and events that can be avoided. It is noticeable in his address that Andrew Bridges talks exclusively about managing and containing risk but never talks about reform.

Following on from this, the second key feature of the 'risk society' is that it promotes a 'precautionary principle', that is it shifts our perception from 'goods to bads' (Mythen 2007). We seek to manage the 'bads' or threats rather than consider the 'goods' such as reform. Risk is not something we can avoid but we have to learn to live with. In the context of dealing with dangerous offenders the focus is on the containment and limitation of danger. Andrew Bridges cites more than once the parameters of what can be realistically expected of supervising dangerous offenders. His key purpose is to see that all that could be done to realistically contain risk was undertaken rather than transform it. This is the resonances of Garland's 'limits of the Criminal Justice state' (2001: 107). We no longer have unquestioned trust in the authorities paid to protect us from harm. There are limits to what we can expect of the state and there is a move to increase public participation in managing the risks dangerous offenders pose. This has links with the concept of 'responsibilisation' (O'Malley 2000) and, in political terms, the emergence of the 'New Right, neo liberal, politics' (James and Raine 1998; Stenson 2001). The role of the Inspector of Probation fits this culture as their aim is to hold to account a publicly funded body for taxpayers. There are recurrent debates and moves to increase public participation in the management of dangerous offenders, such as public notification schemes (Bernardo 2007). We will look at specific schemes in more detail further on.

The third and final point we will highlight is what could be termed the paradox of risk. Given that risk is all pervasive and we all share some responsibility for managing risk then there is a need for as much information as we can to assess the risk we face. However, as Giddens argues, our methods to assess the risk we face outstrips the threats we face. We live, he says in a 'runaway world', in which the threats outpace our ability to keep up with them. In order to manage the risk and dangers we face the more information and controls we demand and the more information there is the greater level of anxiousness we feel and so the process perpetuates itself. In relation to dangerous offenders parallels could be drawn with Garland's concept of the 'strategies of adaptation' (2001). As well as seeking to involve the public more in managing dangerous offenders the state realigns the primary function of the criminal justice system as public protection and as such moves to increase greater control over the management of dangerous offenders. The reassurance of the public is sought and the legitimacy of the criminal justice system is up held through extending greater powers. This may be seen in the introduction and use of indeterminate sentences in the Criminal Justice Act 2003. There are ongoing debates on the powers of the MAPPA system and the detention of those identified with mental health disorders who have not committed a crime.

What we have sketched out here is a brief philosophical, cultural and political landscape in which the challenges of managing dangerous offenders can be best understood. For the sake of brevity and clarity we have simplified a somewhat 'confusing and contradictory' picture (Loader and Sparks 2007) as it involves both increasing state power and control and dispersing it. However, having set the context we examine in more detail the specifics involved in managing dangerous offenders. We have divided this into three sections which we refer to as the scientific (the development and use of risk assessment tools), the administrative and legislative (recent developments in legislation and operational policy such as MAPPA) and security (a shift towards greater use of surveillance and control).

Managing dangerous offenders

Irrespective of the discourse surrounding risk what is evident are the three central features in which risk is managed within England and Wales. These three features, which can also be found across the globe, and especially in western countries in managing risk, can be identified as:

- scientific;
- administration and legislation;
- security.

Scientific approach

Currently within the criminal justice system in England and Wales risk assessment tools are administered by agencies such as probation in order to categorise offenders into high, medium and low risk. This approach is achieved via an actuarial or clinical approach. However, much controversy surrounds these tools on a variety of levels. First, with regard to practice efficacy, while it is claimed that the tools are standardised to ensure consistency in outcome, agencies adopt and use a variety of tools in order to categorise offenders and the variance in efficacy brings into question the reliability with which some offenders are categorised, thus implying that some offenders are not accurately assigned to a group in terms of the level of risk they pose. Furthermore, there is the very nature of actuarial risk assessments which focus on static factors and clinical risk assessments. With the latter focusing on dynamic factors this provides another, yet simple way of demonstrating the variance in assessing offenders who are deemed to pose the greatest risk to the public. Also, it can be further argued that, irrespective of which assessment tool format is adopted to assess risk, what the final outcome of such a measure provides is nothing more than a blanket approach to managing risk in the sense that the tools do not advise on how the risk should be managed and prevented or how this is to be achieved in the short, medium and long term. However, on evaluating the types of tool in use, it is claimed, as pointed out by Nash (2006), that actuarial risk assessments sit better with assessing risk as the huge data sets used to create such assessments lend themselves to certainty more than clinical judgment, due to their scientific nature.

The scientific nature of this approach needs to be questioned though as it is derived from a premise which is inaccurate. Such tools are developed by drawing upon offender and crime data, thus allowing us to claim that if offender 'a' is displaying characteristics such as 'x', then they are deemed to pose a higher risk than offender 'b' who is not. However, to take just one example, data such as the recorded crime figures used to make such an assumption are incomplete due to issues such as under-reporting and no reporting, especially with regard to crimes such as sexual offences. A distinction can be drawn here with research methods, in which if a number of cases within a sample have missing values these missing values can be substituted with the mean, a process known as 'mean substitution'. But as we know when the sample gets larger the use of this mean leads to distorted and inaccurate reports of the actual findings. This can be applied to the categorisation of risk. Due to the fact we do not have all the information at hand in order to establish robust risk assessment tools we substitute the gaps with what we think is missing. As a result this can lead to the incorrect categorisation of offenders. One way of illustrating this point is by asking the question should sex offenders such as paedophiles always be categorised as high risk in comparison to their counterparts 'flashers'? Evidence suggests that in terms of reconviction rates the 'flasher' poses greater risk then the paedophile; up to 70 per cent are reconvicted (Marshall and Barbaree 1990, cited by Fisher and Beech 2004). Abel *et al.* (1987, cited by Fisher and Beech 2004) state that: 'in relation to exhibitionists, a significant number of contact sex offenders have previously exposed themselves before escalating in the seriousness of their sexual offending' (p. 41).

Furthermore, the ethical dilemmas, both approaches to assessing risk demonstrate, brings into disrepute such methods for managing risk posed by the most dangerous offenders within our community. The ethics of actuarial risk assessment centre around the fact that someone is being labelled based on the behaviours of others and ignores individual differences. On the other hand, with the clinical approach, how ethical is it for one person to be judged by another and what is this judgment based upon? If it is professional judgment, isn't this form of judgment developed through professional experience, e.g. based on evidence from working with a significant number of clients? If so, is this different to the premise of an actuarial risk assessment but without the scientific roots?

While these tools can be critiqued from the point of view of managing risk, it is recognised that these assessment tools are only one form of managing risk, but there is no reason why the two types of risk assessments cannot be used in conjunction with each other in a bid to strengthen the outcome of the risk assessment. In Kemshall and McIvor (2004), Grubin calls this approach 'third generation': the use and linkage of both static and dynamic risk assessment tools in a bid to improve the categorisation of offenders.

Administration and legislation

A second feature of managing risk with dangerous offenders can be located within 'administration'. Numerous policy, legislation and HM Inspectorate reports, especially throughout the 1990s and into the new millennium, have been introduced, concerned with the management of risk by criminal justice agencies, including the police and probation (see Kemshall 2002). Some of the significant pieces introduced during this time are highlighted below.

Children's Act 1989

Under this act we saw the establishment of Area Child Protection Committees (ACPCs), now known as Safeguarding Boards. In short, such committees were tasked to ensure the safety of children from harm caused by adults – adults concerned in most cases were involved with criminal justice agencies and could be classified as dangerous offenders.

HMIP, Dealing with Dangerous Offenders: The Probation and Public Protection (1995)

This report identified that the police and probation are involved in the same work and therefore need to work together, and examined areas of good practice where this was already taking place. However, West Yorkshire was the only area in the country at this time in which the police and probation were working together under their own local arrangements in order to assess and manage dangerous offenders in the community.

There were no national guidelines for working together and each area was left to decide how best to achieve this. This lack of local arrangements for working together in order to manage dangerous offenders in the community was blamed upon the police and probation services being separate agencies with different operational and cultural perspectives. However, the report encouraged other areas to follow the best practice of West Yorkshire and begin working together in order to manage such offenders.

Sex Offenders Act 1997

This act significantly informed the legislation creating MAPPA (Multi- Agency Protection Panel Arrangements). It became obligatory for convicted sex offenders to be registered. The register was to be monitored by the police and offenders had to inform the police of changes in their address. There were variations in the requirements for registration depending on the offence. However, registration was usually for five years or more for the majority of offenders that had to register. Under this Act the police and probation had to work in partnership to manage the risk posed by the offenders on the register. This is the first piece of legislation which had made it a statutory duty for the police and probation to work in partnership in relation to the management of dangerous offenders in the community.

One way of managing this risk was via 'Sex Offender Orders' (established under the 1998 Crime and Disorder Act – see Bryan and Doyle 2003) which allowed for restrictions to be placed on certain offenders (see Cobley 2003; Thomas 2005).

HMIP, Exercising Constant Vigilance (1998)

This report was based on the assessment of how well other areas had improved their practice for managing dangerous offenders in the community. The report also advocated the need for specialist workers in order to assess and manage those offenders who posed a high risk of harm to the community.

Criminal Justice and Court Services Act 2000

This is the Act which created MAPPA at a national level and came into force on 1 March 2001. Administered by probation, MAPPAs are responsible for assessing and managing the risk posed by dangerous offenders. Those offenders who are subject to MAPPA are:

- all violent and sexual offenders sentenced to twelve months or more;
- anyone else likely to pose risk of serious harms (Nash 2006).

The Act placed a statutory duty on Responsible Authorities, which at this time were the police and probation but later included the prison service also. Other agencies are under a 'duty of care' to cooperate with the MAPPA process (see Cobley 2003; Thomas 2005).

Sexual Offences Act 2003

This Act revamped the 1997 Sex Offenders Act. New restrictive powers where given to the police in relation to sexual offenders, shifting their role from a 'monitoring' to a 'managing' one. This was achieved via 'Sexual Offenders Prevention Orders' (see Cobley 2003; Thomas 2005). In addition, sex offending was redefined in relation to 'consent' and what that meant, along with the recognition of additional sexual offences e.g. committed via the Internet.

Criminal Justice Act 2003

Through this legislation, two new sentences for dangerous offenders were introduced:

- the indeterminate sentence – this applies to anyone who could be given a life sentence of ten years or more and is similar to life imprisonment;
- the extended licence – this is reserved for those violent and sexual offenders who would attract a sentence of less than ten years.

Of all the above, it has been the Criminal Justice and Court Services Act 2000 introducing MAPPA which has had the most significant impact on managing the risk of dangerous offenders within the community. MAPPA are tasked to work with three categories of clients:

1 registered sex offenders;
2 violent and other sex offenders not registered/sentenced to twelve months or more;
3 other offenders who fall outside of categories 1 and 2, but are deemed to be at risk of causing serious harm to the public (Bryan and Doyle 2003).

Once the category of each MAPPA client is known, a risk assessment is completed in order to allow the offender to be managed in the most appropriate manner through a risk management plan (RMP). For a more detailed account see Bryan and Doyle (2003) and Lieb (2003).

In 2004/5 the annual MAPPA evaluation (http://www.probation. homeoffice.gov.uk/files/pdf/MAPPA) provided the following information:

- 30,000 offenders were deemed to pose a low risk and could therefore be managed effectively by one agency, usually the probation service;

- 12,600 offenders were deemed to pose a medium risk and needed to be managed by two agencies, usually the probation service and the police;

- 3,000 offenders, described as the 'critical few', were deemed to pose the highest risk and were intensively monitored and managed by a number agencies.

However, this management of offenders takes place within the context of an overburden of workload for both police and probation along with resource cuts, and driven by an overzealous performance management culture. Along with the 'pitfalls' of risk assessment tools highlighted above, the question needs to be raised: is this the most effective and safest means to manage the most dangerous offenders within England and Wales in the community?

This therefore leads us to the third feature of managing the risk of dangerous offenders in particular within the community: security – more commonly referred to as 'surveillance'.

Security

Surveillance has been used for some time to manage offenders, in particular within the community, for example the introduction of electronic tagging introduced by the Sex Offenders Act 1997 (see

Thomas 2005: 100–1). However, since then and post 9/11 we have seen an overabundance of surveillance strategies and technologies introduced in a bid to manage high-risk offenders. These developments include 'finger and retinal scans, software which assesses hand geometry and vein patterns, voice and face recognition software' (Hier and Greenberg 2007: 7).

Rule (2007), views surveillance as the way in which we 'identify, locate and apprehend rule breakers' and this enables agencies such as the police to monitor and manage the behaviour and daily lives of violent and sexual offenders within the community.

Surveillance and related technologies create the effect of the panopticon in that those subject to such sanctions are constantly monitored and visible; however, there are ethical and other impacts of such actions. The debate within criminological discourse is rife with discussion of the human rights aspect of utilising such methods as a means of managing offenders (see Nash 2006: 176–93), while further scrutiny of this method can also be found in how effective it is in changing behaviour. While it may be claimed that behaviour can be controlled by means of surveillance, who is this means best serving? Is it the subjects of such technologies who are deemed to pose a risk to the wider community, or is it those claimed to be at risk from such persons? Furthermore, the pitfalls in technology raise further questions for this method in managing the most dangerous offenders within our community: how ethical is it for criminal justice agencies to rely on such methods, first, to protect the public and, second, to manage the risk posed by an individual? As Cobley (2003) points out, such a mechanism does not show who the offender is with, merely their geographical location.

While the debate surrounding such features of managing risk continue, it could be stated that the 'current state of play' for managing the risk of dangerous offenders in the community is as 'good as it gets' for now, and therefore we need to ensure that the provision currently in place to achieve such an outcome is maintained as effectively as possible.

The challenge

Having looked at the administrative, operational and instrumental measures employed in managing the risk of dangerous offenders we will propose that, although these measures have their respective benefits, the most significant challenge lies in how the concept of risk is understood. Returning to the address by Andrew Bridges, we noted how mindful he was of operating in a blame culture and contending with the demand for 'heads on pikes'. We will briefly consider this cultural context further, drawing attention to the implications for the kind of society in which dangerous offenders are managed and the benefits of a broader conceptualisation of risk.

It would be fair to say that one of the dominant themes underpinning various disciplines over the last century is the recognition that reality can be constructed through the use of language. This is one of the foundational principles which informs social analysis such as social constructivism (Parton and O'Byrne 2000) and cultural criminology (Ferrell 2005; Hayward 2004; Greer 2005). One of the common concerns with these schools of thought is not only how social reality is constructed but also by whom, in whose interests and for what purpose. Moreover, they also explore how the concepts which shape reality can be reconfigured – reality is a contestable issue. As indicated earlier risk is not simply a probability calculation but exists within a set of social interactions. As Kemshall and McIvor (2004) point out, the origin of the word risk had two meanings: danger and taking a chance. We noted earlier how risk and dangerousness have become synonymous and we ourselves accepted this for our subsequent discussion. A review of some of the more recent literature on risk would indicate that risk is conceived almost exclusively as 'danger' or 'threats' but not as taking a chance. This singular conception of risk, meaning danger or threats, has particular consequences for shaping the debate on how dangerous offenders should be managed.

This a theme explored by Frank Furedi in his influential study *The Culture of Fear* (1997). His central thesis is how danger or threat of harm has become the pervasive feature of society. One of the consequences is not only do we become accustomed to managing our risks but we also have increasing expectations for greater control measures. It is argued that this can be used as a mandate for extending the powers of the state to restrain offenders (e.g. Nash 2006) In this respect there is a trade off for greater security measures against reducing liberty (Hudson 2003). This also has parallels with a recent argument of 'governing through crime' (Simon 2007) in which it is argued that the danger from crime is promoted to permit greater social sanctions. It can also be likened to Bottoms' seemingly prophetic essay on the 'renaissance of dangerousness' (1977) in which he argued that the promotion of safety from dangerous offenders is used to unify a putatively fragmenting society. The upshot is that, according to Furedi, the fabric of social and civic life is damaged as we become less participatory and more protectionist. The implication is that the dangerous offender becomes the other, the threatening outsider from whom we desire greater protection. Although it would be foolish to argue that dangerous offenders should not be held in check it seems that containment is the only goal. 'Control', as Hayles (2006) argues, undoubtedly has a part to play in relation to offenders who pose a serious risk of harm to the community, but reliance upon it leads to the alienation and brutalisation of individual offenders with little compensatory benefit to the community as a whole in terms of an enhanced sense of security' (p. 72). Hayles explores the significance of separating risk from any social context. It leads to the worst of both worlds. It creates a dehumanising process for offenders which does not promote safety, and, similarly, in seeking greater security, we never feel safe and so demand even more social control. As Hayles subsequently points out, 'The demand for safety cannot be satiated' (p. 72). One question we may consider is that, as we strive for a greater sense of security through expanding social controls, what sort of society could we be creating for ourselves? Perhaps we could be creating prisons in the community.

If we had a concept of risk meaning 'taking a chance' then what could the implications of managing dangerous offenders look like? This would involve offering an alternative vision of the characteristic 'risk society'. We will look at some attempts to revise a social reality which can have significant implications for managing dangerous offenders. We would start with a quote from David Garland early in his study the *Culture of Control* (2001). He says:

> We have to bear in mind, therefore, that the field of crime control involves the social ordering activities of the authorities and also the activities of private actors and agencies as they go about their daily lives and routines. Too often our attention focuses on the state's institutions and neglects the informal social practices upon which action depends. (p. 6)

One interpretation we take from this is that the possibility for social change exists in those 'informal' everyday activities and within the social relationships that are, or could be established. Within this idea the notion of risk as taking a chance may be explored. As indicated above the respective studies of Furedi (1997) and Hayles (2006) respectively show that the increasing demand for formal risk control measures leads to a diminution of civic interaction. One of the things which is sacrificed is trust between people. As Hayles argues, if we are to loosen the tightening social controls we need to rediscover trust and this means learning to take a chance. Hayles challenges the current ethos which characterises the supervision of dangerous offenders. It is argued that the practice is mostly driven by an over-reliance on third-generation assessment tools. While these can have some benefit in supporting professional practice, they actually become for the most part the 'process which drives reality' (p. 70). Moreover this process contributes to an increasingly depersonalised interaction as the offender is subject to a series of overly negative and 'problem-saturated' questions. The key problem, Hayles argues, is that the dangerous offender is constantly aware of what they must not do but has no opportunity to develop a more positive alternative. There is little incentive to actually change. Drawing upon a range of ideas from narratives of desistance (Farrall 2002; Maruna 2001), framing (Strachan and Tallant 1997) and social constructivist theories among others, Hayles develops a model of managing dangerousness through a shared collaborative process in which the positive change can take place. Framing allows the promotion of gains to avoid crime rather than simply being risk averse ('bads to goods'), while 'narratives of desistance' use the transformative nature of language to rewrite the personal narrative thus enabling change. While it does not eschew other formal control measures this approach is predicated on establishing a form of trust as it seeks to explore positive change.

Another possibility we would argue may be found in the study by Loader and Walker, 'Civilizing Security' (2007). This is not primarily concerned with dealing with dangerous offenders per se but looks at issues pertaining to national and international security. Within this they seek to promote the idea of security as a 'thick social good' (p. 4) which involves exploring the idea of 'what may it mean for citizens to live together securely with risk' (p. 5). In brief they seek to outline a conceptual model of risk and security which can be embraced as a unifying social good. Interestingly they also consider the significance of language and meaning in order to reshape society (drawing upon ideas of Charles Taylor and 'retrieval'). They argue that the significance of meaning is linked to the values and beliefs which inform our behaviour. Security is not simply a matter of top-down government controls or a matter of market-driven neo-liberal security services but is developed as a concept in which it can be seen as a shared enterprise. Loader and Walker challenge the tendency of risk measures to create binary oppositions around 'us/them', 'safe/ dangerous' and 'normal/deviant' among others (they refer to these binary oppositions as 'securitising moves', citing Buzan *et al.* 1998).

They point out that the origin of the word 'security' is closely linked to the concept of relationships. Although they do not specifically focus on dangerous offenders it is possible to infer a conceptual framework which promotes a shared, communal goal to manage risk which promotes a model of inclusion.

One possible example of this could be in the use of Circles of Support and Accountability (COSA) (Wilson *et al.* 2007) which began in 1994 in Canada and were instigated by one Reverend Harry Nigh who arranged, with members of his congregation, to befriend, monitor and reintegrate a notorious repeat sexual offender, Charlie Taylor. The goal of COSA perfectly exemplifies the vision of public and community which embraces a shared public good:

> The goal of COSA is to promote successful integration of released men into the community by providing support, advocacy, and a way to be meaningfully accountable in exchange for living safely in the community. In doing so, safety is enhanced for the community, particularly where risk exists for women, children or other vulnerable persons. (Wilson *et al.* 2007: 8)

This could be an example of what David Garland had in mind when he spoke about the 'the activities of private actors and agencies who go about their daily lives ...' (Garland 2001). Perhaps there is another safety paradox at work here: we can maintain community safety by finding a place for our potentially dangerous offenders within it. Within the field of restorative justice there are numerous other examples of attempts to promote reparatory work in relation to dangerous offenders (e.g. Daly 2006).

Conclusions

In conclusion we would return to the point Andrew Bridges made about why be concerned at all about managing dangerous offenders in the community. He offers practical and economic arguments against this proposal but also argues that we do not have, nor should we want, prison in the community. The current cultural and political climate in which dangerous offenders are supervised suggests that this may be a misplaced conviction. As discussed above, there is an increasing shift to extend social controls in the pursuit of satisfying public fears over safety. Ironically this is an approach which may not be as effective in reducing the harm dangerous offenders pose or ensuring public safety. How we manage dangerous offenders may, as Kemshall said, 'raise questions about the types of risks we wish to avoid and manage, those we deem as bad and ultimately the type of society we wish to live in' (2006: 88). This is, perhaps, where the ultimate challenge lies.

References

Beck, U. (1992) *Risk Society*. London: Sage.

Barnado (2007) *A Risk too High? Would Public Disclosure (Sarah's Law) Protect Children from Sex Offenders*. Policy and Research Unit. Available online at: http://www.barnardos.org.uk/a_risk_too_high_public_disclosure_report. pdf

Bottoms, A. (1977) 'Reflections on the renaissance of dangerousness', *Howard Journal of Penology and Crime Prevention*, 16: 70–96.

Bridges, A. (2007) *Dangerous Offenders – What Can Be Achieved?* To an All-Party Parliamentary Group on Penal Affairs, 13 November 2007. Available online at: http://Inspectorates.Justice.gov.uk/hmiprobation/recent-reports!. html/ (accessed 1 December 2007).

Bryan, T. and Doyle, P. (2003) 'Developing Multi-Agency Public Protection Arrangements', in A. Matravers (ed.), *Sex Offenders in the Community*. Cullompton: Willan.

Buzan, B., Weaver, O. and De Wilde, J. (1998) *Security: A New Framework for Analysis*. London: Lynne Reiner.

Cavadino, M. and Dignam, J. (2005) *Penal Systems: A Comparative Approach*. London: Sage.

Cobley, C. (2003) 'The legislative framework', in A. Matravers (ed.), *Sex Offenders in the Community*. Cullompton: Willan.

Daly, K. (2006) 'Restorative justice and sexual assault: an archival study of court and conference cases', *British Journal of Criminology*, 46: 334–56.

Douglas, M. (1992) *Risk and Cultural Theory*. London: Routledge.

Farrall, S. (2002) *Rethinking What Works with Offenders*. Cullompton: Willan.

Feeley, M. and Simon, J. (1992) 'The new penology: notes on the emerging strategy of corrections', *Criminology*, 30 (4): 449–75.

Ferrell, J. (2005) 'Crime and culture', in S. Hale, K. Hayward, A. Wahidin and E. Wincup (eds), *Criminology*. Oxford: Oxford University Press, pp. 139–56.

Fisher, D.D. and Beech, R.A. (2004) 'Adult male sex offenders', in H. Kemshall and G. McIvor (eds), *Managing Sex Offender Risk*. London and Philadelphia: Jessica Kingsley.

Furedi, F. (1997) *Culture of Fear: Risk Taking and the Morality of Low Expectation*. London: Cassell.

Garland, D. (1995) 'Penal modernism and post modernism', in T. Bloomberg and S. Cohen (eds), *Punishment and Social Control: Essays in Honour of Sheldon Messinger*. New York: Aldine de Gruyter.

Garland, D. (2001) *The Culture of Control: Crime and Social Order in Contemporary Society*. Oxford: Clarendon Press.

Giddens, A. (1990) *The Consequences of Modernity*. Cambridge: Polity Press.

Greer, C. (2005) 'Crime and media', in S. Hale, K. Hayward, A. Wahidin and E. Wincup (eds), *Criminology*. Oxford: Oxford University Press, pp. 157–82.

Grubin, D. (2004) 'The risk assessment of sex offenders', in H. Kemshall and G. McIvor (eds), *Managing Sex Offender Risk*. London and Philadelphia: Jessica Kingsley.

Hayles, M. (2006) 'Constructing safety: a collaborative approach to managing risk and building responsibility', in K. Gorman, M. Gregory, M. Hayles and N. Parton (eds), *Constructive Work with Offenders*. London and Philadelphia: Jessica Kingsley, pp. 67–85.

Hayward, K.J. (2004) *City Limits: Crime, Consumer Culture and the Urban Experience*. London: Glasshouse Express.

HMIP (1995) Dealing with Dangerous Offenders: The Probation and Public Protection Report of a Thematic Inspection. London: Home Office.

HMIP (1998) Exercising Constant Vigilance. Report of a Thematic Inspection. London: Home Office.

Hier, S. P. and Greenberg, J. (eds) (2007) *The Surveillance Studies Reader*. Maidenhead: McGraw-Hill.

Hudson, B. (2003) *Justice in the Risk Society*. London: Sage.

James, A. and Raine, J. (1998) *The New Politics of Criminal Justice*. London: Longman.

Kemshall, H. (2002) 'Risk, public protection and justice', in D. Ward, J. Scott and M. Lacey (eds), *Probation Working for Justice*, 2nd edn. Oxford: Oxford University Press.

Kemshall, H. (2003) *Understanding Risk in Criminal Justice*. Maidenhead: Open University Press.

Kemshall, H. and McIvor, G. (eds) (2004) *Managing Sex Offender Risk*. London and Philadelphia: Jessica Kingsley.

Kemshall, H. (2006) 'Crime and risk', in P. Taylor-Gooby and J. Zinn (eds), *Risk in Social Science*. Oxford: Oxford University Press.

Lieb, R. (2003) 'Joined up working: the Multi-Agency Public Protection Panels', in A. Matravers (ed.), *Sex Offenders in the Community*. Cullompton: Willan.

Loader, I. (2006) Fall of the Plantonic Guardians: Liberalism Criminology and Political Responses to Crime in England and Wales. *British Journal of Criminology* 40 (4): 561–586.

Loader, I. and Sparks, R. (2002) Contemporary Landscape and Control: Governance, risk and globalisation in M McGuire, R. Morgan and R. Reiner (eds). *The Oxford Handbook of Criminology*, 3rd edn. Oxford: Oxford University Press.

Loader, I. and Sparks, R. (2007) 'Contemporary landscape of crime, order and control: governance, risk and globalization', in M. Maguire, R. Morgan and R. Reiner (eds), *The Oxford Handbook of Criminology*, 4th edn. Oxford: Oxford University Press.

Loader, I. and Walker, N. (2007) *Civilizing Security*. Cambridge: Cambridge University Press.

Martinson, R. (1974) What Works? Questions and Answers about Prison Reform. *The Public Interest 35*, 22–54.

Maruna, S. (2001) *Making Good: How Ex Convicts Reform and Rebuild their Lives*. Washington, DC: American Psychological Association.

McGuire, J. (1995) What Works: Reducing Reoffending Guidelines from Research and Practice. Chichester: Wiley.

Mythen, G. (2007) 'Cultural victimology: are we all victims now?', in S. Walklate (ed.), *Handbook of Victims and Victimology*. Cullompton: Willan, pp. 464–83.

Nash, M. (2006) *Public Protection and the Criminal Justice Process*. Oxford: Oxford University Press.

National Probation Service (2005) *Annual Evaluation of MAPPA*. Available online at: http://www.probation.homeoffice.gov.uk/files/pdf/MAPPA (accessed 15 January 2008).

O'Malley, P. (2000) 'Risk societies and the government of crime', in M. Brown and J. Pratt (eds), *Dangerous Offenders: Punishment and Social Order*. London: Routledge.

Parton, N. and O'Byrne, P. (2000) *Constructive Social Work*. Basingstoke: Macmillan.

Pratt, J. (2000) 'Dangerousness and modern society', in M. Brown and J. Pratt (eds), *Dangerous Offenders: Punishment and Social Order*. London: Routledge.

Rule, J.B. (2007) 'Social control and modern social structure', in S.P. Hier and J. Greenberg (eds), *The Surveillance Studies Reader*. Maidenhead: McGraw-Hill.

Simon, J. (2006) 'Governing through crime', in M.E. Vogel (ed.), *Crime, Inequality and the State*. London: Routledge, pp. 589–95.

Stenson, K. (2001) 'The new politics of crime control', in K. Stenson and S. Sullivan (eds), *Crime, Risk and Justice*. Cullompton: Willan, pp. 15–28.

Strachan, R. and Tallant, C. (1997) 'Improving judgement and appreciating biases within the risk assessment process', in H. Kemshall and J. Pritchard (eds) *Good Practice in Risk Assessment and Risk Management: Protection, Rights and Responsibilities*, Vol. 2. London and Philadelphia: Jessica Kingsley.

Thomas, T. (2005) *Sex Crime: Sex Offending and Society*, 2nd edn. Cullompton: Willan.

Vanstone, M. (2007) *Supervising Offenders in the Community: A History of Probation Theory and Practice*. Aldershot: Ashgate.

Wilson, R.J., McWhinnie, A., Pichea, J.E., Prinzo, M. and Cortoni, F. (2007) 'Circles of support and accountability: engaging community volunteers in the management of high-risk sexual offenders', *Howard Journal of Criminal Justice*, 46 (1): 1–15.

Index